The Bells of Victory

The Bells of Victory

The Pitt–Newcastle Ministry and the Conduct of the Seven Years' War, 1757–1762

RICHARD MIDDLETON

Lecturer in the Department of Modern History
The Queen's University
Belfast

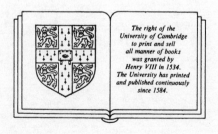

The right of the
University of Cambridge
to print and sell
all manner of books
was granted by
Henry VIII in 1534.
The University has printed
and published continuously
since 1584.

CAMBRIDGE UNIVERSITY PRESS

CAMBRIDGE

LONDON   NEW YORK   NEW ROCHELLE

MELBOURNE   SYDNEY

PUBLISHED BY THE PRESS SYNDICATE OF THE UNIVERSITY OF CAMBRIDGE
The Pitt Building, Trumpington Street, Cambridge, United Kingdom

CAMBRIDGE UNIVERSITY PRESS
The Edinburgh Building, Cambridge CB2 2RU, UK
40 West 20th Street, New York NY 10011–4211, USA
477 Williamstown Road, Port Melbourne, VIC 3207, Australia
Ruiz de Alarcón 13, 28014 Madrid, Spain
Dock House, The Waterfront, Cape Town 8001, South Africa

http://www.cambridge.org

First published 1985
First paperback edition 2002

A catalogue record for this book is available from the British Library

Library of Congress catalogue card number: 84-19840

ISBN 0 521 26546 0 hardback
ISBN 0 521 52132 7 paperback

for Michael Roberts
and
Denys Jacobs

It is common with most men to attribute all events to some one cause. It suits the pedantry of historians, who are for making everything into a system...But no great river arises from one source, but...from an accidental junction of many small streams.

Lord Shelburne c. 1800

CONTENTS

PREFACE

The Pitt–Newcastle ministry was one of the most successful in British history. Under its direction, more battles were won and conquests made than in any other period of conflict. Yet when the coalition took office it faced apparently insuperable difficulty. General Braddock had been killed endeavouring to restore British fortunes in North America; Admiral Byng had been disgraced attempting to relieve Minorca; while at home the country had been humiliated by the use of German mercenaries to face an invasion. When nothing went right, frustration gave way to despair; for as one minister commented, despite every precaution, not a single operation had succeeded. Many reasons were advanced for this deplorable situation: bad luck, ministerial incompetence and the resourcefulness of the enemy. But the most frequently cited of all was that of political instability. Since March 1754 the ministry had been reconstructed three times. Each successive attempt had proved more brittle than the last. The new administration in June 1757 was only formed after eight weeks of political bargaining between men determined to exclude each other. Few predicted that so fragile an entity could last; none that it could succeed.

The triumphs that followed in Europe, America, the East and West Indies, have traditionally been ascribed to the leadership of William Pitt. Basil Williams, author of still the most authoritative biography, reflects the general consensus of opinion when he says: 'The success of the Seven Years' War was almost entirely due to Pitt's torrential energy, to his far seeing preparations, to his wise choice of commanders...above all to his strategic insight into the crucial objects of his world wide campaigns.'[1] Before Pitt, the government had been in the incompetent hands of the Duke of Newcastle, 'an essentially weak man', who nevertheless 'resented any signs of superiority in colleagues abler and clearer in purpose than himself'. Not surprisingly the national cause suffered until rescued by the 'Great Commoner'.[2]

Despite the appearance of a number of works, the picture drawn by

[1] B. Williams, *The Whig Supremacy, 1714–1760* (Oxford, 1962), 358. B. Williams, *The Life of William Pitt, Earl of Chatham* (2 vols., London, 1913).
[2] Williams, *Whig Supremacy*, 341.

Williams is still the most prevalent. One reason for this is the absence of any study of the Pitt–Newcastle ministry since Sir Julian Corbett's, seventy-five years ago.[3] Another is the lack of detailed work on the administrative aspects of the topic, an area that even Corbett neglected. Writers have been prolific with assertions about Pitt's administrative abilities. They have rarely followed these with a convincing analysis of how he made the machinery of government work beyond the bullying of colleagues and the supervision of subordinates. A similar lack of analysis exists concerning the other members of the ministry. Not all of them have been dismissed as incompetent. Suggestions have been made that to Lord Anson must go the credit for expanding the navy; to Sir John Ligonier the acclaim for producing so many successful generals; and even to Newcastle the merit of finding the money. But here too there has been little investigation of their exact contribution to the war.

What follows therefore is not a history of the war, nor a biography of Pitt. The focus is on all the ministers, how they made decisions, planned operations and created resources. Examining their conduct of diplomacy, finance, the army, the fleet, recruitment, the commissary and procurement of munitions ought to show more clearly whether their achievement was due to good luck or effective planning. Battlefield accounts are accordingly limited to those necessary for an appreciation of what the ministers were trying to do.

This book has only been possible through the assistance and advice of many people. I am above all indebted to Denys Jacobs, formerly of the History Department at Exeter University. He first introduced me to the topic through his special subject, 'English Government and Governments, 1751–1770'. Later he encouraged me to do research, acting as my supervisor in the closing stages of the dissertation. He continued to take a keen interest, reading numerous drafts and giving me a great deal of encouragement and judicious criticism. Sadly, his death in November 1977 prevented him from seeing the work come to fruition. It is for this reason that I have made him one of the two people to whom this book is dedicated. Without his support the work might never have been written; without his guidance it would have been inferior.

Another major debt, both intellectual and material, is that to Professor Ian Christie, of University College London. He supervised me in the earlier stages of my research and continued to take a close interest in my work. This included a critical reading of an earlier version of the manuscript before publication. Also valuable was his seminar at the Institute of Historical

---

[3] J. S. Corbett, *England in the Seven Years' War: A Study in Combined Strategy* (2 vols., London, 1907).

Research in Senate House, London, which brought together many students of eighteenth-century government. I should in particular like to mention those three fellow pioneers, David Syrett, Arthur Bowler and Norman Baker, with whom I spent many congenial hours and to whom I am greatly indebted.

Considerable research for this project was done while holding a fellowship at the Institute of Early American History and Culture. I should like to thank the director, Thad Tate and the other members of the staff for their assistance and encouragement. I must also thank the Queen's University, Belfast, for giving me leave to take up the fellowship and for assisting my research in various ways.

I have benefited from the selfless assistance and professional advice of numerous archivists and librarians. It is impossible to name all those who gave of their time and knowledge, but I must mention Bill Ewing and John Dann, of the William L. Clements Library; Anthony Malcomson, of the Public Record Office of Northern Ireland; and William Pearsall, of the National Maritime Museum, who gave me invaluable information about the eighteenth-century royal navy at a formative stage in my career.

My thanks are due also to the Duke of Devonshire for permission to consult the papers of the Fourth Duke at Chatsworth; the Lichfield Trustees for the opportunity of inspecting the Anson papers in the Staffordshire Record Office; and the Duke of Bedford for permission to use some transcripts held by the Northern Ireland Public Record Office. In accordance with the conditions laid down by the Lichfield Trustees, I am instructed to inform readers that they should first obtain the consent of the Trustees before quoting or using any material from these papers. Finally my thanks are due to the staff of the Admiralty Library; the American Antiquarian Society; the British Library; the Houghton Library; the Huntington Library; the London Library; the National Library of Scotland; the Newberry Library; the New York Public Library; the East Riding Record Office; the Public Record Office, London; the Public Record Office of Northern Ireland; the Scottish Record Office; the Staffordshire Record Office; and the William L. Clements Library.

Research is only half the business of producing a book. An author needs many helpers if he is to get his manuscript into shape. Friendly critics are required, who by their judicious comments and countless suggestions make possible a draft that may have some pretensions to scholarship. In this context I should like to thank Peter Blair, John Bossy, Peter Devlin, Jill Finlay, Ian and Judith Green, Martin Ingram, Peter Jupp, Olivia Johnston, John McCusker, Piers Mackesy, Josephine Middleton, Gretchen Oberfranc, Mary O'Dowd, Peter and Yvonne Smyth, Mark Storey, Lewis Warren and Angela Wilcox. In the production stage I have to thank William Davies, Christine Lyall Grant and the staff of Cambridge University Press. Their ability to turn a raw manuscript into a finished work is a considerable one indeed.

At all stages of my work I have been encouraged and supported by my parents. They were always ready to assist me, and many times they provided a roof over my head and a room to work in.

Before the death of Denys Jacobs, this work was to have been dedicated solely to Michael Roberts, formerly Professor of Modern History at Queen's University. As a head of department, a scholar and a person he was an inspiration to all. I shall always be in his debt.

The Queen's University, Belfast   R. M.
January 1984

ABBREVIATIONS

Add. Mss	Additional Manuscripts, British Library
Adm	Admiralty Papers, Public Record Office and National Maritime Museum
BL	British Library
CP	Chatham Papers, Public Record Office
DPC	Devonshire Papers Chatsworth
HMC	Historical Manuscripts Commission
HWK	Hawke Papers, National Maritime Museum
JHC	*Journal of the House of Commons*
Kimball	*The Correspondence of William Pitt, when Secretary of State, with the Colonial Governors and Military and Naval Commissioners in North America*, edited by G. S. Kimball, 2 vols., London, 1906
NMM	National Maritime Museum, Greenwich
PC	Privy Council, Public Record Office
PRO	Public Record Office, London
RA CP	Royal Archives, Cumberland Papers
SP	State Papers, Public Record Office
T	Treasury Papers, Public Record Office
WO	War Office, Public Record Office
Yorke	*The Life and Correspondence of Philip Yorke, Earl of Hardwicke*, edited by P. C. Yorke, 3 vols., Cambridge, 1913

The Outbreak of War and Formation of the Ministry

I

The death of Henry Pelham in March 1754 prompted George II to forecast he would have no more peace.[1] He was thinking only domestically. He was not anticipating the war which was shortly to reduce the House of Hanover to its lowest ebb. Had George II been able to see into the future he would have found that Britain was to be threatened, Minorca lost, the precious Electorate overrun and his favourite son, William Augustus, Duke of Cumberland, disgraced. Equally distressing, though less surprising, the King would have discovered that he was to be the victim of a cabal, whereby his closet was forced and a ministry formed of men personally obnoxious to him. True, the tide of military disaster turned, but it is doubtful if the old King would have found much consolation therein, while the Electorate was beleaguered and the government dominated by men for whom he had, at heart, such scant regard.

The origins of the Seven Years' War between Britain and France are to be sought in the previous 150 years of these two proud nations. To the French, the British were a dangerous people in their constitutional and religious polity: France a country of orthodoxy in both. To the British, the French were perpetrators of despotic monarchy and a persecuting church: Britain a constitutional country nurtured in civil and religious liberty. These differences were highlighted by physical proximity, separated as the two nations were by a narrow band of water. Their rivalry was further increased by an intense competition for trade and empire, especially in North America. As a result, friction on that continent was much increased, for both nations recognized its value in enhancing their power. The differences were sufficiently serious at the Aix-la-Chapelle peace conference to be referred to a separate negotiation. But with such high stakes both powers made only the feeblest attempt to agree. As the diplomats talked, the French in particular took action in the disputed regions of the Ohio, Great Lakes and Nova Scotia. Their operations did not go unnoticed. In August 1753 the

[1] H. Walpole, *Memoirs of the Reign of King George II* (3 vols., London, 1846–47), I, 378.

British colonial governors were instructed to resist 'force with force', and it was while the Virginian authorities were responding to this that the first hostilities occurred, when a small expedition under the then unknown George Washington clashed with a French force guarding the Forks of the Ohio.[2] Minor in itself, the engagement symbolized the determination of both powers to make good their claims in North America. Before the dispute had been settled, most of Europe was at war.

But initially it seemed that domestic problems would be the more contentious as George II pondered the question of a successor to Pelham. Nominally, there were several candidates for the King's favour as First Lord of the Treasury.[3] In the end he chose the dead man's brother, Thomas Pelham Holles, Duke of Newcastle, currently the northern Secretary of State, who by seniority and long service could claim to be the most experienced if not the most accomplished British politician.[4]

The first problem of the Newcastle ministry was America, where some action was required to reverse Washington's defeat. Since the provincials seemed incapable of doing the job, the government decided to dispatch Major-General Braddock with two regiments and officers for raising two more.[5] Unfortunately, this action prompted the French to strengthen similarly their position in Canada which in turn was unacceptable to the British. Trade with the mainland colonies was now more valuable than that with the West Indies, the previous jewel in the nation's empire. A further response was therefore necessary, this time by the dispatch of a fleet under Admiral Boscawen with orders to stop the French reinforcements from reaching Canada. The policy of the administration was simple and logical. Since America was the cause of the dispute, America was where hostilities should occur, though as a precaution steps were taken to mobilize the fleet and army in Britain.[6] A number of warships were taken out of the reserve, press warrants issued and some regiments increased to their wartime strength of 815 men.[7]

Regrettably, there was just one flaw to this policy: Hanover. As the French quickly made clear they would not scruple to extend the conflict to Europe whenever it suited them.[8] The Electorate was Britain's Achilles' heel, for its defence was a commitment that no government could avoid.

[2] T. C. Pease, *Anglo-French Boundary Disputes in the West, 1747–1763* (Springfield, Illinois, 1936), 45.
[3] J. C. D. Clark, *The Dynamics of Change: The Crisis of the 1750s and English Party Systems* (Cambridge, 1982), 45–46.
[4] The best recent biography of Newcastle is that by R. Browning, *The Duke of Newcastle* (New Haven, 1975).
[5] Newcastle to Lord Albemarle, 5 Sept 1754, Add. Mss 32,850 ff 218–224.
[6] Cabinet Memorandum, 18 Mar. 1755, Add. Mss 32,996 ff 48–50.
[7] Charge of Augmenting the Forces, 12 Mar. 1755, Add. Mss 32,853 ff 247, 259. The order to mobilize the fleet was issued by the Admiralty on 16 Jan 1755, Adm 3/63.
[8] Newcastle to William Bentinck, 11 Mar 1755, Add. Mss 32,853 ff 193–199.

The royal succession and, by implication, the settlement of 1689, all depended on this. It had traditionally been protected by an alliance with Austria and Holland. Unfortunately, the Dutch were tired of European strife, claiming that the present conflict was of no concern to them, while the Austrians saw the expulsion of Prussia from Silesia, not the defence of Flanders or the Rhine, as their prime objective.[9]

Another complication was Prussia. Frederick II was allied to France and might join an attack on the Electorate.

It was for this reason that the ministry sought a subsidy treaty with Russia for the use of 50,000 men.[10] Otherwise it could only adopt the less grandiose scheme of assembling an army of Hanoverian and other local forces. A number of German princes were accustomed to support themselves by hiring out their troops. A start was accordingly made with Hesse for 8,000 men,[11] and talks were also conducted with the Danes. The Electoral forces themselves numbered 27,000, so a reasonable defence might yet be provided.[12]

Even so, by the autumn of 1755 the situation of the ministry appeared unenviable. In the first place its American policies had not succeeded. Braddock had got within seven miles of his objective, only to be defeated because he had not had time to accustom his men properly.[13] Elsewhere Boscawen had missed his prey in fog off Newfoundland, while at home the ministry had become involved in naval hostilities that seemed certain to embrace the continent next spring.[14] The nation did not have a dependable ally in Europe. Only one development gave cause for hope. In May 1755 Frederick II had indicated a willingness to talk and subsequent soundings had revealed that he was not happy about his alliance with France.[15] The Anglo-French disputes seemed to him rather pointless, given the barren nature of the contested territory. However, he was anxious that they did not lead to a European war, for he did not relish being asked by France to invade Hanover.[16] Equally, he was concerned at the British negotiation with Russia.

The Convention of Westminster, whereby Britain and Prussia agreed to assist each other in keeping foreign troops out of Germany, initially seemed

---

[9] The diplomatic background to the war is related in D. B. Horn, *Great Britain and Europe in the Eighteenth Century* (Oxford, 1967).

[10] For the terms of the treaty see C. Parry (ed.), *The Consolidated Treaty Series* (New York, 1969), XL, 271–283.   [11] Ibid., 261–267.

[12] Newcastle to Holdernesse, 6 June 1755, Add. Mss 32,855 ff 352–364. Newcastle to Holdernesse, 20 July 1755, Add. Mss 32,857 ff 162–172.

[13] S. M. Pargellis, 'Braddock's Defeat', *American Historical Review*, XLI, 253–269.

[14] J. S. Corbett, *England in the Seven Years' War: A Study in Combined Strategy* (London, 1907), I, 50–62.

[15] Baron Munchausen to Newcastle, 20 June 1755, Add. Mss 32,856 f 70. Holdernesse to Newcastle, 30 July 1755, Add. Mss 32,857 f 452.

[16] Frederick II to the Duke of Brunswick, 14 Aug 1755, Add. Mss 32,858 ff 225–229.

a master-stroke.[17] The French would hardly dare attack Hanover now. Indeed, the treaty apparently completed the isolation of France. What Newcastle and Frederick II did not realize was that their union of January 1756 simply speeded up a realignment of the powers which was already in progress and in no way favourable to either. Austria, convinced that Britain would never be of use in the recovery of Silesia, determined to seek an understanding with France, the traditional foe.[18] In the event, Britain had simply exchanged Austria for Prussia as the main guarantor of Hanover's integrity. Another unforeseen result was that France, prevented temporarily from attacking Hanover, began planning an invasion of Britain as the best means of conducting the war.

Foreign embarrassments, however, were not the only problems to assail the ministry at this time, for internal struggles were also distracting it. The elevation of Newcastle to the Treasury had been secured at the expense of two rivals, Henry Fox and William Pitt, and Fox had subsequently had to be promoted Secretary of State.[19] This, however, bitterly offended Pitt. He was a deeply ambitious man, and for ten years he had loyally served the Pelhams in the hope of ultimate preferment. Seeing no chance of this he had gone into opposition.[20] By good fortune allies were waiting to embrace him at Leicester House, the establishment of the Prince of Wales, which was traditionally hostile to the King and his ministry. The heir's mother, Princess Augusta, and her principal adviser, Lord Bute, were fearful that Cumberland might prove another Richard III. The promotion of Fox, the protégé of Cumberland, was thus a serious blow to the Prince's interest, for the protection of which new allies were required.[21]

Nevertheless, had not foreign disasters intervened, it is likely that Pitt would have spent the rest of the reign in the ranks of the opposition. National disaster was as much the making of him as it was of Winston Churchill, two centuries later. First came the invasion threat of 1756. This found the government short of troops. Though the Newcastle ministry had done its best to expand the army, there was still a shortage of trained men. In this situation, the ministry first requested assistance from the Dutch under the 1713 treaty guaranteeing the protestant succession. When the Republic refused, the ministry had no alternative but to summon the Hanoverians and Hessians, which was possible following the agreement with Prussia. But, though a sensible precaution, Pitt could assert it was a shameful abnegation of the nation's own manhood.[22]

[17] Parry (ed.), *Consolidated Treaty Series*, XL, 293–298. *JHC*, XXVII, 602–603.
[18] Parry (ed.), *Consolidated Treaty Series*, XL, 337–353.
[19] James Earl Waldegrave, *Memoirs from 1754 to 1758* (London, 1821), 31–32.
[20] Remarks, 14 Apr 1755, printed in W. S. Taylor and J. H. Pringle (eds.), *The Correspondence of William Pitt, Earl of Chatham* (London, 1838), I, 134–137.
[21] Walpole, *Memoirs of George II*, II, 36–56. Waldegrave, *Memoirs*, 35–41. Clark, *Dynamics of Change*, 153–195.   [22] Walpole, *Memoirs of George II*, II, 187–189.

The next blow to the ministry came with the loss of Minorca. There was much debate then and since about the responsibility for this. However, some of the blame must fall on Lord Anson, the First Lord of the Admiralty. Rumours of French preparations in the Mediterranean had been rife since the previous autumn. Anson had discounted them. He told Lord Hardwicke, the Lord Chancellor, his father-in-law: 'I think it would be a dangerous measure to part with your naval strength... which cannot be recalled if wanted, when I am strongly of opinion that whenever the French intend anything in earnest, their attack will be against this Country.'[23] The English fleet in the Mediterranean, therefore, was not strengthened until the intentions of the French were clear. The decision was not necessarily unsound. Although British concentration on the Channel permitted the French to land on Minorca, the position could still have been saved had Admiral Byng succeeded in driving off the French fleet under the Marquis de La Galissonière. The British could then have relieved the garrison in Fort St Philip and trapped the besieging army in a snare of its own making.

Unfortunately, Byng was not the man to seize his opportunity. To some extent everything went wrong at the same time. The engagement with La Galissonière left the British force damaged with the enemy still in possession of the waters before St Philip. Because Anson had concentrated the fleet at home, Byng had no reserve of men and ships. He was therefore unable to relieve the garrison which had to surrender after a siege of fifty-six days.[24]

Although the invasion never materialized and the catastrophe at Minorca could be blamed on Byng, this did nothing to strengthen the ministry, for these reverses brought out all the latent tensions between Fox and Newcastle. From the start Newcastle had made it clear that he had resorted to Fox's services with reluctance. Fox had accordingly found his position increasingly intolerable, and, convinced that Newcastle would pass the responsibility for Minorca to him, he determined to resign.[25]

His departure was a double blow to Newcastle, for it was preceded by the loss of one of his most able subordinates, William Murray the Attorney-General, from the Commons to be Lord Chief Justice and a peer as Lord Mansfield.

Initially, Newcastle looked to Pitt to fill the void, even though Pitt had intimated that he would not serve with him and had opposed the Hessian and Russian treaties.[26] Hardwicke, Newcastle's principal confidant, was certain that if Pitt was gratified in the matter of high office, other difficulties would not be allowed to stand in his way.[27] However, on this occasion Pitt

[23] Anson to Hardwicke, 6 Dec 1755, Add. Mss 35,395 f 383.
[24] Corbett, *Seven Years' War*, I, 96–130.
[25] Paper delivered to the King, 15 Oct 1756, Yorke, II, 319.
[26] Newcastle to Hardwicke, 14 Oct 1756, Yorke, II, 321–322.
[27] Hardwicke to Newcastle, 29 Aug 1756, Yorke, II, 310–311.

insisted he could not serve with Newcastle, since all the 'mistakes in the conduct of the war had been committed' while he was 'First Minister'. That he was being insincere was shown by his readiness to retain the other ministers who, as Hardwicke pointed out, were equally culpable for the present situation.[28]

As it was improper to refuse office on grounds of personality alone, Pitt also raised a number of conditions regarding measures. First he insisted that an enquiry be held into the loss of Minorca. Then he wanted the recent incident of a Hanoverian soldier caught stealing a handkerchief to be investigated. In addition, the passing of a Militia Bill had to be made a matter of the highest priority. All these promised political advantage. An enquiry into the loss of Minorca would embarrass Newcastle and neutralize his support. The affair of the Hanoverian soldier would enable Pitt to exploit the intense chauvinism which was such a feature of eighteenth-century English life. Finally, a Militia Bill would have considerable appeal for the Tory Members of Parliament whose support would be crucial for any administration in which neither Fox nor Newcastle was a member. On the conduct of the war, Pitt had few ideas beyond asserting that the policy of the previous government had been too Hanoverian.[29] This also was largely window-dressing, for as Lord Waldegrave, a friend of the King, observed, these 'treasonable falsehoods' were simply bandied about to bring the opposition into power. Once in office they would be ready to 'talk a different language', as Pitt was now doing by his silent acceptance of the treaties with Hesse and Prussia.[30]

In these circumstances Newcastle was unready to brave another session of Parliament, for as Lord Holdernesse, the northern Secretary, later observed, though he had both 'parliamentary strength and confidence at St James's', he could make use of neither for 'want of a leader in the Commons'.[31] Resigning with him were Hardwicke and Anson. Hardwicke wanted to retire after being Lord Chancellor for many years. Anson was too closely identified with the loss of Minorca to contemplate staying.[32]

The way was now open for a more thorough reconstruction of the government. But while it was recognized that Pitt must be given a leading office, neither he nor his immediate faction were to have the key post of First Lord of the Treasury.[33] The new administration could not in any case be composed of one party. As Horace Walpole observed, Pitt did not have

---

[28] Hardwicke to Joseph Yorke, 31 Oct 1756, Yorke, II, 330–334.
[29] Relation of a Conference with Mr Pitt, 24 Oct 1756, Yorke, II, 277–281.
[30] Waldegrave, *Memoirs*, 62.
[31] Holdernesse to Mitchell, 8 Feb 1757, Holdernesse Correspondence, Egerton, 3460 f 167, BL.
[32] Hardwicke to Yorke, 31 Oct 1756, Yorke, II, 333.
[33] Bedford to the Duchess of Bedford, 2 Nov 1756, printed in Lord John Russell (ed.), *Correspondence of John, Fourth Duke of Bedford* (London, 1843), II, 206–209.

enough relatives for this and to survive the new ministry would have to depend heavily on the supporters of Newcastle, though Pitt was hopeful of Tory assistance.[34] In these circumstances it was thought best if the Duke of Devonshire headed the new government, being a non-controversial figure who carried the respect of all the factions. Hence, Pitt became Secretary of State for the southern department; Lord Temple, his brother-in-law, First Lord of the Admiralty; George Grenville, another brother-in-law, a lord of the Treasury; while Henry Legge was given the post of Chancellor of the Exchequer. Pitt initially wanted to be northern Secretary so that he would deal with Hanover. He told Devonshire that if Sir Thomas Robinson, a former holder, was given the southern department, 'the King would find in him an old servant his Majesty would be easy with, and I a colleague very able to rectify my very many and great defects in an office I am a stranger to'.[35] George II, however, refused. It was bad enough having Pitt in office, let alone having him deal with the Electorate.

II

Even his harshest critics in 1756 had to concede that Pitt was a man of unusual gifts. It was of course on his parliamentary abilities that he was judged, for he had had little opportunity to demonstrate his administrative talents. Since his first appearance in the Commons in 1735 he had held only two minor positions, one as Vice-Treasurer of Ireland, the other as Paymaster-General. However, with the exception of Fox and Murray, Pitt had after 1754 no rival in the Commons as a speaker, thrilling his listeners with orations in the style of a Demosthenes or Cicero, whom he had studied avidly and on whom he consciously modelled himself.[36]

Pitt's great love of the classics was not untypical of the age. Rhetorical embellishment in a speech was as acceptable as inlaid marquetry in a commode. But style and rhetoric were not the only qualities admired and some commentators were inclined to be critical of Pitt's excessive attention to form.[37] Such qualities did not become someone who had had little experience outside the narrow world of politics.[38] His career as a soldier had been brief and, unlike many contemporaries, he never studied the law or interested himself in finance. His associations with the City of London were entirely political and confined mainly to the tradesmen element on the Common Council, for with the great financiers he had had few dealings.[39]

[34] Walpole, *Memoirs of George II*, ii, 263–265. Clark, *Dynamics of Change*, 295–300.
[35] Pitt to Devonshire, 2 Nov 1756, DPC.
[36] S. Ayling, *The Elder Pitt, Earl of Chatham* (London, 1976), 106–109.
[37] Notably Mansfield. See his comments in T. C. Hansard (ed.), *The Parliamentary History of England*, xv, *1753–1765* (London, 1813), 606.
[38] Waldegrave, *Memoirs*, 16–17.   [39] Walpole, *Memoirs of George II*, iii, 173.

Curiously, in view of the office to which he aspired, he appears to have shown little interest in writing. He never indulged in that favourite eighteenth-century pastime, political pamphleteering. His correspondence was generally brief and he rarely committed his thoughts to paper, even for speaking in the Commons. On the other hand, he had a good knowledge of French and knew something of Europe, having studied at the University of Utrecht before undertaking a tour of France and Switzerland.[40]

The admission of Pitt to office has usually been presented as a decisive break in the conduct of the war. However, except for the florid tone of the royal speech, the plans of the ministry were little different to those of the previous government when the King unveiled them to Parliament.[41] This was hardly surprising, for the main outlines of the war had been determined. These were the assertion of Britain's claims in America and the security of the King's dominions elsewhere. The only difference was that by the end of 1756 the problems had become more acute, both in Europe and overseas. Except for the consolidation of the British position in Nova Scotia, nothing of consequence had been effected across the Atlantic. Indeed, the previous twelve months had witnessed a further setback, following the destruction in August 1756 of Oswego, the vital trading-post on Lake Ontario.[42] Elsewhere, the East India Company had lost its principal station in Bengal to the forces of Siraj-ud-Daula. Of the Company's personnel, 113 had been suffocated in the Black Hole of Calcutta.

The position was equally bad in Germany, for the Franco-Austrian alliance had prompted Frederick II to invade Saxony to forestall any encirclement of Prussia. The result was what his treaty with Britain was supposed to avoid, a war in Germany. The tsarina, fearful of Frederick II's designs, quickly abandoned the British subsidy for an understanding with France, followed by Sweden and most of the South German princes.[43] The only consolation was that neither Austria nor Russia had so far committed themselves to assist France against Hanover. A war with those powers might still be avoided.

Initially, the ministry had few plans on how to cope with this situation beyond the forming of a militia, though Frederick II was not short of ideas. He suggested establishing an army to observe the French on the Rhine, the making of descents on the coasts of Normandy and Brittany, deploying

---

[40] Ayling, *The Elder Pitt*, 32–35, 41–42.
[41] The text of the royal speech can be found in *JHC*, XXVII, 621, and should be compared with that for the previous year, ibid., 297.
[42] Events across the Atlantic are fully described in L. H. Gipson, *The British Empire before the American Revolution*, VI, *The Great War for the Empire: the Years of Defeat, 1754–1757* (New York, 1946).
[43] J. O. Lindsay (ed.), *The New Cambridge Modern History*, VII, *The Old Regime, 1713–1763* (Cambridge, 1957), 440–464.

British naval forces in the Baltic and Mediterranean and using diplomacy to bring the Dutch and Turks into the struggle.[44]

Such views were too grandiose for the present, though some were to bear fruit later. The need for diplomatic action was recognized, though neither Holland nor Turkey were felt to be practical objectives. The ministry preferred to set its sights lower on Denmark, whose goodwill was a prerequisite for any fleet entering the Baltic.[45] Militarily, the ministry found itself hampered by the small size of the army. Despite the creation of twenty-five new battalions by the Newcastle ministry, the army at home still numbered fewer than 30,000 men.[46] This was partly why the new government wanted a Militia Bill. While the country remained so defence-less, it was inevitable that a large proportion of its military force would be tied down. The proposals of the ministry were presented by George and Charles Townshend and were for 60,000 men. However, suspicion of their political composition led to the number being reduced to 37,000. Many Whigs feared that otherwise Tories of dubious loyalty would infiltrate the government. Even this number would take time to establish.[47]

It was these difficulties that led Cumberland to report to the Earl of Loudoun, the British Commander-in-Chief in America: 'Nothing can be worse than our situation here at home...without a plan or even a desire to have one.'[48] The latter was unfair, though even for America Pitt does not appear to have had any clear views. Like all political figures, he had never been to that continent, nor had he much chance of studying the departmental correspondence. On the first outbreak of fighting in 1754 Pitt had believed that the campaigning ought to be left primarily to the provincials who were better qualified for the backcountry.[49] However, if the ministry was uncertain how to proceed, the commanders in America were not. After the abortive campaign of 1756, knowledgeable observers like Sir Charles Hardy concluded that nothing could be achieved by mounting a series of local attacks on the French outposts as had been done before. The official outbreak of war meant that something more ambitious could be

---

[44] Mitchell to Holdernesse, 9 Dec 1756, SP 90/67.

[45] C. W. Eldon, *England's Subsidy Policy towards the Continent during the Seven Years' War, 1756–1763* (Philadelphia, 1938), 87–88.

[46] Ten new regiments were established at the end of 1755, Newcastle Cabinet Memorandum, 16 Dec 1755, Add. Mss 32,996 f 321. In the summer of 1756 the decision was taken to raise another fifteen battalions, Barrington to James West, 7 Aug 1756, WO 4/52. These were subsequently redesignated regiments. See *JHC*, xxvii, 387–388, 632–633.

[47] J. R. Western, *The English Militia in the Eighteenth Century: The Story of a Political Issue, 1660–1802* (London, 1965), 127–140.

[48] Cumberland to Loudoun, 23 Dec 1756, printed in S. M. Pargellis (ed.), *Military Affairs in North America: 1748–1765: Selected Documents from the Cumberland Papers in Windsor Castle* (New York, 1936), 262–263.

[49] Newcastle to Hardwicke, 2 Oct 1754, Add. Mss 32,737 ff 24–26.

considered against the French in the St Lawrence valley.[50] Loudoun
accordingly suggested to Cumberland the dispatch of a powerful fleet and
10,000 additional troops, though to ensure acceptance he sent a special
emissary, Thomas Pownall.[51]

Loudoun need not have worried. As Pownall shortly reported, his
proposal had 'become the favourite scheme, the thing after the Minister's
own heart'.[52] Pitt had always made the maritime interests of Britain a
principal consideration, if only as part of his anti-Hanover stance. Unfortunately, as he soon discovered, implementing the plan was not so easy.
Anson had left the administration a formidable fleet of 93 ships of the line
and 125 other vessels in commission, manned by 54,000 seamen.[53] The
problem was finding the troops. Pitt had promised Loudoun 8,000 men but
it was not clear where such force could be found. The continuing possibility
of invasion made Cumberland particularly unhappy about sending so many
men away, especially when plans were afoot to return the Hessians and
Hanoverians to defend the Electorate. The Militia Bill was not yet on the
statute-book and many doubted its effectiveness then. At the beginning of
January, Loudoun was warned that, in spite of the ministerial promises, the
reinforcement might yet be denied him.[54] In retaliation Pitt several times
hinted that accommodation here would determine his willingness to help
Hanover.[55]

This situation led the administration to raise men from the clans formerly
loyal to the Pretender. Similar proposals had been made by the Duke of
Bedford during the previous war, but they had been dismissed as too
dangerous. Even now many believed that it would simply arm men for the
Stuarts.[56] However, in the absence of other suggestions, Pitt swept aside
these objections. Two battalions were to be raised for service across the
Atlantic under the supervision of the Duke of Argyle, the initial objective
of the expedition being the fortress of Louisburg.[57]

With regard to Germany, Pitt found that he had little option but to
modify his views. It had been easy in opposition to suggest that Hanover
might be compensated for any harm she suffered: that the treaties with
Russia, Hesse and Prussia were unnecessary.[58] Once in office he found

---

[50] Hardy to Loudoun, 18 Sept 1756. Loudoun Papers, Box 41, Huntington Library.
[51] Loudoun to Cumberland, 29 Aug, 2 Oct, 3 Oct 1756, printed in Pargellis (ed.), *Military Affairs*, 233–242.
[52] Pownall to Loudoun, 7 Dec 1756, Loudoun Papers, Box 54.
[53] Monthly List and Progress of the Navy, 1 Jan 1757, Adm 7/567. See also the estimate in *JHC*, xxvii, 635. Accurate statistics, however, are hard to establish, as the compiler of the Monthly List Book noted.
[54] John Pownall to Loudoun, 8 Jan 1757, Loudoun Papers, Box 59.
[55] Pitt to Devonshire, 30 Jan 1757, DPC.
[56] Hardwicke to Newcastle, 6 Dec 1756, Yorke, ii, 378.
[57] E. M. Lloyd, 'The Raising of the Highland Regiments in 1757', *English Historical Review*, xvii, 466–469. Calcraft to Loudoun, 7 Jan 1757, Loudoun Papers, Box 59.
[58] Walpole, *Memoirs of George II*, ii, 194.

himself looking at affairs from a very different perspective. Britain was at war with France; she required allies and had only one, Prussia. In these circumstances even Pitt realized that he had no choice but to accept the Convention of Westminster and make preparations for carrying out its provisions. Clearly next spring the French would cross the Rhine and attack Hanover as a preliminary to the destruction of Prussia. The previous administration had already begun discussions with Frederick II for a combined force to prevent this.[59] The ministry accordingly arranged for the return of the Hanoverians and Hessians, the whole army to be commanded by Cumberland. But no British troops would be sent and another concession to the new minister was that Hanover would finance its own troops, leaving only the Hessians and other mercenaries to be provided for. Nevertheless, the first action of Pitt when he appeared in the Commons after Christmas was to present a request for £200,000 so that the King could make good his commitments as Elector of Hanover.[60]

These contradictions did not pass unnoticed. Lord Barrington at the War Office reported to Andrew Mitchell, the ambassador in Berlin: 'These measures as declared and explained by Pitt the first day of the session differ in nothing from those of the last administration. Every effort in America consistent with our safety at home, every effort at sea, and whatever this country can do besides, given the support of our allies on the Continent.'[61] Holdernesse similarly found Pitt's 'opinions upon foreign affairs now he is in office...exactly the same with mine, however different they were some time ago'.[62] Pitt later defended his change of heart over Germany by arguing that the arrangements with Prussia were 'dictated by Hanover, not Great Britain'. Under Pitt they had been subordinated to the interests of Britain and had become 'a millstone about the neck of France'.[63] These arguments were largely semantic and accepted as such, though one or two of Pitt's supporters found this cynical acceptance of measures previously condemned hard to accept. Richard Glover, playwright and admirer of Pitt, was especially scathing, castigating the actions of the new administration as being 'all within the old circle, trite, trifling and iniquitous'.[64]

Such criticism was not entirely justified. Despite the lack of troops, Loudoun did get most of his reinforcement, the numbers being made up

[59] An Account of the Anglo-Prussian Correspondence after the Convention of Westminster, CP PRO 30/8/89 ff 148–160. Hanover, an Army in Readiness, 12 Sept 1756, Holdernesse Papers, Egerton, 3430 f 29, BL.
[60] Walpole, *Memoirs of George II*, II, 313. Clark, *Dynamics of Change*, 327–328.
[61] Quoted in O. A. Sherrard, *Lord Chatham*, II, *Pitt and the Seven Years' War* (London, 1955), 172
[62] Holdernesse to Mitchell, 26 Nov 1756, printed in A. Bisset (ed.), *Memoirs and Papers of Sir Andrew Mitchell K.B., Envoy Extraordinary and Minister Plenipotentiary from the Court of Great Britain to the Court of Prussia, 1756–1771* (London, 1850), I, 223.
[63] H. Walpole, *Memoirs of the Reign of King George III* (London, 1894), I, 82–83.
[64] R. Glover, *Memoirs of a Celebrated Literary and Political Character* (London, 1814), 104–106.

by six battalions from Ireland. With them went a squadron of twelve ships of the line to join the four already there, a formidable armament.[65] At the same time three ships of the line were sent under Captain Steevens to help the East India Company. This was especially desirable, since news had arrived that the French were similarly reinforcing their own navy there under the Comte d'Aché.[66]

However, in terms of creating new resources, Glover was right. Little was effected. Among the Chatham correspondence is a paper detailing the naval forces necessary for 'the total Stagnation and Extirpation of the French Trade and Marine'.[67] No attempt was made to implement it. Temple's Board was content to order three new battleships and four frigates, hardly the vigorous start to shipbuilding claimed by one historian.[68] Indeed, Barrington correctly reported: 'The Admiralty change nothing in what they find to have been Lord Anson's plan.'[69] A total of 229 ships was to be in commission, an increase of just 20 on the previous year.[70] As to manning, the main contribution of the administration was the formation of thirty marine companies. Otherwise the manpower of the navy showed only modest growth.[71] Additions to the army were equally limited. Except for the Highlanders, no new units were formed and the army was not expected to increase much beyond that envisaged by the previous government.[72]

Most notable, however, was the failure of the government's financial measures. Legge calculated that the ministry required a supply of £8,500,000, of which £3,500,000 would have to be borrowed, £3,000,000 by the sale of annuities, £500,000 in a simple lottery.[73] The money should not have been difficult to secure, being less than that sought in the last year of the previous war. But Legge had insisted on some unorthodox methods to get his money. The new government was anxious to align the Tory gentry in its support, who had long been distrustful of the City. A frequent panacea of the Tories for curbing the financiers was the adoption of an 'open subscription'. By this method the public would be allowed to subscribe directly to any loan without going through the channel of the monied men. In theory more people would be able to participate at less cost to the

[65] Pitt to Loudoun, 4 Feb, 17 Mar 1757, WO 34/71.
[66] Corbett, Seven Years' War, I, 160, 338–340.
[67] List and Estimate of Vessels Required, 22 Aug 1756, CP PRO 30/8/78 f 76.
[68] B. Williams, The Life of William Pitt, Earl of Chatham (London, 1913), I, 295–296. The orders for new ships can be obtained from the Admiralty minutes in the Public Record Office, Adm 3/63.   [69] Quoted in Yorke, II, 362.
[70] Admiralty to the Navy Board, 26 Nov 1756, Adm 2/221.
[71] Privy Council to the Admiralty, 1 Mar 1757, Adm 1/5164. Seamen Employed, 1756, JHC, xxvii, 844. Seamen Employed, 1757, JHC, xxviii, 128.
[72] Partly because of recruitment for and reliance on the militia: Western, English Militia, 104–145.
[73] L. S. Sutherland, 'The City of London and the Pitt–Devonshire Administration, 1756–1757', Proceedings of the British Academy, XLVI, 148–193.

government, since there would be no need for the intermediary services of the City.[74] However, Legge forgot that he had no network of correspondents for selling the stock and the results of his experimentation were singularly unfortunate. Only a tenth of the money required on the loan was forthcoming, while the lottery part was not much more successful. Scarcely half the tickets were sold.[75]

III

These setbacks not surprisingly made the political atmosphere uncertain. Even before the ministry was formed, Fox had forecast that Pitt would be foolish to act without the support of Newcastle or himself and without the confidence of the King.[76] By March 1757 it was clear how accurate he had been. Pitt had built his administration on sand, not rock. Leicester House and the Grenville family were numerically too small and the Tories too unreliable a basis on which to build a government. Without the confidence of the King, they had no prospect of building a stable majority in the Commons. Even by Christmas Pitt had come to realize that he needed more support and that meant some kind of understanding with Newcastle.[77]

Another reason for the weakness of the ministry was Pitt's ill health. He was stricken with gout just after taking office and it was February before he reappeared in the Commons. Commissions remained unsigned and business was 'greatly retarded'. Holdernesse told Mitchell: 'Many cool thinking people who were once so partial to Pitt' were now discovering 'how unequal he is to the task'.[78] A further problem was his inability to win friends in Parliament. Here Pitt was his own worst enemy. To be an effective leader it was necessary to greet the members with a jocular phrase or courteous salutation. Rhetoric could cajole but hardly endear. As Fox once crudely said, there were times when it was necessary to 'tickle the palm rather than the ear'. In the details of patronage Pitt had no interest. Its effective disposal was another reason why he needed Newcastle.

The latter meanwhile found that, notwithstanding Minorca, his political star continued to shine as brightly as ever. Hardwicke recorded that he had been 'more visited and had greater professions of attachment to him than when he had been at the head of the Treasury'.[79] This might seem surprising, since historians – until recently – have been quick to dismiss Newcastle as incompetent, devious, malicious and corrupt. It has usually been overlooked that the source for most of these charges is the letters and

---

[74] P. G. M. Dickson, *The Financial Revolution in England: A Study in the Development of Public Credit, 1688–1756* (London, 1967), 226–229.
[75] Sutherland, 'City of London', *Proceedings of the British Academy*, XLVI, 166–168, 172.
[76] Fox to Sackville, 4 Nov 1756, HMC, Appendix to the Ninth Report, Part III, 10.
[77] Clark, *Dynamics of Change*, 302–335.
[78] Holdernesse to Mitchell, 4 Mar 1757, Holdernesse Papers, Egerton, 3460 f 193.
[79] Quoted in Yorke, II, 361.

memoirs of Horace Walpole, an inveterate enemy.[80] Newcastle was certainly
idiosyncratic. The fears for his own and his wife's health made him an easy
target for those inclined to lampoon or traduce him. But caricature itself
is no evidence of incompetence in the subject, though it may be of malice
in the author. Corruption in any case was not the basis of his power, for,
as Sir Lewis Namier has shown, this was far less prevalent than was once
supposed.[81] Moreover, the charge of Lord Chesterfield that Newcastle was
'as dilatory in dispatching' business 'as he was eager to engage in it' cannot
be substantiated, for the mismanagement of finance and his other
departmental responsibilities were not among the accusations levelled at
him on his leaving office in 1756.[82] Parliaments tend to produce two kinds
of leader: the masters of rhetoric, of whom Pitt was a notable example, and
the political managers, of whom Fox and Newcastle were conspicuous
examples. The former are as admired as the latter are necessary, for both
are essential to a parliamentary system.

Nevertheless, it required action by Cumberland to terminate Pitt's first
period in office. Cumberland was about to take up his command in
Germany and was anxious that there should be a ministry sympathetic to
him. Distrusting Pitt's recent conversion to continental measures, he pressed
the King to dismiss his lately installed ministers and construct a broader
administration.[83] George II needed little persuading, for he found Pitt and
Temple offensive because of their tendency to harangue him in the closet.
The time was opportune in that the popularity of the new ministry had been
undermined by its seeming readiness to espouse the cause of Admiral Byng.[84]
Unfortunately, George II failed to assess the situation adequately. He did
little beyond sounding Newcastle as to his willingness to come back into
office, which he could hardly do before the Minorca enquiry was over.
Hence, no alternative government had been arranged when Pitt and
Temple were relieved of their offices at the beginning of April 1757. The
government simply continued in the hands of a caretaker administration
headed by Devonshire, with the Earl of Winchelsea in charge at the
Admiralty. Several offices remained unfilled and the country entered what

[80] For a critical analysis of Walpole and his reliability as a source see J. W. Croker, 'Walpole's
      Memoirs of the Reign of George II', *The Quarterly Review*, xxvii, 178–215.
[81] Sir Lewis Namier, *The Structure of Politics at the Accession of George III* (second edition, London,
      1957).
[82] Character of the Duke of Newcastle, by Lord Chesterfield, printed in J. Bradshaw (ed.),
      The Letters of Philip Dormer Stanhope, Earl of Chesterfield (London, 1893), iii, 1425. Many years
      later Burke commented to the Marquis of Rockingham: 'There was nothing I was so much
      surprised at in the late Duke of Newcastle, as that immense and almost effortless ease with
      which he was able to dispatch such an infinite number of letters', L. S. Sutherland (ed.),
      The Correspondence of Edmund Burke (Cambridge, 1960), ii, 40.
[83] Clark, *Dynamics of Change*, 354–358.
[84] Walpole, *Memoirs of George II*, ii, 306–376.

Horace Walpole and historians after him have called the 'interministerium'.[85]

The struggle for power which followed was basically between three main factions. First, there was the King and the court, his principal allies being Cumberland, Fox, Waldegrave and the Duke of Bedford. The issue for George II was one of exercising his right to choose an executive sympathetic to his Electoral interests. Above all he wanted to be delivered from the uncongenial company of Pitt and Temple.

The second faction was made up of a coalition headed by Pitt and Bute, the one leader of the Grenville family, the other of Leicester House. The aims of these two groups were close but not identical. Bute and the Princess of Wales, obsessed about Cumberland, were mainly concerned to keep Fox out of office. Pitt and the Grenvilles, while prepared to indulge their allies in such fantasies, were determined to obtain the offices for which they hungered. As to measures, both groups were suspicious of the war on the continent, though the opposition of Leicester House was the more sincere. For the moment they made a point of stressing the value of the navy and importance of a militia as the main defence of the kingdom.

The third faction was headed by Newcastle and Hardwicke. In parliamentary terms they were much the strongest. Tradition and temperament demanded that they should return to office as soon as the enquiry had removed the stain of losing Minorca. With regard to measures they took a middle course. They dreaded any increase of French power, either in Europe or America, but they saw no conflict between the maritime and continental aspects of the struggle. Both were equally important. As to men, Newcastle had only one condition, namely that he would not work with Fox to whom he was as averse as George II was to Temple.[86]

On the surface the initiative seemed to lie with the King, for he alone had the power of appointing ministers. George II's natural preference was for a coalition between Fox and Newcastle, or an administration headed by one or the other.[87] However, nothing was possible until the Minorca enquiry was finished. Historians have followed Walpole in viewing the proceedings as a farce because Pitt, realizing he needed Newcastle's assistance, declined to press the matter. Recent work has shown this to be untrue.[88] In any case, papers drawn up by Anson and John Clevland, the Admiralty secretary, suggest that the final verdict was not unjustified.[89] The

---

[85] Ibid., III, 20.

[86] The views of the several factions are conveniently summarized in the *Annual Register for 1758*, 9–13. See also Clark, *Dynamics of Change*, 354–447.

[87] Waldegrave, *Memoirs*, 96–109.

[88] Walpole, *Memoirs of George II*, III, 7–9. Clark, *Dynamics of Change*, 375–380.

[89] Naval Preparations, 10 Sept 1756, Add. Mss 33,047 ff 65–76. The materials on which this defence was compiled are in the Hardwicke Papers, Add. Mss 31,959 ff 1–30, 221–260 and

Admiralty had made strenuous efforts the preceding year to mobilize the
fleet. But this effort to keep the various squadrons at sea had taken a heavy
toll, especially in manpower.[90] With an invasion threatening, the home fleet
had necessarily had first priority. Hence the enquiry's conclusion that 'no
greater force could have been sent to the Mediterranean under Admiral
Byng' was not unfounded. Certainly there is no truth to the charge that
Newcastle had 'minced the Navy of England into cruisers and convoys';
for he had not directed the navy and other services were provided.[91]

The result of the enquiry was that Newcastle could now help form a
ministry. He had, however, resolved only to enter the government if an
understanding had been reached with Leicester House. The administration
must not be harassed again because of dissension within the royal family.[92]
To the sense of this George II reluctantly acquiesced. Unfortunately, Pitt's
terms were high. Apart from being Secretary of State, he wanted Legge at
the Admiralty and George Grenville for the Treasury as Chancellor of the
Exchequer. He and Bute recognized the King's antipathy to Temple,
specifying for him only 'some place in the Cabinet Council'. But they also
demanded that Lord George Sackville should replace Barrington as
Secretary at War, which was unacceptable to George II, while Newcastle
was not happy about having Grenville at the Treasury, since it might
threaten his own control there.[93]

About the war there was little disagreement, it being accepted that the
present direction in North America and Germany should continue.

But despite this, Newcastle was still unable to conclude terms, whereupon
George II pressed him to form an administration on his own. Newcastle
hesitated because of his old problem of 'finding proper persons to carry on
the business of the House of Commons'.[94] Nevertheless, the news was
sufficiently alarming for Pitt to moderate his demands. The renewed
readiness to talk was relayed through the Earl of Chesterfield and agreement
was then reached.[95] Unfortunately, none of the King's own conditions were
observed and the negotiation was accordingly ended.[96]

There followed a brief interlude while George II tried to persuade a
reluctant Waldegrave to take the Treasury with Fox and Bedford as his
lieutenants. The scheme might have succeeded had Fox been determined.

have been published by Sir Herbert Richmond (ed.), *Papers Relating to the Loss of Minorca
in 1756*, Navy Records Society, XLII (London, 1913).
[90] State of the Fleet, 1 Jan 1756, Add. Mss 33,047 ff 24–26. The seventy-one ships then at
home had only 17,000 of their 24,000 complement.
[91] Walpole, *Memoirs of George II*, II, 213.
[92] My Present Resolution, 19 Apr 1757, Add. Mss 32,997 ff 135–136.
[93] Clark, *Dynamics of Change*, 380–391.
[94] Hardwicke to Newcastle, 1 June 1757, Yorke, II, 396–398.
[95] Chesterfield to Newcastle, 3 June 1757, Add. Mss 32,871 f 199.
[96] Waldegrave, *Memoirs*, 111–113.

But the weak link was George II himself. He had no faith in the experiment, especially when Holdernesse and others began resigning their offices on the very day that the new ministers were to kiss hands. Instead he decided once more to see whether an administration of Pitt and Newcastle could be constructed.[97] After some discussion, Hardwicke was given this task. The King's only conditions were the Paymaster-Generalship for Fox and a non-executive position for Temple.[98]

Even now three days of bargaining were required before the semblance of an administration took shape; and another two weeks before the final details were agreed. Though respected by all the parties, Hardwicke was by no means a disinterested negotiator. He insisted in an interview with the King on 15 June that some gesture would have to be made to his son-in-law Anson. Fortunately, this proved less of a stumbling-block than might have been imagined. When the King objected to Legge being made both a peer and First Lord of the Admiralty, Hardwicke suggested that Anson might return to his old post. George II quickly agreed, though it was not in the plan originally settled between Pitt and Newcastle.[99] However, no one objected. Pitt was aware of the need for experienced direction at the Admiralty, for Temple's tenure had not been a success. Despite Minorca, Anson's exclusion from office had never been a *sine qua non* with him. Indeed, many years later he confessed how in the ensuing enquiry he had become 'entirely convinced...of the injustice done' to Anson's character.[100] It was quickly agreed, therefore, that Anson should return but with Temple's Board, Legge being compensated with the Exchequer. Newcastle was to be First Lord of the Treasury and Pitt southern Secretary. Temple would hold the prestigious but largely honorary position of Lord Privy Seal; and George II's other conditions were met. Fox was made Paymaster-General. Barrington continued at the War Office.

Other persons to retain their posts or receive appointments were Holdernesse, who was reinstated as Secretary of State for the northern office; Lord Granville, who remained Lord President of the Council; Bedford, who was nominated Lord Lieutenant of Ireland; and the Duke of Marlborough, who continued at the Ordnance as Master-General. Since Hardwicke declined to resume the Lord Chancellorship, Sir Robert Henley was nominated Lord Keeper of the Great Seal.[101]

Inevitably, there had to be some disappointments. George Grenville did not get a position at the Treasury. Lord Halifax was not given a secretaryship for the colonies. Sackville was denied the War Office. Lastly, neither of the

[97] Ibid., 114–129. Clark, *Dynamics of Change*, 413–423.
[98] Hardwicke to Lord Royston, 12 June 1757, Yorke, II, 399–400.
[99] Hardwicke to Anson, 18 June 1757, Yorke, II, 403–406.
[100] Quoted in Yorke, II, 352–353.
[101] Hardwicke to Anson, 18 June 1757, Yorke, II, 403–406.

Townshend brothers was gratified in any way. This was surprising, given their role in the Militia Bill. Being ambitious they were naturally angry and George in particular expressed his disgust to Pitt over the 'ridiculous and dishonest arrangement of men which is now to take place', for which 'not the least adoption of any system of measures had been declared or even hinted at'.[102]

But while there was some truth in Townshend's sentiments, he was not being entirely fair, for underneath the disputes about office was at least one major issue, the extent to which the nation would be committed to a Hanoverian rather than a 'patriot' system. George II was anxious to secure ministers who would do their utmost to help him as Elector of Hanover. Pitt and Bute wanted men to fill the government who would check such tendencies. In the middle were Hardwicke and Newcastle who recognized the King's legitimate expectations, but were concerned to ensure that the nation's other interests did not suffer.

More serious was Townshend's point concerning the incompatibility of the men now being called upon to form a government. As Waldegrave commented: 'The Duke of Newcastle hated Pitt as much as Pitt despised the Duke of Newcastle.' They were only united in that 'nothing should be done for the public service till they were ministers'. These were hardly the ingredients on which a successful administration could be built.[103] True, Hardwicke proudly asserted that the list of names 'is looked upon as the strongest administration that has been formed for many years'.[104] Few shared his enthusiasm. Devonshire thought that on paper the ministry was strong, but doubted how long the two principals could work together, given their fickle natures.[105] Indeed, as late as 28 June it was uncertain whether the ministry would take office at all. Pitt was furious that Newcastle had promised Halifax a third Secretaryship, which seemed designed to undermine his influence. He confessed to Bute: 'I go to this bitter but necessary cup with more foreboding' than ever. He could only promise to do his best 'in that service to which I have the glory, in conjunction with your Lordship, to be unalterably and totally devoted'.[106]

The ministers finally kissed the King's hand for their offices on the afternoon of 29 June. They did so none too soon. The auspices abroad were even more unpromising than those at home.

[102] Sir Lewis Namier and J. Brooke, *Charles Townshend* (London, 1964), 52.
[103] Waldegrave, *Memoirs*, 129–130.
[104] Hardwicke to Anson, 18 June 1757, Yorke, II, 405.
[105] Devonshire to Cumberland, 28 June 1757, DPC.
[106] Pitt to Bute, printed in R. Pares and A. J. P. Taylor (eds.), *Essays Presented to Sir Lewis Namier* (London, 1956), 124–125.

IV

During the negotiations George II complained: 'Ministers are Kings in this country.' His bitterness was understandable. Technically, Pitt and Newcastle were his servants, not masters. Although Parliament had long sought to influence the executive, the ministers were still answerable to the King and his powers were theoretically extensive. As John Chamberlayne, in his ever popular *Magnae Britanniae Notitia*, commented: 'The King alone by his Royal Prerogative hath Power, without Act of Parliament, to declare War, make Peace, send and receive Ambassadors, make Leagues and Treaties with any Foreign States, give Commissions for levying Men and Arms by Sea and Land, or for Pressing Men...disposing of all Magazines, Ammunition, Castles, Fortresses, Ports, Havens, Ships of War, and Publick Monies.'[107]

Historians emphasizing the role of Pitt in the conduct of the war have often overlooked that government at this time was departmental: each minister managed a specific branch of the executive for the King. As George II had previously told Newcastle: 'I have particular persons or ministers for particular branches', and nobody could claim any overall responsibility. Indeed, he rightly affirmed: 'There is no such thing as a First Minister in England', for it was incompatible with his own position as head of the executive.[108]

George II attended to affairs in his closet at St James's in the winter; at Kensington in the summer, when considerations of health made a move from the capital advisable. The closet was a small ante-room to the King's dressing-room and it was the focal point of government.

With the exception of the two Secretaries of State, the King normally saw the ministers individually. However, for some purposes his consent in the closet was insufficient and recourse had to be made to the Privy Council over which he sometimes presided and to which the chief officers of state were summoned. Application to the King in Council, as the procedure was known, was necessary when a department desired to suspend or invoke an act of Parliament for manning the fleet or prohibiting the export of gunpowder. Certain other executive powers were also entrusted to it.

The King was assisted in the dispatch of business by the two Secretaries of State, whose duty it was to ascertain his pleasure and draft his commands. Their letters, when docketed with the royal sign manual and signet seal, became the official notification of the King's commands and a department's legal authority to act beyond its formal commission. This was most often

---

[107] J. Chamberlayne, *Magnae Britanniae Notitia: or the Present State of Great Britain* (London, 1726), 42.
[108] Newcastle to Hardwicke, 2 Jan 1755, Add. Mss 32,852 f 259.

necessary when inter-departmental action was required, a procedure from which the Treasury alone was exempt.[109]

Responsibility for the several concerns of government were thus. The Secretaries, in addition to their domestic duties, looked after foreign relations, the northern incumbent dealing with Holland, Germany, the Baltic States and Russia; the southern with France, Spain, Turkey, Ireland and the colonies. The Privy Council and Board of Trade otherwise administered the colonies' internal affairs; the Treasury, with its subordinate departments of the Exchequer, Customs and Excise, collected the revenue; the Admiralty, with the Navy and Victualling Boards, took care of the fleet; while the War Office supervised the army. Lastly, the Ordnance Board supplied both services with munitions, maintained all forts and provided a corps of artillery and engineers.

The complexity of government meant that British monarchs had long ceased to supervise every detail. It was a far cry from the days when the monarch had surrounded himself with a few boon companions and gone to war with his treasure in a strongbox. Government had become institutionalized, and the very size of some departments meant that his power had had to be widely delegated. The Secretaries of State remained close to the King, for they were responsible for foreign affairs, always an object of great interest to the Hanoverians. They dealt too with other sensitive areas of the royal prerogative. The Hanoverians had also retained supervision of the War Office. Both George I and George II prided themselves on their military prowess and took a keen personal interest in the administration of the army. By contrast, royal control of departments like the Admiralty, Ordnance and Treasury was superficial in the extreme. To have remained in direction, the Kings of Britain had to be not only heads of state and heads of government, but also accomplished performers in the diverse fields of war, diplomacy and administration. William III was the last King to do so. Yet the expansion of government meant that more not less co-ordination was required. Inevitably, the vacuum thus threatened was not long in being filled. If the King was unable to combine these various roles, his principal servants were willing to try.

Ministers had long been meeting to co-ordinate their actions and make recommendations for the better conduct of affairs. In the latter half of the seventeenth century this had been done in a sub-committee of the Privy Council, known as the 'foreign committee' because it dealt primarily with overseas affairs. In time this body, now called the Cabinet Council, had increased in size to the point where it had lost its effectiveness.[110] As a result

---

[109] H. G. Roseveare, *The Treasury: The Evolution of a British Institution* (London, 1969), 63–64. For further information on the eighteenth-century Secretaryship, see M. A. Thomson, *The Secretaries of State, 1681–1782* (Oxford, 1932).

[110] E. R. Turner, *The Privy Council of England in the Seventeenth and Eighteenth Centuries, 1603–1784* (2 vols., Baltimore, 1928). E. R. Turner, *The Cabinet Council of England in the Seventeenth and Eighteenth Centuries, 1622–1784* (2 vols., Baltimore, 1930).

affairs increasingly had come to be considered by yet another body of ministers, usually those with major executive functions like the Secretaries of State, First Lord of the Treasury, First Lord of the Admiralty, Lord President and Lord Chancellor. On the declaration of war in 1756 the direction of affairs had been in the hands of six men: Newcastle, Fox, Holdernesse, Hardwicke, Anson and Granville, with Cumberland attending when military operations were discussed.[111] The Pitt–Devonshire administration had operated with a similar group.[112]

The need for some such body was discussed by Pitt and Newcastle prior to the formation of the coalition. In one of their meetings Newcastle noted that the 'measures relative to the operation of the Army and Navy should be previously concerted and agreed with His Majesty's ministers'.[113] Both men believed that decisions earlier had been taken without proper consultation always. Newcastle in any case was keen to establish an element of collective responsibility. Previously some ministers had concerned themselves only with their own departments. As a result the measures of the government had been weakly supported. That was no way to manage the King's affairs, as Pitt himself had argued during one Commons' debate.[114] Newcastle had accordingly drawn up a paper headed 'Committee of the Cabinet Council to meet on business', containing ten names or posts in all.[115]

Nevertheless, the doctrine of Cabinet responsibility was still far from established. Lord Holland observed that even by 1806 no rules had been established for its conduct. The business most frequently discussed was that of the Foreign Secretary,[116] and similarly now. Except for foreign affairs, the departments generally managed their own business. Military operations had to be discussed because of the need for co-operation and because of their diplomatic implications. Naval matters appeared less frequently. Attention then centred on the condition of the fleet and the orders to it. Building, victualling and manning were almost never broached. The administration of the Ordnance was equally absent. The same was true of the War Office. Recruitment was the one item dealt with regarding the army. Also absent was the business of the Treasury. The raising of loans and even taxation were determined with little or no discussion by the other departments beyond their own estimates. The Treasury lords only brought such matters to their colleagues as might meet with criticism in Parliament. Otherwise they did as they thought best, after approval by the King. Royal involvement, the lack of collective responsibility and the departmental structure of government meant that co-ordinating the executive was not going to be easy for the new ministry, whatever its other problems.

---

[111] Newcastle Cabinet Memoranda, Add. Mss 32,995–32,996.
[112] Pitt Cabinet Memoranda, CP PRO 30/8/95 ff 163–164.
[113] Considerations for the Duke of Newcastle's Conduct, 18 May 1757, Add. Mss 32,997 ff 156–157.   [114] Walpole, *Memoirs of George II*, ii, 189.
[115] Newcastle Cabinet Memoranda, Add. Mss 32,997 f 207.
[116] E. N. Williams, *The Eighteenth Century Constitution, 1688–1815* (Cambridge, 1960), 122–123.

1

A Crisis of Confidence

I

Historians have customarily asserted that Pitt began office with a coherent plan for the defeat of France.[1] However, this was not the case, for the conduct of the war was barely mentioned in the ministerial negotiations and there is nothing in the Chatham correspondence to indicate that Pitt did not believe the war should continue as before, every effort being made in America consistent with the safety of the homeland and the security of the King's German territories.

The aims of the ministry at this time were defensive. Cumberland had no orders to invade France, even if he had had the means. In North America the ministry only sought to recover the rights of the nation as defined by the Treaty of Utrecht, with possession of Nova Scotia, a frontier contiguous to the St Lawrence, and control of the Great Lakes. Admittedly, the futility of attacking every small fort rather than invading the St Lawrence had now been recognized. But permanent possession was not official policy, being a matter of future negotiation.

Elsewhere, the ministry was committed to assisting the East India Company though those operations were too far away to be of much consideration. Otherwise its main concern was the deployment of the navy. Here too the emphasis was defensive, on the protection of the homeland, trade and overseas possessions.

Beyond these objectives even Pitt did not venture. Whatever the war may have subsequently become, it was not yet a war of conquest. Certainly, he had no grand plan for its prosecution. The concept of 'strategy' was limited at this time. The word itself is not to be found in Johnson's dictionary, being a creation of the Napoleonic era.[2] True, there were the maritime and

---

[1] B. Williams, *The Whig Supremacy, 1714–1760* (Oxford, 1962), 356–359. J. S. Corbett, *England in the Seven Years' War: A Study in Combined Strategy* (London, 1907), I, 8, 179–186. W. C. B. Tunstall, *William Pitt, Earl of Chatham* (London, 1938), 168, 193–195.

[2] The word was first used by C. James in the third edition of his *A New and Enlarged Military Dictionary or Alphabetical Exposition of Technical terms* (2 vols., London, 1810), citing a recent French publication. Significantly, there is no such entry in the first two editions. For a further discussion, see the appendix to this book, 223.

continental schools of warfare, but the distinctions were often artificial, for most continentalists readily subscribed to the arguments of their opponents that trade was the ultimate source of a nation's wealth. They only differed in their insistence that a war could not be exclusively maritime. Much British trade was with the continent. By the time enemy commerce had been destroyed, the French were likely to be masters of Europe and thus able to dictate terms. In previous wars all administrations had pursued both philosophies, making a substantial commitment to the continent while trying to destroy the enemy by the seizure of their shipping and colonies. This essentially was to be the policy of the government now. The one apparent disagreement was the deployment of British troops in Germany. Pitt was seemingly firm that Britain did not have the manpower to engage in another such struggle, therefore she could only be an auxiliary: the fighting must be done by others.

The ministers had come to power after the campaign had opened and their capacity for decisive action was necessarily limited. Nevertheless, some initiative was required when they kissed hands at the end of June. Two weeks earlier the French under the Duc d'Estrées had commenced an advance on Hanover. Cumberland was in retreat, outnumbered and outmanoeuvred. Further east the King of Prussia too was falling back from Bohemia after a reverse against the Austrians near Prague. Not the least of his worries was that the Russians were preparing to take the field. Elsewhere, disturbing rumours had been received of a French fleet in the vicinity of Louisburg, so that a further naval and even military reinforcement there might not be amiss to ensure the success of that venture.[3]

Nevertheless, it was the situation in Germany that required the most attention, for unless something was done Cumberland would be driven into the sea, the Electorate overrun and Prussia attacked from the rear. There were two aspects to the problem, one naval, the other military. Frederick II had for some time been demanding a British fleet to protect his Baltic coast.[4] The Convention of Westminster merely committed George II to help Prussia keep foreign troops out of Germany and both the Newcastle and Pitt–Devonshire ministries had prevaricated about a fleet for fear of offending Russia.

Now Frederick II was more insistent.[5] But as Holdernesse informed Mitchell after one of the ministry's first meetings, Sweden and Denmark,

[3] Barrington to Cumberland, 8 July 1757, RA CP, Box 53. Ligonier to Cumberland, 12 July 1757, RA CP, Box 54. See R. Middleton, 'A Reinforcement for North America, Summer 1757', *Bulletin of the Institute of Historical Research*, XLI, 58–59.

[4] Mitchell to Holdernesse, 23 July 1756, SP 90/65. Mitchell to Holdernesse, 26 Feb 1757, SP 90/68. Mitchell to Holdernesse, 19 Apr 1757, printed in A. Bissett (ed.), *The Memoirs and Papers of Sir Andrew Mitchell, K.B., Envoy Extraordinary and Minister Plenipotentiary from the Court of Great Britain to the Court of Prussia, 1756–1771* (London, 1850), I, 241–242.

[5] Mitchell to Holdernesse, 29 June 1757, SP 90/69.

the two powers that controlled the entry to the Baltic, were neither of them negligible and both were inclined to support France. Unless Denmark was secured no ships could be sent, for any fleet would have to be formidable, otherwise it would merely antagonize the Baltic powers without giving Prussia any relief.[6]

The Admiralty at this point had a total of 239 ships in commission with another 25 in reserve and 49 building. Of those in service, 98 were ships of the line.[7] This was a substantial force, since the French had by comparison a mere 72 battleships and many of these were unfit for service.[8] Much of the credit for this must go to Anson. Since becoming First Lord of the Admiralty in 1751 he had done much to make the navy a more efficient service. By a policy of inspection and repair he had ensured that all the fleet was in a good condition, unlike previous peacetime First Lords who had tended to forget about the ships in 'ordinary', as the reserve was known.[9] As a result Anson had been able to commission 82 ships of the line in the first year of mobilization, only 6 fewer than the maximum number during the previous war.[10]

The other means by which Anson ensured that the fleet was adequate was by building. Peacetime economy had not permitted much of this, but the outbreak of hostilities had allowed a large number of orders. Initially, Anson had sought this from the royal yards, but when they proved too busy fitting the ships in commission, he had followed precedent by turning to private builders, though on a larger scale. The result was that over half the 49 ships then under construction were in private hands, many with country builders at Hull, Liverpool, Shoreham and Saltash, places not traditionally associated with such activity.[11]

Unfortunately, not all the ships had crews, even though the fleet now had 62,000 men.[12] Here too Anson had done his best, as the Minorca enquiry showed. Substantial bounties had been offered, legislation passed allowing foreign seamen to serve as replacements in the mercantile marine, and every effort made to create an effective network of press gangs. In

---

[6] Holdernesse to Mitchell, 5 July 1757, SP 90/69.
[7] A List of Ships and Sloops now Building, 13 June 1757, Adm 2/222. Present Disposition of the Naval Force of England, 30 June 1757, RA CP, Box 53.
[8] Abstract of the French Naval Force, 6 July 1757, RA CP, Box 53.
[9] Sir O. Murray, 'The Admiralty', *Mariners' Mirror*, xxiii, 13–35, 129–147, 316–331; xxiv, 101–104, 204–225, 329–352. Clevland to Newcastle, 23 May 1753, Add. Mss 33,046, ff 278–288.
[10] Ships in Commission, 1755, Add. Mss 33,046 f 369. Abstract of Ships in Commission, Admiralty Library, Da. 95.
[11] Admiralty Board Minutes, 23–24 Oct 1755, Adm 3/64. List of Ships and Sloops now Building, 13 June 1757, Adm 2/222. For an account of contract building in the Thames, see P. Banbury, *Shipbuilders of the Thames and Medway* (Newton Abbot, 1971).
[12] Present Disposition of the Naval Force of England, 30 June 1757, RA CP, Box 53. Account of Seamen Borne, *JHC*, xxviii, 128.

addition a marine corps had been formed, this time under Admiralty rather than War Office discipline to end the anomaly of a divided command. Lastly, the official declaration of war allowed the passing of a Prize Act to induce volunteers.[13] These, however, were hard to attract. The duration of the service was uncertain, the conditions harsh, the discipline severe and the pay inferior to that offered by merchants. Thus, although the existing figure was nearly a record, the 116 ships in home waters still wanted 6,000 men. This was the main reason why Anson at least could not agree to a Baltic squadron. Another was that the navy was already stretched by its present obligations with 9 ships of the line in the East Indies; 16 in the Caribbean; 18 in North America; 14 in the Mediterranean; leaving 40 in varying condition for the defence of the British Isles.[14]

On the military front the ministers found that they were even more constricted. Nominally the army had a total establishment of eighty-two infantry battalions and twenty-four cavalry or dragoon regiments. If up to strength this force should have numbered 76,000. However, it was at least 6,000 below this and much of it was scattered, defending the King's dominions at home and abroad. Indeed almost half the force was then overseas and much of the rest unavailable for field operations.[15] In the previous two years the Newcastle ministry had done its best to expand the army by recruiting the ranks and by the creation of new units.[16] Unfortunately the unpopularity of the service had made this difficult. The harsh conditions and lengthy terms of enlistment meant that eligible young men had been slow to step forward, despite the offer of a considerable bounty. Unlike the navy, the army could not impress men unless Parliament passed a special act. The government had been reluctant to do this for fear of exacerbating civilian prejudice. Not until the spring of 1756 had the Newcastle ministry considered the situation sufficiently serious to sponsor a bill permitting the compulsory recruitment of 'such able bodied Men as do not follow any Lawful Calling or Employment'.[17] Then it could only be operated for a few weeks at a time. Hence the experience of the first two

---

[13] S. Gradish, *The Manning of the British Navy during The Seven Years' War*, Royal Historical Society Studies in History Series, No. 21 (London, 1980), 54–88. Gradish however fails to deal with the marines. For this and other aspects of the mobilization, see R. Middleton, 'The Administration of Newcastle and Pitt: the Departments of State and the Conduct of the War, 1754–1760, with Particular Reference to the Campaigns in North America' (Ph.D. thesis, Exeter University, 1969), 73–98.

[14] The Present Disposition of the Naval Force of England, 30 June 1757, RA CP, Box 53.

[15] Disposition of the Army, 1 July 1757, Hotham Papers, DDHO 4/151, East Riding Record Office. The battalions were distributed thus: England 30; Scotland 7; Ireland 12; Guernsey 1; Antigua 1; East Indies 1; Jamaica 1; Gibraltar 8; North America 21.

[16] Middleton, 'Administration of Newcastle and Pitt', 221–226.

[17] An Act for the Speedy and Effectual Recruiting of His Majesty's Land Forces and Marines, *The Statutes at Large*, Ch. IV. 29 Geo II. For a general history of such bills see J. A. Houlding, *Fit for Service: The Training of the British Army, 1715–1795* (Oxford, 1981), 117–118.

years of hostilities suggested that a dramatic increase in the military forces of the nation was not to be expected. Widespread compulsion was thought incompatible with the nation's constitutional forms, while hostility to the military seemed likely to prevent most men joining voluntarily.

It was in these circumstances that the ministers remembered Frederick II's suggestion of an expedition to the coast of France.[18] The idea appealed to Pitt for both political and military reasons. Such a stratagem might alarm the French into recalling some of their men from Germany. It would also avoid the political objections of his supporters to the deployment of British troops for the defence of Hanover. Another advantage was that it would utilize the fleet at home while requiring only a limited number of troops. The other ministers necessarily sympathized. The administration was in its earliest days. No one wanted a crisis of the kind just passed. A coastal expedition seemed a suitable compromise between those who said that the nation would be undone unless the French were stopped in Germany, and those who asserted that the nation would equally be ruined if British troops were the means of doing it. The main problem was where to send the expedition.

A number of possibilities presented themselves, ranging from the coast of Flanders to the western ports of France. Clearly the target must be important if the French were to withdraw troops from Germany. Among the proposals was one from Robert Clerk, an officer in the Engineers, for an attack on the naval base of Rochefort. Clerk had visited the city three years before on his way from Gibraltar, when he found the defence to consist of a single rampart, about 25 feet high, complemented by a ditch. Both were unfinished, making them no great obstacle to a besieging force.[19]

Since Cumberland was absent in Germany, the ministers asked Sir John Ligonier, the Lieutenant-General of the Ordnance, to draw up a plan. He believed that, after providing all the necessary garrison and defence forces, 8,000 men would be available for the expedition. Would the King agree? George II not only did so but proceeded to name the officers: Sir John Mordaunt, Henry Seymour Conway and Edward Cornwallis.[20] Mordaunt, the eldest at sixty, was a nephew of the famous Earl of Peterborough, and had a reputation of being 'a very active, energetic man', well thought of by Cumberland.[21] Conway, the second-in-command, was still only thirty-six. During the previous war he had served as *aide-de-camp* to Cumberland, but had not yet had experience as a field commander, though his bravery was well attested. Cornwallis, nine years Mordaunt's junior, had similarly served in Flanders, though only as a regimental officer. Pitt had earlier wanted to

[18] Mitchell to Holdernesse, 9 Dec 1756, SP 90/67.
[19] Clerk to Ligonier, 15 July 1757, printed in *The Report of the General Officers appointed by His Majesty's Warrant to Enquire into the Causes of the Failure of the Late Expedition to the Coasts of France* (London, 1758), 65–68. (See Mordaunt.)
[20] Ligonier to Pitt, 9 July 1757, CP PRO 30/8/48.   [21] *Dictionary of National Biography*.

send him to America.[22] The ministers thus had no complaints about George II's selection, combining as it did a judicious blend of youth and experience.

The next step was the holding of a more formal discussion at Holdernesse's house on the evening of 15 July 1757. Those invited were Newcastle, Pitt, Hardwicke, Anson and Ligonier. First Ligonier confirmed that the King had consented to the expedition, and had named the commanders and battalions for the service. Then he presented Clerk's paper suggesting Rochefort as a suitable objective. With the situation in Germany continuing to deteriorate, the ministers needed little prompting about the urgency of a decision. The paper from Clerk seemed plausible and the ministers agreed to continue preparations, making Rochefort the target. At the same time they decided to inform the King of Prussia 'under the greatest secrecy with the intended expedition', from which they concluded 'a powerful diversion ought to be expected'.[23]

The plan of the ministry was contained in a dispatch which Holdernesse sent two days later to Mitchell. In this he took the opportunity of explaining the British view of the war. He began by affirming Britain's attachment to the Prussian alliance 'by which alone the cause of Liberty and Religion can be supported'. Little time was spent defining these terms. Liberty, in the context of Europe, meant maintaining the balance of power which in itself was a euphemism for keeping France in check. The inclusion of religion was diplomatically pure sentiment. Holdernesse quickly moved on to express the concern of the ministers at the present course of events in Germany. The Duke of Cumberland was doing his best. He would do a great deal better if given that support from Prussia which the King had been led to believe would be available under the Convention of Westminster. The government for its part regretted being unable to restrain the Russians. It would certainly do its best to secure the Dutch and Danes. There were regrettably limits to what Britain herself could do. Manpower was limited, since there could be no conscription in the manner practised by the King of Prussia. Moreover, Holdernesse explained: 'We must be merchants while we are soldiers...our Trade depends upon a proper exertion of our Marine strength.' Hence there could be no Baltic fleet for the present. However, he could promise two things. Every effort would be made to create a diversion with the proposed expedition. Secondly, George II would do his best to help Frederick II financially. Although 'men are not to be provided from hence, money may at a critical moment enable his Prussian Majesty to supply what is wanting on our part'. This was the manner in which the 'Exertion of the natural strength of this country can be rendered most useful to the Common Cause'.[24]

[22] Pitt to Devonshire, 13 Feb 1757, DPC.
[23] Heads of an Agreement, 15 July 1757, Add. Mss 32,872 ff 204–206.
[24] Holdernesse to Mitchell, 17 July 1757, SP 90/69.

The other ministers now devoted themselves to the details of the operation, for speed was essential if relief was to be afforded to either Cumberland or Frederick II. Pitt had a key role in the assembly of the flotilla. Since government was departmental, a powerful department like the Admiralty could take important decisions about the internal management of the fleet, but could not supply a single Ordnance vessel with naval provisions, unless authorized by a Secretary of State.[25] The task now fell to Pitt rather than Holdernesse, because Rochefort lay in the area for which he was diplomatically responsible.[26]

Assembling the troops was relatively easy. Despite some shortages, the allotted regiments were mainly up to strength. Two days after the ministerial meeting, Barrington was able to inform Pitt that he had given the corps their marching orders with instruction to be at Cowes by 29 July.[27] The preparation of the fleet was also proceeding satisfactorily. Pitt had already had the Channel fleet recalled and all the ships were in port taking on stores and undergoing essential repairs.[28] The only problem was that of men. Sir Edward Hawke, the person designated by Anson to command the squadron, still wanted 1,000 men for his eleven largest ships and the quality of those aboard left much to be desired.[29]

However, this was not the only difficulty still to be overcome. From the beginning the two senior generals, Mordaunt and Conway, had been apprehensive about the project. Their fears were not diminished by the outspoken comments of the two naval commanders, Hawke and Sir Charles Knowles.[30] Both were inclined to think the operation impractical. To iron out these difficulties Newcastle suggested a meeting at Holdernesse's house. Mordaunt and Conway could then question Clerk about Rochefort. In addition, Joseph Thierry, a pilot and native of the area, on whom the government placed reliance, could be present. The apprehensions of the naval officers arose because they were unacquainted with the navigation, and an opportunity to question Thierry should remove their doubts.[31]

However, the news from Germany suggested that the scheme would be too late to help Cumberland. Indeed, Newcastle began to canvass the idea that the troops might have to be diverted if they were to render assistance.[32] He was encouraged in his views by a letter from Mitchell, informing the government that the King of Prussia was of this opinion. Britain had made

[25] Clevland to Rivers, 5 Feb 1757, Adm 2/519.
[26] M. A. Thomson, *The Secretaries of State, 1681–1782* (Oxford, 1932), 2–3.
[27] Barrington to Pitt, 17 July 1757, CP PRO 30/8/18.
[28] Pitt to the Admiralty, 7 July 1757, SP 42/100.
[29] Men wanting to complete, 9–11 Aug 1757, Adm 1/89. Hawke to Clevland, 9 Aug 1757, Adm 1/89.
[30] Newcastle to Hardwicke, 25 July 1757, Add. Mss 32,872 ff 320–324.
[31] Newcastle to Hardwicke, 21 July 1757, Add. Mss 32,872 ff 285–289.
[32] Newcastle to Hardwicke, 25 July 1757, Add. Mss 32,872 ff 320–324.

a formidable military figure on the continent in the days of Marlborough. Surely she could spare 6,000 foot and 3,000 cavalry, for it would be the 'most effectual means to support the common cause'.[33]

Pitt was naturally cool to this proposal, but for the moment said little. Mitchell's letter was dated 9 July, eight days before Holdernesse had written to Frederick II telling him of the administration's plan. The meeting with Clerk and Thierry therefore went ahead. After questioning Clerk, those present then summoned Thierry, who explained that he had been a pilot for twenty years with the French navy before coming to Britain to escape persecution as a protestant. Thierry then described the approaches to Rochefort in the Basque Road, especially the fortifications on the Isle of Aix and the works at the mouth of the River Charante, on which the city stood. He asserted that the difficult navigation of the river excluded any possibility of the fleet attacking Rochefort itself. However, Thierry believed that a landing might be made on the coast opposite Aix, near a small fort called Fouras. If this proved impractical, then a site could be chosen near Chatellaillon, 2 miles to the north. Both places were 5 miles from Rochefort and connected by a good road. He then confirmed Clerk's intelligence about the ditch and rampart not being complete.[34]

After Thierry had withdrawn, Ligonier presented a paper on the state of the French army. At the beginning of the war, he calculated, the French had had 157,000 regular troops. This figure had since increased to 200,000. Of this number, all but 40,000 were in Germany or overseas. After making various deductions for guards and garrisons, the enemy were unlikely to have more than 10,000 regulars for the defence of their western coasts. There was thus little danger of the expedition being overwhelmed on French soil.[35]

This information apparently resolved the doubts of the generals. Newcastle too was more happy. As each day passed there was clearly less point in sending the troops to Germany, for the situation there appeared irreparable. That day, 3 August, news arrived of Cumberland's defeat at the battle of Hastenbeck, seven days earlier. The fate of Hanover was sealed. Though the Duke's army was intact, his right flank had been turned by superior forces and he could do nothing but retreat towards the sea, leaving the Electorate in French hands. In such circumstances it would be foolish to suppose that a few thousand British troops could effect anything decisive.[36] Paradoxically, this reasoning did not lead Pitt and Newcastle to abandon the expedition. Even if the operation was too late to bring relief in Germany it might do something to redeem Britain's reputation. The

[33] Mitchell to Holdernesse, 9 July 1757, SP 90/69.

[34] Minute of a Meeting in Arlington Street, 2 Aug 1757, printed in *The Report of the General Officers*, 68–69.

[35] Mémoire sur la Force Actuelle de la France, 1757, printed in *The Report of the General Officers*, 69–72.

[36] Newcastle to Hardwicke, 3 Aug 1757, Add. Mss 32,872 ff 426–435.

ministry must demonstrate its commitment to Frederick II. Nevertheless, almost unnoticed, the expedition was now something different from what had been originally planned.

When the ministers held their next meeting on 4 August, nine members of the administration were present: Granville, the Dukes of Bedford, Devonshire and Newcastle, the two Secretaries of State, Anson, Ligonier and Legge. Also in attendance were the four senior commanders, Mordaunt, Hawke, Conway and Knowles.[37] The first thing to decide was whether the expedition should proceed. This point was quickly settled in the affirmative. The only doubts came from Devonshire who, along with Newcastle, was uneasy about sending the 'whole naval force of this country away' since the enemy might be tempted to launch a counter-expedition. Pitt then read a draft of the commanders' instructions which he and Ligonier had prepared. These too were unanimously approved, although Devonshire noted they were 'a curious performance, being instead of plain orders, a long and most laborious piece of oratory'.[38] The preamble laid down a number of objectives. Despite recent events, the expedition was still to 'cause a Diversion', compelling the 'Enemy to employ in their own Defence a considerable part of their forces designed to invade and oppress' the powers of Europe. The operation was also if possible to disturb French credit, impair their navy, frustrate their other operations and glorify British arms, while adding 'Life and Strength to the Common Cause'.[39]

The instructions to Mordaunt were entirely discretionary. He was only to land if safe. The same applied to the attack on Rochefort. Ligonier envisaged this as *coup de main* before the enemy had time to organize their defence. A siege was not to be contemplated, since the French might gather a relief force and overwhelm the besiegers. No train of artillery, therefore, would be provided. Everything was staked on the assurances of Clerk and Thierry that the town could be stormed with scaling ladders, given sufficient surprise and panic by the enemy. Ligonier reminded his listeners that Bergen-op-Zoom had been carried in this fashion during the previous war, as had Mahon at the beginning of the present conflict, though he failed to mention that at both, the garrisons had only succumbed after a long siege. However, no one present challenged his statement.[40]

The orders stressed that the attack on Rochefort was not necessarily to be the end of the operation. The commanders had full latitude to turn their attention to other suitable objectives once they had finished in Basque Road. The only limitation was that they must be back by the end of September. This article seemed all the more necessary now, since news had arrived that

---

[37] Minute of the Meeting at Lord Holdernesse's, 4 Aug 1757, Add. Mss 32,997 f 241.
[38] Devonshire to Cumberland, 8 Aug 1757, DPC.
[39] George II to Mordaunt, 5 Aug 1757, printed in *The Report of the General Officers*, 77–80.
[40] *The Report of the General Officers*, 20–22

the French were sending forty battalions to Flanders, ostensibly to enable the Austrians to redeploy their forces against Prussia. Hardwicke believed this might be a strategem to allow the French to launch a counter-attack across the Channel. Victorious in Germany, the enemy might find such course irresistible, if Britain's main force was hundreds of miles away in the Bay of Biscay.[41]

II

Planning the expedition was not the only business to concern the ministers at this time, for arrangements had also been made to strengthen the forces in North America by a draft of 2,000 men from the regiments in the British Isles and the raising of another nine Highland companies.[42] Four more ships of the line were also to go.[43]

Then in an informal discussion outside the King's closet, Pitt, Holdernesse, Granville and Newcastle took two further resolutions. First, in conformity with Pitt's demand about sending money rather than men to Germany, the ministers agreed to allow George II an additional £100,000 to cover the costs of that conflict.[44] As Pitt informed Grenville, this was only reasonable in view of the revenue lost to the King by the occupation of the Electorate.[45]

Pitt then raised the idea of an approach to Spain. Spain occupied a crucial position. If she took an active part against Britain, the royal navy might be driven from the Mediterranean, Caribbean and even the Channel. On the other hand, if the court of Madrid could be brought to a closer understanding, the military prospect would be dramatically improved. Spanish assistance would decisively alter the balance of power in the Mediterranean and West Indies. Above all, the French would be compelled to recall troops from Germany to guard the Pyrenees, and so bring relief to Cumberland. All kinds of blessings might flow, and it was for these reasons that Pitt chose Spain as the field for his first diplomatic initiative on the formation of the coalition. The matter lay with him since it fell within his sphere of diplomatic responsibility.

Traditionally, Spain had been the enemy of Britain, her hostility nurtured as much by colonial rivalries as by her dynastic ties with France. However, since 1748 relations had been on the mend. The war then ended had revealed how dangerous it was for Britain to take on two major naval powers

---

[41] Hardwicke to Newcastle, 22 July 1757, Add. Mss 32,872 ff 300–302. Hardwicke to Newcastle, 4 Aug 1757, Add. Mss 32,872 ff 441–442.

[42] Pitt to Loudoun, 18 July 1757, Kimball, I, 88. For more information on this episode, see R. Middleton, 'Reinforcement for America', Bulletin of the Institute of Historical Research, XLI, 58–72.

[43] Pitt to Holburne, 7 July 1757, Kimball, I, 84–85.

[44] Newcastle to Hardwicke, 9 Aug 1757, Add. Mss 32,872 ff 492–493.

[45] Pitt to George Grenville, 11 Aug 1757, printed in W. J. Smith (ed.), The Grenville Papers: Being the Correspondence of Richard Grenville, Earl Temple, K.G., and the Right Hon: George Grenville, Their Friends and Contemporaries (London, 1852), I, 206–207.

at one time, and the Pelham administration had made special efforts to detach Spain from her old alliance. This policy of dividing the Bourbon powers was aided by dissatisfaction in Madrid at the recent lack of support from France during the war. The overtures from Britain consequently had been well received by the administration of General Wall. Two years later the Treaty of Madrid had been agreed whereby the former causes of dispute were largely settled. Spain paid compensation to the South Sea Company and the latter gave up all claims to trading privileges under the Asiento clause of 1713. The only outstanding questions preventing a closer Anglo-Spanish understanding after 1750 were the problems of Gibraltar and the British logwood settlements along the Honduras coast.[46] Nevertheless, while Wall remained in office, the prospect for good relations seemed more than average and gave some hope that the new initiative might succeed.

Pitt's plan was to offer Gibraltar in return for assistance in the recapture of Minorca. The proposal was not original. Baron Munchausen, the King's German minister, had made a similar suggestion four months before and it had been discussed in at least one London paper.[47] But the crumbling situation in Germany seemed to recommend the scheme afresh when Pitt broached it to his colleagues. The matter, however, was so important that the four men agreed it ought to be discussed at a more formal meeting with Hardwicke, Devonshire and Bedford.[48] At this meeting a minute was drafted stating that, since 'nothing can so effectually tend in the present unhappy circumstances... to the successful prosecution of the present just and necessary war... as a more intimate union with the Crown of Spain', George II should offer Gibraltar to that power in return for help in recapturing Minorca. The ministers recognized that some further induce-ment might be necessary to achieve this desirable union and proposed to offer Spain a favourable settlement of the long-standing dispute on Honduras.[49]

Pitt required all his tact and skill turning this minute into a letter for Sir Benjamin Keene, the British ambassador in Madrid. It was important that the offer should not be made in a manner whereby Spain might construe it as a right to the return of Gibraltar. Nevertheless, the document is a good example of that extravagant prose which had earlier led George II to complain that his dispatches were 'affected, formal and pedantic'.[50] Keene

---

[46] J. O. McLaughlan, *Trade and Peace with Old Spain, 1667–1750* (Cambridge, 1940), 133–146. See also R. Pares, *War and Trade in the West Indies, 1739–1763* (Oxford, 1936), 522–523, 556–557.

[47] *The London Chronicle*, 15–18 Jan 1757. Fox had also aired its possibility the previous year, see J. C. D. Clark, *The Dynamics of Change: The Crisis of the 1750s and English Party Systems* (Cambridge, 1982), 248.

[48] Newcastle to Hardwicke, 9 Aug 1757, Add. Mss 32,872 ff 492–496.

[49] Pitt to Keene, 23 Aug 1757, SP 94/155.

[50] James Earl Waldegrave, *Memoirs from 1754 to 1758* (London, 1821), 95.

was instructed: 'To use the utmost precaution and circumspection...so as to put it beyond the possibility of the most captious and sophistical interpretation to wrest and torture this insinuation of an exchange...into a revival and renewal of any former pretended engagement.' Perhaps not surprisingly the letter took time to write and was only dispatched on 23 August.[51]

So far, relations inside the ministry had been good despite Devonshire's earlier fears. Newcastle informed him: 'We go on very well. Mr Pitt's behaviour at the meetings is as proper as possible.'[52] The only trouble was at the Admiralty. Initially, arrangements there had also worked well. One of the junior lords informed Newcastle: 'Affairs not only go on well...but infinitely better than in my Lord Temple's time.' Now they knew 'what they did, which was not the case formerly'.[53] Legge was similarly complimentary, telling Newcastle that Anson, as a distinguished admiral, was much the best person to keep the service in order. The only mark against him was occasional 'inadvertencies and mistakes in manner', the result of shyness, a quality not always appreciated by an age that often valued wit more than sense.[54] However, this equilibrium was broken in August by the death of Admiral West. Civil appointments to the Board had long been an area of Treasury patronage, and Newcastle immediately arranged to fill the position with Hans Stanley, one of those unrewarded in the recent ministerial reconstruction.[55]

Anson, however, wanted Hawke. Though he had been assured on retaking office that his colleagues would do as he instructed, he seems to have had little confidence in them.[56] In proposing Hawke, he had the support of Pitt who felt that, since the Admiralty was filled with Temple's men, it was only fair that Anson should choose someone himself.[57] Nevertheless, Newcastle was adamant. Since the time of Sir Robert Walpole such appointments had been largely determined by the Treasury and Newcastle was not about to see a diminution of his patronage.[58] The result was nearly a crisis for, although Anson's control of naval affairs was not threatened, he still considered resigning from a Board which, he told his father-in-law, was 'always filled up by the Duke of Newcastle with persons of no use there and no weight or abilities elsewhere'.[59]

[51] Pitt to Keene, 23 Aug 1757, SP 94/155.
[52] Newcastle to Devonshire, 7 July 1757, Add. Mss 32,872 f 116.
[53] Newcastle to Hardwicke, 21 July 1757, Add. Mss 32,872 ff 285–288.
[54] Ibid.
[55] Newcastle to Hawke, 24 Aug 1757, Add. Mss 32,873 f 265. Sir Lewis Namier and J. Brooke, *The History of Parliament: The House of Commons, 1754–1790* (London, 1964), III, 468–469.
[56] Lady Anson to Anson, 18 June 1757, Anson Papers, D615/HMC, Box E, Staffordshire Record Office.
[57] Lady Anson to Hardwicke, 10 Aug 1757, Add. Mss 35,359 f 399.
[58] Sir O. Murray, 'The Admiralty', *Mariners' Mirror*, XXIV, 209–212.
[59] Lady Anson to Hardwicke, 10 Aug 1757, Add. Mss 35,359 f 399.

By now plans for the expansion of the army had been decided. Initially the ministers were inclined to one of two possible schemes: either to add one company to every battalion in Britain; or, more ambitiously, to add a battalion to every regiment that still had only one. The first would amount to an increase of only 4,900 men; the second a rise of about 24,000. However, as Barrington told Cumberland on 15 July, the decision was 'entirely submitted' to him.[60]

Consultation with Cumberland at this time was inevitable. The army was largely his creation. George II had made him Captain-General in 1744 and since then he had vetted all appointments, regulated discipline and issued training instructions. In general he had done a conscientious job, as even the critical James Wolfe admitted.[61] A new system of drill had been introduced; while the artillery and engineers had been given rank to improve their status and morale.[62]

After due consideration Cumberland decided that the scheme for a second battalion was too ambitious, the one for an additional company too modest. By way of compromise he proposed adding two companies to each regiment so that all had an establishment of 1,135 men.[63] But, despite their promise, the ministers were still inclined to opt for an augmentation of only one company to every battalion. In reply Cumberland could only express his amazement when the success of the ministry depended on an expansion of the nation's military effort.[64] The reason, though no one admitted it, was the previous difficulty in recruiting the army. Nevertheless, in the end the sense of Cumberland's ideas could not be denied. On 23 August Barrington informed him that his plans for the infantry at least had been accepted.[65]

At the Admiralty, Anson too was trying to recruit his service, for it seemed that Hawke would have to leave one of his vessels behind and put two battalions of troops aboard the rest to serve as marines.[66] Anson's proposal this time was for a general press, when no regard was paid to protections. Large numbers of these were customarily issued and the system was widely abused. A general press, however, was highly unpopular, not least because many of the government's own departments were inconvenienced. Nevertheless, it was one of the surest ways of securing men in a hurry and this

[60] Barrington to Cumberland, 15 July 1757, RA CP, Box 54.
[61] Wolfe to the Duke of Richmond, 17 Mar 1756, P. L. Carver (ed.), 'Letters of James Wolfe to the Duke of Richmond', *University of Toronto Quarterly*, VIII, 13-14.
[62] Houlding, *Fit for Service*, 198-201. F. Duncan, *History of the Royal Regiment of Artillery* (London, 1879), I, 154-155. W. Porter, *A History of the Corps of Royal Engineers* (London, 1889), I, 180.
[63] Cumberland to Barrington, 22 July 1757, RA CP, Box 54.
[64] Barrington to Cumberland, 8 Aug 1757, RA CP, Box 55. Cumberland to Barrington, 16 Aug 1757, RA CP, Box 55.
[65] Barrington to Cumberland, 23 Aug 1757, RA CP, Box 55.
[66] Hawke to Clevland, 9 Aug 1757, Adm 1/89. Ibid., 22 Aug 1757.

was no exception, 3,500 being obtained.[67] Even so, it is indicative of its ultimate ineffectiveness that a captain at Liverpool stated a further 1,500 men might be raised; but that after he had ignored a few protections he dared not land even to secure his own deserters. Applications for assistance from the magistrates had gone unheeded, emphasizing that on this matter, the civil authorities were often more inclined towards the cause of liberty than the needs of government.[68]

III

While the ministers waited for the expedition to depart, they had to watch a continuously deteriorating situation in Germany. After his defeat at Hastenbeck on 26 July, Cumberland had commenced a retreat towards the sea at Stade by way of Bremen. What happened when he arrived there and could retreat no further was anyone's guess. What everyone feared was that he would conclude some kind of peace that would allow the French to attack Prussia. A Hanoverian neutrality had been a feature early in the previous war. At the beginning of August, George II began to make ominous threats about having to look after himself, since the ministers would do nothing for him, which meant they refused to send British troops to Hanover.[69] Indeed, unknown to his ministers, George II wrote to Cumberland on 11 August authorizing him to make just such an agreement, if there appeared no way of avoiding the destruction of the Electoral army. About the same time he also authorized the Hanoverian Chancellery to enquire in Vienna whether the Empress Queen would mediate for him.[70] Officially he was standing firm, saying that Cumberland would fight to the last. But, although suspecting the worst, the administration constitutionally could do little. Unless invited, it had no right to tell George II how to manage the Electorate, or so Pitt, Holdernesse, Granville and Newcastle concluded when they discussed the problem on 3 August.[71]

However, this did not prevent them from expressing their opinions informally whenever the opportunity arose. Newcastle was especially effective at this. Having been a minister for so many years, he was able to talk to George II and his mistress, Lady Yarmouth, in a way that was impossible for others. His technique was to let the King grumble. Then in a respectful manner he pointed out the disadvantages of the royal plan. Partly as a result of these conversations, George II was made aware of the ministers' strong opposition to a Hanoverian neutrality and of the

---

[67] Admiralty to Captain Schomberg etc., 18 July 1757, Adm 2/79. Seamen Employed, 1757, *JHC*, xxviii, 128.
[68] Robinson to Clevland, 24 July 1757, Adm 1/2385.
[69] Newcastle to Hardwicke, 3 Aug 1757, Add. Mss 32,872 ff 426–432.
[70] George II to Cumberland, 11 Aug 1757, RA CP, Box 55.
[71] Newcastle to Hardwicke, 3 Aug 1757, Add. Mss 32,872 ff 426–432.

disagreeable consequences that must follow.[72] But to stiffen his resolve, Granville, Newcastle, Anson, Pitt and Ligonier agreed, at a meeting on 5 September, that a squadron of ships should be sent to cruise in the vicinity of the Weser and Elbe, and that additional ordnance should be send to assist Cumberland in the defence of Stade.[73] By these measures it was hoped that the Army of Observation could be preserved and the French occupied until the King of Prussia had put his affairs in order. Encouraged by these gestures, the King wrote as late as 15 September to Cumberland that a separate peace would be incompatible with his obligations as King of England. If Stade were untenable, Cumberland should try to link up with the Prussians to the east.[74]

The ministers were perhaps encouraged in their endeavours because the Rochefort expedition was about to sail from Cowes after various delays to the transports. These had taken longer to fit than expected and had then been delayed in the Thames by contrary winds.[75] The news of their arrival now prompted Pitt to remind Mordaunt and Hawke that during the previous war Ligonier had embarked a similar force at Williamstadt in twenty-four hours.[76] But, eager as Pitt was to see the expedition depart, this was hardly tactful handling of men who had been frustrated by events beyond their control. Neither was in a mood to accept it. Mordaunt assured Pitt that not a moment had been lost, pointing out that he was obliged to march the troops and baggage 5 miles to embark, 'whereas at Williamstadt the troops marched directly from the Quay to the Transports, without the least possibility of a Delay'.[77] Hawke was more blunt. He told Pitt that in view of their previous correspondence: 'I should have expected, that before yours was sent, His Majesty would have been fully satisfied that I needed no spur in the Execution of his Orders.'[78] Clearly Pitt had yet to acquire that intimidating manner so often ascribed to him by historians. Nevertheless, the expedition was now on its way. One change made possible by the delay was the instruction to the commanders not to cease their operations after September. The original reason for this had disappeared, since there was no sign of the French organizing a counter-attack from Flanders.[79]

Alas, the orders to Cumberland and the departure of the expedition were too late. The position at Stade was indefensible. Cumberland, armed with the King's previous instructions, had negotiated with the latest French commander, the Duc de Richelieu.[80] By their agreement on 10 September

[72] George II to Cumberland, 15 Sept 1757, RA CP, Box 56.
[73] Ministerial Minute, 5 Sept 1757, Add. Mss 32,997 f 252.
[74] George II to Cumberland, 15 Sept 1757, RA CP, Box 56.
[75] For the correspondence on this see Adm 106/265.
[76] Pitt to Mordaunt and Hawke, 5 Sept 1757, printed in *The Report of the General Officers*, 94–95.
[77] Mordaunt to Pitt, 6 Sept 1757, printed in *The Report of the General Officers*, 97.
[78] Hawke to Pitt, 6 Sept 1757, printed in *The Report of the General Officers*, 95–96.
[79] Pitt to Mordaunt, 15 Sept 1757, printed in *The Report of the General Officers*, 98–99.
[80] Cumberland to Holdernesse, 10 Sept 1757, RA CP, Box 56.

at the village of Klosterseven, the Army of Observation was to be disbanded. The Hessian and Brunswick forces were to be sent home while the Hanoverians were confined to quarters and the Electorate occupied as security for the Convention.[81] The Hanoverian army was thus formally preserved, but effectively disabled, a fact that the miserable old King could not disguise when news of the agreement reached London on 17 September. 'This shameful and ruinous convention', he told Cumberland, had secured none of his essential objectives as Elector.[82] However, when George II tried to claim that Cumberland had acted without authority, Pitt at least had the courage to tell him 'full powers, Sir, very full powers'.[83] Most of the ministers sensibly followed Hardwicke's advice of trying to stay out of what was now a family quarrel, although on the King's insistence they did collectively visit the Duke to hear his explanation on returning home some days later.

The signing of the Convention released the British ministers from the constitutional limbo in which they had been placed. Until now they had had to huddle in small groups whispering among themselves what the King should do. Once the Convention had been announced, their duty was clear. They must advise George II to disown it as being incompatible with his obligations as King of England. A denunciation of some kind was necessary if only to reassure the Prussians. The failure of Cumberland to secure concessions quickly convinced George II of this necessity. A declaration was therefore put out on 18 September by Holdernesse that the Convention had been concluded without the 'participation of the English ministry'.[84] The Prussian ambassador quickly responded that his country would abide by the alliance.

The issue of the declaration, however, did little to solve what was a complex problem. Since the Convention of Klosterseven had been signed on the authority of George II as Elector of Hanover, the announcement from London signified little. The Army of Observation was under the direction of the Hanoverian Chancellery, which still seemed inclined to honour the recently concluded agreement. But, as Newcastle pointed out, the Hessian part of the army was in the pay of Britain and ought not to be disbanded by the Hanoverians. At the very least these troops ought to be sent to help Prussia. The other ministers doubted the utility if not the justice of the proposal.[85] But just when things seemed at their gloomiest, news arrived on 3 October that the Russians had unexpectedly gone home, leaving their sick and a large portion of their artillery in Prussian hands. This miraculous

---

[81] C. Parry (ed.), *The Consolidated Treaty Series* (New York, 1969), XLI, 87–90.
[82] George II to Cumberland, 20 Sept 1757, RA CP, Box 56.
[83] H. Walpole, *Memoirs of the Reign of King George II* (London, 1846–47), III, 60.
[84] Newcastle to Hardwicke, 18 Sept 1757, Add. Mss 32,874 ff 129–136. Newcastle to Hardwicke, 19 Sept 1757, Add. Mss 32,874 ff 148–155.
[85] Newcastle to Hardwicke, 18 Sept 1757, Add. Mss 32,874 ff 129–136.

transformation of the war in the east held out the promise of a similar change in the west. Prussian assistance might now be a possibility. Pitt in particular thought that the Army of Observation should be reconstituted to take advantage of the situation.[86] George II was also ready to escape from the predicament into which he had got himself. But to encourage him, Pitt, Newcastle, Holdernesse, Granville, Anson and Ligonier held a meeting with the King's principal German minister, Baron Munchausen. In an agreed minute, dated 7 October, they reaffirmed that, while they did not presume 'to offer the King any advice on the welfare of Hanover', if George II annulled the Convention, they would recommend that the Army of Observation be taken into British pay the day it recommenced military operations.[87] At a stroke, the ministry had acquiesced in a six-fold increase in spending on the continental war. However, as the *Contest*, a paper favourable to Pitt, had earlier warned: 'We must make good our former treaties and perhaps...enter into new ones till by a course of wise and honest Administration we have gained sufficient strength to stand upon our own footing.'[88]

This offer of assistance had the desired effect. Within twenty-four hours George II had disowned the Convention on the technicality that the French had interfered with the Hessian troops on their way home, contrary to the agreement.[89] The French, who had already transferred a number of their troops to the Prussian Front, were in a poor state to resent such chicanery. For the moment they had to pull their forces back, thus giving the Hanoverians time to put their affairs in order. A first step was the finding of a new commander. As a gesture to the King of Prussia, it was decided to ask Frederick II to release one of his most distinguished generals, Prince Ferdinand of Brunswick. Holdernesse told Mitchell: 'Though his Majesty has many excellent officers there are none who, by their superior quality, or high rank in the army, are equal to such a command.'[90] Fortunately, the expected French counter-attack was delayed longer than anyone anticipated. On 5 November Frederick II smashed part of the French army at Rossbach, and followed this with another victory at the beginning of December over the Austrians at Leuthen. Richelieu dared not expose his flank. Ferdinand had a breathing-space to reorganize his command and the allies could look forward to next year with some hope of survival.[91]

[86] Newcastle to Hardwicke, 3 Oct 1757, Yorke, III, 185.
[87] Cabinet Minute, 7 Oct 1757, Add. Mss 32,999 f 289.
[88] *The Contest*, 2 July 1757.
[89] Newcastle to Hardwicke, 8 Oct 1757, Yorke, III, 186–187.
[90] Holdernesse to Mitchell, 10 Oct 1757, SP 90/69.
[91] Sir Reginald Savory, *His Britannic Majesty's Army in Germany during the Seven Years' War* (Oxford, 1966), 42–60. See also *The Operations of the Allied Army under the Command of his Serene Highness, Prince Ferdinand, Duke of Brunswick...by an Officer who Served in the British Forces* (London, 1764), 1–32.

IV

For the moment all this was in the future. September and October were gloomy months indeed as disasters rained down on the British ministers. In addition to the situation in Germany, news arrived at the beginning of September that the expedition to Louisburg had been thwarted. Like the Rochefort operation, this too had been dogged by delays. Poor weather had prevented the flotilla from leaving England before April. The troops then had to embark at Cork so that Admiral Holburne did not reach Halifax until July.[92] Loudoun himself had done everything possible to have his forces in America ready, having made a risky voyage from New York with minimal protection when a French fleet was rumoured to be in the area. Once at Halifax he had built scaling ladders and instructed his troops in siege techniques.[93]

Alas, all these preparations had been for nothing. By the time Holburne arrived, the French had assembled a superior fleet at Louisburg. This had made proceeding further almost impossible, for if Loudoun had landed on Cape Breton Isle and then lost control of the sea, his army would have faced almost certain destruction. At a council of war, therefore, he had called off the attempt.[94]

Responsibility for this outcome cannot be apportioned to any one individual. It was endemic to the conditions of eighteenth-century warfare. Had the flotilla arrived earlier, Holburne might have defeated the enemy squadrons separately as the prelude to a siege. Equally, success might have resulted had the French been prevented from sending their fleets abroad. Since the beginning of the war Anson had had a squadron cruising in the western approaches. His hope was a repetition of the successes of the previous war, when he and Hawke had inflicted serious loss on the French in the First and Second Battles of Finisterre. The scheme seemed particularly appropriate for the present conflict, since off Ushant the fleet would be able to protect British forces while intercepting enemy traffic with America. Unfortunately, the plan had not so far worked. The area being covered was large and the presence of the fleet spasmodic, for periodic visits had to be made to port to revictual, clean the ships and rest the crews. The result was that at times the entrance to Brest was guarded by little more than a few frigates.[95]

---

[92] Holburne to Clevland, 4 Apr 1757, Adm 1/481. Ibid., 25 Apr 1757. Holburne only left Cork on 8 May, arriving at Halifax on 9 July, ibid.
[93] S. M. Pargellis, *Lord Loudoun in North America* (New Haven, 1933), 226–252.
[94] Loudoun to Devonshire, 5 Aug 1757, Loudoun Papers, Box 91, Huntington Library. See also Minutes of a Council of War, 23–31 July 1757, Loudoun Papers, Box 89. Loudoun to Holdernesse, 5 Aug 1757, Loudoun Papers, Box 91.
[95] Naval Preparations, 10 Sept 1756, Add. Mss 33,047 ff 65–78. The movements of the western squadron in the period 1755 to 1756 can be followed in Adm 1/88–90.

This is what had aborted the present operation. In December 1756 Temple's Board had dispatched a powerful force to cruise in the western approaches under Admiral West.[96] Unfortunately, before West got to his station, a force of six vessels under Admiral Kersaint escaped for Guinea and the West Indies. Then, after the British commander had gone back to port, another five ships of the line departed for the West Indies under Admiral Bauffremont. Later in May, after a second British squadron under Admiral Brodrick had returned home, the main Brest squadron under the Comte de La Motte emerged. All three enemy squadrons had ultimately converged on Louisburg, and in their seemingly disconnected departures lay the seeds of Loudoun's discomfiture.[97]

But this was not the end of the bad news from America. A week later it was learnt that the Marquis de Montcalm, the French commander at Quebec, had taken advantage of Loudoun's absence to seize the strategic post of Fort William Henry. Loudoun had left a substantial garrison under Colonel Monroe, while Brigadier Webb lay in support some miles to the south. Unfortunately, Webb felt unable to advance without the support of the local militias, by which time it was too late to save the beleaguered fort.[98] For a while it seemed that the French might invade the Hudson valley to split the colonies in two. Though this did not happen, the tide of woe continued when, soon afterwards, the fleet of Holburne was dispersed by a hurricane with the loss of two ships and damage to several more.[99]

As though all these setbacks in Germany and America were not enough there came one final humiliation, when the Rochefort expedition returned with nothing accomplished. Initially, the operation had gone as planned, despite the late departure from England. The flotilla entered Basque Road on 21 September and two days later quickly reduced the enemy defences on the Isle of Aix, which guarded the approaches to Rochefort.[100] Unfortunately, the commanders found that there was insufficient water on the mainland side of the Road for the warships to support a landing with their cannon. Then they discovered that the French had a second fortification at the very spot where they were proposing to disembark, a most uninviting proposition. Admittedly, to the north there were no such obstacles, but the water inshore was everywhere shallow and the beaches lined with dunes that could conceal an enemy.[101]

[96] Admiralty to West, 28 Dec 1756, Adm 2/1331.
[97] Corbett, *Seven Years' War*, I, 159–178. M. Le Comte de Lapeyrouse Bonfils, *Histoire de la Marine Française* (Paris, 1845), II, 414–417.
[98] Webb to Loudoun, 5 Aug 1757, Loudoun Papers, Box 91. Ibid., 11 Aug 1757. L. H. Gipson, *The British Empire before the American Revolution*, VII, *The Great War for the Empire: The Victorious Years, 1758–1760* (New York, 1949), 62–88.
[99] Holburne to Clevland, 28 Sept 1757, Adm 1/481.
[100] Hawke to Pitt, 30 Sept 1757, printed in *The Report of the General Officers*, 100–102.
[101] *The Report of the General Officers*, 29–103.

With time slipping by Mordaunt had called a council of war. At this two questions were put. One concerned the feasibility of a landing; the other the possibility of doing anything once the troops were ashore. Clerk in particular was questioned about the value of his information concerning the rampart, ditch and sluice gates. The possibility that Rochefort was in a defensible state was crucial, for without a siege train the expedition was helpless. Finally, after thirty-six hours debate, the council concluded that the attempt was 'neither advisable nor practicable'. The decision concealed a number of differences. Hawke felt that a landing was practicable but was prepared to accept the view about Rochefort. Cornwallis doubted the practicality of a landing but was optimistic that Rochefort was vulnerable.[102]

These disasters not unnaturally created an air of despondency. Lord Shelburne subsequently recalled that there was no one he knew who did not think the nation was undone.[103] Pitt told Sackville that he had 'little less than despair of the public'.[104] Mitchell commented: 'The English 'til now were envied and hated upon the Continent. At present they are despised.' The expedition made them appear 'triflers incapable of acting for themselves or of assisting their allies'.[105] Many close to the administration believed the end to be near. Chesterfield asserted: 'This winter, I take for granted, must produce a peace, of some kind or other; a bad one for us, no doubt, and yet perhaps better than we should get the year after.'[106] To many, the disasters were a sign of divine displeasure at the profligacy of the nation. The general picture was not improved by the widespread threats to public order caused by the continuing high price of grain and by the attempts of the authorities to embody the militia. In October there were reports of flour wagons being seized at Towcester, while mobs at Bakewell demonstrated at the drawing of lots for the Derbyshire levies. Not surprisingly, people were depressed about the general want of discipline, for without discipline no nation could succeed in war.[107]

With frustration came recrimination. People naturally could not understand why such powerful armadas had sailed only to come home without even a landing. Rumours circulated that secret articles regarding Rochefort had been inserted in the Convention of Klosterseven. If a landing was

---

[102] At a Council of War on Board His Majesty's Ship *Neptune*, 25 Sept 1757; printed in *The Report of the General Officers*, 104–106. See also Account of Events, by Admiral Hawke, Nov 1757, Rochefort Slipcase, NMM.

[103] Lord E. Fitzmaurice, *The Life of William, Earl of Shelburne* (London, 1875), I, 74.

[104] Pitt to Sackville, 15 Oct 1757, HMC 9th Report, Part 3, *Stopford-Sackville Mss*, I, 51.

[105] Mitchell to Holdernesse, 1 Nov 1757, printed in Bissett, *Memoirs of Sir Andrew Mitchell*, I, 164.

[106] Chesterfield to Philip Stanhope, 4 Nov 1757, printed in J. Bradshaw (ed.), *The Letters of Philip Dormer Stanhope, Earl of Chesterfield* (London, 1893), III, 1187–1188.

[107] *London Chronicle*, 4/6 Oct 1757. Ibid., 6/8. Sir Edward Fawkener to Cumberland, 23 Sept 1757, RA CP, Box 56.

attempted, Hanover would be put to the sword.[108] Although Pitt publicly
denied the existence of any such agreement, he was privately inclined to
accept a more limited version that 'neither the King nor the Duke wished
success to this expedition', treating 'it as a chimera of Mr Pitt which must
miscarry' to show that the only practical thing 'was to employ our whole
Force in a German War'.[109] These views were repeated by Pitt's supporters
in the press. The inaction of Mordaunt was compared with that of Loudoun,
indicating a plot to discredit the administration.[110] Not all the newspapers
or pamphlets took this line. Some asserted that 'the Expedition was
Chimerical and Impracticable...the production of a Hot Headed Minister'
who foolishly distorted 'our war effort by reason of a Grudge against
Hanover'.[111] Pitt, of course, ignored such abuse. For the moment he was
inclined to order the expedition back to Rochefort to seize the island of Rhé.
He made this point at a meeting of the ministers on 7 October, called to
discuss the breaking of the Klosterseven Convention. He was supported by
Holdernesse and Ligonier. But Anson, Granville, Newcastle and Mansfield
would have none of it. The fleet was wanted for the interception of the
returning overseas French squadrons and in Newcastle's words 'the thought
was dropped very readily'.[112]

Some kind of enquiry was inevitable. The ministers were anxious to know
what had gone wrong, if not to find a scapegoat. The officers too wanted
a chance to clear themselves. As always in times of distress, demands were
made for the guilty to be punished. The Common Council in the City sent
a deputation to the King requesting an enquiry into 'the causes of the failure
of the late expedition'.[113] Most people assumed this would be done through
a court martial. At the beginning of November the King took the unusual
step of establishing a board of enquiry made up of three senior officers: the
Duke of Marlborough, Lord George Sackville and John Waldegrave.

The board went to work in offices near the Privy Garden at St James's
Palace and after a lengthy examination concluded that the prime respon-
sibility for the failure must lie with the Council: 'It does not appear to us
that there were then, or at any time afterwards either a Body of Troops or
Batteries on the Shore sufficient to have prevented the attempting a
Descent.' The same appeared equally true of an attack on Rochefort.[114]

---

[108] H. Walpole to H. S. Conway, 13 Oct 1757, printed in P. Toynbee (ed.), *The Letters of Horace Walpole* (Oxford, 1903), IV, 104–106.

[109] Newcastle to Hardwicke, 8 Oct 1757, Add. Mss 32,874 ff 471–474. For Pitt's public denial see the *London Gazette*, 11/15 Oct 1757.

[110] For analysis of this episode, see R. D. Spector, *English Literary Periodicals and the Climate of Opinion during the Seven Years' War* (The Hague, 1966), 49–55; and M. Peters, *Pitt and Popularity: The Patriot Minister and London Opinion during the Seven Years' War* (Oxford, 1980), 96–103.

[111] Newcastle to Hardwicke, 15 Oct 1757, Add. Mss 32,875 ff 120–125.

[112] Newcastle to Hardwicke, 8 Oct 1757, Add. Mss 32,874 ff 471–474.

[113] *London Chronicle*, 3/5 Nov 1757.   [114] *The Report of the General Officers*, 60–62.

These conclusions could only result in the court martialling of Mordaunt for disobeying orders. The trial began on 14 December in the council chamber at St James's and lasted six days. President of the court was James Tyrawley.[115] Among the witnesses was Pitt. Throughout, Mordaunt remained confident of being acquitted.[116] In this he proved justified. The instructions had left the execution of the project to his discretion. He had acted in good faith. On the charge of disobedience there was no case to answer.[117] But, though acquitted, Mordaunt was by no means exonerated. George II showed his disapproval by removing him, Conway and Cornwallis from his personal staff. They would not be favoured again.[118] The only person to benefit from the affair was James Wolfe, the Quartermaster-General, who gave an impression of vigour without being disloyal to his commander.

Though the verdict of the court martial was technically correct, Hardwicke rightly commented that Mordaunt and his colleagues were a timid lot. Anson later more charitably suggested that the military lacked confidence. Bolder men would have gone ahead and risked a landing.[119] The lack of information about the French defences was unfortunate, though endemic to eighteenth-century warfare. Admittedly more might have been known about the coast, a deficiency Anson only began to correct two years later. But, as Ligonier commented before the start: 'The capacity of the Generals may supply this want of intelligence.'[120] Wolfe certainly believed so. After the expedition he commented: 'Nothing is to be reckoned an obstacle to an undertaking which is not found so upon trial.' In some circumstances 'the loss of a thousand men is rather an advantage', since it might 'redeem the honour of the nation when inaction could be fatal'.[121]

Had Mordaunt attempted a landing he would probably have succeeded, as would an attack on Rochefort itself. When the British fleet appeared the French were quite unprepared, believing the expedition to be bound for Brest. Nothing had been done to the defences since the visit of Clerk. In addition the French had few troops there.[122]

However, it is doubtful if the capture of Rochefort would have been of

---

[115] At a General Court Martial, 14 Dec to 20 Dec 1757, printed in *The Proceedings of a General Court-Martial held in the Council Chamber at Whitehall...upon the Trial of Lieutenant General Sir John Mordaunt* (London, 1758), 7. (See Mordaunt.)

[116] Mordaunt to Tyrawley, Dec 1757, RA CP, Box 57.

[117] *Proceedings of a General Court Martial*, 116.

[118] Ligonier to Sackville, 12 Jan 1758, Germain Papers, I, Clements Library.

[119] Hardwicke to Newcastle, 9 Oct 1757, Add. Mss 32,874 ff 487–490. Anson to Clevland, June 1758, Add. Mss 35,359 ff 410–412.

[120] *The Report of the General Officers*, 20.

[121] Wolfe to Colonel William Rickson, 5 Nov 1757, printed in B. Willson, *The Life and Letters of James Wolfe* (London, 1909), 339–340.

[122] G. Lacour-Gayet, *La Marine Militaire de La France sous le Règne de Louis XV* (Paris, 1902), 304–309.

consequence for the wider objectives of the war. The French navy would have suffered some loss, but the expedition left too late to help Cumberland or the King of Prussia. No troops were withdrawn from Germany, though some units were momentarily dispatched from Paris.[123] The effect on French credit was similarly negligible. Even if Mordaunt and Hawke had departed in July as planned, the results would have been the same. The French were not to be deflected from their main purpose, which was to win the war in Germany. That they did not succeed there had nothing to do with the comparatively minor campaign taking place 800 miles to the west. The opportunity was lost because the French, Austrian and Russian commanders allowed Frederick II and the remnants of Cumberland's army to escape the encirclement then preparing for them.

Thus Pitt's first attempt to alter the course of the war by maritime means had been a failure. So too had his efforts by diplomacy. General Wall proved extremely cool to the idea that Spain could ever be tempted to attack France by an offer of Gibraltar. Indeed, he told Keene that the idea was so offensive that he had not even mentioned it to the King or his colleagues. Wall added that unless the question of the logwood cutters was settled and the trade clauses of the 1667 Treaty between the two countries observed, Spain would have to regard Britain, not France, as the principal threat to her interests and the peace of Europe.[124]

Shelburne commented much later: 'It requires experience in government to know the immense distance between planning and execution. All the difficulty is in the last.'[125] In the summer of 1757 Pitt lacked that experience. It had been easy to suggest an alliance with Spain: quite another to effect it. The episode shows that even for him the scope to change events was limited.

Though the ministry was only partially to blame for the misfortunes in America and Europe, they did lead to one change in its ranks. This was the appointment of a Commander-in-Chief to replace Cumberland as the government's chief military adviser. The move was desired for several reasons. Pitt was convinced that only such action would ensure that commanders did as they were ordered. He was abetted in his determination by his allies at Leicester House, who were still suspicious of Cumberland's designs on the throne. The other members of the administration agreed about the need for a replacement. They had never been enthusiastic about admitting Cumberland to their counsels. He was too close to Fox and as a member of the royal family his presence did not make for informality or freedom of expression. The difficulty was to find a successor who was acceptable to the King and of sufficient standing.

[123] R. Waddington, *La Guerre de Sept Ans* (Paris, 1899), I, 458–524.
[124] Keene to Pitt, 26 Sept 1757, SP 94/156.
[125] Fitzmaurice, *Life of Shelburne*, I, 23.

Fortunately, there did seem to be such a person in Ligonier, who, while not the most senior general in the British army, was certainly the most distinguished. Born in 1680 of Huguenot parents, he had first seen service in 1702 as a volunteer in the army of Marlborough. In 1742 he was appointed deputy to Lord Stair and his subsequent courage at Dettingen won him a knighthood from a grateful George II. During his career Ligonier had participated in twenty-three battles and nineteen sieges without once flinching from the call of duty. But he was not simply a courageous soldier. Through intelligent administration he had made his regiment, the 8th Dragoons, one of the finest in Europe.[126] His general attitude was summed up in a paper he drew up on the tactical deployment of the army: 'In military affairs nothing ought to be left to the Hazard of Fortune, for Industry commandeth Fortune in as much as she Armeth herself' against it.[127]

Nevertheless, the plan to promote him was not without its difficulties. One was his age: he was then in his seventy-eighth year. Hardwicke especially thought he was too old.[128] George II presented another snag. He was sensible that Cumberland was suffering for his own sins. He announced therefore that he would be Commander-in-Chief himself, leaving the position open for his son in the future. This idea was most displeasing to the ministers. As Newcastle noted, unless there was 'some real supreme command', Cumberland would have the 'whole army in his Power without being responsible'.[129] The King's proposal would in any case do nothing to solve the constitutional relationship of the civil to the military power. At the time of the Braddock expedition, Newcastle had commented: 'Since this would be entirely a military operation, we the *civil* Ministers were at a loss, whom to recommend and what measures to take.'[130] Now it was essential that there was 'some person for the ministers to consult', who could 'assist at Council for the Disposition of the Troops' and for the 'Defence of the Kingdom'.[131]

For a few days George II tried to resist. Pitt, however, determinedly badgered both the King and his colleagues. His chance came on Tuesday, 19 October, in an audience at St James's. George II discussed the possibility of the French renewing their invasion and the need for the ministers to take precautions. This gave Pitt the lead he was looking for. 'With whom Sir, must we confer? It will be necessary to have some person to be Commander-

[126] R. Whitworth, *Field Marshal Lord Ligonier: A Story of the British Army, 1702-1770* (Oxford, 1958), 39-48.
[127] 'Some Useful Points of Discipline', Donoughmore Papers, T3459/A3, Public Record Office of Northern Ireland.
[128] Hardwicke to Newcastle, 16 Oct 1757, Add. Mss 32,875 ff 143-145.
[129] Memorandum for the King, 19 Oct 1757, Add. Mss 32,875 ff 191-192.
[130] Newcastle to Sir Horace Walpole, 26 Oct 1754, Add. Mss 32,737 ff 208-211.
[131] Memorandum for the King, 19 Oct 1757, Add. Mss 32,875 ff 191-192.

in-Chief with whom your ministers may consult.' The King, somewhat taken aback, replied: 'I will have no Marshal nor Captain General. There is Ligonier, you may talk to him.' Next day George II told Ligonier that he 'must have the Chief Direction' under himself, finding 'out the Best Officers, as Cumberland had formerly'.[132] But the position still had to be regularized if the Duke's return was to be prevented.[133] Further discussion therefore settled that Ligonier would be given the title of 'Commander-in-Chief of all the land forces in Great Britain', with a patent under the Great Seal. He was also to be made a field-marshal and given a peerage.[134]

Originally, Ligonier's authority was to have extended to America, but this was abandoned when Mansfield suggested that it might conflict with the commission of Loudoun which was also under the Great Seal.[135] Indeed, despite the commendatory language, the appointment was hardly what Ligonier might have wished. The commission issued to Cumberland in 1744 had given the Captain-General authority over 'all the forces at home and overseas'.[136] Ligonier had no such power. He might communicate with the commanders in America, but was not to send them 'orders...independently of the civil Ministers' at home. Elsewhere he was similarly restricted. He could correspond with the forces in Germany and Ireland, might give them advice, but was not to issue commands.[137] The generals overseas were still to communicate with the King through the channel of a Secretary of State, making their own suggestions about operations and promotions. However, for the ministers the important point was the exclusion of Cumberland. They could now run the war their own way.

One event to cheer the ministry as Parliament assembled was the news that Robert Clive had defeated the Siraj-ud-Daula at Plassey. This reversed the previous setback at Calcutta.[138] Though the operations there were the concern of the East India Company, the government's involvement had been increasing for some time. Early in 1754 Admiral Watson had been dispatched with six ships. At the same time the first regular land forces, the 39th Foot, had been sent under Colonel Aldercron. The following year a further step had been taken with the dispatch of four companies of artillery.[139] It was these forces that had enabled Clive to recover the Company's lost ground in Bengal. Nevertheless, it was clear that the struggle was not over and the sending of further aid could not be discounted, despite the recent departure of Steevens. The French were still entrenched in the Carnatic, threatening Madras from their position at Pondicherry.

[132] Newcastle to Hardwicke, 23 Oct 1757, Add. Mss 32,875 ff 222–232.
[133] Whitworth, *Ligonier*, 233–234.
[134] George II to Sir John Ligonier, 29 Oct 1757, Letters Patent, C 66/3659, PRO.
[135] Newcastle to Hardwicke, 23 Oct 1757, Add. Mss 32,875 ff 222–232.
[136] George II to the Duke of Cumberland, 11 Mar 1744, Letters Patent, C 66/3616, PRO.
[137] Newcastle to Hardwicke, 23 Oct 1757, Add. Mss 32,875 ff 222–232.
[138] Sir George Forrest, *The Life of Lord Clive* (London, 1918), I, 435–460.
[139] Ibid., 227–238.

2

A New Start

Parliament was due to meet on 1 December 1757, and the ministers had to settle the content of the King's speech. Even by this time it was the monarch's in name alone. The eighteenth-century version, however, was short, being confined to general sentiments with none of the detailed proposals that have become the hallmark of the twentieth century. Nevertheless, it was still important as an indication of the style and intention of the administration. Newcastle was afraid that if Pitt drafted it, as he intimated he ought at the end of October, he would use it to ride some of his more obnoxious hobby horses, notably the militia. It would also give him an appearance of supremacy. This Newcastle could not admit. For some years he had drafted the speech with the assistance of Hardwicke. As an expedient for keeping the task out of Pitt's hands he suggested that Hardwicke should do it himself.[1]

The former Lord Chancellor was not at all enthusiastic. He was intent on a little peace 'after near twenty years of slavery'. Instead he took the opportunity of giving Newcastle some advice. He was well aware of the latent tensions still in the ministry, but, while inclined to admit that Pitt was 'extremely ambitious', he nevertheless believed the Secretary had sufficient sense of his own interest to realize that he could not go on without Newcastle's assistance. The latter thus ought to have no fears about having to 'act the subordinate part'. As to drafting the speech, Hardwicke thought Newcastle was making too much of it. 'The question of who shall lay it before the King is more material than who shall have the drawing of it, and this only in point of precedence.' More important was the need for the two to take each other into their confidence. Where better to start than on the speech?[2]

Newcastle was not pleased at this reply. Neither was the King. George II was equally anxious to prevent Pitt having the authorship of the document. In a discussion with the two Secretaries, he had indicated that Hanover

---

[1] Newcastle to Hardwicke, 29 Oct 1757, Add. Mss 32,875 ff 289–294.
[2] Hardwicke to Newcastle, 29 Oct 1757, Yorke, III, 38–40.

should not be mentioned until affairs there had been settled. Pitt strongly disagreed, thinking that some reference should be made to the breaking of the Convention of Klosterseven and the determination of the ministers to pursue the war vigorously.[3] Finally, to avoid further altercation, Hardwicke agreed to produce a draft. But, in keeping with his advice to Newcastle, he was careful to give Pitt early notice of its contents. Pitt read the document twice before handing it back to Hardwicke, making a number of complimentary comments and inviting him to compose a formal draft.[4] After showing the speech to Granville, Newcastle then carried it to the King, thus establishing the point of precedence.[5] The incident in fact set the procedure for the rest of the reign. Pitt genuinely seems to have accepted that for this kind of business Hardwicke was eminently more qualified, having the drafting skills that came so naturally to a lawyer.

The speech as finally composed did not mention Hanover or the events of the previous three months. However, it did promise a vigorous prosecution of the war in conformity with the ministry's aims. 'It is my fixed Resolution', George II announced, 'to apply my utmost Efforts for the Security of my Kingdom, and for the Recovery and Protection of the Possessions and Rights of my Crown and Subjects in America and elsewhere.' This would be effected by 'the strongest Exertion of our Naval Forces, as by all other Methods'. The speech continued with the now platitudinous sentiments about the need to defend the 'Protestant Religion' and the 'Liberties of Europe' by alliance with the King of Prussia. The King then noted Frederick II's recent successes and the need to give him financial assistance. Obviously such aid would be expensive. George II could only promise the assembled members that 'the best and most faithful Economy shall be used', consistent with such essential services.[6]

The speech was well received. The success of Frederick II and the distant triumph of Clive, though neither attributable to the ministry, helped suggest that the direction of the war was in able hands, whatever the other setbacks. Besides, no alternative was in prospect. The Foxites, Leicester House and the Tories were all satisfied with the existing arrangement.

By now the ministry had settled down regarding its inner composition. Barrington reported to Mitchell: 'The Duke of Newcastle, the Lord President, Lord Hardwicke, Lord Mansfield, the two Secretaries of State and Lord Anson form what Lord Granville calls the Conciliabulum. They meet continually, and their opinion is the advice given to the King.'[7]

---

[3] Newcastle to Hardwicke, 5 Nov 1757, Add. Mss 32,875 ff 390–398.
[4] Hardwicke to Newcastle, 22 Nov 1757, Add. Mss 32,876 ff 60–61.
[5] Newcastle to Granville, 26 Nov 1757, Add. Mss 32,876 f 134.
[6] *JHC*, xxviii, 3.
[7] Quoted in A. Ballantyne, *Lord Carteret* (London, 1887), 353. Presumably the attendance of Ligonier had been too recent for Granville to include.

The ministers, having announced their intentions, next had to start the detailed planning. One decision already taken was the sending of a second royal battalion to support the East India Company. Though Clive had secured Bengal, the French would most likely try to revive their fortunes by an offensive in the Carnatic. Since no existing unit was suitable for this service, the ministry arranged for Colonel Draper to recruit one. But to assist him several volunteer companies were to be sought from the regiments garrisoned at Colchester.[8]

However, most important was the need to make arrangements for America if the previous delays and disappointments were not to be repeated. Though commerce and the internal administration of the colonies were the concern of the Privy Council and Board of Trade, questions of defence and external relations belonged to the southern Secretary and were therefore Pitt's responsibility.

Traditional accounts of the Seven Years' War have emphasized how Pitt used his office to direct nearly every branch of government: that he was solely responsible for the planning and conduct of the war.[9] This view cannot be sustained. It was only possible through a misunderstanding of the role and function of the eighteenth-century Secretaryship. The days when Thomas Cromwell had used the office to direct practically every aspect of government were long since past. That power had originated because the Secretaries directed the correspondence of the King's most honourable Privy Council. The development of a departmental system of government and powerful bureaucracies like the Admiralty, Ordnance and Treasury meant that many areas of business were withdrawn from the Council and the Secretaries had less scope for wielding influence.[10]

Nevertheless, the Secretaries did have a critical role in wartime, when complex operations had to be co-ordinated. As William Knox, an under-secretary of state, noted in 1776: 'All warlike preparations, every military operation, and every naval equipment must be directed by a Secretary of State before they can be undertaken.'[11] But Knox was only referring to office procedures. This is clear from another definition given at about the same time regarding the collective relationship of the ministers to the Secretariat. ' *The Cabinet*: to consider and determine what expeditions are to take place

---

[8] H. C. Wylly, *A Life of Lieutenant General Sir Eyre Coote, K.B.* (Oxford, 1922), 59.

[9] Reverend F. Thackeray, *A History of the Right Honourable William Pitt, Earl of Chatham* (2 vols., London, 1827). H. Walpole, *Memoirs of the Reign of King George II* (3 vols., London, 1846–47). W. E. H. Lecky, *A History of England in the Eighteenth Century* (8 vols., London, 1878–1890). J. S. Corbett, *England in the Seven Years' War: A Study in Combined Strategy* (2 vols., London, 1907). B. Williams, *The Life of William Pitt, Earl of Chatham* (2 vols., London, 1913). W. C. B. Tunstall, *William Pitt, Earl of Chatham* (London, 1938). For an analysis of the literature on Pitt see the appendix to this book.

[10] On the decline of the Privy Council see E. R. Turner, *The Privy Council of England in the Seventeenth and Eighteenth Centuries, 1603–1784* (Baltimore, 1928).

[11] Quoted in M. A. Thomson, *The Secretaries of State, 1681–1782* (Oxford, 1932), 75.

and at what periods, what troops are likely to be sent abroad, when, where
how and the number. What services are to have the preference. *The Secretary
of State*: to issue timely orders to the Treasury, Admiralty, Ordnance and
the Commander-in-Chief on these heads, so that every necessary preparation
can be made, and no delay nor disappointment happen when the service
takes place'.[12] Although there was no formal Cabinet during the Seven
Years' War, this was essentially the situation now.

Pitt had already been gathering information with regard to North
America. Among those consulted was Sir Charles Hardy, the Governor of
New York and second-in-command of the fleet at Louisburg. Indeed,
Loudoun was told that Hardy 'is every day with the Ministers'.[13] But
equally influential was Loudoun himself. His letters included a number of
observations, of which Pitt and his colleagues were not slow to take note.
Loudoun believed that a major reason for the failure in 1757 had been the
late arrival of the reinforcement from England. The campaign was over
before anything could be achieved. Hence the earliest preparation must be
made.[14]

To meet this criticism Pitt had already arranged for a squadron to winter
in North America. The previous September, Anson had wanted the
majority of Holburne's fleet to come home to refit, pleading a lack of
facilities on the other side of the Atlantic. Pitt had objected for the reasons
now being advanced by Loudoun. To show willing, Anson then agreed to
consult Admiral Boscawen, who was better acquainted with the area.[15] The
result was the leaving of eight battleships at Halifax.[16] But, to meet Anson's
objections, Pitt had taken up the idea of Captain Loring, a transport agent,
to establish a naval base there by arranging for the purchase of Cornwallis
Island in Halifax Bay.[17]

Since any force from Europe might be late, Loudoun advised that a
second offensive overland ought to be undertaken by the troops in America,
if only to protect the backcountry. The point was readily accepted though,
as Hardy informed him, the ministry felt that he ought to have anticipated
this himself the previous year.[18] Nevertheless, the logic and outcome of the
1757 campaign was that not all eggs should be placed in one basket. Staking
everything on a seaborne attack had left the British with nothing to fall back
on. Several assaults would enable the administration to be more certain of

[12] Quoted in P. Mackesy, *The War for America, 1775–1783* (London, 1964), 12.
[13] Calcraft to Loudoun, 29 Dec 1757, Loudoun Papers, Box 113, Huntington Library.
[14] Loudoun to Holdernesse/Pitt, 16 Aug/17 Oct 1757, Loudoun Papers, Box 94. Loudoun
    began the letter believing Holdernesse still to be the sole Secretary, following Pitt's dismissal
    in April.
[15] Newcastle to Hardwicke, 10 Sept 1757, Add. Mss 32,873 f 548.
[16] Pitt to Admiral Holburne, 21 Sept 1757, Kimball, I, 110–111.
[17] Memorandum, 13 Sept 1757, Add. Mss 32,997 f 261. Pitt to the Admiralty, 27 Jan 1758,
    Adm 2/4122.
[18] Hardy to Loudoun, 2 Dec 1757, Loudoun Papers, Box 109.

securing its objective. Only Hardwicke disputed this view. He felt that 'so many Enterprizes going on at once' would 'greatly divide the Forces', remembering that this was one of the points 'objected to after the Event of Braddock's Campaign'.[19]

The next task was to decide the command. A cloud naturally hung over the generalship of Loudoun. He had promised much and a great deal of trust had been placed in him. Initially, Pitt seemed disposed to accept his plea that he had been thwarted by events beyond his control. But as the autumn passed and other setbacks occurred, Pitt affected to see his inaction in a more insidious light.[20] This provided him with an excuse for demanding the removal of a commander who in fifteen months had presided only over disaster, beginning with the loss of Oswego and ending with that of Fort William Henry. He first began suggesting a new person at the same time as moves were being made to have Cumberland replaced by Ligonier. Newcastle advised patience. There were only so many things that George II could be coaxed into doing.[21] But neither Newcastle nor the other ministers wished to protect Loudoun. They could not forget that he was the nominee of Cumberland whose influence they were happy to see diminished. Accordingly, Ligonier was advised to have the name of a successor ready.[22]

Even so, the recall of Loudoun was by no means certain. One difficulty was the lack of a suitable replacement. Several possible candidates had been disgraced at Rochefort or were too close to Cumberland. Yet more did not want to go. As so often with such decisions, chance played a hand. In the third week of December, Pitt gave evidence at the court martial of Mordaunt. In the process he was called to order by the president of the court for deviating from the point. Pitt was furious at this rebuke but powerless to reply. By coincidence, that afternoon the Commons held its annual debate on the army estimates. When William Beckford ventured to ask how so much money had been spent to so little purpose, Pitt responded by stressing the incompetence of the Officer Corps in general and of Loudoun in particular. Most observers agreed that he went further than intended and that this was one of those occasions when he allowed his heart to govern his head.[23] No matter, the damage was done. One of the King's leading ministers had publicly announced his lack of confidence in the general. The administration had little alternative but to find a replacement.

Historians have customarily followed Horace Walpole in crediting Pitt with the selection of Jeffrey Amherst, Wolfe and John Forbes.[24] They may

[19] Hardwicke to Newcastle, 17 Dec 1757, Add. Mss 32,876 f 321.
[20] Newcastle to Hardwicke, 8 Oct 1757, Add. Mss 32,874 ff 471–474.
[21] Newcastle to Hardwicke, 23 Oct 1757, Yorke, III, 191–193.
[22] Newcastle to Ligonier, 10 Dec 1757, Add. Mss 32,876 f 264.
[23] Calcraft to Loudoun, 25 Dec 1757, Loudoun Papers, Box 112.
[24] Walpole, *Memoirs of George II*, III, 91.

have been misled because most commissions in the army were made out in the Secretaries' office. But the writing of these in no way gave them control. Military preferment had long been jealously guarded by the Hanoverians. Only the Secretary at War and Captain-General or Commander-in-Chief assisted the King in these matters. Naturally, pressure to interfere was exerted on the Secretaries as on all the ministers. But generally Pitt took the line that none but military men could decide on military matters. He was wise to do so, for it was over twenty years since he had been an officer himself and there is no evidence that he had maintained his contacts with the military.[25]

All was not well with the Officer Corps when Ligonier began his search for a successor to Loudoun. The failures in North America, Rochefort and Germany had created a crisis of confidence, as was shown by the need to ask Frederick II for a suitable commander for the Army of Observation. Another problem was the bitter quarrelling in the force. Hardwicke blamed this on the aristocratic nature of the Corps and warned that if family connection was to be the only criterion, 'Men of Quality ought not to be let in the Army, for it will ruin the Service'. The public would be 'better served by having more Soldiers of Fortune, and perhaps some foreigners of Service and Experience'.[26]

Hardwicke's assertion that the army was dominated by the aristocracy was of course true of all European armies. Selection from this class was inevitable in such hierarchical societies. The aristocracy had originated as a military order. Martial honours were essential to its meaning and glamour. There was, hence, little that Ligonier could do to change the Corps. He could only see that where possible deserving men were promoted. An outsider himself, he was always sympathetic to those against whom the system discriminated. When a regimental commander during the previous war, he had recommended thirty-seven non-commissioned men for promotion to the rank of officer.[27]

For once he seemingly had an opportunity to ignore the usual claims to command. After the disappointing results of the campaign in North America, George II affirmed that he would do 'all he could to encourage a spirit' there. John Calcraft, the regimental agent, reported to Loudoun: 'The present intention of giving preferment to officers seems to be the promoting those well thought of, without paying the usual regard to

---

[25] Historians have been fond of quoting Pitt's boast to Shelburne that as a young man he had taken 'his military duties seriously and like Wolfe, set himself... to read every military book on which he could lay his hands'. They have not continued to state how Shelburne from his own experience 'never found him...with so much as a book before him', Lord E. Fitzmaurice, *The Life of William, Earl of Shelburne* (London, 1875–76), I, 73–78.
[26] Hardwicke to Newcastle, 16 Oct 1757, Yorke, III, 189–190.
[27] R. Whitworth, *Field Marshal Lord Ligonier: A Story of the British Army, 1702–1770* (Oxford, 1958), 46.

seniority.' However, when Barrington suggested that all the vacant regiments in America should be given to the 'young Lieutenant-Colonels' there, being 'less grating to the old ones here', George II demurred, promising only to consider the idea 'now and then'.[28] Ligonier perhaps failed to press the matter, for, shortly after his appointment, Newcastle suggested he ought to spend more time with the King. Ligonier might dislike waiting in antechambers, but many a government decision was won or lost on the steps of the royal closet. It was something no minister could avoid if he were to be fully in control of his department.[29]

Nevertheless, the names of the men put forward by Ligonier did show considerable imagination. James Wolfe was not known to him personally. But he already had a regimental reputation and his other credentials were also strong. He had an influential patron in the Duke of Richmond and a father who was a lieutenant-general and member of the King's staff.[30]

The selection of Amherst and Forbes was more clearly Ligonier's doing. He had known Amherst since the previous war when he had been one of his aides.[31] The acquaintance with Forbes was even longer. But until 1757 Forbes had been nothing more than a senior officer in the American backcountry. Then in December George Ross, the regimental agent, informed him of Ligonier's promotion: 'In short he has the whole command and direction of the army, and as such is much disposed to serve you.'[32] Soon afterwards, when Pitt told Forbes that he was to command the expedition against Fort Duquesne, Ross asserted it was 'your friend, Marshall Lord Ligonier, who recommended you to the Ministry with great warmth and became answerable for your conduct'.[33]

One reason for the recall of Loudoun was a feeling that his position had been too proconsular. For the 1758 campaign, therefore, Pitt and Ligonier divided the American command effectively into three. The first and ostensibly chief position was given to James Abercromby, Loudoun's senior officer, with Augustus Lord Howe as his deputy. They were to take a mixed force of 25,000 regulars and provincials by way of Lake George, Fort Ticonderoga and Crown Point against Montreal and Quebec.[34] The second operation, an assault on Louisburg, was to be given to Amherst and Wolfe. They were to lead a force of 14,000 men, nearly all regulars, with a powerful fleet under Boscawen on what was clearly the most prestigious assignment.[35]

[28] Calcraft to Loudoun, 25 Dec 1757, Loudoun Papers, Box 112.
[29] Newcastle to Ligonier, 10 Dec 1757, Add. Mss 32,876 f 264.
[30] *Dictionary of National Biography.*   [31] Whitworth, *Ligonier*, 46.
[32] Ross to Forbes, 10 Dec 1757, Dalhousie Papers, GD45/2/20, Scottish Record Office.
[33] Ibid., 14 Jan 1758.
[34] Pitt to Abercromby, 30 Dec 1757, Kimball, I, 143–151. George II to Abercromby, 30 Dec 1757, Abercromby Papers, Box 1, Huntington Library.
[35] George II to Amherst, 3 Mar 1758, CP PRO 30/8/96. The delay was because Amherst had been in Germany attending to commissariat matters.

Lastly, the smallest of the three, an attack on Fort Duquesne, was allotted to Forbes. He too was to be his own master.[36]

In a lengthy memorandum, John Bradstreet, a regular officer who had been in America since 1745, strongly pressed the idea of an attack on Niagara or Fort Frontenac near the entrance to the St Lawrence. He pointed out that British control of either place would make it impossible for the enemy to escape to the west or retain their posts on the Ohio. An attack on the less accessible Duquesne would then be unnecessary.[37]

Such advice was not new. Halifax had made the point in 1754.[38] But the capture of Duquesne had become a point of honour for the British. Its seizure by the French in 1754 had been the original cause of the war and the British were still smarting from the defeat of Braddock and of Washington before him. Although Duquesne might be insignificant in the wider conflict, the ministers had good reason for continuing their plan. Unless some operations were undertaken in the area, the southern colonies might escape making any contribution whatever. A renewal of the attack on Duquesne would at least harness the energies of Virginia and Pennsylvania and bring peace to the backcountry of these two important provinces.

The details of the operations in America were fixed in a series of meetings before Christmas. The ministers then dispersed to their homes for a well-earned rest, except Pitt, who still had to translate the decisions into meaningful orders for the various commanders and civil authorities. So vast was the undertaking that he began to have 'doubts' about his ability to implement it.[39] No sooner had Newcastle reached Claremont, his Sussex country home, than a note arrived from Barrington stating that Pitt would 'not take upon himself to direct the whole plan of American affairs without the assistance of a Cabinet'. Would Newcastle attend at Holdernesse's house, on Wednesday, 28 December?[40] This was too much for Newcastle. America was not his department. As he informed Pitt: 'I think I am fully appraised of Everything that relates to the American Dispositions, and do most entirely approve of them. I am sure I shall approve the *Execution* as much as I do the Plan.' He continued: 'The persons to command in each Place have been settled by us.' If the King consented to Amherst, then the business was as good as done. Newcastle would gladly read any dispatches and if necessary return to London.[41]

Pitt responded by excusing Newcastle from the meeting, but justified its need. Few measures of the government were 'so important...as the

---

[36] Pitt to Abercromby, 30 Dec 1757, Kimball, I, 146. Abercromby to Forbes, 14 Apr 1758, Abercromby Papers, Box 4.
[37] Bradstreet to Lyttelton, 3 Sept 1757, CP PRO 30/8/85 ff 241–248.
[38] Lord Halifax's proposals for North America, 7 Nov 1754, Add. Mss 33,029 ff 138–142.
[39] Business with Lord Hardwicke, 23 Dec 1757, Add. Mss 32,997 f 314.
[40] Barrington to Newcastle, 26 Dec 1757, Add. Mss 32,876 f 439.
[41] Newcastle to Pitt, 27 Dec 1757, Add. Mss 32,876 f 453.

Campaign in North America where England and Europe are to be fought for and where all the *data* on which we are to ground any Plan are so loose and precarious'.[42] The meeting therefore went ahead, but not before Newcastle had read Pitt's drafts in the privacy of his home. These he much approved: 'They are perfectly agreeable to what was the sense of the Lords at our several meetings', and congratulated Pitt 'at being so near the end of this great work'.[43] Two days later Barrington reported that everything was indeed settled except the naming of Amherst. That required another two days of coaxing in the closet.[44]

One difference in the American plans for 1758 was the decision to increase the number of provincials. Pitt in particular felt that their resources had not yet been properly harnessed. But to do this, Hardy warned, more attractive terms would have to be offered. The assemblies needed encouraging.[45] Pitt and the other ministers therefore agreed to offer increased financial incentives. The Treasury would feed and arm their troops, leaving the provincial authorities merely to find the levy money and pay, for which they would be liberally reimbursed. The hope was that the colonists would raise 25,000 men.[46]

Pitt also attempted to solve the vexed question of rank between the provincial and regular officers. At the beginning of the war Cumberland had placed restrictions on the provincials when operating with the latter. The poor calibre of the colonials partly justified this, but it was productive of much trouble, for their pride was deeply wounded. Pitt now arranged that all provincial officers should have equal rank below that of colonel, though the generosity of his measure was somewhat lost when he had all the regular lieutenant-colonels breveted a full rank.[47] Nevertheless, this and the other measures did indicate a change of heart. The result was a greatly increased readiness to help.

Since the regular army in North America numbered 23,000, the ministers decided that only two regiments need be sent from Britain. The French were not thought to have more than 8,000 regulars in Canada, including the garrison at Louisburg, so that the forces there ought to suffice. In any case Britain's military establishment had expanded only modestly during the previous year. The parliamentary estimates were for an establishment of 88,000, an increase of 13,000 on the previous year, most of this being accounted for by the additional companies last summer.[48] Otherwise,

[42] Pitt to Newcastle, 27 Dec 1757, Add. Mss 32,876 f 455.
[43] Newcastle to Pitt, 28 Dec 1757, Add. Mss 32,876 f 461.
[44] Barrington to Newcastle, 29 Dec 1757, Add. Mss 32,876 f 475. Holdernesse to Newcastle, 31 Dec 1757, Add. Mss 32,876 f 499.
[45] Calcraft to Loudoun, 29 Dec 1757, Loudoun Papers, Box 113.
[46] Pitt to the Colonial Governors, 30 Dec 1757, Kimball, i, 136–143.
[47] Warrant for Settling Commissions in America, 30 Dec 1757, SP 44/189.
[48] *JHC*, xxviii, 13–15.

volunteers were still proving hard to attract. This was the reason why Barrington had once more obtained permission from the Privy Council to reintroduce the Act allowing compulsory recruitment.[49] The same difficulties explain why there were no plans to create new corps.

Arrangements for the embarkation of the two regiments were quickly made by Pitt and Barrington.[50] There was more debate on how the forces for Louisburg were to be transported. A paper submitted to Pitt argued persuasively that any shipping hired in England would be too expensive and too late for an early campaign. The tonnage might best be raised in New England or the middle colonies.[51] However, this idea was dismissed by Hardy who knew from experience that American resources were inadequate.[52] Pitt therefore arranged that 20,000 tons would be sent from England, though 'to prevent...any Delays or Disappointment' Abercromby was to raise an additional 6,000 tons locally. To secure this he could authorize an embargo.[53]

As in the previous year a powerful squadron was to escort the flotilla across the Atlantic under the command of Boscawen. Although Anson was planning to reconstitute the western squadron, experience had shown that the protection thus afforded was uncertain. Hence it was essential that the Louisburg expedition was adequately supported. With Boscawen were to sail sixteen ships of the line plus several frigates and bomb vessels to join those already in America at Halifax.[54]

Anson's orders regarding the warships and transports had been issued to the Navy Board on 19 December with instruction that they were to have the preference over every other service.[55] Despite this, Pitt was not entirely happy. At the beginning of January Newcastle reported: 'Mr Pitt in a gentle way seemed to complain a little of the slowness of the Admiralty in the fitting out the ships and transports for America.' Newcastle quickly contacted the secretary, Clevland, and suggested that Hardwicke might also 'give Lord Anson a hint' when he next saw him. The incident was the basis for John Almon's later story that Pitt threatened Anson with impeachment unless some vessels were ready on time.[56]

The orders to Amherst envisaged Louisburg as his main objective, although he could proceed on other operations once he had captured that

[49] Barrington to the High Sheriff of Berkshire etc., 27 Oct 1757, WO 4/1012.
[50] Barrington to the Commanding Officer, 15th Foot Regiment, 30 Dec 1757, WO 5/45. Ibid., 21 Jan 1758. Pitt to Bedford, 27 Dec 1757, SP 63/415.
[51] Memorandum for Mr Pitt, 21 Dec 1757, CP 30/8/95 f 303.
[52] In Sir Charles Hardy's Letter, 14 Dec 1757, CP PRO 30/8/95 f 290.
[53] Pitt to Abercromby, 30 Dec 1757, Kimball, I, 149–150. Pitt to the Admiralty, 3 Jan 1758, Adm 1/4122.　　　　[54] Pitt to the Admiralty, 5 Jan 1758, Adm 1/4122.
[55] Admiralty to the Navy Board, 19 Dec 1757, Adm N/237.
[56] Newcastle to Hardwicke, 3 Jan 1758, Add. Mss 32,877 ff 7–12. J. Almon, *Anecdotes of the Life of the Right Honourable William Pitt, Earl of Chatham, and of the Principal Events of his Time* (London, 1793), I, 310–311. See appendix to this volume.

place. However, the ministers recognized that there might not be time for further operations, in which case the assault on Canada would depend on Abercromby. The Commander-in-Chief was accordingly given instructions to advance 'by way of Crown Point...to an attempt on either Montreal or Quebec', or both if practical. He was to be ready by 1 May.[57] Although Amherst had the cream of the regulars, the ministers calculated that Abercromby would still have about 9,000 British troops with a minimum of 15,000 provincials to face no more than 5,000 French regulars, assisted by perhaps 10,000 militia. On paper the task was by no means impossible, though much would depend on the man leading the force.[58]

II

On completion of the plans for America the next task to confront the ministry was that of mending the alliance with Prussia. Frederick II feared a repetition of the Hanoverian neutrality unless the Army of Observation contained a contingent of British troops. He was angry too because the ministry persisted in its refusal to send a fleet to the Baltic. Relations were also delicate because of Frederick II's financial plight. He had lost considerable territory and with it revenue to the amount of four million crowns or £670,000.[59]

The ministry had already indicated a willingness to help financially.[60] On the conclusion of the campaign Holdernesse had drawn up proposals, assisted by Hardwicke, Mansfield, Pitt and Newcastle.[61] However, in a covering letter he had reaffirmed a number of points on which the British ministers were determined to insist. First, there was no possibility for the present of a Baltic squadron, for negotiations with the Danes had made little progress and the fleet was still insufficient on its own. Secondly, the dispatch of British troops to Germany was not to be expected. The attempt would divide Parliament and put the subsidy at risk. Britain, however, would continue her diplomatic efforts with the Dutch, the Danes, Russians and Turks, though the prospects were nowhere promising. Finally, Holdernesse reminded Mitchell that if the King of Prussia felt ill used, so too did George II. He had expected a substantial contingent of Prussian troops to reinforce the Army of Observation. There was now apparently little prospect of this.[62]

If Holdernesse or the other ministers thought this reply would mollify

---

[57] Pitt to Abercromby, 30 Dec 1757, Kimball, I, 144–146.
[58] On an Expedition to Canada, 1758, CP PRO 30/8/96 f 82. 'Troops destined for an Interruption into Canada by Way of Crown Point, 1758', Abercromby Papers, Box I.
[59] Mitchell to Holdernesse, 31 Aug 1757, SP 90/69.
[60] Holdernesse to Mitchell, 17 July 1757, SP 90/69.
[61] Holdernesse to Mitchell, 23 Sept 1757, SP 90/70. Memorandum for the King, 21 Dec 1757, Add. Mss 32,876 f 363.
[62] Holdernesse to Mitchell, 12 Dec 1757, SP 90/70.

Frederick II they were sadly mistaken. The Prussian monarch was not convinced about the lack of ships and was even more scornful of the reasoning for not sending troops. When Mitchell early in 1758 'urged the impossibility of raising more men without ruining the manufacturers', Frederick II 'laughed and said it was a strange way of reasoning to prefer considerations of trade and manufacturers to our own security and independency'. In previous wars, England had made a major commitment and been a great power. A little assistance now would help occupy the French and assist Britain's operations overseas. When Mitchell tried to show that even a modest force on the Elbe would be incompatible with the services in America, Frederick II replied warmly: 'The way to save America is not to suffer the French to become masters of Europe.'[63] He disliked the idea of having a subsidy and refused to sign the convention. Aside from his distaste about being a pensioner, Frederick II could in no way honour the agreement to send a corps of Prussian infantry to join the Army of Observation, though he was ready to keep some cavalry units with Ferdinand.[64]

This response from Berlin caused dismay in England where the signing of the convention was considered imminent. Pitt suspected that Mitchell had given Frederick II the idea that if he delayed accepting the treaty, a fleet and British troops might still be forthcoming. Though the Prussian correspondence did not lie in his province, he demanded action. Since Holdernesse was incapable of controlling his officials, he lost no time in making the complaint where he knew it would be effective. He bluntly informed Newcastle that the ambassador was 'not fit to be the instrument of the present system'. In spite of the agreement last summer about the use of British troops, 'the tools of another system are perpetuated, marring every hopeful measure of the present administration'. Newcastle was the minister closest to the King and must act by making representations to him. This lurking poison in the vitals of the government had to be flushed out, for Pitt did not intend that 'Andrew Mitchell shall carry me where I have resolved not to go'.[65]

A serious threat to the unity of the administration seemed imminent. The ministers still agreed about the impossibility of a fleet in the Baltic. The 1758 estimate of Anson envisaged a moderate increase of 25 vessels in service, making a total force of 264.[66] Admittedly his building programme meant that these figures would soon be reached or surpassed, for several of the vessels ordered at the beginning of the war had now joined the fleet, including the battleships *Norfolk, Rippon, Lennox, Montague, Dorsetshire,*

---

[63] Mitchell to Holdernesse, 9 Feb 1758, SP 90/71.
[64] Ibid. Bissett, *The Memoirs and Papers of Sir Andrew Mitchell, K.B.*, 1, 389–394.
[65] Pitt to Newcastle, 28 Jan 1758, Add. Mss 32,877 f 256.
[66] Admiralty to the Navy Board, 15 Nov 1757, Adm 2/223.

Shrewsbury and *Warspite*.[67] Even so, the numbers would still be insufficient for such commitment.

But Frederick II's request for British troops in Germany was more contentious. Newcastle, Hardwicke and Devonshire all thought it ludicrous to spend so much on the Army of Observation and put everything at risk by a refusal to send a few regiments from home.[68] However, Pitt remained adamant. He stressed the political nature of the Prussian request. Frederick II wanted British troops to keep the Hanoverians loyal. This was unnecessary now that the army was in British pay.[69] But though he did not say it, Pitt's reasons too were political. He had come to power with the support of the country gentry who were deeply suspicious of a continental war. The previous December he had assured them he would not 'send a drop of our blood to the Elbe, to be lost in that ocean of gore'.[70] This unilateral declaration on so important a matter by a leading minister is a graphic illustration of just how limited was the sense of collective responsibility. But for Pitt the important point was that he had publicly stated his position. He could not go back on it, at least for the present session of Parliament.

The other ministers were thus left with a *fait accompli*. If they ignored Pitt and sent the troops, he might resign and provoke a ministerial crisis. None of them felt the risk would be politically or militarily worthwhile. Troops numbering 10,000 would be a useful addition to Ferdinand's army, but not decisive for the outcome of the campaign. They would only be worth sending if the Prussian monarch dispatched a large contingent of his own army to serve with Ferdinand, and of this there was little hope. The Russians had reappeared across the Vistula, making it likely that Frederick II would require all his men himself.[71] There was thus no point in plunging the King's affairs into confusion. As Hardwicke commented, far more damaging to the campaign than the failure to send British troops would be the defeat of the German supply in the Commons.[72] Consequently, when the ministers met at Pitt's house on 23 February 1758, there was comparative accord. They agreed that no British troops could be provided, nor a squadron sent to the Baltic, unless the administration first gained the support of one of the northern powers, preferably Denmark, with whom negotiations would continue. The ministers recognized that they could hardly insist on the Prussian King honouring his undertaking to keep a contingent with the Army of Observation, though they expressed the hope that Frederick II would permit the existing fifteen squadrons of cavalry with Ferdinand to

---

[67] Monthly List Book and Progress of the Navy, 1 Jan 1758, Adm 7/567. Admiralty Dimensions Book, NMM.
[68] Newcastle to Hardwicke, 29 Jan 1758, Add. Mss 32,877 ff 270–274.
[69] Memorandum for Lord Hardwicke, 16 Feb 1758, Add. Mss 32,997 ff 341–350.
[70] Walpole, *Memoirs of George II*, iii, 88.
[71] Newcastle to Hardwicke, 29 Jan 1758, Add. Mss 32,877 ff 270–272.
[72] Hardwicke to Newcastle, 29 Jan 1758, Add. Mss 32,877 ff 275–276.

stay, subsisted at the expense of the British commissariat. But all this depended on an immediate signing of the convention.[73] These points were to be explained to Frederick II by Sir Joseph Yorke, the ambassador at the Hague, who was to replace Mitchell in Berlin. Since Yorke would require time to get to his post, another letter was advisable. As this would have to be delivered by Mitchell, Pitt determined to help Holdernesse draft it to ensure that this time there was no misunderstanding. Accordingly, after the other ministers had retired, the two Secretaries sat down to transcribe these decisions into a formal dispatch. The exercise lasted until 3.00 a.m., as Holdernesse ruefully reported to Newcastle. The problem was Pitt's excruciating insistence on vetting every word. 'The whole time passed in weighing words more than matter.' However, Holdernesse was confident: 'Though my draft to Mr Mitchell is mutilated so as to be scarce legible even to myself... I think the substance remains pretty much the same as when I sent it to your Grace.' Holdernesse confessed: 'I would not pass such another evening for the King's revenue', adding sarcastically, 'or for what is perhaps more valuable, Mr Pitt's abilities'. One thing the northern Secretary was determined on for the future: his colleague must set down in writing his objections, for he would not 'be detained for hours upon the introduction of a monosyllable'.[74] But, although commiserating with Holdernesse on Pitt's extravagant manner of doing business, Newcastle could not agree on the final outcome. He thought the draft was much improved, especially 'the justification of the present measure of denying English troops'. The letter now emphasized how 'money has always been looked upon as the proper and most effective contribution that England could make to a war upon the Continent'. That was a material point.[75]

Newcastle was confident on this score, since the nation's finances had recovered from Legge's mismanagement. On the collapse of the previous ministry, Devonshire had negotiated a loan for £3,000,000, though only by paying 4 per cent interest. Since then, the market had recaptured its buoyancy, so that Newcastle had been able to secure his requirements for the 1758 supply at the lower rate of 3.5 per cent.[76]

To outsiders, political harmony now seemed the order of the day. Chesterfield commented: 'Everything goes smoothly in Parliament. The King of Prussia has united all our parties in his support... there has not been one single division upon public points.'[77] Unfortunately, not everything was

---

[73] Business for the Meeting, 23 Feb 1758, Add. Mss 32,997 ff 372–374. Holdernesse to Mitchell, 25 Feb 1758, SP 90/71.
[74] Holdernesse to Newcastle, 25 Feb 1758, Add. Mss 32,878 ff 30–32.
[75] Newcastle to Holdernesse, 26 Feb 1758, Add. Mss 32,878 ff 40–42.
[76] L. S. Sutherland, 'The City of London and the Pitt–Devonshire Administration, 1756–1757', *Proceedings of the British Academy*, XLVI, 168.
[77] Chesterfield to Philip Stanhope, 8 Feb 1758, printed in J. Bradshaw (ed.), *The Letters of Philip Dormer Stanhope, Earl of Chesterfield* (London, 1893), III, 1208.

so harmonious inside the administration. George II was bitterly dissatisfied with Pitt at his refusal to deploy British troops in Germany and suggested he be replaced with Fox. Newcastle sensibly refused, telling him in that case he too would have to leave the ministry.[78] Then late in February Newcastle received the estimates for the Army of Observation. These came to over £2,000,000. Pitt was horrified, especially over the Hessian forage contract which had no fixed price, a circumstance the supplier was taking full advantage of. Although the estimates did not concern Pitt departmentally, he could not but be embarrassed at the size of the demands about to be presented to the Commons in view of his previous opposition to the war in Germany. There had to be a limit to the present mood of the Tories to support the government. 'I wish to God I could see my way through this mountain of expense', he informed Newcastle on 6 March. Unless the First Lord could 'prevail to reduce things to a reasonable bulk', Pitt was afraid there would be all kinds of difficulty.[79]

In response to this appeal, Newcastle and his Treasury colleagues managed to scale down the original estimate by some £400,000.[80] These efforts were duly acknowledged by Pitt after an audience with the King: 'In a word I experienced the full effect of Your Grace's conversation in that Place from which alone the preservation of this country from confusion must come.'[81]

Unfortunately, in going over the figures again Nichols, the chief clerk, found it necessary to make some revisions so that the total was almost what it had been. This alteration was too much for Pitt. The right hand of the Treasury appeared unaware of what the left was doing. He accused Newcastle in his most hectoring manner of deliberately allowing the estimate 'to swell beyond all decency'.[82] But Newcastle refused to be bullied. Nothing, he assured Pitt, had been included which was not vital to the campaign. It was grossly unfair to blame the Treasury. The expenses were being incurred because of the decision to take the Army of Observation into British pay. The size of the estimate was a matter for the whole ministry. Newcastle assured Pitt: 'No demand of this sort shall come before Parliament which is not previously approved by the rest of the King's ministers.'[83]

One reason for Pitt's anger was the lack of accountability. Ferdinand did not hold his commission from George II as King of England but as Elector of Hanover. The ministry thus had no direct control over his operations and Pitt was suspicious that the Hanoverians were not being open with their British colleagues on the orders to the Commander-in-Chief. The

[78] Memorandum for the King, 14 Mar 1758, Add. Mss 32,878 ff 210–211.
[79] Pitt to Newcastle, 6 Mar 1758, Add. Mss 32,878 ff 130–131.
[80] Newcastle to Pitt, 17 Mar 1758, Add. Mss 32,878 ff 242–247.
[81] Pitt to Newcastle, 17 Mar 1758, Add. Mss 32,878 f 224.
[82] Pitt to Newcastle, 4 Apr 1758, Add. Mss 32,879 f 46.
[83] Newcastle to Pitt, 5 Apr 1758, Add. Mss 32,879 ff 60–64.

commissariat arrangements were also unsatisfactory. Though the Hessian and Brunswick troops were supplied through a Treasury official, the Hanoverians operated their own system, being reimbursed from London. A divorce of spending and accountability is nearly always a recipe for disaster and this had proved no exception. Clearly the system needed overhauling.[84] On the question of Ferdinand's commission there was little the ministers could do, since the King was constitutionally within his rights. Nevertheless, under Pitt's prompting, Newcastle did extract two concessions from George II. The first was that Holdernesse as the responsible secretary should have the right to correspond with Prince Ferdinand.[85] The other was that, while the Hanoverians continued to have their own commissariat and submit estimates, all other units would be subsisted by two British commissaries, Colonel Boyd and Mr Hatton, who would be directly responsible to the Treasury.[86] Hopefully, for the future the causes of the recent disagreements would be avoided.

Even so, the negotiations with Prussia continued to lag. Contrary to expectation, the ministerial proposals were not appreciated in Berlin where Frederick II continued to press for a Baltic squadron. But after another three weeks he was forced to recognize that further concessions from the English were unlikely. He would still have to fight the Russians and Austrians no matter what he decided about the convention and it would be better to do so with English assistance than without. Accordingly, in the middle of March he instructed his envoys in London to sign the agreement, provided he could spend the subsidy as he thought fit and George II augmented his Hanoverian forces.[87].

During the talks in London, the Prussian envoys made two other proposals: one, that a small corps of British troops should be sent to occupy the port of Emden; the other, that the coastal operations against France should be resumed.

These ideas fell on fruitful ground. Since the ministerial meeting on 5 September 1757, Anson had had a small squadron under Commodore Holmes operating in the River Ems, which had assisted in the capture of Emden and protected Ferdinand's flank. The Prussian proposal would help consolidate the position there, and Pitt quickly agreed, provided 'no future demand in relation to English troops would be founded upon his compliance'. Regarding the renewal of the coastal operations, he was naturally delighted, suggested as it was by the greatest military commander of the day.[88] At the beginning of April the new Anglo-Prussian convention was

[84] Pitt to Newcastle, 6 Mar 1758, Add. Mss 32,878 ff 130–131.
[85] Newcastle to Pitt, 24 Mar 1758, Add. Mss 32,878 f 330.
[86] Treasury Board Minute, 22 Mar 1758, T 29/33.
[87] Mitchell to Holdernesse, 15 Mar 1758, SP 90/71.
[88] Substance of what passed between Mr Pitt and Lord Holdernesse, 27 Mar 1758, Add. Mss 32,878 ff 382–386.

settled, though not before Pitt had alarmed Newcastle with one of his more arrogant displays, saying that he would not see the Prussian ministers again until 'the Ordinary Round of weekly labour begins'.[89]

Technically the convention dealt only with the terms of the subsidy and the conditions the two powers would observe in making peace.[90] But as part of the general understanding, the signing was accompanied by a declaration from George II, stating his intention to keep an army of 50,000 men in Germany at the expense of Great Britain, and promising as Elector to increase this number by as many troops as possible. Moreover, consistent with his American commitments, he would 'employ a considerable Part of his Land Forces, and of the Fleet destined for Channel Service in such manner, as may most annoy the Enemy, and cause a useful Diversion'. George II would also garrison Emden. The failure to send a squadron to the Baltic was not through fear of the powers there, but reflected a lack of ships. He was glad, therefore, that Frederick II recognized the utility of trying 'healing measures with the Courts of Petersburg and Stockholm', for elsewhere he and his ministers intended to stand as one with the King of Prussia, with the same enemies and the same friends.[91]

From the British point of view the agreement was a good one. Though no further Prussian contingent was likely for the Army of Observation, the alliance had been preserved without the necessity of extending the war. Britain could continue to concentrate her forces overseas. The prospects here were generally good. In America the country had 45,000 regular and provincial troops, an overwhelming force if they could but get to the enemy. Geography, not the French, was now the principal obstacle. If the coastal expeditions could divert a substantial number of French troops from Germany and Ferdinand could hold his own, a satisfactory peace might yet be attained, something for which no one had dared to hope six months earlier.

III

The signing of the convention, unfortunately, did not lead to improved relations inside the ministry, for a new issue was dividing it.

The Act for the compulsory recruitment of the army had always carried the danger that the wrong persons might be apprehended. Just before Christmas 1757 a gentleman in casual attire was seized while walking down the Strand. Friends immediately sought his release by writ of habeas corpus in the Court of King's Bench. Mansfield, the Chief Justice, decided he was not competent to grant it. The Habeas Corpus Act merely specified that

[89] Newcastle to Hardwicke, 27 Mar 1758, Add. Mss 32,878 ff 388–389.
[90] C. Parry (ed.), *The Consolidated Treaty Series* (New York, 1969), XLI, 184–186.
[91] Ibid., 189–190.

a person charged with a crime must either be brought to trial or released. The impressed man was not accused of any crime, having been detained for the King's service and the magistrates who committed him must determine the matter.[92] To many, this judgement seemingly rendered ineffective one of the safeguards of liberty. This view was strongly argued by Charles Pratt, the Attorney-General, who brought in a bill making it compulsory for a judge to grant habeas corpus where a man had been wrongly detained because of the Press or Recruiting Acts. Pitt decided to support Pratt, sensing the issue would be popular with the Tories. The rest of the administration took Mansfield's part.[93] Nevertheless, the action of Pitt is surprising since it was bound to affect recruitment, as some speakers stressed. If any man could appeal above the magistrates, the whole point of their being taken would be lost. In an emergency the nation must be able to call on the services of its people.[94] The bill was finally defeated in the Lords by Hardwicke and Newcastle.

Despite these unpleasantries, Pitt was hard at work planning his coastal expedition. His first step had been to issue a general directive to Anson to get as many ships as possible ready for service.[95] However, one restriction on the operation was that it should be confined to the Channel. Several ministers had been uneasy the previous summer at the sending away of the kingdom's primary defence. Anson was anxious too that it should not tie down the western squadron too closely but leave it free to operate against the main French fleet. Regarding an objective Pitt had few thoughts. To help him, Ligonier formed a small committee with Marlborough and Sackville. The choice of these two men was not coincidental. During the Rochefort enquiry they had indicated that more might have been done by commanders with initiative. Ligonier was now giving them a chance to see what they could do.[96]

While the military looked for an objective, Pitt and Ligonier held discussions with Anson and Captain Richard Howe. Howe had been one of Hawke's captains during the Rochefort operation and had impressed everyone with his courage and tact. There could be no question of Anson entrusting the main fleet to a captain. For this Hawke was again the preferred candidate. But if the expedition was limited to the Channel, two fleets would be desirable: a main one to watch the enemy at Brest; and a subordinate one to provide close support and protection for the flotilla. Howe seemed ideal for the latter. Close co-operation between the services

---

[92] *London Chronicle*, 1/4 Apr 1758. Ibid., 20/23 May.   [93] Yorke, III, 1–19.
[94] W. Cobbett (ed.), *The Parliamentary History of England*, XIII, 1752–1763 (London, 1811), 871–926.
[95] Pitt to the Admiralty, 4 Apr 1758, Adm 1/4122.
[96] The end product was a 'Paper signed by Lord Ligonier, the Duke of Marlborough, and Lord Sackville', May 1758, Shelburne Papers, XXXVII, Clements Library.

was essential in such enterprises. At Rochefort it had been absent on occasion.[97]

By the second week of April, discussions were sufficiently advanced for Pitt to begin to assemble the men and materials. Then, if the ministers consented, everything could proceed. On 13 April he ordered the Master-General of the Ordnance to prepare the artillery. This time the expedition would not return empty-handed for want of a siege train. In addition, the Ordnance Board was instructed to provide ammunition for seventeen battalions of foot, at a ratio of 200 rounds to one man.[98] Simultaneously, the War Office began issuing marching instructions. The troops were to set out for Portsmouth on 1 May and be ready to embark by 23 May.[99] The dockyards were also busy, following Pitt's preliminary instructions to Anson. Now more specific orders could be sent. On 21 April the Admiralty informed the captains of seventeen battleships that they were to place themselves under Hawke's command. At the same time a number of other captains were told they would shortly receive orders from Howe.[100]

The preparation of the transports too was well advanced and for this Pitt can claim the credit. The Rochefort expedition had been delayed several weeks by the need to hire, fit and get its transports down the Thames.[101] On the return of the flotilla, therefore, he had ordered its shipping to Southampton, where, fully manned and seaworthy, it had remained under the watchful eye of an agent, pending further instructions.[102] Most of this had subsequently been allocated to the Louisburg expedition, but Pitt had quickly had it replaced so that at the end of March the Navy Board reported 17,000 tons were ready for service.[103] Hence the only tonnage required for the expedition was that for some cavalry.[104] Arrangements for this were soon made, and by the first week of May Anson was able to order Howe to Portsmouth to take charge.[105] His dispatch did not reassure Pitt entirely,

---

[97] *Report of the General Officers appointed by His Majesty's Warrant to Enquire into the Causes of the Failure of the Late Expedition to the Coasts of France* (London, 1758), 9–64. (See Mordaunt.)

[98] Pitt to the Master-General, 13 Apr 1758, Shelburne Papers, xxxvii. Many papers in this collection are the originals, which Shelburne possibly collected to write an account of a campaign in which he participated. For convenience I have cited, where possible, these papers rather than those scattered in the Public Record Office.

[99] Pitt to Barrington, 13 Apr 1758, SP 44/191.

[100] Admiralty to Captains Various, 21 Apr 1758, Adm 2/80.

[101] For further information on this see Adm 106/265, Correspondence of Captain Pryce and the Navy Board.

[102] Admiralty to the Navy Board, 24 Oct 1757, Adm N/237. Ibid., 3 Nov 1757. For further details see R. Middleton, 'The Administration of Newcastle and Pitt: The Departments of State and the Conduct of the War, 1754–1760' (Ph.D. thesis, Exeter University, 1969), 175–176.

[103] Pitt to the Admiralty, 31 Dec 1757, SP 44/230. James Randall to the Navy Board, 29 Mar 1758, Adm 106/266.

[104] Pitt to the Admiralty, 1 Apr 1758, Shelburne Papers, xxxvii.

[105] Admiralty to the Navy Board, 9 May 1758, Adm N/238.

for Robert Wood, the under-secretary, informed Clevland on 9 May: 'Mr Pitt hopes the Admiralty, because of Mr Howe's journey, won't wash their hands of this affair.'[106]

The other development to result from the lessons of Rochefort was the design of a new landing craft. The rafts used then were cumbersome things which 'plainly pointed out a great Imperfection in that Part of the Equipment'.[107] Anson now attempted to rectify this by the construction of an entirely new vessel. The craft would be manned by sailors and marines who would sit round the edge. In the middle would be seventy soldiers, muskets in their hands, ready to leap ashore in formation. The vessels would be of shallow draught so that they could approach the water's edge. The new craft promised both to speed up landings and put the troops ashore in better order.[108] Two prototypes were constructed at Woolwich. On 26 April Anson and a number of dignitaries went down the Thames in the Admiralty barge to view them.[109] The inspection was apparently satisfactory, for the Navy Board were shortly instructed to build as many of them as possible by 17 May.[110]

The only thing to mar these otherwise smooth preparations was the command of the fleet. Hawke was absent with the western squadron when the naval arrangements had been made. Indeed, he was at that moment engaged in one of its more successful cruises, for early in April he had discovered that the French were preparing a large convoy of forty merchantmen in Basque Road, escorted by five ships of the line and seven frigates, to reinforce Canada. Luckily Hawke had taken the precaution of forming a line, as his own force was made up of no more than eight battleships when he entered the Road. The enemy, however, were in no mood to resist. Since the tide was out most of them had to jettison their guns and stores to make their escape, which they succeeded in doing, much to Hawke's dismay. However, the damage to the French was considerable. Their forces in the West Indies and North America would want for men and supplies more than usual; while five battleships had been temporarily immobilized.[111]

The action was significant, since it followed Admiral Osborne's success in the Mediterranean, where he had smashed another part of the French plan to help their colonies. Since the loss of Minorca, successive Admiralty Boards had maintained a strong British presence in the area, first under Hawke and later Admiral Saunders. Osborne had first chased part of the

---

[106] Wood to Clevland, 9 May 1758, Adm 1/4122.
[107] T. M. Molyneux, *Conjunct Expeditions or Expeditions that have been carried on Jointly by the Fleet and Army* (London, 1759), I, 211–212.
[108] Ibid., 213.   [109] *London Chronicle*, 27/29 Apr 1758.
[110] Admiralty to the Navy Board, 27 Apr 1758, Adm 2/222. There is a model of one of these craft in the National Maritime Museum, Greenwich.
[111] Hawke to Clevland, 11 Apr 1758, Adm 1/89.

Toulon fleet into the Spanish port of Cartagena and then defeated a force sent to relieve it, capturing in the process the flagship of the Marquis Duquesne and a second ship of the line.[112] The result of these actions by Hawke and Osborne was that any British attack on Louisburg was unlikely to be thwarted this time by a concentration of the enemy navy.

Unfortunately, the first news to greet Hawke on his return was that an expedition was preparing, the immediate command of which had been given to a junior. Worse, rumour suggested that its destination was Rochefort, which if true would be a public declaration of the Admiralty's lack of confidence in him. Although Hawke would have command of the covering force, Howe was to reap all the credit: 'He is to make his demands and I am to comply.' He had accordingly struck his flag, for no consequence would permit him to fly it 'one moment with discredit'.[113]

Hawke was promptly summoned to the Admiralty to explain his conduct. He was duly penitent on learning the expedition's true destination. But although Anson and his colleagues had high regard for Hawke, they could hardly allow such conduct to go unpunished. If commanders could resign at will, naval discipline would cease.[114] The Admiralty apparently faced a dilemma. It did not wish to lose Hawke by relieving him of his command. On the other hand it could hardly place him under another officer, for there was no one seemingly of sufficient stature.

In this assumption the Board proved wrong, for Anson suddenly put his own name forward. He had long wanted another command. When the western squadron had first been formed in 1755 he had visited it to see how mobilization was going. The sight at Spithead had stirred a desire to take command. He had told Holdernesse sadly: 'When I mentioned it to the Duke of Newcastle he asked me what was then to become of the Admiralty.' It had been a good question. Nevertheless, Anson confessed: 'I am certain I sacrifice the one thing that would give me the greatest pleasure.'[115] Unlike Pitt or Newcastle, he found administration a drudgery, pestered as he was by colleagues and politicians. Indeed, it may have been at this time that he had been embroiled with Newcastle after the latter had obtained a plan from one of the Admiralty lords, taken it to the King for approval and then produced it 'at a Cabinet meeting without making the least mention of it to the Person at the head of that Board'.[116] Such action broke the convention of departmental responsibility and Anson had threatened to resign. Now he had an opportunity to escape such altercation by serving with the fleet, for, although the ministry was alarmed at his prospective absence, his offer

[112] Corbett, *Seven Years' War*, I, 237–238, 255–260.
[113] Hawke to Clevland, 10 May 1758, Adm 1/89.
[114] Admiralty Board Minute, 12 May 1758, Adm 3/66. R. F. Mackay, *Admiral Hawke* (Oxford, 1965), 196–197.
[115] Anson to Holdernesse, 9 May 1755, Holdernesse Papers, Egerton 2444 ff 42–43, BL.
[116] Lady Anson to Lord Royston, [undated], Add. Mss 35,376 ff 182–183.

was too convenient to refuse. Within a few days he was at Portsmouth unfurling his flag with Hawke dutifully in attendance as his second.[117]

Formal approval, meanwhile, still had to be given to the scheme. Another meeting had been held at the end of April, attended by Marlborough, Sackville and Howe.[118] However, the ministers made no decision beyond requesting the designated commanders to write down their ideas so that they could be considered more precisely. The project hung fire partly because of Pitt's health. During the first two weeks of May he was incapacitated by gout. Although there was no reason why the other ministers should not take charge, Pitt was apprehensive of what they might do. However, on 11 May he was finally compelled to go into the country for a few days to recover his health. Since no time was to be lost, he asked Newcastle to get the King's approval for the draft outline of the generals' paper.[119] Newcastle duly reported the results of this initiative to Pitt at Hayes, his country residence. On the desirability of the expedition, the King remained as taciturn as ever: 'He would neither advise it nor oppose it.' However, George II concluded that the appearance of a British flotilla off the French coast might prove useful. Therefore, Pitt was to 'prepare a Draught of the Instructions for the Duke of Marlborough, upon the plan proposed in the paper, signed by the General Officers'. Then the whole project should be considered at a final meeting of the ministers.[120]

This was enough for Pitt. Within a week he had drafted the instructions and was back in London, his health apparently mended. A ministerial meeting was fixed for the evening of Friday, 19 May.[121] Any doubts about the expedition were quickly removed. The ministers had already agreed in principle some weeks ago: now they were gathered to select a target and ensure that the orders drafted by Pitt were proper for approval by the King. The meeting began with a reminder from Pitt that there must be hazard in the best-concerted operation.[122] The ministers then turned to the paper which Ligonier, Marlborough and Sackville had drawn up. The generals recommended an attack on the fishing and privateer port of St Malo. The town was situated on a small island at the mouth of the River Rance and was joined to the mainland by a narrow peninsula, 800 yards long. A regular siege therefore would not be possible. However, the generals were confident they could reduce the place with mortars and red-hot shot, especially since they believed the town's water supply ran along the causeway and could be cut. Once in British hands it might be possible to

---

[117] W. V. Anson, *The Life of Admiral Lord Anson, the Father of the British Navy, 1697–1762* (London, 1912), 151–153.
[118] Newcastle to Hardwicke, 26 Apr 1758, Add. Mss 32,879 ff 310–317.
[119] Pitt to Newcastle, 11 May 1758, Add. Mss 32,880 ff 5–6.
[120] Newcastle to Pitt, 11 May 1758, Add. Mss 32,880 ff 9–10.
[121] Pitt to Newcastle, 18 May 1758, Add. Mss 32,880 f 128.
[122] Newcastle to Hardwicke, 21 May 1758, Add. Mss 32,880 ff 170–176.

hold St Malo, in which case the French would have to dispatch a powerful army for its recapture. Even if it was not taken, the army might still inflict much damage, and so by 'making Feints, or really landing in different Parts, oblige the Enemy to keep a great Force' upon the coast, thus inhibiting their operations elsewhere. But all activity would be confined to the Channel so that the expedition could be recalled to the defence of Britain, should the need arise.[123]

These suggestions were faithfully incorporated in the instructions prepared by Pitt. They were prefaced once more with arguments about the need to prevent the French from oppressing the 'Liberties of the Empire' and subverting the 'Independency of Europe'. More emphasis was placed this time on 'Protecting the Commerce of Our Own Subjects by striking at the Principal Seat of their Privateers'. Another difference from the orders to Mordaunt was the absence of any provision for a council of war. Each of the principal commanders, Marlborough, Howe and Anson, was to be responsible for his own sphere of operations. There was to be no collective shelving of responsibility, which Pitt rightly felt had occurred at Rochefort. This did not mean that there would be no consultation, which remained essential. But in military matters Marlborough must make his own decisions. The duties of Howe were limited to landing and re-embarking; those of Anson to protecting the whole. All three were to correspond with Pitt.[124]

It has often been suggested that orders were issued in this manner to preserve secrecy and ensure Pitt's control.[125] But the real reason was the need to minimize inter-service rivalry. The Admiralty could hardly issue orders to the generals, nor the Commander-in-Chief to the fleet. The Secretary was the one person who could do this with the fullest authority of the King and his ministers. There is no substance to Almon's often-repeated anecdote that Pitt placed a sheet of paper over Admiralty orders to prevent its members from learning the contents. The story was simply the invention of a one-time bookseller and pamphleteer who gossiped with Temple some years after the events he was supposedly describing.[126] In any case, Howe and Anson were instructed to correspond with both Pitt and the Admiralty.[127] This was necessary since their squadrons could only operate effectively with support from the yards at home. The general practice on these occasions was for the Secretaries of State to issue operational orders, the Admiralty to deal with

---

123 'Paper signed by Lord Ligonier, The Duke of Marlborough, and Lord Sackville, May 1758', Shelburne Papers, XXXVII.
124 George II to Marlborough, 20 May 1758, Shelburne Papers, XXXVII. George II to Howe, 20 May 1758, Shelburne Papers, XXXVII. George II to Anson, 23 May 1758, Shelburne Papers, XXXVII.   125 Corbett, *Seven Years' War*, I, 181.
126 Almon, *Anecdotes of Pitt*, I, 307. See R. Middleton, 'Pitt, Anson and the Admiralty, 1757–1761', *History*, LV, 189–198.
127 George II to Howe, 20 May 1758, Shelburne Papers, XXXVII. George II to Anson, 23 May 1758, Shelburne Papers, XXXVII.

logistical matters. Both responsibilities necessarily overlapped and required close consultation. But once the operation was completed, the fleet was returned to the Admiralty.[128]

The orders to Anson were that he should cruise so as 'to prevent any Ships of the Enemy, from Brest or Elsewhere, from molesting the Operations' of the flotilla. But Anson was also to use every opportunity to 'annoy and distress the Enemy, taking due Care to protect the Trade'. Moreover, should he learn that the enemy were about to sail from Brest, he was to 'use the utmost endeavours to attack and destroy the same'. He was not tied solely to watching the expedition.[129]

The plan of the generals and the instructions to the commanders were approved unanimously. Pitt could now take the final drafts to the King for his signature, before handing them to the commanders. Within twenty-four hours Marlborough was heading for Portsmouth, where he arrived on 21 May. Here he found everything ready for embarkation.[130] Howe was at that moment testing the landing craft, with gratifying result. The craft could navigate waters where even ships' boats had difficulty in passing. The army seemed in good spirits, helped by the warm sunny weather. All seemed to augur well.[131]

[128] Pitt to the Admiralty, 8 Dec 1758, Shelburne Papers, xxxvii.
[129] George II to Anson, 23 May 1758, Shelburne Papers, xxxvii.
[130] Marlborough to Pitt, 21 May 1758, Shelburne Papers, xxxvii. Ibid. 24 May 1758.
[131] *London Chronicle*, 27/30 May 1758. Howe to Pitt, 27 May 1758, Shelburne Papers, xxxvii.

3

The Broadening Effort

I

There was a lull now while the ministers waited for news from France. In the meantime the Privy Council came to a resolution concerning a spy, Dr Hensey. This man had been attached to the Spanish embassy as a Jesuit priest and had been detected passing information from an Admiralty clerk to the French. Indeed, it was believed that the enemy had first received news of the British designs on Rochefort from this source. Hensey had been closely interrogated by the ministers as members of the Privy Council. The accusations about Rochefort were not substantiated, but there was evidence that Hensey had collaborated with the enemy and should stand trial.[1]

When the news came from France it was not discouraging. Although St Malo had not been taken, considerable damage had been inflicted on the French. Marlborough and Howe had landed on 5 June at Cancalle Bay, nine miles to the east. Here the shore was sandy and steep with a sufficient depth of water to allow the frigates to silence any batteries, in contrast to the coast at Rochefort.[2] Unfortunately, the site had proved less useful for any advance on the town. The countryside around Cancalle was dissected by thick hedges and high walls, making excellent cover for marksmen, and was in general 'entirely different' from what Marlborough 'had heard it represented'.[3] Worse, the roads were so narrow as to prevent the movement of stores and artillery, thus making any siege of St Malo impossible. However, at the village of St Servan, on the south side of the town, the army found 30 privateers and 100 other vessels. The destruction of these meant that one objective at least had been accomplished.

Marlborough was conscious, on re-embarking four days later, that the expedition had not entirely answered the expectations of its architect.

---

[1] Details of the interrogation are to be found in the Newcastle Papers, Add. Mss 32,998 ff 71–131. Hensey was reprieved after he agreed to make a full confession, Holdernesse to George II, 11 July 1758, Egerton 3425, BL.

[2] Marlborough to Pitt, 6 June 1758, Shelburne Papers, xxxvii, Clements Library. Account of the Expedition to St Maloes, by Colonel Charles Hotham, Hotham Papers, DDHO 4/172, East Riding Record Office. Hotham served as adjutant-general.

[3] Marlborough to Pitt, 11 June 1758, Shelburne Papers, xxxvii.

Nevertheless, he asserted that much damage had been done, while reports of French troops on the march persuaded him that a considerable diversion must have taken place.[4]

Marlborough need not have worried. The ministers and the public were well pleased with his report. The objects laid down by Pitt were closer to being realized. His letter coincided with the news that Prince Ferdinand had not only completed the liberation of Hanover, but had pursued the French across the Rhine. Chesterfield commented: 'The face of affairs is astonishingly mended', when Newcastle informed him of the double event.[5] Also pleasing were reports that a considerable number of French troops were being recalled from Germany. Newcastle privately believed these to be exaggerated, but was still satisfied at what had been achieved.[6] Ligonier too was pleased, though disappointed that Marlborough had not marched to meet a French force reputed to be on its way from Granville. He was confident that the British would always win any engagement between nearly equal forces.[7] George II also affected to approve of what the generals had done. At a meeting on 20 June the ministers accordingly recommended that the operation should continue. Some additional shipping would be provided to avoid overcrowding, and a further supply of provisions found.[8]

To expedite these matters, Pitt for once bypassed the normal channel of communication by getting his under-secretary, James Rivers, to write direct to the Comptroller of the Navy Board, George Cockburne. Anson was with the fleet, while Clevland and the other lords were away for the weekend. Rivers, however, was careful to assure Cockburne that formal orders would be sent as soon as Clevland returned.[9]

The incident emphasized the importance of the Admiralty secretary to the smooth running of the navy. Since 1727 he had been permitted to issue instructions after consultation with one lord only.[10] Clevland was well qualified for such responsibility. The son of a dockyard official, he had spent his entire career in the yards, rising from humble foreman to commissioner at Portsmouth, and then to secretary at the behest of Bedford. He was a considerable figure, being a Member of Parliament, and occasionally attended ministerial meetings.[11] The extent of his influence had not passed unnoticed. During the Minorca crisis, one pamphleteer cast him in the role

---

[4] Ibid.

[5] Newcastle to Chesterfield, 10 June 1758, Add. Mss 32,880 f 387.

[6] Newcastle to Anson, 7 July 1758, Add. Mss 32,881 ff 189–190.

[7] Ligonier to Sackville, 21 June 1758, Ligonier Letter Book, Clements Library.

[8] Pitt to Marlborough, 21 June 1758, Shelburne Papers, xxxvii. Ligonier to Sackville, 21 June 1758, Ligonier Letter Book.

[9] Rivers to Cockburne, 26 June 1758, Shelburne Papers, xxxvii.

[10] F. Wickwire, 'The Admiralty Secretaries and the British Civil Service', *Huntington Library Quarterly*, xxviii, 243.

[11] D. A. Baugh, *British Naval Administration in the Age of Walpole* (Princeton, 1965), 82. Sir Lewis Namier and J. Brooke, *The History of Parliament: The House of Commons, 1754–1790* (London, 1964), ii, 599.

of an Iago, suggesting that Anson had been 'grossly...hoodwinked and abused, by one whose influence...has in great measure been the source of misfortune to the nation, and of perdition to yourself as minister'.[12]

No new instructions were sent to Marlborough, the next objective being left to him. Nevertheless, affairs were on the verge of a dramatic turn, for Pitt was about to do a *volte face* on the question of British troops in Germany. There had been several straws in the wind, though all seem to have gone unnoticed. During the habeas corpus dispute Pitt hinted to Lady Yarmouth that if the measure was allowed to pass, he would do everything the King might wish on Hanover. He also indicated to Holdernesse that his Tory support would be expendable once the appropriate gestures had been made.[13] The swing in public opinion over the war on the continent made some change desirable. Historians who have talked about Pitt's strategy have overlooked the political calculation in everything he did. The victories of Frederick II at Rossbach and Leuthen and the recent success of Ferdinand had created a climate that was more favourable to British participation on the continent. British troops could now safely be sent. Nevertheless, Pitt waited for Parliament to rise before making his conversion known.[14]

The first direct hint of a change in Pitt's views about the war was given to his colleagues at the meeting on 20 June, where it was agreed that when Marlborough had finished his operations, the administration 'might spare 6,000 men to be employed where they could be of most service', meaning Germany. The expectation was that this would be in the autumn. Newcastle therefore was astonished when three days later Pitt proposed the immediate dispatch of some cavalry units, since they were presently unemployed in Britain. Newcastle readily agreed.[15] The suddenness of the decision meant that Ligonier had to be hastily summoned from his country home at Cobham to settle the details. Privately he thought the measure would weaken the forces at home, but loyally agreed to do as he was asked.[16] The episode illustrates that if Pitt and Newcastle agreed on something the consent of the other ministers could largely be anticipated. During the next couple of weeks the number of men for Germany was increased to almost 9,000 and was made up of both infantry and cavalry.[17]

Since the troops' destination lay within the northern department it was Holdernesse who ordered transports and saw to their departure.[18] Before

---

[12] Anon., *A Letter to the Right Honourable Lord A...* (London, 1757), 22–29, Admiralty Library, P/230.
[13] Newcastle to Hardwicke, 21 May 1758, Add. Mss 32,880 ff 170–176.
[14] Parliament was prorogued on 20 June 1758, *JHC*, xxviii, 314.
[15] Newcastle to Lord Rockingham, 24 June 1758, Add. Mss 32,881 ff 37–40.
[16] Conway to Devonshire, 7 July 1758, DPC.
[17] Monthly Totals of British Troops in Germany, Hotham Papers, DDHO 4/44.
[18] Holdernesse to the Admiralty, 29 June 1758, SP 44/228. Holdernesse to Barrington, 29 June 1758, SP 44/190.

they left, Newcastle made arrangements for their subsistence in a series of meetings at the Treasury. The main emphasis was on the need for 'a better economy than was used in the course of the last war'. Continental conflicts were unpopular, and Marlborough must do everything possible to keep costs down, if his command was not to incur criticism. For this reason, Newcastle wanted to issue the men with rye bread, advertising the contract for the most competitive tender. However, he was overruled on both matters. Ligonier declared that more men had been killed in earlier wars by rye bread than by the enemy. The objection to advertising, Barrington stressed, was that it obligated the authorities to accept the lowest bid, which was most undesirable, since the character and reliability of the contractor was crucial.[19]

The decision of Pitt to deploy troops on the continent was surprising, since to effect it three of the regiments with the expedition would have to be withdrawn.[20] It was a tacit admission that Germany was where the European war would be decided. Not that Pitt had given up all belief in coastal operations. The war on the continent was at a critical stage: after driving the French across the Rhine, Ferdinand had inflicted a sharp defeat on them at Kreveld, and they were now trying desperately to reverse the situation. Hence, if coastal operations could be effective, this was the time to demonstrate it.

Nevertheless, Pitt's modified attitude could not but be welcome to the other ministers. They accepted that maritime and continental warfare complemented each other and that Ferdinand might gain some benefit from the operations along the Channel. But to Newcastle and most of his colleagues, the expeditions could never be more than a diversion, born of political expediency. As he commented to Anson: 'We must play a little with Expeditions' to secure the operations in Germany. These were 'the only true solid ones, from whence any great and real advantage can come', though Newcastle believed 'the Enemy should at the same time be entertained with Expeditions, if a diversion could be procured'.[21] Happily Pitt now seemed to agree.

This dispatch of forces to Germany created a problem of command. George II had exercised his prerogative regarding the army to nominate Lieutenant-General William Bligh, with James Whiteford, John Granby and William Kingsley as senior officers.[22] This was quite unacceptable to Marlborough and Sackville, who, since the visit to St Malo, had spent a fruitless two weeks inspecting Caen and then Cherbourg.[23] When bad

---

[19] Treasury Board Minute, 10 July 1758, T 29/33. Ibid., 13 July 1758. Ibid., 20 July 1758.
[20] Pitt to General Ancram, 11 July 1758, Shelburne Papers, xxxvii.
[21] Newcastle to Anson, 7 July, Add. Mss 32,881 ff 189–190.
[22] Conway to Devonshire, 7 July 1758, DPC.
[23] Marlborough to Pitt, 24 June 1758, Shelburne Papers, xxxvii. Ibid., 30 June 1758.

weather and failing supplies necessitated a brief return to Portsmouth, the first news to greet them was that British troops were going to Germany under the command of a 74-year-old 'superannuated' officer. This was both stirring and mortifying. The continent was where the first Duke of Marlborough had made his reputation and where Prince Ferdinand and Frederick II were creating new legends. Apparently this chance of glory was to go to a nonentity, while the grandson of the great duke and his equally ambitious deputy spent their time digging sandcastles along the French coast. The result was a demonstration of that aristocratic intrigue so deprecated by Hardwicke, for the two men used all their influence to have the command structure changed so that their names were substituted for Bligh's.[24]

This outcome was communicated to Howe on 11 July. No mention was made of a successor. The reason, though Pitt did not say, was that no replacement could be found. Newcastle commented to Anson: 'Our Generals have found that it is better fighting upon Land than beating about at Sea.' Possible candidates like General John Mostyn were quick to make their preference for service in Germany known. It was no strong testimony to the efficacy of such operations.[25]

At last, when everyone else had declined, Bligh consented to take the position. Though mortified at his treatment, he decided it was better to serve his King than return home to Ireland. A veteran of the War of Spanish Succession, Bligh was hardly in his prime.[26] Pitt, however, affected to be impressed. He commented to Bute on 18 July: 'I like our general extremely, and never saw a more soldier like man.'[27] One event to cheer Bligh was the announcement that Prince Edward, the younger brother of the Prince of Wales, would accompany the expedition.[28] This was intended by Leicester House as a demonstration of its disapproval for the German war. The announcement, however, was good for the morale of the troops.[29] The Prince boarded the *Magnanime* on 27 July, albeit with lessened pomp, the salutes being reduced to conserve gunpowder.[30]

With the problem of the command settled, the ministers were able to issue instructions to the new general. These were once more drafted by Pitt. In

---

[24] Lady Anson to Anson, 12 July 1758, Anson Papers, D 615/HMC, Box F, Staffordshire Record Office. H. Walpole, *Memoirs of the Reign of King George II* (London, 1846–47), III, 125–126.
[25] Newcastle to Anson, 7 July 1758, Add. Mss 32,881 ff 189–190. Mostyn to Newcastle, 10 July 1758, Add. Mss 32,881 f 338.
[26] *Dictionary of National Biography.*
[27] Pitt to Bute, 18 July 1758, printed in R. Pares and A. J. P. Taylor (eds.), *Essays Presented to Sir Lewis Namier* (London, 1956), 159.
[28] Pitt to Bute, 14 July 1758, printed in Pares and Taylor, *Essays to Namier*, 157.
[29] Anon., *A Journal of the Campaign on the Coast of France* (London, 1758), 73.
[30] An Order in Council on the matter of naval salutes had been issued to the fleet on 14 April 1758, Adm 1/5164.

scope they were similar to those of Marlborough. Bligh was to create a diversion from which it was hoped the usual cornucopia of results would follow. Only the target was changed. Cherbourg now seemed the best objective. Thereafter, Bligh was to use his discretion. The most essential requirement was haste. Bligh was to put to sea as soon as he heard that Anson was back on station.[31] The First Lord had taken advantage of the lull to do some victualling and repairs to his squadron at Plymouth.[32]

Anson's cruise had so far been uneventful. At first he had chosen the island of Bas as his station but had then moved to Ushant to be closer to Brest. The French, however, had not stirred and his main concerns had been logistical. Early on he concluded that his vessels were too cluttered with stores to be easily manoeuvred.[33] Then he found a lack of frigates was impeding his efforts at intelligence, because of the time spent cleaning these vessels at Plymouth.[34] Next it was the quality of the victuals that received his attention.[35] But most noteworthy was the poor discipline of the fleet. He told Hardwicke: 'I never saw such awkwardness in going through the common manoeuvres.' The first few weeks, therefore, had been spent running out the guns, working the sails and doing all the other things necessary to fight an action.[36]

Otherwise his only problem had been that of subordinate commanders. After two weeks Hawke had fallen ill and had been sent ashore.[37] This mishap left Anson with no flag officer for a fleet whose operational size required division into three. As a temporary measure Anson had chosen two of his senior captains to command the rear and van, giving them the rank of commodore. He duly notified the King of these arrangements, expecting the Admiralty to devise a more permanent solution.[38] He was accordingly disconcerted when Pitt informed him that George II had approved his action, 'which will it is not doubted answer for the present'.[39] However, the failure to send him a flag replacement was quite inadvertent. As Lady Anson informed her brother-in-law: 'No Admiral has been sent out to your brother, both the Board and the King thinking it better to confirm his Commodores til he applies for any particular Admiral, imagining they do in that what will be most agreeable.'[40] As soon as Anson appreciated this, he penned a letter to the Board suggesting that three of the most senior and

[31] George II to Bligh, 17 July 1758, Shelburne Papers, xxxvii.
[32] Anson to Pitt, 16 July 1757, Shelburne Papers, xxxvii.
[33] Anson to Clevland, 13 June 1758, Adm 1/90.
[34] Anson to Clevland, 20 June 1758, Adm 1/90. Ibid., 29 June 1758.
[35] Anson to Clevland, 20 June 1758, Adm 1/90.
[36] Anson to Hardwicke, 22 July 1758, Add. Mss 35,359 f 413.
[37] Anson to Clevland, 18 June 1758, Adm 1/90.
[38] Ibid., 20 June 1758.
[39] Pitt to Anson, 21 June 1758, Shelburne Papers, xxxvii.
[40] Lady Anson to Sir Thomas Anson, 27 June 1758, Anson Papers, G 615/HMC, Box G.

deserving captains in the navy, Charles Steevens, Philip Durell and Charles Holmes, be promoted to the rank of Rear-Admiral, and that one of them, Holmes, should be sent to join him immediately. These proposals were no sooner received than accepted.[41]

II

Despite the return of the expedition to French waters, the hopes for continued success on the continent soon proved illusory. An attempt by the King of Prussia to advance into Moravia was beaten back, while substantial French reinforcements compelled Ferdinand to remain on the defensive.[42] Moreover, the troops supposedly withdrawing from Germany had merely done so to reform their ranks. All the indications were that the enemy were about to make a renewed effort, with one army on the lower Rhine to confront Ferdinand, and another to attack his flank by way of Hesse. To counter this, Ferdinand proposed to create a separate corps, but he required yet more men. His request of the British was small: two extra regiments to garrison Stade.[43] However, coming after so considerable a reinforcement it inevitably fuelled Pitt's suspicions that any continental commitment was bound to be limitless.

Newcastle, naturally, did not agree. Indeed, Pitt's attitude made him comment: 'Mr Pitt looks too much to his own part of the world *only*. That is and ought to be a great object, but not the only one even for the sake of that Object itself. Ministers in this Country, where every part of the world affects us, in some way or other, should consider the *whole Globe*.' Pitt should stop confining himself to the concerns of his own department.[44]

A meeting was accordingly arranged on 1 August to discuss the matter at Holdernesse's house in Arlington Street. The number present was small. Anson was absent, Ligonier was sick, while Hardwicke declined to attend. This left the decision to Granville, Pitt, Holdernesse and Newcastle.

Prior to the meeting the King appealed to Newcastle to support Ferdinand's request. Aside from the troops, the Prince wanted further ships on the Weser and the Elbe, together with some transports to hold the 7,000 prisoners then in his hands. At the discussion the ships and transports were agreed to. But on the additional regiments Newcastle found his colleagues opposed. Pitt pointed out that Britain already had in pay on the continent 50,000 men exclusive of the substantial reinforcement now on its way from the national army. No further men could for the present be spared, though as a willing gesture he suggested hiring 6,000 troops from the Elector of

41 Pitt to Anson, 7 July 1758, Shelburne Papers, xxxvii.
42 Newcastle to Holdernesse, 22 July 1758, Add. Mss 32,882 f 37.
43 Newcastle to Hardwicke, 2 Aug 1758, Add. Mss 32,882 ff 200–209.
44 Newcastle to Holdernesse, 25 July 1758, Add. Mss 32,882 ff 65–66.

Bavaria. This cut no ice with Newcastle, since the Bavarians were firmly
in the pay of Austria. Newcastle could only go home and complain how
invidious it was 'to meet with three persons, two of which will always take
part against me'.[45] In the ensuing weeks he made several pleas to
Hardwicke, Devonshire and Mansfield to come and support him, but to no
effect.

Nevertheless, the ministry was at last beginning to reap the rewards for
its work. In the second week of August came word of the capture of
Cherbourg. The previous visit of Marlborough had revealed the town was
undefended on the landward side, so that once the troops were ashore its
capture was likely. The coast to the east was rocky, but to the west there
were several suitable bays. Here the French had a number of strong posts
linked by a continuous entrenchment for a few miles, the assumption being
that any attacking force would approach fairly close to its objective. In this
they proved wrong, for Bligh and Howe, knowing that a landing was the
most difficult part, decided to outflank the French by disembarking at a
place called Urville, even though this entailed an additional march of
several miles. The opposing force was mainly militia and little resistance was
encountered, either at the beach or towards the town where the mayor and
leading inhabitants were waiting to surrender.[46]

The spoils proved considerable. In the harbour were thirty-five ships
including several privateers. There was also much ordnance. Twenty-two
brass cannon were loaded on a vessel for display in London.[47] More
important was the destruction of the harbour. This had been constructed
under the direction of Vauban in 1687 to make Cherbourg a naval base.
The sum of £1,000,000 had reputedly been spent before the project was
abandoned through lack of water for the larger ships. Since then Cherbourg
had been a commercial centre used by privateers in wartime.[48] A start
therefore was made on levelling the causeway with powder captured from
the enemy.

The capture of Cherbourg did much to raise the pride of the nation: the
newspapers noted that it was the first successful landing of any size in France
since the Hundred Years' War.[49] The captured cannon were paraded
through Hyde Park and Pitt was able to tell Bligh that the King was well
pleased. As a mark of confidence some of the troops sent to Germany would
be replaced.[50] However, as Lady Anson commented, the spoils were modest
compared to those of the First Battle of Finisterre; and a letter to the *London*

---

[45] Newcastle to Hardwicke, 2 Aug 1758, Add. Mss 32,882 ff 200–209.
[46] Bligh to Pitt, 7 Aug 1758, Shelburne Papers, xxxvii.
[47] Bligh to Pitt, 8 Aug 1758, Shelburne Papers, xxxvii.
[48] *London Chronicle*, 12/15 Aug 1758.
[49] Walpole, *Memoirs of George II*, iii, 133.
[50] Pitt to Bligh, 12 Aug 1758, Shelburne Papers, xxxvii.

Chronicle reminded readers that the French government was unlikely to feel concerned in Paris.[51] Indeed, the ministers now knew that the expeditions were having little effect on the operations in Germany. Ferdinand had informed them that the army of the Marquis de Contades was growing daily. Unless the government could find extra means of supporting him, he was doubtful of holding his position on the Rhine.[52]

The next news, this time from America, was also good. Louisburg had fallen. Amherst had assembled his forces at Halifax in time for a landing on Cape Breton Isle to the west of the fortress by 8 June. The landing itself had proved risky in the rough seas and a number of men had been lost. Nevertheless, a vital foothold had been obtained and the isolation of Louisburg was completed by the establishment of a blockade.[53] Before a siege could begin, however, stores had to be landed, the enemy driven from their outposts, roads built and trenches dug. The last was subject to harassment from the cannon of the five ships of the line marooned in the harbour. The result was that these tasks were not completed until 22 July when the British batteries opened with their full fury.[54] Soon several of the French vessels were alight and by 26 July the French were ready to surrender. The capture of the fort was the single greatest success of the British to that point. Not only had they captured the gateway to the St Lawrence, they had also inflicted a considerable defeat on the French navy. Five ships of the line had been captured or sunk along with four frigates, and 3,000 Frenchmen were prisoners of war.[55]

However, the news from America was mixed, for shortly afterwards came information of a setback at Ticonderoga. Abercromby had initially made good progress: a supply train had been established, naval control of Lake George attained and stores forwarded so that he had been able to advance against Ticonderoga on 5 July. He would have started earlier but for the delay of the provincials, their first units only arriving at the beginning of June, a month after Pitt had stipulated.[56]

Originally, Abercromby had expected to conduct a formal siege at Ticonderoga. However, Montcalm with the main French army had arrived a few days before and was busy entrenching in front. Thus to get to the fort Abercromby first had to drive away Montcalm. When a prisoner erroneously reported that the enemy were expecting a reinforcement of 3,000 men, he

---

[51] Sir John Barrow, *Life of George, Lord Anson* (London, 1839), 314. *London Chronicle*, 19/22 Aug 1758.
[52] Newcastle to Hardwicke, 14 Aug 1758, Add. Mss 32,882 ff 344–350.
[53] Amherst to Pitt, 11 June 1758, Kimball, I, 271–275.
[54] Amherst to Pitt, 23 June 1758, Kimball, I, 281–284. Amherst to Pitt, 6 July 1758, Kimball, I, 291–293. Amherst to Pitt, 23 July 1758, Kimball, I, 302–305.
[55] Amherst to Pitt, 27 July 1758, Kimball, I, 305–307. Boscawen to Pitt, 28 July 1758, Kimball, I, 307–309.
[56] Abercromby to Pitt, 29 June 1758, Kimball, I, 284–287.

decided to act quickly without waiting for his artillery, which would require
several days to deploy. As Abercromby told the ministers back home, if he
could have breached the enemy lines 'even at the expense of some good
officers and men, we should have forced the Marquis of Montcalm to have
retired to his boats, leaving the garrison to be besieged'. The British could
then have captured the fort at their leisure.[57]

The action proved a fatal miscalculation. Montcalm's breastwork was
higher than expected, being at least 8 feet from the ground. Moreover, the
front was obstructed by numerous trees with sharpened stakes pointing
towards the attackers. The result was that after several ferocious attacks and
four hours of bitter fighting Abercromby had had to call off the assault,
having lost 1,600 regulars and 300 provincials. Indeed, the regular corps
were so shattered that Abercromby, fearing the enemy might try to disrupt
his communications, had retreated to the other end of Lake George to reform
his army before contemplating another move.[58]

The difficulties of the terrain and the lateness of the provincials led many,
like Robert Napier, the Adjutant-General, to excuse him. Others were more
critical, for instance Wolfe believed that Abercromby had missed a golden
opportunity to end the war at a single blow by capturing Montcalm's
army.[59] Such a verdict was harsh, as Abercromby did have to contend with
almost the entire force of Canada. Whatever historians have said about Pitt's
co-ordinated strategy, Abercromby received no assistance from the attack
on Louisburg. On the news of the expedition there, Montcalm was able to
concentrate on the threat from New York.[60] A three-pronged offensive had
not been a magic formula for success.

The setback Abercromby suffered made it clear that the ranks in North
America would have to be reinforced, especially if subsequent operations
were to be undertaken against the French in the Caribbean, as Pitt was
hoping. Even before the disaster at Ticonderoga was known, Pitt wanted
to dispatch recruits. Accordingly, it was agreed, as last year, to draft 2,000
men from the regiments at home and raise another battalion of Highlanders,
amounting in all to 3,000.[61]

This decision was not ideal, for drafting was recognized as a most
unsatisfactory method of recruitment, which broke regimental loyalties and,
being usually for service overseas, was regarded as a form of punishment
without the formality of a court martial. The receiving corps too were not

[57] General Abercromby, 19 Aug 1758, Add. Mss 32,884 ff 362–366.
[58] Abercromby to Pitt, 12 July 1758, Kimball, 297–302.
[59] Napier to Abercromby, 7 Sept 1758, Abercromby Papers, Box 12, Huntington Library.
   Wolfe to Colonel Rickson, 1 Dec 1758, printed in B. Willson, *The Life and Letters of James
   Wolfe* (London, 1909), 402.
[60] G. Fregault, *Canada: The War of the Conquest* (Toronto, 1969), 214–223.
[61] Barrington to Abercromby, 8 July 1758, WO 4/56. Newcastle to Holdernesse, 25 July 1758,
   Add. Mss 32,882 ff 65–66. Pitt to Barrington, 21 Aug 1758, WO 1/857.

usually benefited, since the regiments at home invariably disposed of their least wanted men.[62] However, no other course seemed available, as 1758 had proved a difficult year for recruitment. The furore stirred up by Pratt meant that the Recruiting Act could not be renewed and volunteers were proving hard to get. Even in Ireland, a traditional source of men, the regiments were having to send parties to England to avoid the illegal recruitment of Roman catholics.[63] The corps were also being reduced by desertion. Although most of those serving in the ranks were volunteers, enough were missing for Barrington to be constantly writing to the magistrates and commanding officers about their return.[64]

The mixed news from America was not the only setback suffered by the ministry at this time, for misfortune now overtook Bligh. After the successful withdrawal from Cherbourg, he and Howe determined on another visit to St Malo. Bligh's instructions left him free to attempt any place between Havre and Morlaix.[65] The latter was too close to the forces at Brest while Caen, the other most tempting target, had been reconnoitred and found unsuitable. An attack on St Malo offered the prospect of surprise, for the French would hardly expect another visit so soon. Bligh's plan had been to approach this time from the west by way of St Briac. After establishing himself on the opposite bank, he would cross the River Rance to reoccupy St Servan and Paramé. St Malo would then be surrounded and have to surrender.[66]

Unfortunately, the Rance had proved unnavigable. Another problem was the landing site at St Lunaire; the rocks and shoals there had compelled Howe to look for an alternative anchorage before resuming his operations. The nearest place appeared to be St Cast, 9 miles to the west. This was too distant to support an investment of St Malo and Bligh had had to abandon his attack.[67]

The fleet had accordingly gone to its new anchorage while the army followed on foot. This meant a march inland, during which time communication was completely severed. However, few reports had been

---

[62] Loudoun commented to Cumberland on the news of one such reinforcement: 'I do not doubt we have got the whole Vices of the Irish Army', 5 Jan 1757, printed in S. M. Pargellis (ed.), *Military Affairs in North America: 1748–1765: Selected Documents from the Cumberland Papers in Windsor Castle* (New York, 1936), 292. See J. A. Houlding, *Fit for Service: The Training of the British Army, 1715–1795* (Oxford, 1981), 120–125.

[63] Bedford to Pitt, 29 Aug 1758, printed in Lord John Russell (ed.), *Correspondence of John, Fourth Duke of Bedford* (London, 1843), ii, 360–365.

[64] The correspondence is to be found in WO 4/593–595.

[65] George II to Bligh, 17 July 1758, Shelburne Papers, xxxvii. Accusations were subsequently made that St Malo had been improperly chosen as a target by Leicester House, Hardwicke to Newcastle, 7 Oct 1758, Add. Mss 32,885 ff 289–291.

[66] Bligh to Pitt, 8 Sept 1758, Shelburne Papers, xxxvii. Account of the Expedition, by an Officer thereon, 17 Sept 1758, RA CP, Maps xii.

[67] Bligh to Pitt, 8 Sept 1758, Shelburne Papers, xxxvii. Colonel John Irwin to Sackville, 21 Sept 1758, HMC 9th Report, Part 3, *Stopford-Sackville Mss*, i, 298.

received of enemy troops. Not until the army had almost reached its destination did a prisoner confirm that a French force of between 7,000 and 10,000 men was closing in from the west under the Duc d'Aiguillon.

At this critical juncture Bligh held a council of war. Clerk suggested bringing the artillery and cavalry ashore so that a vigorous attack could be launched. But the other officers pointed out that if Bligh was defeated, the entire army would be lost. Common sense dictated an immediate retreat to St Cast to forestall the French.

The more cautious advice prevailed. Unfortunately, the French appeared before the Guards had been ferried to safety. The British were then at their most vulnerable, being too weak to counter-attack, but still too numerous for one embarkation. In the ensuing battle, 750 were killed, wounded or taken prisoner, despite the heroic efforts of Howe and the fleet to save them in the landing craft.[68]

This disappointing end naturally led to controversy. Bute and Princess Augusta were most embarrassed at the turn of events. They had committed themselves heavily in sending Prince Edward to serve with Howe. In addition they had taken Clerk under their patronage. Bute disingenuously tried to exculpate his protégés by suggesting that the government had undermined the expedition to discredit the heir.[69] Few believed him, particularly the officers. Those who served on the expedition blamed Clerk, asserting he had lured Bligh on a dangerous wild-goose chase.[70] The ministers for their part criticized Bligh. Ligonier in particular felt that he should not have declined an engagement on the terms offered by Aiguillon.[71]

As for Bligh, he played down the misfortune. If the nation was going to engage on such risky warfare, then losses must be expected. He personally had no regrets. Everyone knew it was not easy to land on a hostile coast, however weak the opposition, and once ashore, re-embarking was inevitably difficult, ten times so in the presence of a foe who was well equipped and determined to attack.[72]

Amid all these recriminations the reasons for the disaster were clear. The expedition had been launched on faulty information. Had more been known about the River Rance and the navigation at St Lunaire, Bligh would not

[68] Bligh to Pitt, 13 Sept 1758, Shelburne Papers, XXXVII. Irwin to Sackville, 21 Sept 1758, HMC, *Stopford-Sackville Mss*, I, 299. Anon., *A Letter from the Honourable L--t G--l B--gh to the Right Honourable W--m P--t Esquire* (London, 1758), 18–19.
[69] Newcastle to Hardwicke, 5 Oct 1758, Add. Mss 32,884 ff 260–270.
[70] Account of the Expedition, 17 Sept 1758, RA CP, Maps XII. Irwin to Sackville, 21 Sept 1758, HMC, *Stopford-Sackville Mss*, I, 296–301. Napier to Hotham, 1 Nov 1758, Hotham Papers DDHO 4/8.
[71] Ligonier to Pitt, 18 Sept 1758, CP PRO 30/8/58.
[72] Bligh to Pitt, 13 Sept 1758, Shelburne Papers, XXXVII. *A Letter from the Honourable L--t G--l B--gh*, 25–29.

have been tempted into a second visit. Even so the landing need not have ended in this manner and for this Bligh must accept some responsibility. Throughout he had been surprisingly casual in the presence of the enemy.[73] Both Mordaunt and Marlborough had rigidly insisted that no operation could begin until the army had a secure retreat. In this insistence events at St Cast had proved them right. One charge from which Bligh can be exonerated was his failure to attack Aiguillon. Few of those serving with the expedition thought this would have been possible. All the British regiments were under strength, with many sick and wounded, some men with no food or clothing. The countryside too was difficult to penetrate. An advance on the enemy would have been a recipe for disaster.[74]

Shelburne, who served on the expedition as adjutant-general, believed that had an officer of Prince Ferdinand's calibre been appointed, the operation would have been successful. He erroneously blamed Pitt for this situation, suggesting that he left Ligonier to find officers in the manner of a valet selecting a shoemaker.[75] In reality, the matter did not lie with Pitt or even Ligonier, and the choice of commanders would always be a lottery when men of Prince Ferdinand's calibre were so rare.

Though no enquiry or court martial was held, Ligonier curtly informed Bligh that the King would not receive him at court. This spiteful treatment of a faithful servant, who had been chosen for one command and given another less congenial, was not lost on the public. Within a week the edict was withdrawn, but the change of heart at St James's came too late to mollify Bligh. He resigned all his appointments and retired to his estates in Ireland.[76] Another casualty was Clerk. His rise had been meteoric: he had enjoyed the patronage of Pitt, Ligonier and Leicester House, and had risen from lowly engineer to colonel. But, although Leicester House adopted his cause, his career was finished. Pitt had no use for failures and George II never forgave men who squandered his precious Guards.

The episode completed the break between Pitt and Leicester House which had been in the making for some time. Bute and the heir disapproved Pitt's readiness to deploy British troops in Germany and were displeased at his handling of the St Cast affair.[77] But what really rankled was Pitt's failure to consult them. As Prince George commented shortly afterwards, Pitt treated them with 'no more regard than he would do a parcel of children'.[78] There would be no more intimacy with him.

---

[73] Irwin to Sackville, 21 Sept 1758, HMC, *Stopford-Sackville Mss*, i, 296–297.
[74] Ibid.
[75] Lord E. Fitzmaurice, *The Life of William, Earl of Shelburne* 2nd edition, revised (London, 1912), i, 75–76. [76] Walpole, *Memoirs of George II*, iii, 137.
[77] Prince George to Bute, 2 July 1758, printed in R. Sedgwick (ed.), *Letters from George III to Lord Bute, 1756–1766* (London, 1939), 10–11. Hardwicke to Newcastle, 7 Oct 1758, Add. Mss 32,884 ff 268–269.
[78] Prince George to Bute, 8 Dec 1758, printed in Sedgwick (ed.), *Letters from George III*, 18.

The mishap at St Cast inevitably influenced attitudes to such operations. Many outside the administration agreed with Fox that they were expensive futilities, like 'breaking windows with guineas'.[79] Even those in favour of maritime operations began to denigrate this type of warfare. A correspondent in the *London Chronicle* had earlier commented: 'The true objection to these expeditions is their utter insignificance', since they were ineffective even as a 'diversion in favour of our friends and allies in Germany'. The administration should devote its attention to more worthwhile objectives in North America and the West Indies.[80]

There was no denying some of these points. The day after the news of St Cast, Newcastle reported to Hardwicke: 'Mr Pitt talked very reasonably to me on the subject.' Coastal operations against France would be abandoned.[81] Pitt as always said little about his feelings. One of his virtues was that he would always try something new. He did not brood over past mistakes, however obstinate he might be about future plans. On this occasion the men, if not the concept, had been found wanting. Militarily, coastal expeditions were risky. Pitt would not repeat the mistake again. There was no need to. The expeditions had been a useful compromise between sending troops to Germany and not doing anything there. Secure now in the Commons and administration, he no longer needed such gestures.

The coastal expeditions of 1757 and 1758 were Pitt's most distinctive contribution to the war. In other directions he found policy already determined by events. The concept was not his but he was almost alone in getting it accepted in the ministry. Indeed, the expeditions reveal Pitt as the traditional portrait would have him: a man of action, capable of carrying his colleagues against their inclination. Some years later Shelburne asserted that the orders were 'all oratory and no substance'; that 'Mr Pitt's great aim was to draw them up so as to throw all the blame in the case of any failure on the military commander'.[82] Such criticism might have been true of the Rochefort expedition. The 1758 operations showed that he could learn. The formation of the transport pool and stockpiling of provisions at Portsmouth had helped the departure and revictualling of the force.

Nevertheless, as an effective contribution to the war they were disappointing. Despite the ambitious language of the instructions and later claims of historians, the French withdrew hardly a soldier from Germany.

[79] Chesterfield to Philip Dormer, 27 June 1758, printed in J. Bradshaw (ed.), *The Letters of Philip Dormer Stanhope. Earl of Chesterfield* (London, 1893), III, 1227–1228.
[80] *London Chronicle*, 27/29 July, 1758. For a more detailed analysis of the press concerning this incident, see M. Peters, *Pitt and Popularity: The Patriot Minister and London Opinion during the Seven Years' War* (Oxford, 1980), 128–131.
[81] Newcastle to Hardwicke, 18 Sept 1758, Add. Mss 32,884 ff 79–85.
[82] Fitzmaurice, *Life of Shelburne*, I, 74.

When news of the expedition reached Versailles in the spring of 1758, the French were primarily worried that the troops might be sent to Flanders to strike at the lower Rhine. News that Marlborough had gone to St Malo actually produced relief.[83] The fifteen battalions later reported to be withdrawing from Germany did so to reform their ranks, after being mauled by Prince Ferdinand.[84] There were two reasons for the enemy's failure to act as desired. First, Pitt's schemes were not part of a co-ordinated strategy, being essentially rationalizations of domestic needs. Secondly, the French recognized their diversionary intent. Just as the British later refused to change plans in 1759 under the threat of invasion, so the French declined to bring back their forces from Germany in 1758, recognizing that the decisive theatre in Europe was the Rhine, not Brittany. Victory there could make them masters of Hanover, complete the destruction of Prussia and enable France to concentrate on the maritime war. The coastal provinces must fend for themselves.[85]

Pitt had already noted the call for more expeditions overseas, and was busy preparing two: one to Goree, the other to Martinique. The former was suggested by a London merchant, Thomas Cumming. A small force had already been sent out in February to the neighbouring French station of Senegal and the capture of Goree would consolidate British control of the African slave trade, thus appealing to mercantilist sentiment.[86] The proposal was to send a small squadron of ships together with a battalion of troops. Planning the operation had not gone entirely smoothly. Samuel Touchet, a merchant with extensive interests in Guinea, wanted to warn Pitt of the danger of sending troops to the area during the rainy season. However, Lady Anson reported to her husband: ' Mr Touchet has been four times with Mr Pitt; once sent by the Duke of Newcastle, once by Mr Pitt's own appointment, but has never been able to see him.'[87] After these difficulties had been settled, the ministry then had to find a commander. Since the operation would be mainly naval, Pitt wrote to Anson for a suitable person. Augustus Keppel was suggested and subsequently approved by the King.[88]

More important was Pitt's plan for an expedition to Martinique. By dispossessing the French of this rich sugar island their trade would suffer, their revenue decline and with it their ability to fight. Such a measure was traditional in British military thinking. Nevertheless, its proposal represented

---

[83] R. Waddington, *La Guerre de Sept Ans* (Paris, 1899), III, 86. Moreover, so great was the French concern for Flanders that they actually moved forces from the maritime provinces, ibid., 119–120.   [84] Ferdinand to Holdernesse, 31 Aug 1758, SP 87/33.

[85] Waddington, *Guerre de Sept Ans*, III, 119–120.

[86] Corbett, *Seven Years' War*, I, 157, 337.

[87] Lady Anson to Anson, 21 June 1758, Anson Papers, G 615/HMC, Box F, Staffordshire Record Office.

[88] Pitt to Anson, 5 Sept 1758, Shelburne Papers, XXXVII. Anson to Pitt, 11 Sept 1758, Shelburne Papers, XXXVII.

a subtle shift in the ministry's aims. Until now everything could be presented as being defensive: the coastal operations were punishment for the French for their aggression in Europe; the invasion of Canada was the necessary result of the attempts to secure the King's territories there. Of course, while the French persisted in their aggression, their colonies could be seen as legitimate targets, especially if such attacks weakened their ability to fight. Additionally, the British still had the problem of Minorca, whose recovery was a point of national honour. The capture of one of France's most valuable overseas possessions offered the prospect of an exchange. Nevertheless, the plans to seize both Goree and Martinique did represent a move from a basically defensive to a more offensive view of the war, since they were directed at areas where there was little territorial dispute.[89]

This went unnoticed inside the ministry where there was strong support for the measure. Everyone agreed that damage might be inflicted on the French by striking at their Caribbean possessions. The plan was to use the 3,000 recruits that Pitt and Ligonier had earlier scheduled for North America, plus another 2,000 men from the expedition. Other troops were for the moment unavailable.[90] In the event, the premature return of the coastal force allowed the sending of five regiments, plus the recruits.[91] This was good news for the designated commanders, though less so for the generals in North America, whose forces would be correspondingly depleted.

The furore over the commanders for Germany induced George II to leave the initial selection this time to Ligonier. He suggested either Henry Conway, Lord Albemarle, John Mostyn, Thomas Hopson or Edward Cornwallis.[92] Originally, George Elliot had featured high on the list; he was well respected by the troops, having just served on the final expedition to France with distinction. However, his health was not good and when Pitt heard that he would have to visit Bath his name was removed.[93] In such appointments, the main considerations were naturally experience, seniority and reputation. But political and personal considerations could never be absent. Conway was a favourite of Ligonier; Cornwallis had been well thought of by Pitt. Albemarle was connected with Cumberland; Mostyn with Newcastle. In the event it was Hopson who carried the prize. Conway

---

[89] The only disputes concerned the so-called neutral islands in the Windward group, notably Granada and Nevis. In theory these had been left to the native Carib Indians; in practice both Britain and France had been seeking to settle them. For more detail, see L. H. Gipson, *The British Empire before the American Revolution*, v, *Zones of International Friction: The Great Lakes Frontier, Canada, the West Indies, 1748–1755* (New York, 1942), 207–230, 312–314.

[90] Newcastle to Holdernesse, 4 Sept 1758, Add. Mss 32,883 ff 273–274.

[91] Barrington to Hopson, 6 Oct 1758, WO 4/56.

[92] Newcastle to Hardwicke, 5 Oct 1758, Add. Mss 32,884 ff 260–270.

[93] General Mostyn to Newcastle, 4 Oct 1758, Add. Mss 32,884 f 248.

and Cornwallis were almost certainly not chosen because of their failure at Rochefort. Albemarle was passed over because Cumberland was still out of favour. Mostyn was too young and wanted to go to Germany. The choice of Hopson to some extent reflected the preference of both George II and Ligonier for senior men, for Hopson had had a long and distinguished career as a regimental commander.[94] Regrettably, he was, as Hardwicke noted, 'quite worn out', though, to balance this, his deputy was the youthful John Barrington, brother of the Secretary at War.[95]

In the absence of Anson the naval details for Martinique were settled by Pitt with the assistance of Clevland.[96] This was one reason why Pitt now wanted Anson to return. Indeed, even Newcastle was unhappy about the Admiralty's management, for all his packing of the Board.[97] Accordingly, in September Pitt had informed Anson: 'The King thinks it is for his service that your Lordship should attend the Board of Admiralty.'[98] Anson himself was ready to come in. His ships were in a miserable condition, but even so he remained at sea until Howe left the French coast. News of the setback at St Cast reached him shortly afterwards, and on 18 September he was back at Spithead, ready to resume his office.[99]

Anson on his return was dubious about the Martinique project. He was concerned that too many ships were being sent overseas 'when we may have occasion for them at home'. He was undoubtedly thinking, with some prescience, of the possibility of a renewal of the French invasion threat. Nevertheless, he loyally accepted the plan as 'a measure already agreed upon', although formal approval was only given in October.[100] Present then was a Mr Burt who had been on the island during the previous war and claimed to have a good knowledge of the terrain. Hardwicke had earlier expressed some unease at the lack of more up-to-date information.[101] Anson now spoke up in support of the project and assured the ministers, from his own personal experience, that Martinique offered few obstacles to an invading force. There was a good beach with a safe retreat should one be necessary. The expedition accordingly went ahead, and the dangers of an invasion were for the moment dismissed.[102]

[94] *Dictionary of National Biography.*
[95] Hardwicke to Newcastle, 7 Oct 1758, Add. Mss 32,882 f 289. M. T. Smelser, *The Campaign for the Sugar Islands, 1759: A Study of Amphibious Warfare* (New York, 1955), 19.
[96] Newcastle to Holdernesse, 4 Sept 1758, Add. Mss 32,883 ff 273–274.
[97] Newcastle to Anson, 2 Aug 1758, Add. Mss 32,882 f 205.
[98] Pitt to Anson, 1 Sept 1758, Shelburne Papers, xxxvii.
[99] Anson to Pitt, 9 Sept 1758, Shelburne Papers, xxxvii. Ibid., 18 Sept 1758.
[100] Newcastle to Hardwicke, 18 Sept 1758, Add. Mss 32,884 ff 79–83.
[101] Hardwicke to Newcastle, 21 Sept 1758, Add. Mss 32,884 ff 98–102.
[102] Newcastle to Hardwicke, 5 Oct 1758, Add. Mss 32,884 ff 260–270.

III

Although the attention of the ministers was focused on the more visible parts of the war, other aspects were no less critical, for since the summer Newcastle had been experiencing difficulties at the Treasury.

Historians have been fond of repeating Shelburne's comment that Newcastle was like the fly on the chariot wheel in imagining he made the machinery of government go round.[103] The analogy was misconceived. All the plans of the ministry would be unavailing if the money or credit was not found to hire the transports, pay the seamen, raise armies, produce munitions and provide a commissariat. No responsibility was more important.[104]

It cannot be pretended that Newcastle had any special aptitude for finance. However, so long as the ministry enjoyed the confidence of the City, the details could be left to others, for the principles of public finance had long been established.[105] Indeed, Newcastle's lack of pretension may have been a blessing, for it meant he was not given to the kind of experimentation that had been Legge's undoing.

The raising of the supply for 1758 had not proved difficult. The Commons had voted £10,000,000, half to be found from the customary land, malt and customs duties, the other half by borrowing.[106] The latter had readily been raised in the City, £4,500,000 in 3.5 per cent annuity stock, £500,000 in a lottery.[107] New taxes to fund the loan had also been voted. On the advice of John Page, a former director of the Sun Fire Company, Newcastle adopted an additional stamp duty together with a tax on places and pensions, which had Pitt's approval.[108]

But negotiating the loan and finding the taxes were not the end of the matter. In wartime a vote of credit had to be obtained so that unforeseen contingencies could be met. The money was usually secured by an issue of Exchequer bills through the Bank of England. Each July a contract was signed to circulate bills to the value of £2,500,000, for which the Bank received 3 per cent interest.[109] The vote of credit for 1757 had been no more

---

[103] Fitzmaurice, *Life of Shelburne*, I, 85–86.
[104] R. Browning, 'The Duke of Newcastle and the Financing of the Seven Years' War', *Journal of Economic History*, XXXI, 344–377.
[105] P. G. M. Dickson, *The Financial Revolution in England: A Study in the Development of Public Credit, 1688–1756* (London, 1967).
[106] Supply for 1758, Add. Mss 33,039 f 87. *JHC*, XXVIII, 7–34.
[107] J. J. Grellier, *The History of the National Debt from the Revolution in 1688 to the Beginning of 1800* (London, 1810), 241–242. After the draw the lottery tickets were converted into normal 3 per cent stock.
[108] Page to Newcastle, 31 Oct 1757, Add. Mss 32,875 ff 340–350. West to Newcastle, 1 Apr 1758, Add. Mss 32,879 ff 1–2. These proposals were implemented in an Act for granting to His Majesty several rates and duties upon offices and pensions etc., *Statutes at Large*, Ch XXII, 31 George II.
[109] Sir John Clapham, *The Bank of England: A History* (Cambridge, 1944), I, 58–79. See also Dickson, *Financial Revolution*, 382–388.

than £1,000,000 and no trouble was anticipated when Newcastle was advised to seek the slightly smaller sum of £800,000 for 1758.[110]

However, business confidence was low, even though the war was going better than at any time. Of the consolidated 3 per cent stock, £100 was now worth only £90.[111] Hence, when Newcastle asked the Bank's Governor and his co-directors on 28 August to honour the contract, the company demurred. Although the number of bills in circulation was below the stipulated limit, the directors professed to be fearful that if they accepted another £800,000 worth of bills their credit would be severely extended. In the event of a further decline in market prices, the Bank might have to redeem both the bills and the specie value of its own notes. This it would not be able to do.[112]

Various reasons were ascribed for the slide in confidence. Some attributed it to the massive shipments of specie overseas to Germany and America, which meant a lack of money for domestic investment. Others accused the financiers of manipulating the prices.[113] But Sampson Gideon, a Jewish financier on whom Pelham had sometimes relied, believed that the Treasury's own shortage of cash was the cause. The government was failing to keep pace with the accumulating debt of the navy. The Treasurer of the Navy customarily issued bills on the completion of work or the delivery of materials, and from 1754 to 1757, the maximum time between the issue of the bills and their settlement had been six months; now, the delay was a year. To many observers this suggested a real shortage of money in the government. Not unnaturally the merchants were hastening to sell their bills at a discount and their action was affecting the price of the long-term stocks. The danger was that if the decline continued investors might not subscribe to further loans. Higher interest in these circumstances would only be a palliative, for this would merely depress the existing funds yet further, putting everything at risk. There was real danger that the government's credit might fail, in which case bankruptcy and a humiliating peace must be the result.[114]

Regarding the stocks, Newcastle could only hope that confidence would return and prices revive. For him the most pressing problem was still realizing the vote of credit. Something had to be done, for by the end of September the demands on the Exchequer were in excess of funds to the amount of £1,000,000.[115] Gideon had previously suggested that Newcastle should raise the money himself by the issue of interest-bearing tallies. In the end he undertook to use his good offices with the Bank, successfully as it

---

[110] *JHC*, xxvii, 90. Newcastle to Hardwicke, 3 June 1758, Yorke, iii, 53.
[111] *London Chronicle*, 15/17 Aug 1758. W. H. Beveridge, *Prices and Wages in England from the Twelfth to the Nineteenth Century* (London, 1939), i, 523.
[112] Treasury Board Minute, 28 Aug 1758, T 29/33.
[113] Legge to Newcastle, 4 Sept 1758, Add. Mss 32,883 ff 276–277.
[114] Gideon to Newcastle, 28 Aug 1758, Add. Mss 32,883 ff 148–150.
[115] Treasury Board Minute, 27 Sept 1758, T 29/33.

turned out. The directors agreed to accept £1,200,000 of Exchequer bills on the security of next year's land tax, plus a further £750,000 on the revenue of the malt. But as an inducement Newcastle had to pay 4 per cent on the bills, a full point higher than the normal figure.[116] Temporarily the cash crisis of the Treasury was over, but the difficulties with the Bank and the higher rate of interest were a foretaste of possible problems to come. Not unnaturally Newcastle began to think of peace, though he affirmed to Hardwicke that he was 'at present for pushing on the war most vigorously', to obtain a satisfactory settlement later.[117]

One reason for the lack of money was the cost of the war in Germany, as Pitt was quick to note. When Munchausen presented the 1759 estimates for the Electoral forces, they amounted to over £1,800,000, exclusive of the Hessian and Prussian demands. Pitt was infuriated, not least because the numbers to be provided for had risen from 38,000 to 50,000 men. 'In the name of God,' he thundered, 'how comes such an idea on paper?' Unless Newcastle could bring 'things to some reasonable bulk...the whole must go into Confusion', for the demands were politically inadmissible. Pitt, however, was careful to add: 'This is particularly your Grace's province.' He alone had the necessary influence in the closet to revise these demands.[118]

Newcastle replied that he personally was not responsible for the figures. The Hanoverian numbers were the consequence of the convention with Prussia in April 1758 which called for an increase in the King's forces. The estimates were in any case preliminary ones. Everything was still open to discussion. Pitt, however, made no response except to complain of a lack of notice.[119] The reason for his sensitivity was that Parliament was about to reassemble.

Cost, however, was not the only problem regarding the war in Germany, for Newcastle had been experiencing problems with the British part of the commissariat. Despite the exhortations to economy, Marlborough had signed an exorbitant agreement with a local contractor for the supply of forage.[120] The details had horrified Newcastle and his Treasury colleagues and led them to insist that in future all contracts must be referred to the Commissary-General, Abraham Hume, in London.[121] But the episode had underlined the unsatisfactory nature of the arrangements in Germany. Newcastle and the Board were aware that at times the military must have power to make agreements without waiting weeks for confirmation of their

---

[116] Gideon to Newcastle, 21 Nov 1758, Add. Mss 32,885 f 475.
[117] Newcastle to Hardwicke, 26 Aug 1758, Add. Mss 32,883 ff 114–121.
[118] Pitt to Newcastle, 22 Nov 1758, Add. Mss 32,885 ff 482–485.
[119] Newcastle to Pitt, 22 Nov 1758, Add. Mss 32,885 ff 490–491. Pitt to Newcastle, 22 Nov 1758, Add. Mss 32,885 ff 492–493.
[120] Marlborough to Newcastle, 29 Aug 1758, Add. Mss 32,883 ff 154–155.
[121] Treasury to Marlborough, 30 Oct 1758, T 27/27. Martin to William Hatton, 27 Oct 1758, T 27/27.

plans: the war assuredly would not wait. For this reason Newcastle suggested that Hume himself should go to Germany 'to inspect the accounts, contracts and everything relative to the British troops, which could properly come under the cognizance of the Treasury'. The Commissary-General declined on health grounds.[122] Nevertheless, the need for some kind of supervision by a senior official was clearly established.

Before making any decision, Newcastle ascertained the views of the commanders in Germany, which was desirable, since there had been a change following the death of Marlborough and his succession by Sackville. Newcastle accordingly wrote on 31 October emphasizing the need for the 'greatest frugality and strictest economy'. Regarding the future shape of the commissariat Newcastle insisted: 'I have no favourites in things of this kind; whoever will serve the public best and the cheapest shall be preferred.' However, this did not mean that economy would supersede the well-being of Sackville's command, for Newcastle had the success of the army much at heart.[123]

Sackville proved noncommittal and in the event Newcastle followed the advice of James West, the Treasury secretary, to appoint a civilian with the title of 'Superintendent or Director of the Commissary'.[124] The position, as Samuel Martin, the other Treasury secretary, later pointed out, was entirely new. No official before had had such authority.[125] The superintendent was to have powers both of account and of supply. Though the day-to-day management would be under Boyd and Hatton, the new man would make all the major contracts, inspect those already made, and look for fraud. He could muster the army, check the magazines and inspect the wagon train. Finally, he would have the power to issue drafts on the deputy paymasters, a responsibility that until now had been exclusive to the Commander-in-Chief. To assist him in the execution of these tasks, the superintendent was to have a full complement of clerks and inspectors.[126]

Clearly, someone of exceptional standing was required to fill this important position. The man Newcastle finally selected was Thomas Orby Hunter, one of the Admiralty lords and Member of Parliament for Winchelsea. Though not politically associated with Newcastle, he was a natural choice. He had been a deputy paymaster with the forces in Flanders during the previous war, and thus was acquainted with the business to which he was going. In the Commons and as a paymaster he had acquired a reputation for honesty.[127] The feeling that Hunter would heed the Treasury's

[122] West to Newcastle, 20 Oct 1758, Add. Mss 32,884 ff 445–446.
[123] Newcastle to Sackville, 31 Oct 1758, Add. Mss 32,885 ff 148–152.
[124] West to Newcastle, 27 Oct 1758, Add. Mss 32,885 ff 97–98.
[125] Martin to Hatton, 24 Apr 1760, T 64/96.
[126] George II to Thomas Orby Hunter, 6 Jan 1759, Letters Patent C 66/3663, Public Record Office.
[127] Namier and Brooke, *History of Parliament*, II, 656–657.

exhortations was a powerful consideration with Newcastle, now that the expenses of fighting in Germany were running at between £3,000,000 and £4,000,000 a year.

The other business to concern the ministers in the autumn of 1758 was mainly diplomatic. During the discussions in the spring, Frederick II had told Yorke several times that the allies must stop living from day to day. They must mend their relations with the Dutch.[128] Holland had been traditionally Britain's ally, and the alliance had ended only when the Dutch refused help in 1756 on the grounds that the dispute was none of their concern, being solely about America. However, there was some reason to believe that the decision of Austria in 1757 to allow the French to garrison the barrier fortresses – to release their own men for service in Germany – had not pleased the Dutch, whose own security was imperilled thereby.[129] If the Republic could be brought into the war on the side of the allies, the operations of Prince Ferdinand would be materially assisted: his flank would be secured, thus allowing him to carry the war towards France.

Unfortunately, though the government of the Princess Royal was anxious to renew the old understanding, the Republic itself was hopelessly divided. Many deputies in the Estates General, where all money bills had to pass, were strongly opposed to the Princess's government and all that it stood for. British observers were in the habit of ascribing this to the machinations of France. French agents were undoubtedly busy, but little gold was needed to fan the flames of Anglophobia. From the beginning, resentment had been growing in commercial circles at the activities of the royal navy and British privateers. The complaints were of various kinds: some, that the captains and their vessels were being plundered; others, that they could get no redress in the Vice-Admiralty courts; yet more, that their ships should have been stopped at all. As Yorke explained, in these circumstances it was easy for the French party 'to raise a flame against the union with England and Prussia'. Unless the commercial disputes were resolved, it was vain to hope for any agreement.[130]

These points were readily acknowledged in London. However, as Holdernesse observed, a major cause of the disputes was the blatant disregard of the Dutch for the laws of neutrality. Trade with the French West Indies was not open to them in peacetime. Permitting it now was simply a device by the French to enable their sugar colonies to survive. By carrying on this intercourse, the Dutch were giving aid and comfort to the enemy. This the British could not condone, as they had made clear in their Order in Council of September 1756. It was pointless, Holdernesse argued, for the Dutch to appeal to the provisions of the Anglo-Dutch treaty of 1674.

---

[128] Yorke to Holdernesse, 4 Apr 1758, SP 90/71.
[129] A. Carter, *The Dutch Republic during the Seven Years' War* (London, 1871), 86–87.
[130] Yorke to Holdernesse, 4 July 1758, SP 84/481.

Whatever the wording, the document had never been intended to cover such blatant partiality. That the Dutch merchants knew they were acting dubiously was shown by their readiness to resort to fraudulent bills of lading. Where detected, such practices would do them no good. Both ships and cargo would be confiscated. Though the government was sincere in its desire to resolve these disputes, the Dutch must first do their part by regulating their trade and augmenting their army, after which the old intimacy might be resumed. For the moment, therefore, Holdernesse instructed Yorke to concentrate on the maritime aspects of the dispute.[131]

These views were put forcefully by Yorke to a delegation of the deputies. The matter was urgent since Prince Ferdinand was now being threatened by the two armies of Contades.[132] Unfortunately, the atmosphere was not improved by the news in August that a Dutch convoy from Surinam had been detained by British privateers. Opinion was so inflamed that some members of the Estates demanded a complete break with Britain.[133] Not until September were the deputies ready with their proposals and when they presented them Yorke could not hide his disappointment. The deputies insisted on claiming the fullest protection for their commerce, as they saw it, under the Treaty of 1674, which prohibited trade with an enemy only in respect to contraband of war. This was narrowly defined as comprising weapons, money, victuals or 'any other necessaries for making war'.[134] Essentially, the deputies were taking the classic stand of all neutral powers that free ships meant free goods, no matter what their origin or destination.

On receipt of the resolutions, Holdernesse requested the advice of the government's legal experts, Hardwicke, Mansfield and Henley. Anson, Legge and Newcastle were also consulted for their departmental views. The verdict of the lawyers was unanimous. If the Dutch based their claims on the Treaty of 1674, then they must respect the other agreements between the two countries, notably that of 1678 which committed the Republic to a defensive alliance with Britain in the event of a war with France. Since the Dutch had failed to honour that treaty and other conventions for the defence of the barrier fortresses, they could hardly expect the King to do anything but consider the Treaty of 1674 as void.[135]

Holdernesse duly replied to Yorke on 28 November. However, he added that if the Dutch would give up their clandestine trade with the French West Indies, the King would admit the rest of the 1674 Treaty respecting their commerce. The Secretary of State also held out the inducement of a stricter

---

[131] Holdernesse to Yorke, 21 July 1758, SP 84/481.
[132] Sir Reginald Savory, *His Britannic Majesty's Army in Germany during the Seven Years' War* (Oxford, 1966), 85–101.
[133] Yorke to Holdernesse, 22 Aug 1758, SP 84/481.
[134] Yorke to Holdernesse, 26 Sept 1758, SP 84/482.
[135] Newcastle to Yorke, 17 Nov 1758, Add. Mss 32,885 ff 365–367.

regulation of the British privateers.[136] But although it followed the opinion of his colleagues, Holdernesse's draft came in for considerable criticism. Newcastle thought it wanted 'an appearance of a conciliatory disposition here, to enable the Princess Royal and the sound part of the Republic to put their good intentions into Execution'. He was supported by Pitt, who suggested that a separate letter be added for the Dutch ministers, giving them support and assurances of good will. Holdernesse duly complied.[137]

That Pitt took these disputes seriously was reflected in the fear he expressed to Newcastle that the Dutch and the Danes might enter the Channel in concert with the French. To forestall this, he thought there ought to be constantly 'a sufficient force at home, and a certain means of making up a...number of ships in all events'. Special care should also be taken to ensure that the fleet was properly manned.[138] Momentarily he seemed to be coming round to the views of Anson about the dangers of the French renewing their invasion plans. In fact that part of the western squadron with Admiral Holmes had already been reinforced, following a meeting which Anson had called at Pitt's house.[139] Manning was a problem of which the latter needed no reminding. As mentioned earlier, 1758 had not been a good year, and total manpower had increased only marginally from 66,000 to 69,000.[140] All the traditional methods for securing men had been tried, including a general press from protections which had yielded barely 800 men.[141] Fortunately the operations of the navy had not been interrupted, and those difficulties that did occur were mainly early in the year when the fleets had been setting out for America and the western approaches. Boscawen, Hawke and Anson had all had to take troops on board in lieu of marines, and Anson had only got to sea after leaving one of his 100-gun ships behind.[142] However, Pitt's concern now was only momentary. He had no proposals to make.

While negotiations with Holland were coming to a halt, Holdernesse was also suffering disappointment elsewhere. One power whose friendship had been mentioned as the precondition for a British fleet in the Baltic was Denmark. The administration had agreed at the time of the Anglo-Prussian convention that a renewed attempt should be made to secure that court. The desirability of this had been given fresh impetus by the difficulties of

[136] Holdernesse to Yorke, 28 Nov 1758, SP 84/482.
[137] Newcastle to Yorke, 1 Dec 1758, Add. Mss 32,886 ff 98–101. Holdernesse to Yorke (Secret), 28 Nov 1758, SP 84/482.
[138] Memorandum for the King, 22 Dec 1758, Add. Mss 32,886 f 431.
[139] Holdernesse to Newcastle, 1 Nov 1758, Add. Mss 32,885 f 170.
[140] Seamen Employed, 1758, JHC, xxviii, 405.
[141] Admiralty to the Regulating Captains, 20 June 1758, Adm 2/80. Seamen Employed, 1758, JHC, xxviii, 405.
[142] Pitt to Barrington, 5 Jan 1758, SP 44/191. Hawke to Clevland, 7 Mar 1759, Adm 1/89. Anson to Clevland, 27 May 1758, Adm 1/90.

Prince Ferdinand and his request for support.[143] Holdernesse was not optimistic about a treaty with Denmark, and with good reason, as he had been trying to negotiate one since the spring of 1757 when it had been an object of the Pitt–Devonshire administration.[144] Any hopes now were immediately dashed by the news that France had already negotiated a subsidy agreement with the Copenhagen court.[145] British diplomats habitually blamed the machinations of the French party at the various courts of Europe for their setbacks. They failed to realize that to small nations like Denmark, France was not a dangerous threat but a possible friend to be used to secure trade and influence for them.

A similar lack of realism led to the failure of the ministry's attempts to detach Russia from the opposition. The ministry hoped that peace might be negotiated between Russia and Prussia. The pressure on Frederick II would then be relieved and he would have less reason for demanding a Baltic fleet. The first attempt at realigning the balance of forces was made in early 1758 when Robert Keith was dispatched as ambassador to St Petersburg.[146] Unfortunately, his arrival coincided with the fall of the Grand Chancellor, Bestucheff, who was favourable to Britain. Keith initially could do nothing more than attempt a renewal of the lapsed Anglo-Russian treaty of commerce.[147]

However, in the next few months, Keith detected a desire among some members of the court to contract out of the war. They felt that the Hapsburgs had not been sufficiently vigorous, leaving the Russians to bear the brunt of Frederick II's forces. The fear was also expressed that Austria might not be able to pay her share of the Franco-Austrian subsidy which had replaced that from Britain.[148] This news prompted a new initiative from the British. Holdernesse was momentarily at Bath for the recovery of his health, so Pitt began matters by ordering Keith to befriend the Russian Cabinet Secretary, Count Alsufiev, who was thought to be well disposed to Prussia.[149] Holdernesse himself then sent more detailed instructions. Keith was empowered to offer the Russian court a new subsidy agreement of £80,000 for two years, though he could raise this figure to £100,000 if an understanding seemed likely, since a Russian withdrawal from the war was 'an Object of such immense consequence'.[150]

---

[143] Newcastle to Holdernesse, 22 July 1758, Add. Mss 32,882 ff 37–42.
[144] Holdernesse to Walter Titley, 18 Jan 1757, printed in J. F. Chance (ed.), *British Diplomatic Instructions, 1689–1789*, III, *Denmark*, Camden Society Publications, Series 3, XXXIV (London, 1926), 160–161. C. W. Eldon, *England's Subsidy Policy towards the Continent during the Seven Years' War, 1756–1763* (Philadelphia, 1938), 88, 94–95.
[145] Eldon, *England's Subsidy Policy*, 111–112.   [146] Ibid., 122.
[147] Keith to Holdernesse, 3 Mar 1758, SP 91/66. Ibid., 14 Mar 1758.
[148] Keith to Holdernesse, 6/17 Oct 1758, SP 91/66.
[149] Pitt to Keith, 2 Jan 1759, SP 91/67.
[150] Holdernesse to Keith, 13 Feb 1759, SP 91/67.

These orders were no sooner written than they were undermined, for Holdernesse's letter crossed with one from Keith informing the ministry that the Austrians had just made a considerable subsidy payment. Nevertheless, Keith proceeded to do his best. He had an initial success when he succeeded in bribing Alsufiev with 500 ducats and the promise of more to come.[151] The negotiation, however, was quickly ended at the suggestion of Frederick II. He was convinced that talks now would seem like timidity to the Russians and only encourage them in their hostility. The time to negotiate would be after they had been defeated.[152] Nevertheless, the instability of Russian politics and the uncertain health of the tsarina sustained the hope that the policies of that court might be changed by the bribery of its ministers or the death of its monarch.

The only success enjoyed by Holdernesse or Pitt during this period was the renegotiation of the Hessian subsidy treaty. This was due to expire early in 1759. There were fears that the elderly Landgrave might not renew the agreement, taking with him his 14,000 troops. In reality the Landgrave, now a refugee in Hamburg, had little option but to agree. Hesse was destined to be a battleground whichever side he supported. The one advantage of the British connection was the certainty of payment. Negotiations for a new agreement were accordingly begun in London by Holdernesse and the Hessian minister, with Pitt and the Prussian envoys, Monsieur Michel and Baron Knyphausen, in attendance. After some difficulty a new agreement was reached, though not before Pitt had suggested that the subsidy be increased by £50,000.[153] The treaty was finally signed on 17 January 1759 and was to continue for two years after the current hostilities had ceased.[154] The offer was a handsome one and showed that British money was not totally despised. More important, the allied effort in Germany could be sustained, leaving Britain to continue her operations elsewhere.

Overall, the year had been satisfactory in terms of results. Some impression had at last been made in North America, while at home the fleet had had the better of the French navy. In Germany the allies had held their own against the odds. Nevertheless, the situation was finely balanced and there was no guarantee that the war would end successfully, especially in view of the disappointing expansion of the nation's forces. Here the performance of the ministry was hardly outstanding. Except for Draper's regiment, no unit of battalion strength had been formed, while the navy had shown only modest growth in its manpower.

---

[151] Keith to Holdernesse, 8/19 Jan 1759, SP 91/67. Ibid., 30 Mar/10 Apr 1758.
[152] Mitchell to Keith, 14 Mar 1759, SP 91/67.
[153] Newcastle to Yorke, 12 Dec 1758, Add. Mss 32,886 ff 283–285. Eldon, *England's Subsidy Policy*, 112–117.
[154] C. Parry (ed.), *The Consolidated Treaty Series* (New York, 1969), XLI, 269.

4

The Threat of Invasion

I

Parliament meanwhile had reassembled amid scenes of harmony. The recent military and naval success had seemingly eliminated all opposition. The King's speech, outlined by Newcastle, drafted by Hardwicke, and polished by Pitt, naturally made the most of these, mentioning Louisburg, Frontenac, Senegal and Cherbourg.[1] But more remarkable were the reasons attributed for these successes. Frederick II and Prince Ferdinand had given the French such full employment that Britain's 'operations both by Sea and in America have derived the most evident Advantage'. Here was eloquent testimony that all now accepted maritime and continental operations as complementary, not exclusive. America was being conquered in Germany, as Frederick II had suggested. Other advantages too were noted. For while the French had sent forth their armies to disturb the peace of Europe, their own coasts had not escaped inviolate. And while the trade of France was languishing, the commerce of Britain had flourished, judiciously protected as it was by the navy.[2]

In the debate that followed there were congratulations all round. Even Beckford, one of the bitterest opponents of the continental war, commended the proposed expenditure of £2,000,000 there. Pitt himself, ever the political animal, was careful not to be too closely identified with such expense. He did however praise the First Duke of Marlborough, commenting that 'if he had been suffered to end the war which he so gloriously carried on, we should not have had the wars we have had since'. Nevertheless, America remained the primary objective even if Germany cost more. On the subject of expense he could only say it was 'not his department'. He could truthfully add, however, 'there was no naval strength, ships or men, that had not been employed either in America or in defence of our Trade and Commerce'.[3]

---

[1] Newcastle to Hardwicke, 8 Nov 1758, Add. Mss 32,885 f 222. Newcastle to Pitt, 15 Nov 1758, Add. Mss 32,885 f 342. For the background to the capture of Frontenac, see below, pp. 99–100. [2] *JHC*, xxviii, 317–318.
[3] Mr West's account of the debate, 23 Nov 1758, Add. Mss 32,885 ff 524–526. H. Walpole, *Memoirs of the Reign of King George II* (London, 1846–47), iii, 149–151.

These assurances were enough for the House. There was a feeling that the nation now had the measure of its old foe. As Chesterfield reported to his son, it was taken for granted that the estimates 'are necessary and frugal; the members go to dinner', leaving the Treasury secretaries, West and Martin, 'to do the rest'.[4]

With regard to the war, the ministers realized that much remained to be done before the nation's objectives were attained. The fortunes of the King of Prussia were at a low ebb, following another setback, this time against the Austrians at Hochkirk.[5] However, no one doubted his ability to recover. Frederick II remained the hero, commonly compared to Caesar the poet, general and statesman. On the Rhine the prospects of Ferdinand were not discouraging. Although the French were expected to renew their efforts to seize Hanover, there was a general confidence that the Prince could surmount the crisis. Not that Ferdinand himself was so optimistic. He emphasized that if the ministers expected a decisive turn to the campaign it was imperative they secure the Dutch and Danes. Success with those courts would enable him to form a separate corps to protect Hanover while he moved with his main force of 60,000 men against the enemy. Alternatively, a large reinforcement should be sent from Britain.[6]

That for the moment was not to be contemplated. The army during the previous twelve months had grown by only 3,500 men. The estimates Barrington was then preparing actually registered a decrease for the home establishment, though the number overseas was higher so that the total establishment was for 91,000.[7] Clearly, no further commitments could be considered.

The shortage of manpower was one reason why the ministry could not contemplate further help for the East India Company, though permission was shortly given to Colonel Eyre Coote to raise a regiment for its service. As far as was known the French were still massing their forces for an attack on Madras. However, the situation in the Carnatic was not as critical as it had been earlier. Draper's battalion had now arrived, while Rear-Admiral Pocock, Watson's successor, had compelled the squadron of Aché to retire to its base in Mauritius.[8]

With regard to America, the ministers realized that they could not relax while British claims to Crown Point and the Great Lakes were still unsatisfied. The best means of ensuring these was by seizing the St Lawrence valley, the centre of French power and influence.

Few plans, however, were possible until more was known about the

---

[4] Chesterfield to Philip Stanhope, 27 Feb 1759, printed in J. Bradshaw (ed.), *The Letters of Philip Dormer Stanhope, Earl of Chesterfield* (London, 1893), III, 1248.
[5] Mitchell to Newcastle, 8 Jan 1759, Add. Mss 32,887 f 61.
[6] Newcastle to Yorke, 12 Dec 1758, Add. Mss 32,886 ff 211–218.
[7] Estimate of Guards and Garrisons for 1759, *JHC*, XXVIII, 327–330.
[8] J. S. Corbett, *England in the Seven Years' War: A Study in Combined Strategy* (London, 1907), I, 344–350.

campaign just finished. Nothing had been heard from Abercromby since mid-September so that a successful renewal of the attack on Ticonderoga could not be discounted. News of the fall of Fort Duquesne was still weeks away. Even by mid-December Pitt was not certain what operations would be required to complete the conquest of New France. He only knew that a further campaign would be necessary for which orders must soon be given. It was with this in mind that he wrote to the colonial governors on 9 December, hinting at a renewal of the offensive by way of Ticonderoga. The colonists were to exert themselves beyond their efforts of the previous year – for which they would be compensated – and everything was to be ready so that an early start could be made.[9]

One decision that had been taken was the removal of Abercromby, despite Pitt's initial sympathy for him. This was not because of any understanding of his difficulties. Rather, here was a general whose failure was the result of action, not inactivity.[10] But when the nature of Abercromby's mistake was more fully appreciated, Pitt had no hesitation in demanding his recall. This was comparatively simple, for Abercromby had few protectors.[11] Within a few days agreement was reached that Amherst should be his successor. Copies of Pitt's letters to the governors were sent, together with a note explaining why it had not been possible to send Amherst more specific orders. This would be done as soon as circumstances permitted.[12]

When the full details were known it was clear that the campaign in America had disappointingly made little further progress. On the fall of Louisburg, Boscawen had insisted that it was too late to navigate the St Lawrence. It had accordingly been agreed that Amherst should take six battalions and go to the assistance of Abercromby, while Wolfe with some naval units explored the Gulf and reduced the outlying French settlements.[13]

Unfortunately, Amherst had been unable to leave before the end of August because of the need to secure Louisburg. Then he inadvertently failed to take the quickest route by sea to Albany, going instead via Boston which necessitated an overland march of two weeks. As a result he did not reach Abercromby before the beginning of October, by which time it was too late to contemplate any further offensive.[14] However, the summer

[9] Pitt to the Colonial Governors, 9 Dec 1758, Kimball, I, 414–420.
[10] Newcastle to Hardwicke, 17 Sept 1758, Add. Mss 32,884 ff 27–36.
[11] Pitt to Abercromby, 18 Sept 1758, Abercromby Papers, Box 13, Huntington Library.
[12] Pitt to Amherst, 9 Dec 1758, Kimball, I, 422–424.
[13] Resolutions of Admiral Boscawen and General Amherst, 8 Aug 1758, Add. Mss 32,882 f 245. Amherst to Pitt, 10 Aug 1758, Kimball, I, 312–314. Wolfe to Sackville, Aug 1758, HMC 9th Report, Part 3, *Stopford-Sackville Mss*, I, 262–267.
[14] Amherst to Abercromby, 3 Sept 1758, Abercromby Papers, Box 12. Amherst to Abercromby, 25 Sept 1758, Abercromby Papers, Box 13. Amherst to Pitt, 13 Oct 1758, Kimball, I, 364–365.

had not been entirely wasted on this front. While waiting for Amherst, Abercromby had commissioned Bradstreet to lead a force of provincials against Fort Frontenac on Lake Ontario, which guarded the western entrance to the St Lawrence.[15] There was no question of Bradstreet holding so distant a place. But during his occupation he destroyed a large amount of stores and several vessels, thus weakening the enemy's control in a vital area.[16] The episode led Newcastle to comment that Bradstreet was one of those 'alert fellows whom the Duke of Cumberland would never encourage'.[17] His success now was one more indication that the Officer Corps under Ligonier had regained its confidence.

The ministry were not in receipt of all the relevant information until the end of December. Only then could Pitt give Amherst specific orders, which, in outline, were similar to the plans of the previous year. Simultaneous offensives would again be launched on several fronts to ensure proper recognition of 'His Majesty's just and indubitable Rights'. As last year, an amphibious operation would be made to the east. The difference was that this time the expedition would start rather than finish at Louisburg. Quebec would be the primary objective. Simultaneously, a new attempt would be made to enter Canada by land, with Montreal as target. The route for this was left to Amherst, a belated recognition by Pitt and Ligonier that they were not competent to decide every detail. In addition there was to be an expedition against Niagara. This important post controlled the Great Lakes and was a link in the French communication with the Ohio, therefore its capture would be a severe blow. Finally, an expedition would be undertaken on the southern frontier to harness the energies of Virginia, Pennsylvania and Maryland. Since the ministers did not yet know whether Duquesne had fallen, this too was left to the commanders on the spot.[18]

As in 1758 each expedition was to be an independent operation, though Ligonier hoped that if the two main armies started together, a diversion 'equally advantageous to both', would occur.[19] But until the two forces arrived in the St Lawrence co-operation between them would not be possible, as events the previous year had demonstrated. The important thing was that each army was capable of looking after itself and of fulfilling its tasks. Thus, if one failed the other could still succeed and Britain's objectives be attained.

The bulk of the regular forces were to be used once more for the amphibious operation, because the regulars were more experienced for this type of warfare. In addition this would allow the government to use the

[15] Minutes of the Council of War, 13 July 1758, Abercromby Papers, Box 9.
[16] Bradstreet to Abercromby, 31 Aug 1758, Abercromby Papers, Box 12.
[17] Newcastle to Yorke, 31 Oct 1758, Add. Mss 32,885 ff 146–149.
[18] Pitt to Amherst, 29 Dec 1758, Kimball, I, 432–442.
[19] Ligonier to Amherst, 12 Feb 1759, Ligonier Letter Book, Clements Library.

provincials in the backwoods and terrain of their own country. The command of the St Lawrence expedition was allotted to James Wolfe. A paper on the subject by Ligonier suggested that Amherst ought to remain on the mainland to direct operations there, lending his authority as Commander-in-Chief to the provincial effort.[20] Another reason was that for this type of operation Amherst was eminently qualified. The main problem was that of getting to the enemy. In the art of logistics Amherst had already demonstrated his abilities. Conscientious and painstaking, he would do nothing rash to end the war.

Amherst was undoubtedly disappointed not to receive the command of the Quebec expedition. While he agreed that the British must take both routes 'to be sure of prospering in one', he confided to Sackville 'Quebec is everything'. Nevertheless, he loyally accepted the role for which he had been designated, being optimistic that one more campaign 'in this country must do all that is to be done here for this war'.[21]

James Wolfe, the man chosen for the Quebec expedition, was a precocious choice indeed, being just thirty-two years of age. One reason for his appointment, as Wolfe confessed, was the 'backwardness of some of the older officers'.[22] Wolfe himself had come home hoping to serve in Germany, telling a friend: 'It is my fortune to be cursed with American services, yours to serve in an army commanded by a great and able Prince.'[23] But this was only part of the story. Since early youth he had been in the army, serving with distinction in Flanders during the War of Austrian Succession. Enthusiasm and industry secured him rapid promotion. By 1750 he was lieutenant-colonel of Sackville's regiment, and enjoyed the reputation of being one of the most thorough officers in the army. At Louisburg, Wolfe had proved himself to be a dynamic corps commander showing considerable flair, of which he was not unconscious, especially when comparing himself with Amherst.[24]

The exact date on which Wolfe was informed of his mission cannot be established, but it would seem to have been in the third week of December. By the 20 December he was contacting one of his old comrades 'to know

[20] Proposals for an Expedition to Quebec, 1759, Germain Papers, i, Clements Library. The document is unsigned, but Sackville's receiving a copy suggests Ligonier was the author, since the two men regularly corresponded.

[21] Amherst to Sackville, 19 Jan 1759, HMC, *Stopford-Sackville Mss*, ii, 267.

[22] Wolfe to Major Walter Wolfe, 29 Jan 1759, printed in B. Willson, *The Life and Letters of James Wolfe* (London, 1909), 417–418.

[23] Wolfe to Captain Henry Parr, 6 Dec 1758, printed in Willson, *Wolfe*, 404–405. Wolfe was prepared to serve as a volunteer in Ferdinand's army, but Ligonier had tersely informed him: 'The King will not give leave for anyone to serve in Germany without an Employment', 9 Nov 1758, Ligonier Letter Book.

[24] *Dictionary of National Biography*. An example of Wolfe's critical attitude to Amherst at Louisburg can be found in his letter to Colonel William Rickson, 1 Dec 1758, printed in Willson, *Wolfe*, 402–403. There has been no decent modern biography of Wolfe.

if I may mention you for a distant, difficult, and disagreeable service'.[25] Four days later he was writing to Pitt himself, making points he thought essential for the success of the operation. Most important was the need to get a fleet early into the river. The French would not then be able to reinforce their colony. At the same time the advance guard, operating from the Island of Bic, could navigate the St Lawrence to Quebec and prepare a way for the army. The task of exploring the river would rest with the squadron already in America under Philip Durell. On this point Wolfe was not happy. He informed Pitt that from his own personal experience he knew this officer to be 'vastly unequal to the weight of business; and it is of the first importance to the country that it doth not fall into such hands'.[26] Despite this bluntness no change occurred. The matter did not lie in Pitt's department, but he did ensure that the orders to Durell were among the first to be drafted and were repeated more than once.[27]

Wolfe of course was not the only person consulted by Pitt and Ligonier. Equally important was the advice of Patrick Mackellar, a major in the Engineers, who had been captured at Oswego in 1756 and held at Quebec until his release the following year. While there he had sought to observe the defences and on his return wrote down his impressions, using Charlevoix's *History of New France* as a guide.[28] His views now became the basis of the ministerial plan. The cliffs along the river and above the harbour made him think that a frontal attack on the town would be unsuccessful. Even if the troops got ashore, progress up the narrow streets was unlikely. Only an assault from the rear promised success. Mackellar was encouraged in this view from a belief that the fortifications on the upper side of Quebec were incomplete, and, once the army took possession of the high ground to the west, the town would in all probability fall. The main difficulty would be getting there: a landing just below Quebec could not be covered by the men of war because the water was shallow. Mackellar therefore believed the invading force ought first to establish itself on the Island of Orleans, from where the commanders could look for a place on the north shore to begin their operations. As to the dangers of navigating the St Lawrence, Mackellar was inclined to think these had been exaggerated. Provided due care was taken the fleet ought to have no difficulty of the kind experienced by Admiral Walker and General Hill in 1711 when part of their armada was destroyed on the rocks.[29]

The force allotted to Wolfe was made up of ten infantry regiments, some

[25] Wolfe to Colonel George Warde, 20 Dec 1758, printed in Willson, *Wolfe*, 406–407.
[26] Wolfe to Pitt, 24 Dec 1758, printed in Willson, *Wolfe*, 407–408.
[27] Pitt to Durell, 29 Dec 1758, Kimball, I, 444–445.
[28] C. P. Stacey, *Quebec, 1759* (Toronto, 1959), 44–46. P. F. X. de Charlevoix, *Histoire et description generale de la Nouvelle France* (3 vols., Paris, 1744).
[29] Major Mackellar's Description of Quebec, printed in C. V. F. Townshend, *The Military Life of Field Marshal George, First Marquis Townshend, 1724–1807* (London, 1901), 60–67.

light infantry and six companies of American rangers. If up to strength the total should have been 12,000 officers and men.[30] However, as Wolfe was to discover, all the units were under strength, because the intended reinforcement of Highlanders and drafts from England, amounting to 3,000 men, had been diverted to Martinique. The ministerial hope was that they would still be available once General Hopson had finished his operations in the Caribbean.[31] Since all the units were then in America the full extent of the problem was not appreciated in England. Attention here was focused on getting the ships of war and transports ready to carry the army to its destination. Once again Pitt was taking no chances: 20,000 tons of shipping were to be raised in England. Another 6,000 tons would be found locally.[32] Fourteen ships of the line, six frigates, three bomb vessels and three fireships were to escort this vast flotilla across the Atlantic, joining the ten battleships and four frigates already with Durell.[33]

As Wolfe's brigadiers, Ligonier nominated Robert Monckton, James Murray and Ralph Burton.[34] All three were experienced officers holding the rank of colonel and all had seen service in America, where they had distinguished themselves at different times. Monckton had commanded the expedition against Beausejour, whose capture in 1755 was the only British success that year. He had subsequently served as governor of Nova Scotia. Murray had arrived in America at the same time as Wolfe. He commanded one of the brigades at Louisburg, and, according to Wolfe, had acted with 'infinite spirit'.[35] Burton, colonel of the 48th Regiment, had first come to America with Braddock. But though well thought of he was not to get the position initially designated. The name of George Townshend was preferred instead. The change was probably Pitt's doing. Townshend had previously applied to him for an opportunity to serve,[36] and Pitt felt obliged to assist, if only to make good his failure to do anything for him on the formation of the ministry. Ligonier in any case could have little reason to object. Townshend had proved an able officer until his career was blighted by a dispute with Cumberland. Accordingly, on 21 December, he was summoned to London and informed: 'Lord Ligonier was yesterday in the closet; your affair was mentioned and very graciously agreed to by His Majesty.'[37]

Wolfe of necessity had to accept, though from the start he made his dislike

[30] Pitt to Amherst, 29 Dec 1758, Kimball, I, 433.
[31] Pitt to Hopson, 13 Nov 1758, Kimball, I, 396. M. T. Smelser, *The Campaign for the Sugar Islands, 1759: A Study of Amphibious Warfare* (New York, 1955), 20–21.
[32] Pitt to Amherst, 29 Dec 1758, Kimball, I, 432–442.
[33] Admiralty to Saunders, 9 Jan 1759, Adm 2/82.
[34] Proposals for an Expedition to Quebec, Germain Papers, I.
[35] Wolfe to Sackville, Aug 1758, HMC, *Stopford-Sackville Mss*, II, 263.
[36] Townshend, *Life of Townshend*, 142.
[37] Sir Richard Lyttelton to Townshend, 28 Dec 1758, printed in A. Doughty and G. W. Parmelee (eds.), *The Siege of Quebec and the Battle of the Plains of Abraham*, v, *The Townshend Papers* (Quebec, 1901), 191–192.

clear. Some historians have suggested that Townshend's aristocratic background made Wolfe uneasy, but this seems to be only a partial explanation. Both Monckton and Murray were of noble family and many of Wolfe's friends were aristocrats. A more likely reason was that Townshend lacked experience, as Wolfe tactlessly noted.[38]

Wolfe also had trouble in naming his personal staff. He wanted Colonel Guy Carleton as quartermaster. The King objected because Carleton had once made disparaging remarks about the Hanoverian army. Pitt only succeeded in having him accepted by getting Ligonier to tell George II that the best means of making a 'General completely responsible for his conduct' was by complying with whatever he requested. He could then have no excuse for any setback.[39]

The Admiralty meanwhile was busy with the naval preparations. The man chosen for the command of the escorting squadron, Charles Saunders, had been one of Anson's officers on his voyage round the world. Augustus Hervey had some bitter words on this subject, claiming that Anson 'ever sacrificed the interest and service of the country to the interest and favour of a few individual favourites'.[40] But the men on that journey had been a picked group, the best the navy could provide, and it was only natural that twenty years later they should be given positions of responsibility. Hervey was in fact allowing loyalty to his former commander, John Byng, to cloud his judgement, for many others enjoyed Anson's favour. For the western squadron Anson consistently chose two men of almost equal reputation who had risen independently of him, Boscawen and Hawke. Younger men too were given their opportunity. George Rodney, Richard Howe and Robert Duff all enjoyed important assignments: Samuel Hood, Richard Kempenfelt and John Jervis received their first ships. In the matter of appointments Anson had fulfilled his responsibilities well. The Pitt–Newcastle ministry had reason to be grateful.

Indeed, nothing so well illustrates Anson's ingrained professionalism as his attitude to appointments. Throughout the period he remained insistent that all candidates for a commission must first do their six years' apprenticeship before obtaining a lieutenancy.[41] He was equally stringent about more senior appointments. When Newcastle shortly made a particularly inappropriate request, Anson responded: 'I must now beg your Grace will seriously consider what must be the condition of your fleet, if these Borough recommendations...are to be complied with.' It was 'captains of that cast' which had necessitated Bedford's revising the articles of war in 1748.[42] He

---

[38] Wolfe to Townshend, 6 Jan 1759, printed in Willson, *Wolfe*, 414.
[39] Willson, *Wolfe*, 411.
[40] D. Erskine (ed.), *Augustus Hervey's Journal* (London, 1953), 253.
[41] Admiralty to the Navy Board, 5 Oct 1758, Adm 2/224.
[42] An Act for Amending, Explaining and Reducing into One Act of Parliament, the Laws relating to the Government of His Majesty's Ships, *Statutes at Large*, Ch xxxiii, 22 George II.

could only reaffirm that while he remained in charge he would 'promote the Lieutenants to command, whose ships have been successfully engaged upon equal terms with the enemy, without having any friend or recommendation'. This was the only policy to follow if his successors were to 'have a fleet to depend on'.[43]

The man now selected to the North American station was certainly an officer after Anson's own heart, being someone who believed in actions rather than words. Even Horace Walpole, who usually had little good to say of anyone, commented of Saunders: 'No man said less, or deserved more.'[44] The other flag officers chosen by Anson, Philip Durell and Charles Holmes, were also able, despite Wolfe's reservations about the former. Durell had already served in America, being the senior officer there. Holmes had commanded the squadron that forced the passage of the Ems in March 1758 and enabled Ferdinand to capture Emden, a feat that naturally recommended him for the present operation. He had latterly been flag officer with Anson on the western squadron.[45] Both men had seemingly the right experience and qualifications.

Even before Saunders reached London, the Admiralty was hard at work. Initial instructions were issued on 14 December to the Navy Board for preparing a number of battleships, bomb vessels and fireships for foreign service.[46] Various other instructions followed, all emphasizing the need for haste. Pitt in particular could not forget that delays in the past had contributed to several abortive campaigns. On 1 January Clevland wrote to Holburne, the port admiral at Portsmouth, telling him 'in the most pressing manner, to get the ships ordered to be fitted for Foreign Service out to Spithead with all the expedition that is possible'. Similar instructions were sent to Admiral Harrison at Plymouth.[47] Not that Pitt was riding roughshod over the navy departments as is often depicted. When he and Saunders decided that the number of frigates ought to be increased, he got Robert Wood, one of the under-secretaries to enquire of Clevland 'what difficulties there may be in the way of this proposal'.[48] The availability of ships was strictly the concern of the Admiralty. The demand for haste, nevertheless, seems to have been observed. By the end of January Saunders reported that all his squadron were ready at Spithead, except for some Folkestone cutters which he had requested for exploring the St Lawrence, whose masters refused to go on the service.[49]

[43] Anson to Newcastle, 15 June 1759, Add. Mss 32,892 ff 96–97.
[44] Walpole, *Memoirs of George II*, III, 230–231.
[45] Corbett, *Seven Years' War*, I, 242, 246–252.
[46] Admiralty to the Navy Board, 14 Dec 1758, Adm 2/224. Admiralty to Captains various, 14 Dec 1758, Adm 2/81.
[47] Clevland to Holburne, 1 Jan 1759, Adm 2/524. Admiralty to Harrison, 2 Jan 1759, Adm 2/82.   [48] Wood to Clevland, 11 Jan 1759, Adm 1/4123.
[49] Saunders to Pitt, 26 Jan 1759, Kimball, II, 19. Saunders to the Admiralty, 11 Feb 1759, Adm 1/482.

Progress in raising the 20,000 tons of transports, however, was not quite so smooth. The practice of having a pool of shipping had proved a mixed blessing. The navy made difficulties about having it at Portsmouth because it diverted services for the fleet. Southampton, on the other hand, had few facilities. Moreover, ships fitted out for Channel service were not necessarily suitable for operations across the Atlantic. Finally, there was the constant pressure from Newcastle to reduce the expense. Accordingly, on 14 November Pitt had ordered all the vessels to be discharged.[50]

The Navy Board, therefore, had to look elsewhere for its shipping. The first order for 10,000 tons had been given on 30 November, with a second similar order six days later, both lots to be victualled for four months' service at the rate of one and a half tons a man. Forty landing craft were also to be found.[51] In response, the Navy Board reported on 5 December that 10,000 tons had been secured from a Mr Ward of the collier trade. Four days later it wrote that the whole tonnage had been secured at the rate of 12s 9d a ton a month.[52] Even so, Anson and the Admiralty could not have the shipping too soon. On 14 December 1758, they instructed the Navy Board 'to use the utmost dispatch'; and to ensure compliance, they told the Commissioners to send 'an account of the...Transports every other day'.[53] Later, when some Ordnance vessels failed to move, Anson ordered the Navy Board to send an officer to chase them out of the Thames.[54] Despite the urgency, some of these vessels had not arrived at Portsmouth by the end of January.[55]

With the fleet nearly assembled, Pitt could now give Wolfe his final orders. The British commander was to rendezvous at Louisburg and assemble his forces there. Then, as soon after 7 May as 'the season of the year shall permit', he was to proceed to Quebec and use every endeavour to take the city. Should he be successful, he was to appoint a governor and 'put the place into a position of defence', after which he could 'determine what ulterior operations, higher up the St Lawrence' should be undertaken. But in that case, Wolfe must first inform Amherst and 'as far as may be...concert the same with our said general'; any opportunity for co-operation should not be missed. But only when the two armies actually joined was Wolfe to revert to the command of Amherst. Otherwise he was to maintain a good

---

[50] Pitt to the Admiralty, 14 Nov 1758, Adm 1/4122. See R. Middleton, 'The Administration of Newcastle and Pitt: The Departments of State and the Conduct of the War, 1754–1760, with particular reference to the campaigns in North America' (Ph.D. thesis, Exeter University, 1969), 175–176.

[51] Admiralty to the Navy Board, 30 Nov 1758, Adm N/238. Ibid., 6 Dec 1758. Admiralty to the Navy Board, 8 Dec 1758, Adm 2/225.

[52] Navy Board to Clevland, 5 Dec 1758, Adm B/161. Ibid., 9 Dec 1758.

[53] Admiralty to the Navy Board, 14 Dec 1758, Adm N/238.

[54] Clevland to the Navy Board, 5 Jan 1759, Adm 2/524.

[55] This necessitated some reorganization of the Ordnance stores, Pitt to Saunders, 20 Jan 1759, Kimball, II, 11–12.

understanding with Saunders and the other naval officers, whose assistance would be of the 'utmost importance'. And he was to send 'constant and particular accounts of his proceedings to the Secretary of State'.[56]

The fleet finally weighed anchor on 14 February. Just before it did, word was received that Fort Duquesne had fallen.[57] Until the end the success of this operation had been in doubt, for in October the advance guard under Major Grant had suffered a reverse which had placed the whole mission in jeopardy. Nevertheless, Forbes, now sick and confined to a stretcher, had pushed bravely on. The enemy, short of supplies, had at length evacuated the fort on 25 November.[58] It was a good omen for the expedition just setting out.

II

The administration could thus look forward confidently at the beginning of 1759. With 45,000 regulars and provincials in America under proven generals, a final success could hardly be doubted. Good news could also be expected from the West Indies, where Hopson had arrived. Though the prospects were less promising in Germany, they were by no means hopeless. Finally, at home the army and navy appeared to be in a satisfactory condition, ready to protect the homeland if need be. Nevertheless, any threat always caused apprehension and this was certainly the case when rumours began to circulate in February that the French were preparing a descent on Britain.[59]

The plan of the enemy was a direct response to the disappointing performance of their armies in Germany and America the previous year. The Duc de Choiseul and Marshal Belleisle, mindful of the disruption caused in 1756 by the apparently defenceless state of Britain once its maritime defences had been pierced, began to reconsider the idea of an invasion. Their scheme was limited in that they did not envisage conquering the country or restoring the Stuarts. Rather it was to secure a foothold in Scotland and capture London. Such action would disrupt the flow of supplies to America, destroy public credit and compel the British to sue for peace without antagonizing the other protestant powers of Europe.[60]

Various methods for executing this design were considered until the ministers decided that the invasion should involve two forces: one to sail

---

[56] Instructions to General Wolfe, 5 Feb 1759, WO 34/23. Wolfe's commission as Major-General and Commander-in-Chief in the St Lawrence was issued on 12 Jan 1759, SP 44/191.   [57] *London Chronicle*, 18/20 Jan 1759.

[58] Forbes to Pitt, 27 Nov 1758, Kimball, I, 406–409. Forbes's tribulations are well documented in A. P. James (ed.), *The Writings of General John Forbes* (Wisconsin, 1938).

[59] *London Chronicle*, 30 Jan/1 Feb, 1759.

[60] G. Lacour-Gayet, *La Marine Militaire de la France sous le Règne de Louis XV* (Paris, 1902), 318–322. J. O. Lindsay (ed.), *The New Cambridge Modern History*, VII, *The Old Regime, 1713–1763* (Cambridge, 1957), 475–476.

from Brittany for the west coast of Scotland; the other to cross from Normandy and Flanders to Essex. Choiseul and Belleisle hoped that a union of the Atlantic and Mediterranean fleets would secure them a temporary naval superiority, allowing the flotillas to reach their destination. To help them, a small diversionary force would sail from Dunkirk for Ireland under Commodore Thurot. First, the united fleets would escort the Brittany force to the Clyde. Then, they would proceed round Scotland to Flanders to pick up the main force for London.[61] The operation would be hazardous, as Choiseul admitted to the Swedish court, whom he was attempting to involve in the scheme. However, the often chaotic conditions of eighteenth-century warfare meant that the English fleet might be blown off course or sufficiently incapacitated to give the French the time they required. Besides, Louis XV's ministers could think of nothing else to redeem the situation. Unless some action were taken the French possessions in North America and the Caribbean would be irredeemably lost.[62]

Britain's defences were one of the ministers' most important concerns and it behoved them to ensure that the army and navy were in a proper condition to resist any threat. A meeting was accordingly arranged at Anson's house on 19 February. Present were Granville, Newcastle, Holdernesse, Hardwicke, Pitt and Ligonier.

The first and most important business was to hear from Anson about the state of the fleet. Fortunately, this was in a good condition, with 275 ships in commission and another 82 in 'ordinary'. However, squadrons were required in the Mediterranean, the East and West Indies, North America, as well as at home. Thus 59 of the 100 ships of the line were abroad or on their way, leaving only 41 at home, of which 21 were manned and prepared. But several more would soon be ready. By comparison, the French were thought to have 43 ships of the line at home, with another 30 overseas. However, the respective home figures were not comparable, for the French total included their Mediterranean fleet, the British did not. Also, many of the French ships were unfit for sea. Anson on the other hand was confident of having 41 battleships ready for the Channel by the beginning of May. His only concern was a shortage of men.[63]

Anson had achieved this impressive force by two means. First, there had been more deliveries from the yards. Since June 1757 ten ships of 50 guns and over had joined the fleet or were about to be launched.[64] Secondly, the fleet had grown because of seizures from the French. Up to the end of 1758 the navy had captured seven battleships, including the 80 gun *Foudroyant*, which Osborne had taken the previous February.[65] Not that Anson was

[61] Lacour-Gayet, *Marine Militaire*, 318–322.
[62] Corbett, *Seven Years' War*, II, 17–23.
[63] At Lord Anson's, 19 Feb 1759, Add. Mss 33,047 ff 249–252.
[64] Admiralty Dimension Book, 1660–1760, NMM.
[65] A List of French Ships taken since 1755, April 1762, Holdernesse Papers, Egerton 3444 f 268, BL.

complacent. The previous December the Admiralty had determined that twelve of the battleships then in service would reach the end of their usefulness by 1761 and had ordered nine new vessels, five from the royal yards, the others from contractors; included in the number were two ships of 64 guns. Several of these had been captured from the French, but none had been built for the navy.[66] Their attraction was their manoeuvrability.

This was not the first time that Anson had introduced new ships to the service. Most important had been his patronage of the two-deck 74 gun ship which was large enough to engage the best of the enemy but sufficiently manoeuvrable to remain at sea in bad weather, unlike the three-deck 80, 90 and 100 gun ships. Bedford had wanted to introduce such vessels in 1745, but the Navy Board had been against the plan, doubting if the new class would fit the existing docks.[67] Its opposition was only overcome in 1747 after the capture of several 74 gun ships in the First and Second Battles of Finisterre. Peacetime economy meant that only two such vessels had been built before the war.[68] However, by June 1757 Anson had six in service with another ten building, of which five had now been launched.[69] The value of these vessels was shortly to be proved.

A similar improvement had also been attempted with the frigates. Prior to 1755 many of the navy's 24 and 44 gun ships were either too small or too slow.[70] After the opening of hostilities, Anson introduced several new types of vessel with 28, 32 and 36 guns apiece. The first of these, a 28 gun ship, was launched in 1756. By 1757 no fewer than twelve 28, six 32 and two 36 gun ships were under construction.[71] These too were to play an important role in the coming campaign.

The main problem in the present emergency was likely to be manning. By February 1759 the navy had 71,000 men, a record for any war.[72] This was still insufficient for all the vessels being pressed into service, especially for the battleships, where 9,500 men were wanted to complete the crews.[73] The prospects of rectifying this were uncertain, for all the traditional recruiting methods had been tried.

Various reasons accounted for the slow increase in manpower. A major problem for Anson and his colleagues was desertion. During the first three

---

[66] Admiralty to the Navy Board, 13 Dec 1758, Adm 2/225.
[67] D. A. Baugh, *British Naval Administration in the Age of Walpole* (Princeton, 1965), 251–252.
[68] Sir Herbert W. Richmond, *The Navy in the War of 1739–1748* (Cambridge, 1920), III, 1–50, 78–115. The first 74 built in British yards was the *Culloden* in 1747; the next the *Shrewsbury* in 1750. Not until 1757 was another 74, the *Norfolk*, launched, Admiralty Dimension Book, 1660–1760, NMM.
[69] A List of Ships and Sloops as are now Building, 13 June 1757, Adm 2/222. Admiralty Dimension Book, 1660–1760, NMM.
[70] J. Charnock, *A History of Marine Architecture* (London, 1802), III, 203. For the navy's establishment in the period 1742–51, see Baugh, *British Naval Administration*, 515–530.
[71] Admiralty Dimension Book, 1660–1760, NMM. A List of Ships and Sloops as are now Building, 13 June 1757, Adm 2/222.
[72] Seamen Employed, 1759, *JHC*, XXVIII, 765.
[73] At Lord Anson's, 19 Feb 1759, Add. Mss 33,047 ff 249–252.

years of the war over 12,000 men fled the service because of the harsh conditions and poor pay.[74] But equally deleterious was sickness and disease. During the same period no fewer than 13,000 men had been lost in this way when by contrast a mere 143 were slain in combat.[75] The state of the hospitals was in part the cause, though improvements were on the way. In 1758 Anson had appointed James Lind to be senior physician at Haslar Hospital, following the publication of his *Essay on Preserving the Health of Seamen*. But, as Lind pointed out, a major reason for the outbreak of diseases was the method of securing men. Pressing the flotsam of the seaports was bound to result in widespread sickness.[76]

However, the worst malady was scurvy, and the cause of this was the poor quality of the victuals. Unfortunately, Anson and his colleagues believed too much salt was the reason. They thought that by cutting down the issue of pickled meat the disease might be reduced.[77] But although fresh meat was undoubtedly beneficial, they failed to realize that it was insufficient to prevent scurvy. Only a more balanced diet with fresh vegetables could achieve this, as Lind has explained in his earlier *Treatise of the Scurvy*. But, despite a dedication to Anson in the book, none of Lind's findings were looked at seriously.[78]

In defence, Anson did not have the most imaginative or dynamic group of men in the Victualling Commissioners. Indeed that Board provides one of the worst examples of the eighteenth-century patronage system. Practically all its members were placemen to whom hard work and administrative dedication were uncongenial. Typical was Sir Francis Stiles, the Commissioner of the Bakehouse. Stiles was a cultured man, an amateur scientist and Fellow of the Royal Society. Baking was the last thing to interest him. The post, however, lay within the patronage of the Treasury and had been a rung on a ladder that would take him to greater things.[79] Anson had certainly done his best to avoid such men. In 1755 he had insisted on the appointment of Robert Pett to the position of hoytaker, which had always of necessity been filled by a seafaring person. Newcastle had wanted

[74] An Account of the Number of Men taken into the Service of His Majesty's Navy, 10 Jan 1759, Adm B/161, NMM. For a fuller discussion of this problem see S. Gradish, *The Manning of the British Navy during the Seven Years' War*, Royal Historical Society Studies in History Series, No. 21 (London, 1980), 111–116. For a graphic contemporary account of why the service was so unpopular, see 'A Sailor's Observations on the Government of the Navy', *Gentlemen's Magazine*, 1759, 566–567.

[75] An Account of the Number of Men taken into the Service of His Majesty's Navy, 10 Jan 1759, Adm B/161.

[76] C. Lloyd (ed.), *The Health of Seaman: Selections from the Works of Dr James Lind, Sir Gilbert Blane and Dr Thomas Trotter*, Navy Records Society Publications, CVII (London, 1965), 26–130.

[77] Clevland to the Victualling Board, 18 May 1756, Adm C/542. Admiralty Board Minute, 5 Oct 1758, Adm 3/66. See R. Middleton, 'The Administration of Newcastle and Pitt', 193–194.   [78] Lloyd (ed.), *Health of Seamen*, 2–25.

[79] Stiles to Newcastle, 24 Sept 1760, Add. Mss 32,912 ff 82–83.

to choose a relative of the influential Lord Powis. Anson commented: 'His Lordship might as properly have asked to have him made a Captain of a Man of War' and appealed that in future 'more people of business should be appointed' to the victualling. The appointment of Pett was to prove especially fortunate.[80]

With regard to impressment, Anson had been reluctant to change the system, since the remedies seemed worse than the faults. Two solutions were favoured outside the service. One was a register whereby the period of service would be rotated, thus making the merchants and their crews readier to co-operate. The other was to treat the seamen better so that they would volunteer and do away with the need for compulsion. During 1758, attempts were made in both directions. A group of Bristol and Newcastle merchants proposed a registry of all seamen, those on the list drawing lots as to who should serve. The scheme, however, did not meet with general support in the Commons and had to be dropped.[81] The other measure was a bill by George Grenville for the more effective payment of the seamen's wages, especially regarding remittances to their wives and dependants. The justice and humanity of the scheme was accepted by all, for prior to this families were all too often left to starve or seek assistance from their parish. However, Anson and his colleagues remembered the ineffectiveness of an earlier measure in 1728 which had been difficult to administer and had encouraged fraud.[82] Undeterred, Grenville went ahead and succeeded in having the bill passed. But Anson's scepticism about its encouraging recruits was so far well founded. The numbers in service had increased only marginally.[83]

To meet the present crisis Anson did have a number of suggestions. Some of the frigates could be stripped to produce 1,000 hands. A similar number might be squeezed from the hitherto protected coastal trades and from the privateers, if curbs were placed on them. The buccaneers had long been a nuisance to the authorities, stealing men from the navy and causing endless trouble with the neutral powers. Anson thought a general embargo would be too controversial, as had been demonstrated in the spring of 1756, though one might be tried selectively at ports like Bristol. Finally, appeals ought to be issued by the Privy Council asking all mayors and magistrates to secure men for the navy. Every effort would be made to equip 300 vessels for the first time in the navy's history.[84]

---

[80] Anson to Newcastle, 15 Feb 1755, Add. Mss 32,852 ff 485–486.

[81] Gradish, *Manning of the British Navy*, 107–110.

[82] Observations on the Bill for the Payment of Seamen's Wages, 1758, Add. Mss 33,047 ff 175–179. For the debate in parliament, see W. Cobbett, *The Parliamentary History of England*, XV, *1752–1763* (London, 1811), 839–870.

[83] Gradish, *Manning of the British Navy*, 87–92, 116–120. Baugh, *British Naval Administration*, 227–229.

[84] At Lord Anson's, 19 Feb 1759, Add. Mss 33,047 ff 249–252. Authority to do so was confirmed by Pitt in a letter to the Admiralty, 22 Feb 1759, SP 44/230.

During these deliberations Anson and the ministers appreciated that the French would attempt to unite their Mediterranean and Atlantic fleets and that this ought to be prevented. He readily agreed therefore to dispatch a further six ships to join the squadron under Admiral Brodrick.[85] He did not want to repeat his mistake of 1756 when Admiral Byng had gone belatedly with too small a force. Because of the great responsibility, Anson determined to appoint one of his most trusted officers, Boscawen, to this command. His orders were simple. He was not to let the French Mediterranean squadron pass the Straits of Gibraltar. Should they succeed he was to follow. Quite how he effected this, by a close watch on Toulon or positioning himself at Gibraltar, was left to him to decide.[86]

After Anson had finished, Ligonier introduced the condition of the army. Officially the home establishment stood at 52,000 men, but this figure included the forces in Germany and at Gibraltar. The regulars in England only numbered 20,000 men. But there were 5,000 in Scotland and a further 4,000 serving with the fleet. Ligonier could also call on 4,000 invalids who were too old for the field, but fit for garrison duty. The units in England, however, wanted 4,000 recruits and after provision had been made for the defence of London and the naval ports, Ligonier would have barely 10,000 men to resist the French on their landing.[87]

Nevertheless, for the moment neither Ligonier nor the other ministers had any proposals to make, other than the formation of Coote's battalion for service in India and one of dragoons under General Elliot for dispatch to Germany.[88] Previous recruiting difficulties seemed to preclude any fresh initiative. The main suggestion was that of Pitt for embodying the militia to guard the prisoners of war and release more regulars for the field. Otherwise the four battalions serving with the fleet were to be brought ashore and every effort made to recruit the regiments.[89] The prospects here were not encouraging. Indeed, Hardwicke reported to Newcastle: 'Some people... think that a new Recruiting Act is necessary.'[90] However, after the habeas corpus dispute the ministers agreed this was politically too sensitive. Hence recruitment had to proceed as before. But Ligonier insisted the emergency was not to lead to any lowering of standards. Men must be not less than 5 ft 4½ ins to be enlisted and must be aged between seventeen and forty-five. All supernumeraries were to be retained, for every man would be needed.[91]

[85] At Lord Anson's, 19 Feb 1759, Add. Mss 33,047 ff 249–252.
[86] Admiralty to Boscawen, 7 Mar 1759, Adm 2/82.
[87] At Lord Anson's, 19 Feb 1759, Add. Mss 33,047 ff 249–252.
[88] Barrington to Fox, 17 Mar 1759, WO 4/57.
[89] At Lord Anson's, 19 Feb 1759, Add. Mss 33,047 ff 249–252. J. R. Western, *The English Militia in the Eighteenth Century: The Story of a Political Issue, 1660–1802* (London, 1965), 154–156.
[90] Hardwicke to Newcastle, 21 Feb 1759, Add. Mss 32,888 ff 206–207.
[91] Ligonier to Lord Beauclerk, 4 Apr 1759, Ligonier Letter Book. Beauclerk was the commanding officer of the North Britain area.

III

Meanwhile, not everyone's attention was focused on the invasion, for Newcastle was having difficulties once more with the nation's finances. The underlying problem this time was the increasing expense of the war, as the estimates for 1759 revealed. The navy, £3,250,000 for the last year, was £5,000,000 this time; while the transport service, never more than £350,000 for the last war, now exceeded £600,000.[92] Though trade and the receipts of the Sinking Fund had continued to flourish, the extra revenue was only a fraction of the £12,000,000 required for 1759, of which £6,500,000 would have to be borrowed.[93] The size of the loan and the uncertainty of the market meant that by the end of 1758 it had been impossible to keep the rate of interest to 3.5 per cent, even though many thought this would destroy the existing funds as people sold to buy the new issue. After consultation with Legge and Gideon, Newcastle had attempted to surmount the dilemma by offering the stock at 3 per cent with a douceur of a £10 lottery ticket and £5 additional capital for every £100 subscribed.[94] Thus, to secure the fiction of lower interest rates Newcastle had added an extra £1,000,000 to the national debt, and because the real cost of the money was still 4 per cent it had done nothing for the existing funds. The loan itself, however, had been a success, £200,000 being subscribed over the £900,000 required on the first instalment.[95]

Unfortunately, this was merely the prelude to a new problem, that of finding the taxes to fund the new loan. Initially, Newcastle had wanted to raise the revenue by an increase of 3s on a bushel of malt.[96] The duty would be easy to collect and had the support of the Excise Commissioners. The previous August, Newcastle had requested them to recommend what additional duties, if any, could be laid. The Board replied that only beer, ale or malt could support an additional levy; all other forms of excise would bear too heavily on the manufacturing interest.[97] The idea, however, found little favour with Legge, who was now showing renewed confidence in financial matters. Since he would have to introduce the new tax into the Commons, Newcastle agreed to leave the decision to him. It was a gesture he would regret.

The scheme initially favoured by Legge was a refinement of Walpole's

---

[92] Estimate of the Supply for 1759, Add. Mss 33,039 ff 214, 232. Newcastle to Hardwicke, 17 Sept 1758, Add. Mss 32,884 ff 27–36.

[93] Estimate of the Supply for 1759, Add. Mss 33,039 f 217.

[94] Considerations upon the mode of raising the 1759 Supply, Add. Mss 33,039 ff 223–224. Gideon to Newcastle, 21 Jan 1759, Add. Mss 32,887 ff 274–275. Legge to Newcastle, 25 Jan 1759, Add. Mss 32,887 f 333. Grellier, *History of the National Debt*, 243–244. As in the previous year, the lottery tickets were convertible into 3 per cent stock after the draw.

[95] Newcastle to Hunter, 16 Feb 1759, Add. Mss 32,888 ff 138–139.

[96] Newcastle to Hardwicke, 17 Sept 1758, Add. Mss 32,884 ff 27–36.

[97] Excise to the Treasury, 23 Aug 1758, Add. Mss 32,883 ff 66–67.

old excise plan for a duty on tobacco.[98] The idea, however, threatened to be both complicated and controversial. Hardwicke returned Legge's proposals to Newcastle without comment because the subject was too technical.[99] The political objections were even greater. Many had not forgotten the controversies aroused by the previous attempt at such a measure. All the fears about excise officers invading homes and threatening liberty were certain to be revived, and indeed were raised by Pitt when he came to give his opinion. No matter how exaggerated such views might be, they were still latent and Legge was quickly convinced that another source of revenue must be found. His second choice was a 5 per cent *ad valorem* duty on sugar, tea, linen and certain luxuries from the East.[100]

If Legge thought that his alternative proposals would be acceptable he was greatly mistaken. In the first place the dispute gave Pitt a pretence for continuing his vendetta against the Chancellor. For almost a year, relations between the two men had been deteriorating, following Pitt's discovery of some clandestine negotiations by Legge during the coalition with Devonshire.[101] In addition, the plan to tax sugar immediately ran foul of the West Indian lobby, with whom Pitt was associated by virtue of his acquaintance with William Beckford, the Jamaican planter and London alderman. While Pitt privately made his views known, the West Indians lobbied the ministers in turn.[102] Faced with such opposition, Legge began to vacillate. The other Treasury officials then tried to find a compromise. Martin suggested a stamp duty, but this found little favour with the two protagonists.[103] By the beginning of March nothing had been resolved and Legge muttered that he would retire to the country and present no taxes at all unless Pitt assured him of support in the Commons. An open rupture seemed likely.[104]

Fortunately, Pitt began to have second thoughts. He had no wish to destroy the administration and accordingly intimated to Hardwicke and Newcastle that he would not oppose Legge in the House. Beckford would have to fight his own battle. On 9 March, therefore, Legge introduced his budget. Beckford duly expressed his opposition in a speech which according to one City observer showed an appalling lack of knowledge.[105] The House responded with laughter, especially at an attempt to appeal to the writings of an eminent seventeenth-century theorist, Sir Joshua Child. This jocularity

[98] Mr Legge's Paper, 5 Feb 1759, Add. Mss 33,039 ff 185–190.
[99] Hardwicke to Newcastle, 7 Feb 1759, Add. Mss 32,888 f 17.
[100] Taxes now suggested [1759], Add. Mss 33,039 ff 196–200. Memorandum for the King, 28 Feb 1759, Add Mss 32,888 ff 275–276.
[101] B. Williams, *The Life of William Pitt, Earl of Chatham* (London, 1913), I, 310, 320; II, 52.
[102] West to Newcastle, 20 Feb 1759, Add. Mss 32,888 f 194.
[103] Martin to Newcastle, 26 Feb 1759, Add. Mss 32,888 ff 250–252.
[104] Hardwicke to Newcastle, 1 Mar 1759, Add. Mss 32,888 ff 287–289.
[105] Joseph Watkins to Newcastle, 22 Mar 1759, Add. Mss 32,889 ff 197–198.

was too much for Pitt. For much of the debate he had maintained a sulky silence. Now, summoning all his awesome rhetoric, he asked whether the members would have laughed so heartily had Beckford been discussing corn and land, not sugar and trade. He then proceeded to turn the knife in the Chancellor, making the gratuitously offensive remark that none of the present difficulties were of his making. If the proposals were controversial or late, that was the fault of the Treasury. He, Pitt, had not been consulted.[106] The speech did nothing to strengthen confidence in the government, either at Westminster or in the City, since appearances suggested imminent disintegration. Indeed, the aftermath of the debate was a request from Legge to resign, even though his taxes were finally accepted by the House.[107]

The discord came at a most inopportune time for Newcastle. While the administration's spokesmen were fighting in the Commons and an invasion was threatening, a renewed shortage of specie had occurred, caused by the shipments of money to Germany and America. All the portents suggested a financial crisis.[108] Rumours that the Bank of England was about to call in its loans were already rife and the City was not surprisingly nervous as the 3 per cent stock plunged below eighty-five and the discount on navy bills reached 4.5 per cent.[109] Then at the beginning of April a 3 per cent discount appeared on the current subscription, giving fears that the loan would not be completed.[110] If that happened the government's credit must certainly fail, because it would be impossible to secure any further money.

Newcastle as First Lord faced an apparently insuperable situation. However, like many another man he sat down to work things out on paper. The result was a two-part memorandum on the state of the government, incorporating an analysis of its financial and political position. Financially, the most pressing problem was the next vote of credit, which at the very minimum would have to be for £800,000. Unless this was secured, the Treasury would find itself in difficulties later in the year. Fortunately, there were a number of alternatives should the Bank refuse to assist. An approach might be made to other financiers in the City. Another possibility was the non-payment of the seamen's wages, although such action would require parliamentary approval suspending Grenville's recent bill, which sought to prevent just such juggling by the Treasury.[111]

On the future prospects of the government there was also cause for hope.

---

[106] Mr West's Report on the Commons' Debate, 9 Mar 1759, Add. Mss 32,888 ff 428–430. Walpole, *Memoirs of George II*, III, 176–178.
[107] Memorandum for the King, 13 Mar 1759, Add. Mss 32,889 f 44.
[108] Memorandum for the King, 28 Feb 1759, Add. Mss 32,888 ff 275–276.
[109] Stock prices were regularly quoted in many newspapers, notably the *London Chronicle*.
[110] Newcastle House, 12 Apr 1759, Add. Mss 32,890 f 37.
[111] Considerations on the Present State of Affairs at Home and Abroad, 18 Apr 1759, Add. Mss 32,890 ff 130–136.

Newcastle was convinced that the French would not attempt their invasion before October. A good result ought to be expected in America, while in Germany Prince Ferdinand had made a promising start despite the superiority of the French. Nevertheless, there had to be 'some consistency in the Administration'. Above all Newcastle wanted to see 'the not wasting our Force by sea and land with Useless and Expensive Expeditions'. Newcastle did not specify which expeditions he was thinking of; the only one then being undertaken of any consequence was that against Martinique, which he had approved.[112] But at heart his complaints were political, rather than financial or military. Newcastle was angry at Pitt's failure to support him in the difficult task of financing the conflict. The Secretary was being unreasonable in saying that finance was not his department and then asserting that the Treasury was responsible for any failure. He commented: 'It is indeed amazing that a person who by his own measures has thrown the nation into an immense expense...shall think to lay the blame on the Treasury.' If the ministry were to survive, Pitt must behave more reasonably. Collective responsibility had to be acknowledged. However, there was no escaping the real cause of the present difficulties: 'We are engaged in Expenses infinitely above our strength...Expedition after Expedition, Campaign after Campaign', with no end in sight. For this reason Newcastle was doubtful whether the nation could continue the war beyond the present year. Perhaps the King of Prussia should be warned thereof.[113]

If Newcastle had any doubts about what he was writing they were quickly dispelled, for he received a sharp reminder of all that dissatisfied him about Pitt's conduct. The Secretary thought it a good idea to reform the transport pool, since it might be necessary to send troops either to Scotland or Ireland. Such a ploy might also usefully alarm the French into thinking a counter-expedition was intended. However, on this occasion he failed to consult his colleagues, simply asking Anson to get the necessary order from the King. Pitt was suffering from gout, which may account for his erratic behaviour. Whatever the reason, when Anson went into the closet he found George II equally uninformed. Newcastle was appalled. 'This is a most abominable and most unheard of measure,' he told Hardwicke, 'to send orders to the Admiralty for such an expense without condescending to tell either the King or Ministry what that service should be.'[114] Newcastle wanted the order revoked. Anson, for the sake of ministerial harmony, let it stand while he ascertained what Pitt intended. The Secretary, perhaps conscious of his misdemeanour, kept to his bed, communicating only through his under-

[112] Newcastle to Holdernesse, 4 Sept 1758, Add. Mss 32,883 ff 273–274.
[113] Considerations on the Present State of Affairs, Part 2, 19 Apr 1759, Add. Mss 32,890 ff 137–151.
[114] Newcastle to Hardwicke, 17 Apr 1759, Add. Mss 32,890 ff 114–117.

secretary, Robert Wood.[115] The advisability of the pool, once explained, was soon obvious and agreement readily given, despite the expense.[116]

Regarding the financial aspects of the crisis, Newcastle circulated his memorandum to that small but diverse group to whom he usually turned for such advice. Among these was Gideon. He had no panaceas to offer. The best way of reviving public credit was to make a further payment on the course of the navy; the government would then seem unembarrassed and the fears for its solvency unfounded. Appearances were everything: they could calm apprehensions and restore confidence. Once that was done money for the vote of credit and completion of the subscription would be readily available.[117]

Legge's views were very different. He believed that the way to restore confidence was by cutting expenditure: £5,000,000 to £6,000,000 was the maximum the country could borrow in one year. However, Legge affected to see in the crisis a plot on the part of the monied men. By withholding credit and depressing prices, the financiers were hoping to extract better terms from the government. The remedy was clear: by reducing its borrowings the government would show it was not to be coerced.[118] Indeed, Legge's message was one of firmness all round, for the unco-operative attitude of the Bank led him to suggest that the Company's privilege of circulating Exchequer bills be offered instead to the South Sea Company. The Bank was undermining the structure of public credit and had to be brought to terms.[119]

Legge's views were as usual extreme and not well thought out. For the sake of a victory over his old adversaries he was proposing to default. However, as Page pointed out, the massive nature of the loan and uncertain appearance of the war made it unsurprising that the stocks had fallen, the Bank was unco-operative and despondency prevailed. Page's advice was essentially the same as Gideon's. Newcastle should wait until the outlook had brightened and the market was less nervous. Any necessary finance would then be secured.[120] The only snag, as Newcastle told Mansfield, was that if the supply was not completed, he could expect abuse from Pitt. The Secretary was sure to argue that as the money had been voted by the Commons, any delay in securing it could only be owing to the incompetence of the Treasury.[121]

In the event Gideon and Page were right. Newcastle and Legge had

---

[115] Anson to Newcastle, 18 Apr 1759, Add. Mss 32,890 f 170.
[116] Admiralty to the Navy Board, 18 Apr 1759, Adm N/239.
[117] Gideon to Newcastle, 21 Apr 1759, Add. Mss 32,890 f 233.
[118] Legge to Newcastle, 21 Apr 1959, Add. Mss 32,890 ff 223–226. See also his letter to Martin, 18 Apr 1759, Add. Mss 32,890 ff 166–167.
[119] Legge to Newcastle, 24 Apr 1759, Add. Mss 32,890 f 229.
[120] Mr Page's Paper, 20 Apr 1759, Add. Mss 32,890 ff 216–218.
[121] Newcastle to Mansfield, 22 Apr 1759, Add. Mss 32,890 ff 255–256.

exaggerated the crisis, though the problems outlined in the memorandum were real enough. This was the reason why Newcastle was anxious to settle the disputes with Holland. The Dutch had always been big investors in British funds and agreement there might unlock an extra £1,000,000.[122]

Unfortunately, Holdernesse and Yorke had made little progress in their negotiations. When the deputies presented a new set of resolutions in January 1759 they differed little from those of August 1758 and had to be rejected.[123] The release of several ships by the Vice-Admiralty courts momentarily created a more favourable climate, and towards the end of March 1759 the British envoy was able to inform his chief that the deputies were planning to send a mission to London.[124] But, despite the initial hopes, the assignment was to prove a failure. The deputies continued to insist on complete freedom for their trade. In any case the heart had gone out of the British negotiators. The aim of the talks was to secure a closer union. That objective was as far away as ever.[125]

As news of the French preparations continued, so concern mounted inside the ministry, particularly about Ireland. It was to discuss this that the ministers held a meeting at Holdernesse's house on 8 May. Present were the usual conciliabulum together with Bedford, the Lord-Lieutenant. Only Ligonier was absent, because of a cold. The proceedings were opened by Pitt. He said there had been conflicting reports about the French preparations, which he personally thought were groundless. However, since the administration 'had given the alarm' the ministers must 'now make the people easy, by taking proper measures for their security'. The other ministers ignored these histrionics and got down to business. According to Bedford, the condition of Ireland was deplorable. There were scarcely 5,000 men available for the island's defence. But despite the obvious dangers the ministers could offer no immediate assistance. The British army was too small to send any reinforcement. All the ministers could presently do was to recommend the gathering of a strong naval force in Torbay under Hawke to proceed to Brest on the first reports of French activity.[126]

This by no means satisfied Bedford and ten days later a second meeting was held. Here Pitt's mood was significantly different. Hardwicke attributed this to his 'sensibility of having sent so great a part of the strength of the Kingdom to so great a distance', adding that 'the Southern Department seems to have no channel of intelligence at all'.[127] A number of decisions

---

[122] Newcastle to West, 13 May 1759, Add. Mss 32,891 ff 115–117. For earlier Dutch investment, see P. M. G. Dickson, *The Financial Revolution in England: A Study in the Development of Public Credit, 1688–1756* (London, 1967), 306–331.
[123] Holdernesse to Yorke, 7 Feb 1759, SP 84/483.
[124] Yorke to Holdernesse, 20 Mar 1759, SP 84/483.
[125] Holdernesse to Yorke, 8 June 1759, SP 84/484.
[126] Memorandum for the King, 9 May 1759, Add. Mss 32,893 ff 102–103.
[127] Hardwicke to Newcastle, 18 May 1759, Add. Mss 32,891 f 171.

were now taken which gave Bedford a measure of consolation. First, the ministers agreed that the squadron at Torbay under Hawke should proceed immediately to Brest to watch the French, and, in addition, plans were made for an encampment on the Isle of Wight. Also adopted was Pitt's scheme for a number of transports to be in attendance to alarm the enemy and be ready for carrying men to Scotland or Ireland. Finally, the militia should start to be called out so that more regulars would be available for the field army.[128]

Anson's orders to Hawke were similar to those previously issued to the western squadron. Hawke was to proceed to Ushant to observe as accurately as possible the 'enemy's force in Brest', making sure he was not driven to the west. Throughout his cruise he was 'to defeat any designs the enemy may have conceived for invading these Kingdoms', always doing everything 'to protect the trade'. He was to continue thus for fourteen days, after which he was to return to Torbay, unless the enemy were about to sail. At Torbay he would find fresh meat and provisions, so that he would not have to put into port, and after he had revictualled he was to hold his vessels in readiness for further service.

Anson at this point was thinking of short cruises, with interludes for resupply and the refreshment of the crews. He did not want the fleet staying out and all the ships being incapacitated as on some previous occasions. Otherwise the only article that was different from previous instructions was the need to prevent supplies reaching Brest. The French fleet was believed to be short of stores. Hawke was accordingly instructed to 'appoint such of the smaller ships of the line and frigates as you shall think sufficient to cruise on the most likely stations for intercepting' the same.[129] The implications of this had yet to be revealed as the fleet weighed anchor on 20 May.

IV

Inside the ministry relations were again fractious, because Newcastle and Holdernesse had fallen out. Holdernesse was tired of Newcastle's domineering attitude and resented his correspondence with the ambassadors abroad. Newcastle in turn began to complain of Holdernesse's rudeness. He was especially upset by a conversation whispered between the northern Secretary and Lady Yarmouth to which he was a witness but not participant.[130]

Newcastle was an inordinately suspicious man, constantly worrying that other ministers had longer receptions with the King and thus had more influence. Such sensitivity among politicians was not uncommon. Sir Robert

---

[128] Bedford to the Primate of Ireland, 22 May 1759, printed in Lord John Russell (ed.), *Correspondence of John, Fourth Duke of Bedford* (London, 1843), II, 373–377.

[129] Admiralty to Hawke, 18 May 1759, Adm 2/1331.

[130] Newcastle to Hardwicke, 12 June 1759, Add. Mss 32,892 ff 26–27.

Walpole's twenty years of power were a record of men being dismissed for appearing to challenge his authority.

Newcastle has often been charged with having no political principles: that he was only interested with the nuts and bolts of patronage, a point made by George III shortly after his accession.[131] However, as George III came to appreciate, Newcastle's interest in such matters was not entirely misplaced. Most politicians and public figures had their share of vanity which was only appeased by the same trifles that Newcastle was accused of trafficking in. Besides, as Hardwicke commented on the first outbreak of war: 'There had to be some principal person... to hear the wants and wishes of mankind.' Otherwise, the government so precariously built up might collapse.[132]

One item to cheer the ministry at this time was the news of the capture of Guadeloupe.[133] The force had originally been sent to seize Martinique. That objective had proved too difficult, the garrison being numerous and well entrenched. On the advice of Commodore Moore, the naval commander, Hopson, had then shifted his operations to neighbouring Guadeloupe where the enemy were less formidable.[134] An immediate success had been gained at Basseterre, but after this the army had got bogged down defending the town. At this point Hopson died, leaving the command with Barrington.[135] The latter immediately transferred his operations to the other side of the island, with spectacular result, for by early May the French were ready to surrender.[136] Guadeloupe was the second most productive sugar island after Martinique, and its capture was hence a damaging blow to the French marine and its possession something that might be traded advantageously at the peace.

The news from the Caribbean prompted Anson to suggest that some of the battleships with Moore be recalled. He was aware that the French would probably bring back their own West Indian squadron under Monsieur Bompart to reinforce their invasion effort. But Newcastle accurately forecast that Pitt would not 'easily part with any ships from hence'.[137] The southern Secretary was anticipating further operations there and felt that the navy had sufficient ships at home for any emergency. In the end Anson had to be satisfied with the recall of three of the larger vessels.[138]

Otherwise the ministerial attention was focused on Brest, where Hawke

[131] George III to Bute, 18 Nov 1761, printed in R. Sedgwick, *Letters from George III to Lord Bute, 1756–1766* (London, 1939), 70.
[132] Hardwicke to Newcastle, 3 Jan 1755, Yorke, II, 225–226.
[133] Newcastle to Devonshire, 14 June 1759, Add. Mss 32,892 f 55.
[134] Hopson to Pitt, 30 Jan 1759, Kimball, II, 20–26.
[135] Barrington to Pitt, 2 Mar 1759, Kimball, II, 45–50.
[136] Barrington to Pitt, 9 May 1759, Kimball, II, 94–105.
[137] Newcastle to Hardwicke, 14 June 1759, Add. Mss 32,892 ff 58–59.
[138] Memorandum for the King, 19 June 1759, Add. Mss 32,892 f 137.

had the dual problem of how to supply his fleet and sustain an effective watch on the French. Severe winds had already compelled him once to shelter in Torbay, leaving Captain Robert Duff and four frigates to keep vigil. Fortunately the wind that drove Hawke up the Channel effectively imprisoned the French.[139] The ministry was thus able to accept his detention with reasonable equanimity, especially since he could resupply from the vessels promised by Anson. Since then, Hawke had arranged for some of the victuallers to go to Ushant so that he would not have to return to port so frequently. But it was not certain how feasible this would be in such blustery conditions.[140]

The other problem, that of preventing supplies from reaching the French fleet, Hawke had solved by creating a separate inshore squadron under Augustus Hervey. This was composed largely of frigates which were better able to navigate the rocky coast and dangerous lee shore. The main fleet remained off Ushant ready to provide support.[141] Hence, by the middle of July Hawke was able to report that Brest was 'blocked up in the strictest sense', the first time this had been done in such waters.[142] This went against the conventions of international jurisprudence which understood blockade to include only vessels of belligerents or ships with contraband of war, narrowly defined as money, arms or ammunition. But, as in the disputes with the Dutch, such limitation was no longer acceptable to the British.[143]

Nevertheless, the need to conciliate neutral opinion was the main reason why the ministry continued its plan for a bill to curb the activities of the privateers before Parliament rose for the summer. As Pitt told the Commons: 'The misfortunes accruing to this country from the robberies committed by the privateers are such that unless a step is timely made, the country is undone.' The nation must act quickly before the storm, for 'then concession would be taken for fear'.[144]

If a total blockade was a restriction for neutral shipping, it was a new and humiliating experience for the French. Never before had they suffered the indignity of having enemy cruisers sailing unchallenged at the entrance to their principal base. As Hervey exultantly commented to Hawke a few days after the French had made a vain attempt to drive him away: 'I think, Sir, you have insulted them in a manner that they were never before used to, or that any history can give an account of.'[145] The French were rapidly

---

[139] Hawke to Clevland, 6 June 1759, Adm 1/92.
[140] Hawke to Clevland, 8 June 1759, Adm 1/92. Anson had received a cargo of beer the previous year, but this had hardly been an adequate test, Anson to Clevland, 4 Aug 1758, Adm 1/90. Ibid., 12 Aug 1758.
[141] Erskine, *Augustus Hervey's Journal*, 303.
[142] Hawke to Clevland, 16 July 1759, Adm 1/92.   [143] See Yorke, II, 312–314.
[144] Quoted in Williams, *Life of Pitt*, I, 402. For details of the measure, see An Act to Explain and Amend an Act...for the Encouragement of Seamen etc., *Statutes at Large*, Ch. xxv, 32 Geo. II.
[145] Hervey to Hawke, 23 July 1759, Hawke Papers, HWK/VII, NMM.

becoming discredited in the eyes of Europe, especially since their fleet was almost equal to that of the British.

The main concern now was that of keeping the fleet at sea. At the beginning of July the squadron had entered the sixth week of its cruise. As Newcastle had earlier written to Devonshire, the number of ships was sufficient. The problem was: 'Hawke can't keep that station without often coming in' to refit. He continued: 'I own I don't like this; tho' I hope there is no real Danger for I think their flat bottomed boats will find great difficulty in Landing, as Admiral Rodney will have a small squadron constantly upon the watch for them.'[146] This latter was a reference to a detachment that Anson had sent to Le Havre, where the invasion craft were being constructed.[147]

The state of Hawke's fleet was accordingly discussed at a meeting of the ministers on 16 July. Newcastle noted in a memorandum: 'What orders should be sent to Sir Edward Hawke?' The ministers wanted to know whether 'he could be enabled, by a small additional number of ships, to send home to clean and refit, six ships of the line at a time, which might enable him to continue his station before Brest'.[148] Happily, Anson was able to tell the ministers that a reinforcement had now been sent. A cleaning rota ought to be possible, as Hawke himself had earlier suggested.[149] Unfortunately, as the British commander was even then discovering, the vessels sent to Plymouth were so long away that he was already being forced 'to alter my Plan'.[150] The enemy were reported as having at Brest twenty-two battleships compared to his twenty-three. For the present, therefore, such ships as had to be sent in should have their hulls boot-hosed-topped only, being keeled over in shallow water with a mixture of tallow and resin applied as a temporary protection.[151]

The navy was apparently about to suffer for the lack of development to its yards at Portsmouth and Plymouth. Basically the fleet was using the same facilities as at the turn of the century.[152] One useful, though minor, reform had been the raising of Plymouth to the status of Portsmouth. Anson realized that in any war with France it was likely to be crucial to a squadron in the western approaches. Additional officers had accordingly been appointed and salaries raised to end what had been 'an Obstruction to carrying on

---

[146] Newcastle to Devonshire, 14 June 1759, Add. Mss 32,892 ff 55–57.

[147] Admiralty to Rodney, 26 June 1759, Adm 2/1331.

[148] Business for the Meeting Tomorrow, 15 July 1759, Add. Mss 32,893 ff 58–59.

[149] Hawke to Clevland, 3 July 1759, Adm 1/92. Three additional ships of the line had been ordered to join Hawke in mid June, Clevland to Hawke, 16 June 1759, HWK/vii, NMM.

[150] Hawke to Clevland, 23 July 1759, Adm 1/92.

[151] Hawke to Clevland, 24 July 1759, Adm 1/92.

[152] The origin and development of the yards can be traced in King's Mss, 44, BL, which was written for George III early in his reign. See also J. Ehrman, *The Navy in the War of William III: Its State and Direction, 1689–1697* (Cambridge, 1953); and Baugh, *British Naval Administration*.

the business, and a Discouragement to the officers themselves'.[153] Unfortunately, this commendable attempt to improve the facilities at Plymouth had not been pursued. Even the dry dock, ordered in 1753, was still barely started because of the failure to complete one of the men of war.[154]

However, another reason for the shortage of vessels was a want of seamen. An Admiralty survey of 2 August revealed that only seven of the fifty-two ships of fifty guns or more in port had proper crews: and of the fifty-two frigates, only twenty-two were even partially manned. These figures included all those vessels in the reserve, many of which were mere hulks. Nevertheless, some could have been deployed, if the manpower had been available, especially among the frigates, which were now of the greatest importance to the blockade.[155]

Since the meeting on 19 February, Anson had been doing his best to deal with the problem. To offset the loss of the 4,000 troops he had requested permission of the Privy Council to add one lieutenant, a corporal and twenty-three privates to every marine company, raising the strength of the corps from 11,000 to 14,000 men.[156] At the same time he had instituted a vigorous recruiting drive. The magistrates and regulating captains were to round up any idle hands fitting the description of seamen.[157] By the end of May about 5,000 had been secured but this was still insufficient.[158] Accordingly, the bounty for volunteers was increased. Then in June Anson had ordered a general press from all protections.[159] But apart from disrupting many of the navy's own supply services, the result was to increase opposition from the merchant and seafaring community.[160] By the end of July the number of men in service as a result of this last effort had risen by only 1,000.[161]

Despite these difficulties, Hawke still blamed his want of battleships and frigates on Anson's arrangements for cleaning and refitting, which he felt was detaining them unnecessarily in port.[162] Earlier, the master shipwright at Plymouth had introduced a new method of cleaning the ships' hulls, but this had upset the labour force and he had been told to return to 'the ancient practice of the navy'.[163] A more likely reason for the slow turn round was

[153] Admiralty to the Privy Council, 2 Mar 1756, Adm 1/5164.
[154] Navy Board to Clevland, 12 Jan 1758, Adm/B, NMM. See Middleton, 'Administration of Newcastle and Pitt', 134–135.
[155] Musters of Ships in Port, 2 Aug 1759, Adm 7/420.
[156] Privy Council to the Admiralty, 3 Mar 1759, Adm 1/5165.
[157] Admiralty to the Officers at the Cinque Ports etc., 9 Mar 1759, Adm 2/82.
[158] Seamen Employed, 1759. *JHC*, xxviii, 765.
[159] *London Gazette*, 12/15 May 1759. Admiralty to the Regulating Captains, 21 June 1759, Adm 2/83.
[160] Middleton, 'Administration of Newcastle and Pitt', 89–95.
[161] Seamen Employed, 1759, *JHC*, xxviii, 765.
[162] Hawke to Clevland, 28 Aug 1759, Adm 1/92.
[163] Navy Board Minute, 30 Jan 1759, Adm 106/2565. However, according to Charnock, *History of Marine Architecture*, iii, 204, a new method of sheathing was introduced.

Anson's refusal to hire more hands. The total workforce during the war had not exceeded 8,500, an increase of just 40 per cent on the peacetime establishment, when by contrast the work-load had risen fourfold. The only additional workers recently recruited were some foreign sailmakers at the beginning of the year.[164] The main reason for this was the firm control that had to be exercised in the interests of economy. Anson knew that once a post had been created or a precedent set, they were exceedingly difficult to abolish. Hence, requirements were judged not on present need but on what had sufficed previously; and remedies lay in greater attention to business, longer working hours and the dismissal of offending employees.[165]

One solution to the cleaning problem was to use the crews. But to this Hawke was opposed. As he pointed out at the beginning of August: 'The relief of the squadron depends more on the refreshment of the ships' companies than on the cleaning of the ships.' The men 'would be so harrassed and fatigued, that they would return to me in a worse condition than they left'. But concern for the welfare of his crews led him to return to the question of the victualling. It was pointless delivering victuals to the fleet if the quality left so much to be desired. What was needed was a senior officer at Plymouth to oversee the arrangements.[166]

Anson duly complied by sending Robert Pett.[167] Earlier, he had ordered the Commissioners for Sick and Wounded Seamen to send Hawke a number of sheep and bullocks for the refreshment of the sick.[168] However, what was really needed was a method of keeping the crews healthy. Hawke therefore replied by proposing that any returning ships should bring as much fresh meat as they could carry.[169] The sense of this suggestion was readily recognized. Indeed, Anson went further by ordering the Navy Board to hire four transports. At the same time he took the task from the Commissioners for Sick and Wounded Seamen, placing it with the Victualling Board and its representative at Plymouth.[170] But this was not all, for Pett soon afterwards suggested that fresh vegetables should also be sent to Hawke. Almost unperceived, a revolution in the victualling was taking place. On 14 August Hawke was able to report that he had been joined by no fewer than nine victuallers, carrying live cattle, turnips, carrots, onions, cabbages and beer.[171] The good effects of even a little fresh food were quickly noted.[172]

[164] Navy Board Minute, 23 Jan 1759, Adm 106/2569.
[165] Middleton, 'Administration of Newcastle and Pitt', 137–139.
[166] Hawke to Clevland, 4 Aug 1759, Adm 1/92. Hawke to Clevland, 23 July 1759, Adm 1/90.
[167] Clevland to Hawke, 7 Aug 1759, HWK/vii, NMM.
[168] Clevland to Hawke, 19 July 1759, HWK/vii, NMM.
[169] Hawke to Clevland, 24 July 1759, Adm 1/92.
[170] Admiralty to the Navy Board, 2 Aug 1759, Adm 2/225. Victualling Board to Hawke, 10 Aug 1759, HWK/vii. Admiralty to the Victualling Board, 20 Aug 1759, Adm 1/83.
[171] Hawke to Clevland, 14 Aug 1759, Adm 1/92.
[172] Hawke to Clevland, 28 Aug 1759, Adm 1/92.

Unfortunately, the improvements did not include one vital article, for as Hawke told Clevland laconically on 4 August: 'Our daily employment is condemning the beer from Plymouth.'[173] The supply there had been an object of complaint since 1756.[174] The problem had been compounded inadvertently by Anson's well-meant decision to cease issuing malt spirits in the interest of the men's health, which meant an increase in brewing capacity was required. But this was not all. Beer brewed in summer would not keep because of bacteria in the fermenting process. Hence, if the fleet was to receive a wholesome supply, a policy of winter brewing and summer storage was required. This Anson and his Admiralty colleagues had failed to provide. Though they had agreed to an increase in the brewery near Portsmouth, nothing had been done at Plymouth, with the results that were now being seen.[175] But, as Hawke was warning, unless a good supply was obtained, the likely result must be the return of the squadron to port, especially once the autumn weather made victualling at sea difficult.[176]

The departmental nature of government meant that the ministers were largely oblivious to these developments. Indeed, it is indicative of the general satisfaction that Pitt's correspondence with the Admiralty was only half that of the previous year.[177]

Also discussed at the meeting on 16 July was the state of the army. Until then no serious attempt had been made to consider its recruitment. As before the ministers seemed content to let traditional methods take their course. One reason for the lack of urgency may have been Anson's assurance that the French would not be ready to invade before the autumn.[178] This had helped Pitt to recapture his old self-confidence, so that he now affected to despise the French preparations while admitting the genuineness of their intent.[179] Yet another reason was the past difficulties of recruiting the army, and a third may have been the lack of a single head regarding the administration of the army. Ligonier's duties were primarily those of personnel and discipline; Barrington's of housing and the minutiae of recruitment. No one was responsible for the overall development of the service, so that initiatives often had to come from elsewhere in the ministry. Hence it was Pitt who decided to explore the possibility of securing more Highlanders with Argyle; and Devonshire who put forward the idea of forming regiments by the nobility.[180] Clearly these ideas needed discussing,

---

[173] Hawke to Clevland, 4 Aug 1759, Adm 1/92.
[174] Boscawen to Clevland, 16 May 1756, Adm 1/90. Anson to Clevland, 16 July 1758, Adm 1/90.
[175] Middleton, 'Administration of Newcastle and Pitt', 194–197.
[176] Hawke to Hanway, 8 Sept 1759, HWK/ix, NMM.
[177] See his Naval Entry Books in the Public Record Office, SP 44/229–230.
[178] Newcastle to Hardwicke, 14 June 1759, Add. Mss 32,892 ff 58–59.
[179] Newcastle to Hardwicke, 12 June 1759, Add. Mss 32,892 ff 26–30.
[180] Newcastle to Hardwicke, 27 June 1759, Add. Mss 32,892 ff 256–257.

but it was Newcastle who finally arranged a 'meeting of the usual Lords', at Holdernesse's house on the evening of Monday, 16 July, to which Argyle and Devonshire were invited.[181]

The expedient of regiments raised by members of the nobility was not new: it had been tried with success during 1745.[182] An advantage was that the nobility could appeal to their retainers and tenants; another that the prospective colonel met the initial levying expense. A number of such offers had been made since the start of hostilities, but had been politely declined, not being popular with the King or Ligonier.[183] To the King, the practice meant the loss of patronage over which the old man still took an immense if erratic pride. To Ligonier it meant another opportunity for the privileged to buy promotion. Indeed, despite all his hopes, members of the aristocracy were continuing to leapfrog over their less well-connected brethren.[184] Nevertheless, the present emergency meant that the ministers had no option but to consider the idea. One possible solution was that the scheme might be limited to infantry companies or troops of cavalry. A chance also existed that the army might yet be recruited by more normal means. Barrington, Napier and William Sharpe, Secretary to the Privy Council, were preparing a proclamation, promising potential recruits that their service would be limited to the emergency and that they would not be sent out of the kingdom.[185]

Newcastle believed that Pitt's activity at this time was the product of a guilty conscience about sending so many troops away during the previous twelve months, which made him 'very pressing for trying all tricks by Highlanders, Volunteer Regiments, Light Troops...to strengthen ourselves at home'.[186] At the meeting itself a number of schemes were accepted. Among them was a plan for a regiment of two battalions of Highland fencibles, to be raised under the auspices of the Earl of Sutherland and General Campbell for service in Scotland.[187] Newcastle wanted the men to wear red coats, but Argyle argued this would retard the scheme.[188] Details were also completed for a regiment of infantry under Colonel Crawford, and one of light horse under John Burgoyne.[189] One solution to the weakened ranks of the existing corps was that of attaching militia companies to them.

---

[181] Newcastle to Holdernesse, 7 July 1759, Add. Mss 32,892 ff 460–461.
[182] Sir John W. Fortescue, *A History of the British Army* (London, 1899), II, 132–133. Memoranda of the Extraordinary Measures to Raise men 1708–1745, Add. Mss 33,046 ff 382–384.
[183] Details of the various schemes can be found in WO 1/869.
[184] Ligonier to Amherst, 28 Jan 1759, Ligonier Letter Book.
[185] Lord Barrington, The War Office, 15 July 1759, Add. Mss 32,893 f 62.
[186] Newcastle to Andrew Stone, 1 Aug 1759, Add. Mss 32,893 ff 403–412.
[187] Barrington to Fox, 7 Aug 1759, WO 4/58.
[188] Newcastle to Hardwicke, 21 July 1759, Add. Mss 32,893 ff 189–192.
[189] Barrington to Fox, 23 July 1759, WO 4/58. For a list of new units raised in 1759 see *JHC*, XXVIII, 646–651.

However, the jealousies between the two groups were thought to be too great, though the Duke of Rutland assured Newcastle that the Lincolnshire men were willing to participate in the scheme.[190] More useful was a move by the City of London for a subscription to assist the recruitment of the existing regiments so that they could compete against the high bounties of the new corps.[191]

One change in the ministry at this time was the promotion of Ligonier to the Master-Generalship of the Ordnance. This position had remained vacant since the death of Marlborough. The delay had occurred in part because of the feeling that the authority of the Master-General over the other members of the Board was excessive, especially with respect to finance.[192]

Ligonier had originally shared these views. Now a different prospect was in the offing, for he was aware that as Lieutenant-General he had the best claim to the vacant post. The Master-Generalship was still one of great honour and some power. On Marlborough's death, accordingly, he had suggested that it ought to be 'kept in the military branch' and not given to some titled lord.[193] Now he pointed out: 'Experience teaches the necessity of such an officer, especially in time of war, when Preparations and Expeditions' had to be made in secrecy.[194] Newcastle agreed, commenting to Pitt a few days later: 'We shall not have things carried on in that material office with that Expedition that the present critical situation of affairs requires.' Ligonier's appointment was accordingly announced in the second week of July.[195]

Overall the Ordnance had run smoothly enough, with or without a Master-General. Supplies of weapons and munitions had been sufficient, though the Board had had to request the Privy Council in February 1758 to reduce courtesies at sea to preserve gunpowder.[196] Since the beginning of the war there had been a ban on all exports.[197] Cannon had generally been plentiful, in part because the Surveyor had endeavoured to regulate deliveries from the contractors,[198] and a similar practice had been adopted with small arms. From 1757 Marlborough and the Board had tried to ensure

---

[190] Rutland to Newcastle, 29 Aug 1759, Add. Mss 32,894 ff 448–449.
[191] Newcastle to Devonshire, 19 Aug 1759, Add. Mss 32,894 ff 287–294. This prompted Newcastle to organize a similar scheme for Middlesex and Nottinghamshire – of which he was the Lord-Lieutenant – being the minimum, he told Rutland, that could be expected from those counties where the militia had not yet been organized, 23 Aug 1759, Add. Mss 32,894 ff 291–294. For his attempts at organizing a subscription in Middlesex see the *London Chronicle*, 8/11 Sept, 25/27 Sept 1759.
[192] Queries concerning the Ordnance, June 1759, Ligonier Letter Book.
[193] Ligonier to Sackville, 12 Nov 1758, Ligonier Letter Book.
[194] Ligonier to Newcastle, June 1759, Ligonier Letter Book.
[195] Newcastle to Pitt, 23 June 1759, Add. Mss 32,892 f 187. *London Gazette*, 10/14 July 1759.
[196] Ordnance Board Minute, 27 Mar 1758, WO 47/51.
[197] This had been effected by An Act to impower His Majesty to prohibit the Exportation of Salt Petre etc., *Statutes at Large*, Ch xvi, 29 Geo. II.
[198] Ordnance Board Minute, 17 Feb 1756, WO 47/47.

that 50,000 muskets were always at the Tower.[199] The same had been done for stores for the navy. Unfortunately, the Board had not always been assisted by the Admiralty, which rarely gave notification of its requirements, especially for new ships. The Board pointed out with some irritation now that as no account of these had been given since 11 February 1758, the Admiralty should contact the Ordnance immediately, if 'timely provision were to be made'.[200] Nevertheless, when the first rumours of an invasion began to circulate, Ligonier was able to promise Anson that every ship of English construction at least would find their cannon ready.[201] These views were shared by Sir Charles Frederick, the Surveyor, who told Sackville in May: 'As to what relates to the Civil part of the Ordnance, I am certain we are in a condition to issue whatever may be required at home or abroad.'[202]

Frederick significantly did not include the military branch in his assessment. However, the Royal Artillery Regiment had generally performed well. Its main problem, as for the army, had been to increase its ranks. At the beginning of the war it had one battalion of ten companies.[203] Various additions were subsequently made and during the Pitt–Devonshire ministry the force was divided into two.[204] Now, following the addition of yet more companies, Ligonier was able to create a third battalion, also of ten companies.[205] A good start too had been made in the creation of a unit in Ireland. Indeed, Ligonier was even then requesting a draft of sixty men to strengthen the corps in England.[206] In the field the regiment had generally been praised.[207]

The situation of the Engineers was less happy. Here too a shortage of personnel was a problem. At the beginning of the conflict the establishment had been about fifty. But so many had been dispatched overseas, especially to America, that early in 1759 there were only five qualified personnel left in Britain.[208] To meet this challenge it had been agreed to create another eleven posts, making a total of sixty-one.[209] Nevertheless, this was hardly sufficient for all the demands on the service and is a principal reason why the Board was unable to provide an early-warning system of beacons.[210] The

---

[199] Ordnance Board Minute, 9 Sept 1757, WO 47/50.
[200] William Bogdani to Clevland, 31 Aug 1759, Adm 1/4011.
[201] Ordnance Board Minute, 27/28 Jan 1759, WO 47/53.
[202] Frederick to Sackville, 15 May 1759, Germain Papers, II.
[203] Almanacs, *Court and City Register for 1754*, 162.
[204] Pitt to Marlborough, 8 Mar 1757, SP 44/189.
[205] Pitt to Ligonier, 20 Aug 1759, SP 44/191.
[206] Ligonier to Richard Rigby, 2 June 1759, Ligonier Letter Book.
[207] Fortescue, *British Army*, II, 597.
[208] List of Engineers in North America, 24 Dec 1758, Amherst Slipcase, Clements Library.
[209] Establishment of Engineers, 3 Mar 1759, King's Mss 70, ff 145–147, BL.
[210] The Privy Council had requested such a system in 1756, Privy Council to the Master-General, 3 Feb 1756, PC 1/6/43. Ibid., 2 Mar 1756, PC 1/6/44. Ordnance to the Master-General, 13 Mar 1759, PC 1/6/52.

siting of these depended on a proper knowledge of the countryside. This the Board did not possess, for its survey, begun in 1746, had made only modest progress.[211]

The quality of the corps was also criticized. Despite the dispatch of a large proportion of the force to America, Loudoun confessed that he did not have a senior man in whom he could trust; and General Tyrawley was equally condemnatory of the corps for its attempts to fortify Gibraltar.[212] More recently, both Wolfe and Abercromby had made derogatory remarks.[213] However, in March 1758 Marlborough had drawn up a list of reforms, including provision for a more thorough instruction of the cadets in the art of attacking, defending and building military installations. At the end each cadet was to be examined by the chief engineer, Colonel Skinner, who was to have more access to the Board's plans and surveys in the Tower.[214] It was hoped a better class of engineer was in prospect.

[211] W. Porter, *A History of the Corps of Royal Engineers* (London, 1889), II, 228–229.
[212] Loudoun to Cumberland, 22 Nov 1756, printed in S. M. Pargellis (ed.), *Military Affairs in North America, 1748–1765: Selected Documents from the Cumberland Papers in Windsor Castle* (New York, 1936), 277. Tyrawley to Barrington, 1 Dec 1756, RA CP, Box 48.
[213] Wolfe to Major Walter Wolfe, 27 July 1758, printed in Willson, *Wolfe*, 384–385. Abercromby asserted that he had only launched his attack on Ticonderoga after receiving the advice of 'two very expert engineers', Abercromby to Mr James Abercromby, 19 Aug 1759, CP PRO 30/8/98 f 27.
[214] Ordnance Board Minute, 1758, WO 47/51.

5

The Bells of Victory

I

The situation of the nation and the ministry in the summer of 1759 was finely balanced. The fleet was adequate, but no one knew whether it could stay at sea and prevent the enemy from launching an invasion. The army was growing but was still seemingly insufficient to resist a formidable assault by the French. So far there had been no news from North America, though few doubted ultimate success there. Elsewhere, Prince Ferdinand was battling manfully. However, since June he had been on the defensive, facing a pincer movement by the army of Contades. The dangers seemed all the greater when on 11 July the enemy took the town of Minden, a key approach to the Electorate.[1]

This misfortune unexpectedly prefaced success, for on 5 August news arrived of Ferdinand's victory over the French four days earlier. The Prince had exploited a weakness in the enemy's position to lure them into a premature attack. His victory was considerable; not only had he recaptured Minden and several thousand prisoners, he was also pushing the French back towards the Rhine.[2] Here was one cloud removed, though the ministerial joy was slightly diminished by rumours of misconduct by Sackville. Nevertheless, as the enemy fled from the battlefield there was much satisfaction, which not even the news of a bloody and largely unsuccessful encounter between Frederick II and the Russians at Kunersdorf could dispel.[3]

There is still much dispute in accounting for Sackville's conduct. The popular verdict then and later was cowardice.[4] This seems unconvincing, since Sackville had never been slow to maintain his honour.[5] The most likely explanation stems from Ferdinand's obsessive secrecy which committed Sackville to an operation in which he had not been adequately briefed.

---

[1] Sackville to Holdernesse, 18 July 1759, Add. Mss 32,893 ff 112–113.
[2] Holdernesse to Newcastle, 8 Aug 1759, Add. Mss 32,894 f 25.
[3] Hardwicke to Newcastle, 15 Aug 1759, Add. Mss 32,894 f 211. Newcastle to Devonshire, 19 Aug 1759, Add. Mss 32,894 ff 287–292.
[4] H. Walpole, *Memoirs of the Reign of King George II* (London, 1846–7), III, 196–197.
[5] *Dictionary of National Biography*.

Hence when ambiguous orders arrived to sustain some of the infantry, Sackville hesitated to commit his forces, especially since his view of the battlefield was obscured by a wood. Unfortunately, Ferdinand jumped to the conclusion that Sackville was being deliberately disobedient, depriving him of a more complete victory.[6]

Ferdinand made no formal charge, but his public comment that the British cavalry would have matched the infantry had they been under different leadership was enough to destroy Sackville's standing. He left a few days later to clear his name in a court martial, his position as British commander being filled by Lord Granby. The episode was embarrassing for the ministry, since Sackville had been an ally of Pitt and Leicester House in 1757. Pitt, however, had no use for failures and declined to assist. Leicester House more predictably expressed sympathy, ready to seize a handle against the continental war. The affair could only further damage relations between Pitt and Bute, though for the moment this was not a matter of concern while George II remained in good health.[7]

Even success brought its problems. With an invasion still threatening, the condition of the army was critical, for the demands on it were unceasing. The battle at Minden had cost several hundred British casualties which would require replacing if the momentum was to be sustained. On the advice of Ligonier, the ministers agreed to a draft of 430 men plus the raising of another 600 Highlanders under Major Keith.[8] No alternative seemingly existed to the undesirable draft.[9]

In the meantime there was no want of offers to form new corps. Lord Lauderdale proposed a regiment recruited around Edinburgh and Lord Pulteney one in London. The Duke of Richmond suggested a regiment of chasseurs. A plan was also afoot to raise, in lieu of militia, three battalions from the environs of Westminster, financed by subscriptions similar to those being collected in the City.[10]

Nevertheless, men were still proving hard to find for the established corps, which were 6,000 short of their complement.[11] Some of the reasons were explained to Newcastle by his correspondents. In Leicestershire, Rutland commented, a turnpike was being built and this attracted labour. Similarly, in Yorkshire, the general opinion was that 'there never was so great a

---

[6] P. Mackesy, *The Coward of Minden: The Affair of Lord George Sackville* (London, 1979), 83–142.

[7] Ibid., 142–233.

[8] Memorandum for the King, 21 Aug 1759, Add. Mss 32,894 f 333.

[9] Napier to Hotham, 24 Aug 1759, Hotham Papers, DDHO 4/10, East Riding Record Office.

[10] Plan for a Regiment from Midlothian, 4 Aug 1759, Add. Mss 32,893 f 485. Ligonier to Richmond, 24 Aug 1759, Ligonier Letter Book, Clements Library. Scheme for Three Battalions from Westminster, 18 Aug 1759, Add. Mss 32,894 f 275.

[11] Newcastle to the Duke of Rutland, 23 Aug 1759, Add. Mss 32,894 ff 391–394.

demand for Manufactures, especially Woollens as at this time'.[12] Even so Newcastle blamed the militia for the lack of recruits, tempting the young men by its easier terms. This was especially irksome when the military value of these corps was so questionable, as a serious mutiny at Plymouth demonstrated, where a militia regiment was guarding the dockyard.[13]

Soon more successes were being announced, notably the defeat of the French Mediterranean fleet of the Marquis de La Clue by Boscawen. Initially Boscawen had maintained a watch in the vicinity of the enemy's main base at Toulon. However, at the end of June he had been compelled to retire to Gibraltar for repairs.[14] Four weeks later La Clue determined to try and sail through the straits at night. In this manoeuvre he was only partially successful, for Boscawen saw him and was waiting to follow. The British commander finally caught up with his quarry off the Portuguese coast near Lagos. In the ensuing engagement two French ships of the line were destroyed and three taken, while the rest fled to the sanctuary of the Tagus. Here they were blockaded by Brodrick, while Boscawen set out for home with his captures. A serious blow had been struck against the French plans to invade Britain.[15]

The defeat of La Clue came at an opportune time, for the ministry had received some ominous news about troopships at Bordeaux and Nantes. The first warning had come from Duff, who had chased a convoy of thirty vessels into the Morbihan, an alluvial basin inside Quiberon Bay. The response of Anson on hearing this was to send Hawke another four frigates, promising him in addition some bomb vessels if he thought them of use in getting at the French.[16] Later another sixty transports managed to get into the Morbihan from Bordeaux. Their destruction now seemed so important that Anson informed Hawke he was to make this his principal priority, along with the watch on the enemy fleet at Brest.[17]

Meanwhile, good news at last began to flow from America. Almost simultaneously came information that Niagara, Ticonderoga and Crown Point had fallen.[18] The taking of Niagara by a mixed force of provincials and regulars not only consolidated British control of the Great Lakes, but also promised an early advance from the west to seal the fate of the enemy in the St Lawrence. Equally crucial was the capture of Ticonderoga and

[12] Rutland to Newcastle, 29 Aug 1759, Add. Mss 32,894 ff 448–449. Lord Kinnoull to Newcastle, 28 July 1759, Add. Mss 32,893 ff 331–334.
[13] Newcastle to Hardwicke, 21 July 1759, Add. Mss 32,893 ff 189–192. Account of the Mutiny, 24 Aug 1759, Add. Mss 32,895 f 28.
[14] Boscawen to Clevland, 8 Aug 1759, Adm 1/384.
[15] Boscawen to Clevland, 20 Aug 1759, Adm 1/384. See J. S. Corbett, *England in the Seven Years' War: A study in Combined Strategy* (London, 1907), II, 31–40.
[16] Duff to Hawke, 6 Aug 1759, HWK/VII, NMM. Clevland to Hawke, 22 Aug 1759, HWK/VII.
[17] Reynolds to Hawke, 19 Sept 1759, Adm 1/92. Clevland to Hawke, 5 Oct 1759, HWK/VII, NMM.   [18] *London Chronicle*, 8/11 Sept 1759.

Crown Point. These guarded the principal route from the south to Canada and had long stood in the way of British control of the backcountry there.

Nevertheless, although the French had finally given up Ticonderoga and Crown Point without a siege, the campaign had not been without its problems. A continual shortage of money had hindered the supplying of the forces.[19] Amherst had only been able to continue his operations by an appeal to the Governor and Assembly of New York for an issue of paper money.[20] Other problems had also interposed. Bad weather made the transport of supplies north of Albany difficult; and the provincials were again late in arriving, despite Pitt's having sent his instructions nearly three weeks earlier than for the 1758 campaign.[21] But Amherst had also lost time through his mistaken assumption that the appearance of Wolfe in the St Lawrence would lead to the virtual abandonment of Ticonderoga. This did not happen, therefore a siege was seemingly necessary for which artillery would be required: to transport it Amherst needed a special raft, and its construction was only begun in July after everything else was completed.[22] The importance of this, though the ministers did not realize it, was that the campaign was already behind schedule. Amherst still had to win command of Lake Champlain before being able to join Wolfe in the St Lawrence to give the final blow to Canada.

So far no news had been received from Wolfe since his setting out from Halifax on 6 June.[23]

At home the militia was drilling and Ligonier began to consider the defences. Little had been done to these since the last scare in 1756. On that occasion additional earthworks were thrown up at Chatham, Portsmouth and Plymouth, together with further entrenchments at Dover and Pendennis Castle.[24] More land had subsequently been purchased at the three former places, since the defences there were too close to the facilities they were designed to protect.[25] The programme now was even more modest. Eight sites had been selected for the construction of batteries along the Kent and Sussex coast at Arundel, Brighton, New Haven, Seaforth, Hastings, Rye, Hythe and Folkestone. Not all of them were new, being repairs or extensions to existing emplacements. The whole programme was costing a mere £6,000. To each battery the Board had appointed a master gunner and

[19] Amherst to Bradstreet, 4 Feb 1759, WO 34/58. Ibid., 5 Mar 1759, Amherst to Gage, 28 Mar 1759, Amherst Papers, IV, Clements Library.
[20] Amherst to Governor James De Lancey, 8 June 1759, WO 34/30. Ibid., 8 July 1759.
[21] Amherst to Pitt, 19 June 1759, Kimball, II, 120–129. Amherst to De Lancey, 20 June 1759, WO 34/30. J. C. Webster (ed.), *The Journal of Jeffery Amherst* (Toronto, 1931), 112, 117.
[22] Webster (ed.), *Amherst Journal*, 132–139.
[23] Wolfe to Pitt, 6 June 1759, Kimball, II, 118–120.
[24] Fox to Marlborough, 12 April 1756, SP 44/189.
[25] An Act for the purchase of certain Lands etc., *Statutes at Large*, Ch XXXIX, 31 Geo. II.

assistant 'to teach the people...how to Load, Fire and Point the Guns'.[26]
How effective these makeshift works would prove seemed in doubt. Even
so, Ligonier did not consider a tour before the late summer to assess the
chances of repelling the invasion at its inception.

One reason for the delay may have been poor health. That his duties were
beginning to be too much for him is evidenced by his writing to the Earl
of Shaftesbury asking him if he had thanked him for some recent services.
Ligonier was unable to remember 'because of the multiplicity of business'.[27]
In these circumstances his inspection had to be leisurely, and each evening
the group amused themselves with whist and amateur theatricals. The trip
however was useful. Apart from inspecting the works, Ligonier visited
several encampments in Kent and Sussex to see the condition of the field
force.[28] All seemed in good array.

So far the further expansion of the army had been limited to an
augmentation of the Guards, while Ligonier evaluated the schemes agreed
at the ministerial meeting on 16 July. But further corps were not long in
being accepted, if only because of the needs of the army in Germany.[29] Lord
Aberdour was given permission to recruit a regiment of light dragoons from
the Scottish lowlands and another corps of Highlanders was to be raised
by Captain Morris for service in the Carnatic.[30] Then John Hale was named
colonel of a dragoon regiment. The terms agreed with Hale were typical
of those now being offered. He could name the officers but not promote them
above their present rank. No levy money was to be paid and the new corps
were to be ready in two months. On disbandment the officers would be
entitled to half pay.[31]

Similar plans were afoot in Ireland where the demand for men was
equally acute. Bedford reported to Pitt: 'I know of no other resource' for
making good the want of 1,600, 'but that of raising new corps, which can
only be effected by giving the nobility and gentry in this Kingdom the like
encouragements which have been given in Great Britain'. Whatever the
reservations of Ligonier, Bedford had no doubt as to the advantages of such
schemes, for the nobility were in a position 'to prevail on their tenants and
dependents to enter into the army and thereby bring into it a better class
and rank of people than would otherwise enlist'. Shortly afterwards he
gratefully accepted the plan of Sir Richard Gore and Richard Clements for
raising a corps of 900 protestant foot.[32]

[26] Estimate of the Charge of erecting Batteries to oppose an Enemy Landing, King's Mss
      70, f 81, BL.
[27] Ligonier to Shaftesbury, 15 Sept 1759, Ligonier Letter Book.
[28] Major Frederick Ramsden to Charles Hotham, 20 Oct 1759, Hotham Papers, DDHO
      4/10, East Riding Record Office.
[29] Calcraft to Amherst, 12 Oct 1759, WO 34/99.
[30] Barrington to Morris, 16 Oct 1759, WO 4/59. New Corps, 1759, *JHC*, xxviii, 646–651.
[31] Barrington to Hale, 17 Nov 1759, Add. Mss 32,898 ff 162–163.
[32] Bedford to Pitt, 1 Nov 1759, printed in Lord John Russell (ed.), *Correspondence of John, Fourth
      Duke of Bedford* (London, 1843), ii, 373–377. Bedford to Pitt, 5 Dec 1759, SP 63/416.

II

Though warlike activity predominated, peace and diplomacy were never entirely absent from the ministry's thoughts.

Since June the Prussian envoys in London had been intimating the desire of their master for an opening of talks. Frederick II was increasingly wearied by the attacks of the Austrians and Russians and saw negotiation as a means of escaping ruin.[33] The British ministers were divided on the question, being unsure to what extent the nation's objectives in North America had been attained. Pitt thought the present campaign must be completed before an honourable settlement could be secured. He was also anxious that there should be provision for any conquests made prior to the conclusion of the talks. But the question was one for all the ministers and for the moment he did not insist.[34] Though doubtful about the timing, he realized that it would be impolitic not to listen to the Prussian proposals. He also recognized that it would take time to get the combatants round the conference table. By then the military situation might have improved in Britain's favour.

On the question of peace, Pitt was less intransigent than has been supposed. In an interview with the Prussian envoys he revealed that he was still undecided about Louisburg, whether to keep it or hand it back demilitarized. He was equally flexible on the question of Quebec. The main object was to secure for Britain her original claims in North America to the Ohio, Great Lakes and the region of Crown Point. The one thing he insisted on was that the nation must not abandon its ally for short-term advantage. There must be no repetition of the charges about perfidious Albion, as on the signing of the Treaty of Utrecht.[35] He also ridiculed George II's idea of keeping everything, though his refusal to identify himself with the King may have stemmed from a realization that for George II no peace could be satisfactory without some compensation for Hanover.[36] On that point at least all the ministers agreed. It was inadmissible. Britain had spent millions of pounds and much blood to protect the Electorate. George II might make what charges he liked about ministerial ingratitude; they could not cede gains made elsewhere simply for his benefit.[37]

Serious discussion between the allies on the subject of peace therefore did not begin until the end of September, when Pitt, Holdernesse and Newcastle met Knyphausen and Michel in London. Even then there was little progress, for on the British side only Newcastle was wholeheartedly in favour of talks.

---

[33] Newcastle to Hardwicke, 3 June 1759, Add. Mss 32,891 ff 399–403.
[34] Newcastle to Hardwicke, 21 July 1759, Add. Mss 32,893 ff 189–192.
[35] Pitt to Mitchell, 12 June 1759, printed in W. S. Taylor and J. H. Pringle (eds.), *The Correspondence of William Pitt, Earl of Chatham* (London, 1838), I, 100–101.
[36] Newcastle to Hardwicke, 31 Oct 1759, Yorke, III, 241–242. Memorandum for the King, 28 Aug 1759, Add. Mss 32,894 f 499.
[37] Newcastle to Hardwicke, 16 Nov 1759, Add. Mss 32,898 ff 284–288. Newcastle to Hardwicke, 21 Nov 1759, Add. Mss 32,899 ff 5–7.

The Treasury was in the middle of another financial crisis, having £1,000,000 to meet anticipated demands of £2,000,000.[38] Accordingly, the only agreement was on the mode of procedure. Holdernesse was to write to Prince Lewis of Brunswick, the Dutch regent, asking him if he would issue a formal invitation to the belligerent powers to attend a congress at Augsburg.[39]

On the battle front there was for the moment a lull. Hawke continued the vigil off Brest, even though the beer from Plymouth had not improved.[40] Fortunately, Anson and the victualling authorities were alive to the problem and arrangements were being made to send a supply from the other ports.[41] In addition, Pett was arranging for the hire of larger transports to meet the adverse conditions.[42] The value of victualling at sea was later commented on by Lind: 'It was hardly ever known before that ships could cruize in the Bay of Biscay much above three or four months without suffering from the scurvy.' Now, after six months, 14,000 men were enjoying a better state of health than the like number anywhere in the world.[43] As a consequence there had been no weakening of the blockade.

Nevertheless, it was no time for complacency, for news now arrived that Thurot had escaped from Dunkirk with 1,500 men on board, while at the Morbihan all attempts to attack the transports had proved unavailing.[44] A principal reason for this had been the lack of knowledge about the navigation.[45] This led Anson and the Admiralty to undertake something that had long been overdue, a systematic charting of the French coast. As their circular of 27 October 1759 admitted: 'The King's Service has suffered very much during this war for want of due information and knowledge of harbours, roads and accessible places on the coast of France.' In future, each captain or master was to keep a book of sketches with pertinent hydrographical information. Anyone failing to do this was to have his pay docked.[46]

Disappointment was seemingly in prospect in America too, for the next letter from Wolfe reeked of stalemate and despondency.[47] Initially the expedition had gone well. The navigation of the St Lawrence had proved relatively easy and Saunders had accompanied the flotilla on the entire journey with most of his ships. A landing had been effected on Orleans

[38] Treasury Board Minute, 31 July 1759, T 39/33. Memorandum for the King, 28 Aug 1759, Add. Mss 32,894 f 496.
[39] Holdernesse to Prince Lewis of Holland, 30 Oct 1759, SP 84/486.
[40] Hawke to Clevland, 1 Oct 1759, Adm 1/92.
[41] Victualling Board to Clevland, 31 Oct 1759, Adm 110/19.
[42] Admiralty to the Victualling Board, 22 Oct 1759, Adm 2/83.
[43] C. Lloyd (ed.), *The Health of Seamen: Selections from the Works of Dr James Lind, Sir Gilbert Blane and Dr Thomas Trotter*, Navy Records Society Publications, cvii (London, 1965), 121.
[44] Newcastle to Devonshire, 18 Oct 1759, Add. Mss 32,897 ff 199–201.
[45] Duff to Hawke, 18 Oct 1759, Adm 1/92.
[46] Admiralty to all Captains, 27 Oct 1759, Adm 2/83.
[47] Wolfe to Pitt, 2 Sept 1759, Kimball, ii, 149–158.

and possession taken of nearby Point Levis and the east bank of the Montmorency river. However, as Mackellar had warned, a landing on the north shore in the vicinity of Quebec had proved difficult. The enemy had entrenched from the city past the village of Beauport to the Falls of Montmorency, and everywhere the water was too shallow for the warships to support an engagement.

Most of July was accordingly spent considering alternatively an attack above or below the town. In the end, Wolfe had determined to attempt the French positions opposite his own camp at Montmorency: unfortunately, his plans had gone awry. The initial attempt to possess two redoubts had proved unavailing. Then the forces coming from across the St Lawrence had hit a sandbank while the grenadiers, instead of waiting for the main body, had rushed ahead and been repulsed. With the tide turning Wolfe had had to abandon the attack.[48]

Despite this, Wolfe was confident that his general scheme had been right. However, towards the end of August he contracted a fever and had to ask his senior officers to consider the situation. The brigadiers – with Saunders – were unanimous that as a considerable number of ships had now run the gauntlet past Quebec's batteries, the army should transfer its operations above the town so as to come between the enemy and their supplies in the interior.[49] Wolfe necessarily had to agree, though he had little confidence in the plan. Indeed, he confessed to Pitt: 'There is such a choice of difficultys that I own myself at a loss how to determine'.[50]

This was the gloomy picture that the ministers received at the beginning of October, giving little prospect of a final success, unless Amherst could get through.[51] The surprise was all the greater, therefore, when two days later dispatches arrived announcing the fall of Quebec, though at the cost of Wolfe's life. The initial attempt to land above the town had been thwarted by bad weather and high tides.[52] However, in the interval Wolfe had found another site closer to Quebec, called the Anse du Foulon, where a path traversed the steep cliffs along this part of the river.[53] Despite the risk of detection the army had scrambled ashore early on 13 September and established itself on the cliffs above.[54]

[48] Ibid., 152–155.
[49] At a Council of War, 29 Aug 1759, Diary and Papers of an Officer with the Expedition, DOD/678, Public Record Office of Northern Ireland. C. V. F. Townshend, *The Military Life of Field Marshal George First Marquis Townshend, 1724–1807* (London, 1901), 60–67.
[50] Wolfe to Pitt, 2 Sept 1759, Kimball, II, 158.
[51] Saunders to Clevland, 5 Sept 1759, Adm 1/482.
[52] The *Sutherland* off Cape Rouge, 8–9 Sept 1759, printed in *The Northcliffe Collection: Papers presented to the Government of Canada by Sir Leicester Harmsworth* (Toronto, 1926), 163–164.
[53] Journal of General George Townshend, 10 Sept 1759, printed in A. Doughty and G. W. Parmelee (eds.), *The Siege of Quebec and the Battle of the Plains of Abraham* (Quebec, 1901), V, 266–267.
[54] Townshend's Rough Notes, 13 Sept 1759, printed in the *Northcliffe Collection*, 424. Journal of Patrick Mackellar, 13 Sept 1759, printed in Doughty and Parmelee (eds.), *Siege of Quebec*, V, 50–54.

Although the two armies had been numerically equal in the subsequent battle, the entire British force was composed of regulars, whereas much of Montcalm's army was made up of militia and Indians.[55] These had quickly broken and run when confronted by the redcoats. It was at this moment that Wolfe was killed, otherwise the victory would have been complete, for by the time Townshend had taken charge, another detachment of the French army had appeared under Louis Bougainville from the west, thus necessitating a redeployment. In the event Bougainville had made no attempt to attack, once he realized that the battle was lost.[56]

Townshend apologized to Pitt for not having engaged Bougainville, but was quickly vindicated.[57] The army was now before Quebec on its weakest side. Montcalm had been mortally wounded and the French army, temporarily under the command of the governor, was in precipitate retreat, leaving the city to its fate. Not surprisingly, the commander of the garrison had four days later intimated a desire for terms.[58]

The victory had in fact been a close thing. At the Heights of Abraham, Wolfe gambled everything on a last throw. The chances of success were slim, not least because the lateness of the season made even success on the battlefield inconsequential without a place to winter in. On the other hand he had been proved right not to wait for Amherst, for the Commander-in-Chief was not destined to get to the St Lawrence this year. Just before the capture of Ticonderoga, Amherst had dispatched Brigadier Thomas Gage to complete the siege of Niagara as the prelude to an advance down the St Lawrence from the west.[59] Unfortunately, Gage found that the supply services were not sufficient to support an initiative in that region.[60] Then Amherst made a further miscalculation, this time over the French naval strength on Lake Champlain. A superiority here was essential if the army was to progress to the enemy position at the Isle aux Noix. Amherst had twice to increase his force on receiving news of the French strength. The second augmentation was only decided on 3 September with the result that one of the vessels, a sixteen-gun sloop, was not finished before 1 October. The French vessels still had to be destroyed; the first frosts had been experienced; and Amherst's provincial troops were getting homesick. With an ever-lengthening supply line and little prospect of joining Wolfe, Amherst had no choice but to end the campaign, which he did on 19 October.[61] Hence another offensive would be necessary if the conquest of Canada was to be completed.

The near failure of Wolfe and non-completion of the campaign was

[55] C. P. Stacey, *Quebec, 1759* (Toronto, 1959), 81–84.
[56] Townshend to Pitt, 20 Sept 1759, Kimball, II, 164–169. Stacey, *Quebec*, 150–151.
[57] Townshend to Pitt, 20 Sept 1759, Kimball, II, 167–168.
[58] Stacey, *Quebec*, 156–158.
[59] Amherst to Gage, 28 July 1759, Amherst Papers, IV, Clements Library.
[60] Amherst to Pitt, 22 Oct 1759, Kimball, II, 196.   [61] Ibid., 186–202.

naturally overlooked in the chorus of acclaim which followed the fall of Quebec. Everyone was quick to acknowledge Wolfe's achievement and the heroic manner of his death. The ministry responded by announcing a public funeral in Westminster Abbey. Among all the encomiums it was noticed that Wolfe's colleagues had not joined in the praise of the deceased man. Indeed, Townshend's letter to Pitt was implicitly critical. But, however justified, Townshend was savagely condemned in the press for wanting to carry off the laurels himself, though Pitt paid tribute to his services and those of the other brigadiers.[62]

III

Wolfe's success arrived regrettably at a time when the ministry was threatened by a dispute over patronage.

Although Temple's comment that Pitt was the 'Minister of Measures' and Newcastle the 'Minister of Numbers' is a gross oversimplification, it is true that until the autumn of 1758 Pitt himself had shown little interest in the subject of promotions and management.[63] On occasion he even allowed Newcastle to recommend men to his own department, especially if he was prepared to endure the tedium of getting the King's permission. Nevertheless, Pitt could not but at times be irritated at the extent of Newcastle's influence. Early in January 1758 he petulantly complained how he had had to tell a 'Doctor Morton who came to him about the Deanery of Chester, that he had no credit in those things, that he must get himself recommended to the Duke of Newcastle'.[64] But Pitt had only himself to blame for this situation, which stemmed from an unreadiness to interest himself in the details of patronage. He could have no complaint against the Treasury. Newcastle studiously mentioned all the more important requests and promotions to him. Even for appointments to his own Board, Newcastle consulted Pitt, as happened in 1759 when he wanted to bring in his nephew, Lord North, to strengthen the membership.[65]

Despite these efforts, Pitt and Temple were now to be at the centre of a dispute that for a moment threatened the existence of the government. The discord arose out of a request by Temple to be made a Knight of the Garter. Since the formation of the ministry, Temple had been ignored even by Pitt once his position was secure. He may thus have been ready to

---

[62] Walpole, *Memoirs of George II*, III, 229–230.
[63] Temple to Wilkes, 16 Oct 1759, printed in W. J. Smith (ed.), *The Grenville Papers: Being the Correspondence of Richard Grenville, Earl Temple K.G., and the Right Honourable George Grenville, Their Friends and Contemporaries* (London, 1852), I, 405–406. According to Walpole, Pitt repeated these sentiments in Parliament at the end of 1761, when he said of the previous ministry that 'he had borrowed their majority to carry on their own plan', *Memoirs of the Reign of King George III* (London, 1894), I, 82–83.
[64] Newcastle to Hardwicke, 3 Jan 1758, Yorke, III, 40.
[65] Newcastle to Pitt, 24 May 1759, Add. Mss 32,891 f 271.

humour Temple because of his own neglect of him. Another reason may have been earlier newspaper articles suggesting Pitt might be replaced.[66] The bestowal of such a prestigious award would help stifle such rumours.

Membership of this exclusive order was in theory at the invitation of the monarch. However, the usual procedure was for prospective candidates to get the First Lord of the Treasury to submit their names to the King. The first intimation of Temple's interest was displayed in September 1758. Newcastle, knowing the King's dislike of him, prevaricated, pointing out that Prince Ferdinand could not be overlooked much longer. Others in the running for the two unfilled places included the Marquis of Rockingham, the Earl of Halifax, Lord Bristol and Holdernesse.[67] There for the moment the matter rested, though Newcastle was privately informed that Temple had by no means given up his claim. Unless he was gratified there would be trouble.[68] These threats do not seem to have worried Newcastle. When news was received of Ferdinand's victory at Minden in August 1759, the problem of who would fill the other vacancy did not seemingly cross his mind.

If Newcastle thought he could simply ignore the matter he was in for a shock. At the end of August, Pitt began to mutter ominously about the failure to gratify Temple and the lack of attention to his own requests. He could not even secure the appointment of a customs officer: he would not stay on this footing.[69] In an interview on 21 September, he good-humouredly told Newcastle that the securing of the Garter would settle everything. Pitt himself had no desire to interfere in patronage or the management of the Commons: all that he left to Newcastle. But he must have some public mark of the King's confidence, which could be best effected by giving Temple the Garter. Unless this were done he would confine himself to his own department, stop coming to court and generally cease being a member of the administration in a meaningful sense. Though very civil, Pitt was, as Newcastle noted, extremely determined. So too was the King.[70] On renewing Temple's application for a Garter, George II categorically told Newcastle that he would not accede to the request, for 'my Lord Temple had insulted him'. The King several times acknowledged that he might be forced, but he had one important advantage in this war of nerves. He was well aware that what Pitt 'wanted was the Garter given not taken; that if it came by force, it wanted the only merit of it, viz; the mark of His Majesty's approbation'.[71] He determined accordingly to remain obdurate.

[66] *London Chronicle*, 7/9 Nov 1758. Ibid., 3/5 May 1759.
[67] Temple to Newcastle, 19 Sept 1758, Add. Mss 32,884 f 71. Newcastle to Temple, 28 Sept 1758, Add. Mss 32,884 ff 181–183.
[68] Memorandum of a Conversation with Count Viry, 16 Mar 1759, Add. Mss 32,889 ff 110–112.
[69] Memorandum for the King, 9 Sept 1759, Add. Mss 32,895 ff 288–290.
[70] Memorandum, 21 Sept 1759, Add. Mss 32,896 f 21.
[71] Newcastle to Hardwicke, 27 Sept 1759, Yorke, III, 60–63.

For Newcastle the crisis was very real. The stability of the administration was at stake. As he reminded George II, Pitt might vent his anger by attacking the Treasury in the Commons. He would certainly press his quarrel with Legge, perhaps forcing the Chancellor to resign. If that happened George Grenville might succeed him. Newcastle melodramatically predicted: 'Pitt had the Foreign Affairs, he was meddling with the Army every day, he would then have the Treasury also.' Endless scope for mischief existed and all because of the Garter.[72]

In the event Pitt chose to make trouble in another direction. Since his days as Secretary of State, Newcastle had corresponded with Yorke and a number of other ambassadors abroad, as was well known. Indeed, Newcastle claimed to have the King's permission, so that it was not unconstitutional, despite the convention of departmental responsibility. The correspondence was in any case fairly personal and not intended to infringe the duties of either Secretary. When one of the Dutch ministers sought to involve him in the maritime disputes, Newcastle replied: 'You know very well it is not my province to enter into these matters. The Secretary of State is the only person who does and can send the King's orders to His Majesty's minister at the Hague.'[73] However, by the autumn of 1759 neither Secretary was prepared to be so tolerant of the matter. Pitt was angry with Newcastle for his failure to secure Temple his Garter. Holdernesse was increasingly resentful at the snubs he had of late received from Newcastle. The opportunity to make trouble occurred late in September 1759, when Yorke casually informed Newcastle that he had been approached by a mysterious lady concerning the possibility of peace with the French. Since this *Dame Inconnue* appeared to have no authority of any kind, Yorke did not inform Holdernesse, merely sending the details to Newcastle 'for his amusement' and that of the King.[74]

Unluckily for Yorke, details of the affair reached Holdernesse who promptly informed Pitt. The latter was determined not to let so useful an opportunity pass. He wrote to Newcastle reminding him that it was the indispensable 'right of a Secretary of State to be informed instantly of every transaction of this nature'. Otherwise, 'the King's service and the public good must be essentially and incurably prejudiced'. Pitt had to admit: 'I know not how far your Grace may have had the King's orders for this clandestine proceeding.' But, even if authorized, it created such an intolerable situation that Pitt of necessity would have to resign.[75] When Newcastle tried to make light of the whole affair, Pitt affected to be even more enraged.[76]

[72] Newcastle to Mansfield, 3 Sept 1759, Add. Mss 32,895 ff 145–146.
[73] Newcastle to William Bentinck, 29 June 1759, Add. Mss 32,892 ff 299–304.
[74] Yorke to Newcastle, 9 Oct 1759, Yorke, III, 65.
[75] Pitt to Newcastle, 23 Oct 1759, Yorke, III, 68.
[76] Pitt to Newcastle, 23 Oct 1759, Yorke, III, 69–70.

Holdernesse simultaneously vented his spleen on Yorke. He commented: 'An irregular correspondence of this kind must create confusion in business and uneasiness to those who carry it on.' To punish the envoy for his transgression, Holdernesse proposed to exclude him from participation in the Anglo-Prussian peace initiative, now being aired at the Hague, an unparalleled snub.[77] The northern Secretary had long resented the correspondence between Newcastle and Yorke as a reflection of his own impotence. Here was a chance to demonstrate to everyone the penalties for not confiding in their superior.

But the real cause of Pitt's displeasure had not escaped Newcastle. As he explained to George II: 'It is not Yorke's correspondence that is the point; it is, Sir, another object which has been refused and thus it will be, now and then one thing, now and then another, if his great objective is not attained.'[78]

Despite this shrewd analysis, George II refused to listen, even though it was a most inopportune time for a ministerial crisis. In spite of the recent successes at Guadeloupe, Minden and Lagos, the situation overseas remained critical. The King of Prussia had been defeated at Kunersdorf. The French were still apparently bent on an invasion. And at home the Bank of England once again would not raise the vote of credit to help the Exchequer out of its difficulties. Lord Dupplin believed that George II was deliberately provoking a crisis to be rid of Pitt. The King had recently learnt that his Secretary of State would never agree to territorial concessions for Hanover in any future peace.[79] Throughout October the threats and refusals continued to be exchanged, with the unhappy Newcastle caught in the middle. Then on 14 November Temple broke the deadlock by resigning his position of Lord Privy Seal.[80] Suddenly the King awoke to the danger confronting him; after one further attempt to extract concessions on Hanover, he gave way. Temple should receive his Garter.[81]

The resolution of Temple's affair was fortunate, for, unknown to the ministers, that day the French fleet had put to sea. Several reasons prompted the Marquis de Conflans to sail at this moment. A few days earlier a fierce westerly gale had forced Hawke off his station. The French commander assumed that the British had finally had to return to port, as all previous such fleets. Equally important, the same gale brought into Brest the French West Indian squadron of Admiral Bompart, giving Conflans much-needed reserves of men and materials.[82] But Choiseul and the French court were

[77] Holdernesse to Yorke, 2 Nov 1759, Yorke, III, 83. Hardwicke to Newcastle, 24 Oct 1759, Yorke, III, 71–72.

[78] Newcastle to Hardwicke, 25 Oct 1759, Yorke, III, 73.

[79] Kinnoull to Hardwicke, 30 Oct 1759, Add. Mss 32,897 ff 500–503.

[80] Newcastle to Hardwicke, 14 Nov 1759, Add. Mss 32,898 ff 249–250.

[81] Newcastle to Hardwicke, 16 Nov 1759, Add. Mss 32,898 ff 284–290.

[82] R. Waddington, *La Guerre de Sept Ans* (Paris, 1899), III, 368.

also urging that he do something to rectify France's miserable situation. The first part of the invasion at least ought to be attempted: Conflans should head for the Morbihan, pick up the transports and sail for Scotland via the west coast of Ireland. Clearly the time was opportune, with the British fleet absent and an engagement seemingly unnecessary for the accomplishment of this plan.[83]

Unfortunately the situation was not as Conflans thought. The good condition of Hawke's crews and partial rotation of the ships meant that the British had merely gone to shelter in Torbay. When news of Conflans's escape with eighteen ships of the line arrived, Hawke was then in Plymouth Sound, battling his way back down the Channel. Although Admiral Geary had taken some vessels in for repair, Hawke still had twenty-three battleships. Of the result of a meeting with the French he had no doubt.[84]

The news of Conflans's escape caused excitement ashore. Anson had additional workmen rushed to Portsmouth and Plymouth so that every vessel was ready for sea.[85] Nevertheless, behind all the bustle the ministry was quietly confident of victory. Newcastle asserted to Bedford: 'It is thought almost impossible that Mr Conflans should escape from Sir Edward Hawke.' He continued: 'As to fighting him, which is given out by the French, my Lord Anson treats that as the idlest of all notions.'[86] This confidence increased, and with reason, as Newcastle shortly informed Yorke. Not only had Geary got back to sea, but the 'brave and judicious Admiral Saunders' with the North American fleet had arrived to join him. A massive force was gathering in the Bay of Biscay ready to give the '*Coup de Grace* to the French Marine'. Following the victories at Lagos, Minden and Quebec, this would truly be a glorious ending to the year.[87]

These expectations did not go unrewarded. Although Conflans had two days start on Hawke, the poor state of his crews and variable weather meant that by the evening of 19 November the two fleets were a mere 25 leagues apart just west of Belleisle. Early next morning they were not long in sighting each other. Conflans thereupon decided to continue for Quiberon Bay. He reasoned that Hawke would not dare enter its rocky waters in such blustery conditions. But the French Admiral had mistaken the character of the man now opposed to him. Hawke had spent four years waiting for such an opportunity and he was not about to allow the uncertainties of the navigation to deflect him from his chance. Moreover, Conflans found that having sailed into Quiberon, he did not have room to make an orderly turn.

[83] G. Lacour-Gayet, *La Marine Militaire de la France sous le Règne de Louis XV* (Paris, 1902), 325–329.
[84] Hawke to Clevland, 17 Nov 1759, Adm 1/92. Hawke to Geary, 17 Nov 1759, HWK/IX, NMM.
[85] Admiralty to Admiral Holburne, 19 Nov 1759, Adm 2/84. Admiralty to Commodore Hanway, 19 Nov 1759, Adm 2/84. Navy Board Minute, 22 Nov 1759, Adm 106/2570.
[86] Newcastle to Bedford, 18 Nov 1759, Add. Mss 32,898 ff 339–340.
[87] Newcastle to Yorke, 23 Nov 1759, Add. Mss 32,899 ff 50–51.

As a result his vessels became hopelessly tangled, both with themselves and with the British now pressing into the Bay. As the winter darkness increased, the engagement became a confused mêlée with both fleets fighting to destroy each other while trying to avoid disaster on the surrounding shoals.[88]

In this confusion the superior seamanship and determination of the British proved decisive. By 4.00 o'clock the first successes were being registered, three of them by ships of seventy-four guns, a testimony to their design and Anson's building programme.[89] Unfortunately, for the British, firing then had to stop because of darkness.[90]

The outcome at this point was still not clear, whatever historians have suggested. The British had to ensure that the action did not end on the rocks. When dawn came it brought first relief, then surprise, ultimately disappointment. The relief came in the realization that all but one of their vessels were safe. The surprise was the discovery that Conflans's flagship was anchored in their midst. The disappointment came with the recognition that except for the four vessels already taken, the remainder had escaped into the River Vilaine or got to sea. Better knowledge of the navigation had assisted the French in this respect.

Though Conflans's flagship was duly attacked and destroyed, a second British vessel was lost in the process. Consequently, when Hawke sat down on 22 November to write his report to Anson, his tone was distinctly apologetic. The score so far as Hawke knew was five enemy ships captured or sunk for the loss of two of his own. Knowledge that a sixth had foundered near the mouth of the Loire would have been some but not much consolation, for Hawke was greatly distressed by the escape of the rest. The reason for this disappointing result was clear: 'In attacking a flying enemy it was impossible in the space of a short winter's day that all our ships should be able to get into action.' Otherwise the whole French fleet must have been 'destroyed or taken'.[91]

Still caught in the turmoil of the action, Hawke was unable to be objective. But if he had doubts as to the achievement of the fleet, this was not the case with the Admiralty or the public. Parliament and the nation demonstrated their joy by voting their thanks to the Admiral and his brave crews.[92] While Hawke measured his success solely by the ships taken or destroyed, the public noted that not only had the French fleet been dealt a severe blow, the threat of invasion was also no more. The year of victories was truly ending on a successful note. As Hawke came to appreciate, the damage inflicted on the French was greater than he initially supposed. The enemy had saved seven of their vessels only by immobilizing them in the

[88] Conflans to Monsieur Berryer, 24 Nov 1759, printed in M. Le Comte de Lapeyrouse Bonfils, *Histoire de la Marine Française* (Paris, 1845), II, 470–476.

[89] The British 74s were the *Magnanime, Torbay* and *Resolution*; their captures, the *Héros, Thésée* and *Formidable*.

[90] Hawke to Clevland, 24 Nov 1759, Adm 1/92.

[91] Ibid.   [92] Walpole, *Memoirs of King George II*, III, 237–238.

Vilaine. Although the rest of the fleet escaped to Rochefort, the once mighty Brest squadron was hopelessly scattered. Moreover, unknown to Hawke and the public, this latest disaster strengthened those persons in the French government who wanted to concentrate on the struggle in Germany. For the rest of the war, the French made no further effort with their navy. Although the occasional squadron was fitted out, British control of the sea was not challenged again.[93] As a result, when Spain came into the war the French were unable to exploit the potential advantages of the new alliance. This was the true measure of what had been accomplished on 20 November.

None of this would have been possible but for Anson's perseverance with the western squadron. The success at Quiberon was a vindication of his policy. Nevertheless, until 1759 the operation of the squadron had been too spasmodic. Only after improvements had been made to the victualling and types of ships in service had victory come. In the development of the blockade itself Hawke was guided by no strategic theory. His action was a pragmatic response to a specific problem. Nothing better illustrates the eighteenth-century approach to such matters. The results were nonetheless dramatic. Until 1759 the fleet was rarely able to stay out for more than a few weeks before sickness, lack of victuals or leaking ships necessitated a return to port. By November 1759 Hawke's fleet had been almost continuously at sea for six months, though much still remained to be done if the new capability of the navy was to be fully realized.

Inside the ministry the readiness of George II to give Temple the Garter had led to a dramatic change of atmosphere. Within days Newcastle was able to report to Yorke: 'All ill humour is removed; my Lord Temple and Mr Pitt are in the best disposition imaginable.' Pitt was now treating the matter of the *Dame Inconnue* as the 'slightest thing in the world'. Even Legge had given up the idea of resigning.[94] To cement the union, Newcastle shortly afterwards suggested that Temple ought in future to be 'informed of every branch of the King's business' like the other ministers, through the circulation of the departmental papers and summons to the meetings.[95]

The only casualty in this affair was seemingly Holdernesse, for, once Pitt had obtained his objective, he was quick to disclaim any connection with his fellow Secretary. He told Newcastle: 'We live civilly together', but added: 'I have avoided anything further, even to see his letters before they are produced at the meetings.'[96] As a result, when Holdernesse drafted his invitation to Prince Lewis to initiate talks, the ministers agreed that Yorke should be fully informed of the letter and be named one of the plenipotentiaries to the congress at Augsburg.[97] The northern Secretary's mortification was complete.

[93] Lacour-Gayet, *Marine Militaire*, 342–356. Waddington, *Guerre de Sept Ans*, III, 374–379.
[94] Newcastle to Yorke, 20 Nov 1759, Yorke, III, 97–100.
[95] Newcastle to Pitt, 7 Dec 1759, Add. Mss 32,899 ff 362–364.
[96] Newcastle to Hardwicke, 21 Nov 1759, Add. Mss 32,899 ff 5–7.
[97] Newcastle to Hardwicke, 20 Nov 1759, Yorke, III, 95–96.

Newcastle was naturally delighted, commenting to Hardwicke that Holdernesse 'looks like what he is, and every day makes the Mean Figure, to see Mr Pitt and me settling everything and he either in that or the next room, no more informed than a page of the backstairs'.[98] Soon he was talking of the need to replace Holdernesse, but in this he found little support from Pitt. The southern Secretary had no desire to replace a colleague he could dominate for one he perhaps could not. The plan was accordingly not encouraged. But it was doubtful whether Holdernesse could recover from this affront to his authority, even though he shortly tried to buttress his position by courting the favour of Leicester House.

So ended what is customarily called the year of victories. Traditional accounts, based on Horace Walpole, have given the impression that under Pitt's leadership success was almost pre-ordained. That except for the fussy and timorous Newcastle, the nation sat back confident of victory. However, as the last two chapters have tried to show, this was not the case. The ministry had worries until almost the last. The desperate plight of Prussia, the defenceless state of Ireland, uncertainties over the naval campaign, the probability of a setback in America and the financial stringencies all seemed to presage disaster. Only afterwards was it discovered that the church bells were in Walpole's words, 'threadbare with ringing for victory'.[99] Only then did contemporaries realize what a remarkable year it had been.

---

[98] Newcastle to Hardwicke, 17 Dec 1759, Add. Mss 32,900 ff 120–122.

[99] The phrase was used by Walpole in a letter to George Montagu, 21 Oct 1759, P. Toynbee (ed.), *The Letters of Horace Walpole, Fourth Earl of Oxford* (Oxford, 1903), IV, 314. Walpole affected a flippant attitude throughout the crisis. In this he was very much the exception. See the coverage given by papers like the *London Chronicle*.

6

Consolidation

The victories of 1759 meant that Britain's war aims were now achieved. The conflict therefore was entering a new phase in which the momentum of victory had to be sustained until a satisfactory peace could be arranged. This would clearly be no easy matter, for the enemy first had to be convinced of the need for a settlement. Even Pitt confessed the making of a peace to be a daunting prospect.[1]

Parliament meanwhile had met to deliberate on yet another royal speech drafted by Hardwicke. Despite the internal wrangling, adumbrating the speech had not proved difficult. The objects of the war had not changed, even if its fortunes had. The first part of the speech was accordingly little more than a recital of the recent successes at Quebec, Lagos and Minden. The second half mentioned, for the first time, peace and the desire of the King 'to see a stop put to the Effusion of Christian Blood'. But Hardwicke did not elucidate what constituted a 'just and honourable' settlement, except that it must have the consent of the nation's allies and provide for the security of her dominions. The truth was that the administration had still no clear ideas on the subject beyond the need for a satisfactory settlement in North America, the return of Minorca and the evacuation of Hanover.[2]

Pitt was now intimating to Newcastle that he was ready to go on in a different fashion than before. Like all the ministers he was delighted at the recent successes, for which he could claim much of the credit. It was time to relax and be more considerate of the hardworking if maladroit First Lord, whom he had often treated as little more than a verbal punchbag for relieving his own frustrations and humours, themselves the product of a continuing ill health. Ministerial quarrels could only be to the advantage of Bute and others inimical to the government. Moreover, the nation was united as never before: even the *Monitor*, the most patriotic of the Tory

---

[1] H. Walpole, *Memoirs of the Reign of King George II* (London, 1846–47), III, 226.
[2] Newcastle to Hardwicke, 6 Nov 1759, Add. Mss 32,898 ff 143–144. *JHC*, xxviii, 628–629.

papers, supported the German war in the belief that it really did distract the French from the protection of their colonial interests.[3]

The first sign of Pitt's new humour came during the debate on the Address to the Speech. For once he was generous in his praise of others. He acknowledged that when he had first come into the administration he 'had found America the first object'. He had not been alone in advising the King thereon. As to the future 'he thought to pursue the war in all parts was the only way to procure a safe and honourable peace', since the least omission 'might be fatal to the whole'. He then praised the King of Prussia, without whom nothing could have been done, and pronounced himself in favour of reinforcing Prince Ferdinand. Though public credit was a tender plant, he affected to believe the nation could fight on for several more years. But he assured his listeners they were in the position of a man who had almost rolled a large stone to the top of a hill: one more push and the job was done.[4]

This was the first time he had suggested that the overseas and continental theatres of the war were linked or that his operations had been anything other than a series of *ad hoc* blows. These views were only fully developed after he left office when, in a Commons' debate in November 1761, he declared: 'Had the armies of France not been employed in Germany, they would have been transported to America... America had been conquered in Germany.' Such statements were mere rationalizations after the event.[5]

Nevertheless, Newcastle and the other ministers could not but be pleased at these sentiments of Pitt. While disagreeing on the extent of the nation's financial strength, Newcastle was delighted with Pitt's wholehearted support for all the theatres of the war, especially for Germany. Even on the financial condition of the country, the two men were not so far apart. Following the recent victories, money had again become plentiful if not cheap. Newcastle agreed with Pitt. It was time for pushing on with the war: 'Expense now may secure us such a Peace as may put us above danger for some years.'[6]

The general satisfaction was reflected in the conduct of business in Parliament. All the estimates were received with minimal questioning, and it seemed that the nation was ready to accept any burden.[7]

The spirit of co-operation was reflected in one of the last meetings of this memorable year of 1759 when the ministers gathered to consider an offer of mediation from the Spanish court, plus a request from Ferdinand for a reinforcement. On both subjects there was complete harmony. The Spanish proposal was deemed improper and rejected, though in a conciliatory

---

[3] From the Monitor, *London Chronicle*, 20/22 Sept 1759.
[4] Mr West's Account of what happened in the House, 13 Nov 1759, Add. Mss 32,898 ff 223–224.
[5] H. Walpole, *Memoirs of the Reign of King George III* (London, 1894), I, 76.
[6] Newcastle to Yorke, 25 Dec 1759, Add. Mss 32,900 ff 312–315.
[7] Newcastle to Page, 27 Dec 1759, Add. Mss 32,900 ff 357–358.

fashion, to keep Spain out of the war. Regarding Ferdinand's request, no detachments from home could be presently sent, for an invasion was still a possibility in 1760. However, the ministers, led by Pitt, quickly decided to secure an additional 7,000 men from Hanover, Brunswick and Hesse.[8]

The benign attitude to the war in Germany was reflected in the lack of ministerial protest when Ferdinand sent a detachment to assist the King of Prussia in Saxony. He did this without consulting either George II or his Hanoverian ministers. The decision might have had serious consequences, bringing British and Hanoverian troops into conflict with the Austrians, with whom neither country was technically at war. But for the moment the Prince could do no wrong.[9]

In previous years, December had been a time of planning and preparation for the next campaign in America. This time there was less to do. Although the conquest had not been completed it was accepted that Montreal ought to be taken and would soon fall. Amherst might not be the most dashing general, but everyone appreciated his thoroughness and judgement, which were the only qualities that could bring lasting success. The conduct of the campaign was therefore left to him. He could proceed with one army or several, a latitude that had been denied to either Loudoun or Abercromby. The ministry did no more than lay down Montreal as the objective and set 1 May as the date on which the campaign should begin.[10] The provincial governors were given similar instructions and promises of reimbursement, as in 1759. The one thing that Pitt did insist was that they were not to weaken in their efforts by thoughts of peace.[11]

Naval affairs, however, did require attention. In the aftermath of the battle of Quiberon Bay, Hawke had instituted a close watch on the French vessels in the River Vilaine, with a separate squadron under Keppel to observe those at Rochefort.[12] However, recent reports made it clear that the ships with Hawke were in a poor condition after almost seven months at sea. Some replacement or alternative plan was necessary if the watch was to be maintained.[13]

Anson accordingly requested a meeting of the ministers for the night of Monday 31 December, when he outlined his plans for the dispatch of a relief squadron under Boscawen. Newcastle mistakenly thought the purpose of the meeting was 'to settle the general disposition of the fleet for the ensuing year'. He was hoping that a decision might at last be taken about a Baltic

---

[8] Memorandum on the state of affairs, 10 Dec 1759, DPC. Newcastle to Yorke, 14 Dec 1759, Add. Mss 32,900 ff 70–74. For the Spanish negotiations, see below, pp. 160–161.

[9] Newcastle to Yorke, 18 Dec 1759, Add. Mss 32,900 ff 151–154. According to P. Mackesy, *The Coward of Minden: The Affair of Lord George Sackville* (London, 1979), 50, authority had been given to a similar operation the previous year.

[10] Pitt to Amherst, 7 Jan 1760, Kimball, II, 237–242.

[11] Pitt to the Colonial Governors, 7 Jan 1760, Kimball, II, 234–237.

[12] Hawke to Clevland, 9 Dec 1759, Adm 1/92.   [13] Ibid., 19 Dec 1759.

squadron for the King of Prussia.[14] He was soon disabused of the idea. A new ruler had come to the Spanish throne and there could be no such extension of the navy's commitments while his intentions were unclear.[15] Nevertheless, the general state of the fleet could not but impress the ministers. Anson shortly expected to have 73 ships of the line ready for service at home, in addition to those still overseas. Indeed, the naval estimate was for 301 ships manned by 85,000 seamen, a reflection of the tremendous efforts of the previous year.[16]

The orders to Boscawen were to keep a diligent watch on the enemy in Quiberon and to use his 'utmost endeavours to prevent their joining each other or getting to sea separately with any number of Transports'. Because of the latent fears of invasion Boscawen was to 'keep a lookout for the ships expected from Cadiz', and to prevent supplies from reaching the French fleet. In the execution of these tasks Boscawen was left to decide where to station his ships.[17] In the event he followed the dispositions of Hawke, placing part of his fleet in Quiberon and the remainder in Basque Road, except for some cruisers at Brest and the other west coast ports.[18]

The main task of the ministry in the new year seemed likely to be the recruitment of the army. The estimates presented by Barrington to Parliament for 1760 were for an army of 109,000 men, an increase of 18,000 on the previous year, the largest rise of the war. The number of foreign troops in British pay was also a record at 65,470, making a grand total of 174,000.[19] Even so, none of these men would be surplus. After the disappointments of 1759 the French were certain to renew their effort in Germany as the best means of improving their position. They were likely to be encouraged in this by the desperate condition of Prussia. Frederick II doubted if he could field more than 100,000 men to face the combined Austrian and Russian forces of 230,000. The situation was not hopeless. The Russians were apparently concerned at their previous losses, attributing them in part to a lack of assistance from the Austrians. This year they would not move before their allies had committed themselves.[20]

There was also the possibility of peace, though the hopes for a successful outcome to the talks at Augsburg were not high. While the Austrians had a chance of destroying Prussia it was likely that they would fight, not talk. The chances of separate negotiations with France were better, but there was no guarantee of any settlement.

[14] Newcastle to Hardwicke, 29 Dec 1759, Add. Mss 32,900 ff 399–406.
[15] Hardwicke to Newcastle, 30 Dec 1759, Add. Mss 32,900 ff 424–428.
[16] Newcastle to Yorke, 1 Jan 1760, Add. Mss 32,901 f 18. Monthly List and Progress of the Navy, 1 Jan 1760, Adm 7/567.
[17] Admiralty to Boscawen, 4 Jan 1760, Adm 2/1331.
[18] List of Ships with Admiral Boscawen, 2 Mar 1760, Adm 1/90.
[19] *JHC*, xxviii, 636–638, 645–651.
[20] Mitchell to Holdernesse, 13 Feb 1760, Add. Mss 32,902 ff 129–133.

Preparations for a new campaign would soon have to proceed. The ministers at length realized that the only sensible course was to reinforce Ferdinand again. It was essential that the Prince should be able to resist the full weight of France's military force. Ferdinand was still pressing for more men, so that he could divide his army into two corps.[21] During the second week of January, Ligonier suggested sending two regiments of horse from Ireland, to which Pitt was agreeable.[22] However, nothing was done, though the ministerial indecision was soon shaken when news arrived at the beginning of February of the death of the Landgrave of Hesse. There were fears that his successor would not honour his commitments, but terminate the subsidy agreement, taking his 14,000 troops away.[23] A hasty meeting was arranged by Holdernesse to discuss the problem.[24] Fortunately, information arrived shortly that the new prince was well disposed and would recruit another 3,000 men. Here was good news, raising as it did the total augmentation to over 10,000 men. Ferdinand must surely now have enough troops to form his two corps, one to contain Marshal Broglie on the lower Rhine, the other to deal with the Prince de Soubise further up the river.[25]

The success of the negotiation confirmed the ministers that they had been right to refuse a request from the King of Prussia for 10,000 men. Britain was certainly doing her share to keep Germany free of foreign troops, as required by the Convention of Westminster.[26]

Nevertheless, a further expansion of the army seemed desirable, given the likely intensity of the fighting in the next few months. The shortage of recruits inevitably tempted the ministry to accept fresh offers from the nobility. But the uncertain advantages of such schemes inclined Ligonier at least to try an idea that had been discussed the previous July, namely the forming of independent companies under private sponsorship.[27] The advantages of this were twofold. Smaller units would mean a reduction in the loss of patronage. At the same time, new sources of manpower would be tapped in a more flexible manner, for the units could either reinforce existing corps or be linked together to provide additional battalions. They would also be easier to disband, not having the staff of the larger units. The scheme would still have appeal, especially for the more junior officers anxious to emulate their superiors, albeit on a reduced scale. The first commissions were accordingly issued in February. By March 1760 twenty companies were in the process of formation and the army at home totalled

---

[21] Memorandum for the King, 9 Jan 1760, Add. Mss 32,901 ff 164–165.
[22] Pitt to Newcastle, 11 Jan 1760, Add. Mss 32,901 f 194.
[23] Newcastle to Yorke, 12 Feb 1760, Add. Mss 32,902 ff 120–126.
[24] Holdernesse to Newcastle, 14 Feb 1760, Add. Mss 32,902 f 163.
[25] Newcastle to Yorke, 15 Feb 1760, Add. Mss 32,902 ff 179–184.
[26] Newcastle to Yorke, 8 Feb 1760, Add. Mss 32,902 ff 92–94.
[27] Business for the Meeting, 15 July 1759, Add. Mss 32,893 ff 58–60.

33,000 men, of which 23,000 were available for the field.[28] Both figures were a record for the war.

One minor cloud removed from the ministerial vista was the news that Thurot had finally been defeated. Since escaping from Dunkirk the previous November nothing had been heard of him; the reason being that he had been driven by a storm to seek shelter in Norwegian waters. Not until the New Year was he ready to renew his venture with a reduced force of three frigates. After seizing Carrickfergus Castle in the north of Ireland he had put back to sea, only to fall in with a number of British cruisers. In the ensuing engagement all Thurot's vessels were taken and he himself was killed.[29]

II

Not all the ministerial worries were over, however, for Newcastle was once more having trouble with the commissariat. Despite every care, the superintendency of Hunter had not been a success.

The previous year Ferdinand had complained of difficulty getting supplies from the peasantry.[30] Newcastle had accordingly given him a floating sum of £50,000 and Hunter a monthly allowance of £100,000, as the preliminaries to a more efficient and economical system.[31] But the intensity of the fighting had necessitated an increase in the allowance to £150,000, despite the protests of the Treasury.[32]

The result was that Hunter wanted to quit, for the job had proved more onerous than he had expected. Newcastle was not sorry to see him go, for another arrangement might do as well.[33] But the situation was complicated because Ferdinand also wanted some improvements in the commissariat. Essentially, he wanted more money and less Treasury interference.[34]

Someone, however, was required to keep the commissariat in order and avoid the situation that had occurred under Marlborough. Newcastle therefore attempted a compromise. A new superintendent would be appointed, but he would be the Guards officer, Richard Pierson, a friend of Granby. This went against West's advice about the need for a civilian, yet what better way of pleasing Ferdinand than by entrusting the commissariat to a soldier?[35] But Newcastle took the precaution of making Pierson's

[28] Barrington to Lt Richards *et al.*, 23 Feb 1760, WO 4/60. Calcraft to Amherst, 8 Mar 1760, WO 34/90. Effectives now in South Britain, March 1760, Add. Mss 33,048 f 26.
[29] J. S. Corbett, *England in the Seven Years' War: A Study in Combined Strategy* (London, 1907), II, 88–91.
[30] Hunter to Martin, 25 Jan 1759, T 64/96. Treasury Board Minute, 31 Jan 1759, T 29/33.
[31] Martin to Hunter, 6 April 1759, T 64/96. Newcastle to Hunter, 12 June 1759, Add. Mss 32,892 ff 19–20.
[32] Treasury Board Minute, 25 Sept 1759, T 29/33. Hunter to Martin, 18 Dec 1759, T 64/96.
[33] Treasury Board Minute, 26 Mar 1760, T 29/33.
[34] Prince Ferdinand's Notes, 26 Mar 1760, Add. Mss 32,904 ff 48–50.
[35] Newcastle to Granby, 6 May 1760, Add. Mss 32,905 ff 294–295.

commission less sweeping than Hunter's. The power of issuing money was returned to the British Commander-in-Chief.[36] However, Pierson could issue warrants and make necessary payments when separated from the army. Newcastle was determined that over money Ferdinand should have no further complaint, for additional credit would be available in Holland.[37]

The expenses in Germany were a reason why Newcastle was shortly to experience renewed difficulties over finance. Initially arrangements for the 1760 supply had gone smoothly, despite the record nature of the demands, the total being £14,000,000, of which half would have to be borrowed. The military successes had for once put the money market in a cheerful mood and Newcastle had been able to agree terms for a loan at 4 per cent, with a douceur of a £3 lottery ticket for every £100 subscribed.[38] This was quite an achievement, for the terms were only slightly higher than those of the previous year and were remarkably cheap compared to the rates commanded by the French. These facts were reflected by the lack of opposition in the Commons, the House accepting the terms and voting an additional duty on malt for funding the loan 'with scarce a negative'.[39] Newcastle was elated, telling Yorke: ''Til this year I own that I have been very economical as to expenses. . . But now I am as extravagant as anybody. . . This year I grudge nothing.'[40]

Unfortunately, within a few days Newcastle was alarmed to hear that the price of the new subscription had fallen below par, raising the spectre once more of default and bankruptcy. Various reasons were offered for the decline. Newcastle himself preferred to ascribe it to 'roguery in the Alley'.[41] Others noted the disappointing response from Holland. Newcastle sought the cause of this restraint from Yorke at the Hague: surely the Dutch did not think the British would default on their loans? That was inconceivable 'so long as land lasts and beer is drunk'.[42] But, as one City adviser commented shortly, the real reason for the market's nervousness lay elsewhere. 'Our expenses are now extended infinitely beyond our capacity' was his despondent analysis.[43] Newcastle was not helped by the inadequate procedure for calculating the departmental estimates, which were always for establishments in being rather than those likely in a few months time. The result was that Newcastle found it necessary to begin negotiations for

[36] George II to Richard Pierson, 10 June 1760, Letters Patent, C 66/3678, Public Record Office. See also Instructions to Lieutenant Colonel Pierson, 9 May 1760, Add. Mss 32,905 ff 358–361.
[37] Newcastle to Granby, 9 May 1760, Add. Mss 32,905 ff 349–350.
[38] J. J. Grellier, *The History of the National Debt from the Revolution in 1688 to the Beginning of 1800* (London, 1810), 246.
[39] Newcastle to Page, 27 Dec 1759, Add. Mss 32,900 ff 357–358.
[40] Newcastle to Yorke, 25 Dec 1759, Add. Mss 32,900 ff 312–316.
[41] Newcastle to Legge, 5 Jan 1760, Add. Mss 32,901 ff 94–96.
[42] Newcastle to Yorke, 18 Jan 1760. Add. Mss 32,901 ff 343–346.
[43] Joseph Watkins to Newcastle, 8 May 1760, Add. Mss 32,905 ff 341–342.

securing the vote of credit as early as February 1760.[44] But knowledge that the government was short of money did nothing to assist confidence in Threadneedle Street. The Bank was quick to intimate once more that it was in no position to help, leaving the Treasury no alternative but to issue Exchequer Bills on its own account. The number floated amounted to £1,000,000.[45] Fears were expressed that the new issue might be destructive of existing credit, but this did not prove to be the case.[46] A second issue for £1,500,000 was equally successful, despite concern in the City about the volume of paper in circulation and the anticipation of the Sinking Fund to Michaelmas 1761.[47] For the moment a substantial new source of credit appeared to have been secured.

The financial difficulties provided one reason for pressing the exploratory peace talks with the French which had resulted from the initiative at the Hague. Unlike the Austrians and Russians, the French had indicated a willingness to talk. Another hopeful development was the readiness of the Prussians to sanction this. Frederick II now accepted that a separate negotiation between Britain and France offered the best way of ending hostilities. His only condition was that any understanding must end the French presence in Germany.[48] The situation therefore seemed sufficiently promising for Holdernesse to authorize Yorke to speak to the French ambassador at the Hague, Monsieur d'Affry. This he proceeded to do in two long discussions, one of them held in d'Affry's coach. The talks revealed that there were still wide differences, especially over the treatment of the two powers' respective allies. The French were willing to separate the maritime and the continental disputes, but would not unilaterally abandon their European allies. However, they were ready to assist Frederick II in an attempt to accommodate his disputes with the Empress Queen. The French believed that once agreement had been reached on the maritime disputes the other powers would be more inclined to negotiate. With this in mind, Choiseul, the French Secretary of State, was for sending an intermediary, Mr Dunn, to London to open talks on America.[49]

Yorke himself said little except to reaffirm that Britain would not abandon her allies. His reticence, as he informed Newcastle, was in part because he had not had a letter from Holdernesse for over a month and was

[44] Memorandum for the King, 8 Feb 1760, Add. Mss 32,902 f 100.
[45] Treasury Board Minute, 13 Feb 1760, T 29/33. Memorandum, 13 Feb 1760, Add. Mss 33,039 ff 382–388.
[46] Watkins to Newcastle, 13 Feb 1760, Add. Mss 32,902 f 155. Watkins to Newcastle, 17 Mar 1760, Add. Mss 32,903 f 338.
[47] West to Newcastle, 10 May 1760, Add. Mss 32,905 ff 391–392. Grellier, *History of the National Debt*, 251–252.
[48] Minute with the Prussian Ministers, 13 Mar 1760, printed in W. S. Taylor and J. H. Pringle (eds.), *The Correspondence of William Pitt, Earl of Chatham* (London, 1838), II, 29–31.
[49] Yorke to Holdernesse, 21 Mar 1760, Add. Mss 32,903 ff 421–424.

at a loss to know whether his talks with d'Affry were approved or not.[50] The reason for the silence was illness, which had incapacitated both Secretaries. The reply to Yorke's letter of 21 March, therefore, came from Newcastle, this time acting officially as the King's amanuensis. Since the negotiations involved the French ambassador, any correspondence on the matter lay primarily with the southern Secretary and it was to Pitt that Newcastle turned before replying to Yorke. The discussion took place at Pitt's bedside in London. He thought the initiative should be pursued, and liked the idea of a minister being sent to London. Dunn, however, as a former Jacobite, would not do. Indeed, the mention of Dunn made Pitt doubt Choiseul's sincerity.[51] These fears were seemingly confirmed in Yorke's next letter of 4 April. The French now wanted to exclude Prussia from any negotiation. Indeed, they were prepared to try their fortunes on the continent in another campaign, no matter how desperate their situation overseas.[52] Such terms were unacceptable to the British, who continued to insist that any accommodation must include the King of Prussia, even though this meant that France would in turn have to abandon her allies. The French tried to keep the door open for further talks at the Hague, but it was clear by the middle of April that there would be no peace for the moment.[53] Another campaign was inevitable.

No one could be blamed for this failure. The ministers had tried to respond to the French opening. Certainly Choiseul's suggestion of Dunn as intermediary was a mistake. Even for the eighteenth century, when a man could serve another country in good faith, the choice was unfortunate. A French nobleman close to the court would have been a more convincing demonstration of French readiness to talk. But the real obstacle was the commitment of the two powers to their allies. Unless either side reneged on their obligations, the question of peace seemed to lie in other hands. Thus, although Britain and France were ready to talk and could have negotiated a satisfactory agreement, the fighting was to continue another two years.

The failure of these talks inevitably increased the pressure for a further strengthening of Ferdinand, especially as there was no sign of the French renewing their invasion threat. If Ferdinand could defeat the enemy's designs this summer then the French at least must be brought to the peace table. To these arguments even Pitt seemed to acquiesce, though his enthusiasm for the German war was already cooling under this constant stream of demands. Still, as he reportedly told Granby at the beginning of

---

[50] Yorke to Newcastle, 14 Mar 1760, Add. Mss 32,903 ff 252–254.
[51] Newcastle to Yorke, 25 Mar 1760, Add. Mss 32,904 ff 9–14. Newcastle to Holdernesse, 27 Mar 1760, Add. Mss 32,904 ff 52–55.
[52] Yorke to Holdernesse, 4 Apr 1760, Add. Mss 32,904 ff 192–194.
[53] Newcastle to Yorke, 22 Apr 1760, Add. Mss 32,905 ff 28–29.

April, 'if the other ministers were of opinion that more English troops should be sent, he should not . . . be displeased'.[54] Newcastle accordingly proposed a meeting for 15 April when it was agreed to send a minimum of three or four regiments, with the possibility of six not ultimately discounted.[55] But to secure even the lower figure it was necessary to do some hard political bargaining over the renewal of the Militia Bill, which Pitt was seeking.[56] Nevertheless, Newcastle was well satisfied and, with Holdernesse, Anson and Ligonier, proceeded to hasten the dispatch of the necessary instructions. At this Pitt protested that the orders 'ought to have been submitted to a meeting'. Another one was therefore arranged for 1 May, this time at Kensington at which Pitt, Holdernesse, Legge, Barrington, Ligonier and Newcastle were present. Pitt, still suffering from an attack of gout, facetiously refused to give any opinion. Ligonier, however, reaffirmed that four battalions could be spared, though doubtful about six. In the end Newcastle, Holdernesse and Legge persuaded Ligonier to agree to six, together with a regiment of horse from Ireland. However, the ministers accepted that the men should return home by the end of the year or sooner if there was any renewal of the French invasion threat. To fill the gap Pitt then suggested that the best regiments of the militia should take the field with the regulars, a flattering recognition of the part they had played the previous year.[57]

Even this reinforcement, however, proved insufficient to allow Ferdinand to take the offensive. At the beginning of June he informed the ministers that he was remaining on the defensive. His position had been weakened by the withdrawal of the last units of Prussian cavalry that had been with him since October 1757. Politically, Ferdinand's plan of campaign was quite unacceptable. A large force of national troops had been sent to him and the public were expecting some return for their expense. Pitt was especially uneasy at the possible reaction, and Newcastle tried to reassure him, pointing out that Ferdinand had spoken in a similar manner prior to the battle of Minden.[58] It was perhaps this remark that a few weeks later prompted Pitt to suggest the sending of three battalions of the Guards to reinforce Ferdinand. Newcastle readily agreed, though the King made some difficulty because the men might arrive too late. Pitt replied: 'If we beat the French, this Reinforcement may make an end of the affair at once. If we are beat, it will be of use to the Army'. The essential consideration, Pitt insisted, was that everything was done to 'make this campaign decisive and the last'.[59]

[54] Newcastle to Hardwicke, 9 Apr 1760, Add. Mss 32,904 ff 278–282.
[55] Newcastle to Granby, 15 Apr 1760, Add. Mss 32,904 ff 378–382.
[56] Newcastle to Hardwicke, 19 Apr 1760, Add. Mss 32,904 f 437. Hardwicke to Newcastle, 20 Apr 1760, Add. Mss 32,904 ff 454–455. The Act passed in 1757 was for five years only.
[57] Newcastle to Hardwicke, 1 May 1760, Add. Mss 32,905 ff 196–201.
[58] Newcastle to Pitt, 1 June 1760, Add. Mss 32,906 ff 408–409.
[59] Newcastle to Hardwicke, 21 July 1760, Add. Mss 32,908 ff 398–401.

One unexpected setback at this time was the discovery that the French had nearly recaptured Quebec. With the coming of spring the Chevalier de Lévis, the French commander, had gathered his forces at Montreal for one final attempt to dislodge the British before the ice on the river melted and allowed them to send relief. Murray, exuding the confidence the British now felt, decided to engage Lévis on the open ground above the city rather than trust to his weakened defences. The ensuing battle was almost a complete reversal of the previous battle, for this time it was the British who fled. For a few days it seemed that Wolfe's work might have been in vain. Murray was short of stores after a long winter and was faced by the French on his most vulnerable side.[60] There was of course little that Pitt or Ligonier could do except to urge Amherst to send relief and to hope that the vessels already on their way arrived before the French forced Murray to capitulate.[61] Fortunately, this is what occurred. The British fleet appeared, bringing Murray supplies and making a continuation of the siege impossible because of the threat to Lévis's communications. But the episode was a sobering reminder that nothing could be taken for granted.

Ministerial relations generally remained harmonious. One sign of this was the absence of consultation between Newcastle and Hardwicke, to whom the former invariably turned at the slightest difficulty. It may have been to these months that Pitt was referring when he told Shelburne some years later: 'There were no party politics and consequently no difference of opinion.' The ministerial discussions were the most pleasant he ever remembered.[62] Statesmen have notoriously bad memories. Two items to cause trouble at this time were the Scotch Militia Bill and the Qualification Bill. The latter was a sop to the Tory gentry. With so many men of new wealth trying to enter Parliament, there was a desire among established members to impose tighter landed qualifications for election.[63] The Militia Bill arose out of events the preceding year which had revealed the weak state of Scotland's defences. A number of members wanted to rectify this by creating a militia similar to that in England. Though Pitt was inclined to humour his allies, the latter measure was anathema to most Whigs. Armed Scotsmen had twice threatened the Hanoverian succession.[64] Finally, a compromise was agreed. The Qualification Bill would be supported, but not the Scotch Militia Bill. Pitt seemed satisfied along with the majority of his supporters, and, as Newcastle reported to Dupplin, the session ended satisfactorily, amid scenes of cordiality.[65]

[60] Murray to Pitt, 25 May 1760, Kimball, II, 291–295.
[61] Pitt to Amherst, 20 June 1760, Kimball, II, 303–305.
[62] Lord E. Fitzmaurice, *The Life of William, Earl of Shelburne* (London, 1875), I, 85.
[63] An Act to enforce and render more effectual the laws relating to the Qualifications of Members, *Statutes at Large*, Ch XX, 33 Geo. II.
[64] J. R. Western, *The English Militia in the Eighteenth Century: The Story of a Political Issue, 1660–1802* (London, 1965), 162–167.
[65] Newcastle to Kinnoull, 1 June 1760, Add. Mss 32,907 ff 15–22.

Nevertheless, the ministry now faced some difficult problems. The decision to reinforce Ferdinand's army meant that the field force at home was almost halved, despite the formation of nearly forty independent companies.[66] Moreover, because of drafting, all the units wanted men, even though some colonels were offering bounties of £6 to complete their corps.[67] As a result, the ministry had to refuse yet another request from Granby for a reinforcement of 1,800 men to make good his losses in August. Ligonier told the British commander: 'We have no more than two Regiments of Cavalry and those full of old men... The rest are boys, hardly able to manage their horses. The eight regiments of Foot, two thirds of them recruits, will if drafted, become entirely useless.'[68] But Granby believed that behind the ministerial negative lay the parsimonious influence of the Treasury. He accordingly pleaded with Newcastle not to consider 'how large a number has been sent already upon any service; but whether, if more are wanting, there is a possibility of reinforcing the service that requires it'.[69] But Barrington in a special paper showed that the army had no spare men. After the guards and garrisons had been provided, barely 9,000 men remained for the field force. The administration could do nothing for the moment.[70]

Equally worrying was the financial condition of the nation. With little prospect of peace, it was clear that the next session of Parliament must begin with new records in government expenditure for the army, navy and the German war. A total supply of at least £18,000,000 could scarcely be avoided, of which the Treasury must borrow £12,000,000. The sum seemed beyond belief, being more than twice the amount raised during the War of King William. The effect on interest rates could only be imagined.[71] Also sobering was the question of taxes. Legge believed that the taxing capacity of the nation had been reached: funding on this scale would be impossible. The only alternative was to use the unappropriated revenues of the Sinking Fund. This would mean breaking a fundamental tenet of eighteenth-century finance that such revenues must be available for the redemption of the Debt and not tied up to other subjects. Admittedly, the rest of the Treasury were not so despondent, as they thought that a further tax could be levied on spirits. Nevertheless, money might have to be found from the Sinking Fund, which all agreed was a 'terrible consideration'.[72]

[66] Lord Barrington's Paper, 25 Aug 1760, Add. Mss 32,910 ff 274–275.
[67] Robert Napier to Charles Hotham, 13 June 1760, Hotham Papers, DDHO 4/11, East Riding Record Office. Ibid., 14 June 1760.
[68] Ligonier to Granby 26 Aug 1760, printed in W. E. Manners, *Some Account of the Military, Political and Social Life of the Right Honourable John Manners, Marquis of Granby* (London, 1899), 144.
[69] Granby to Newcastle, 5 Sept 1760, Add. Mss 32,911 ff 66–67.
[70] Lord Barrington's Paper, 25 Aug 1760, Add. Mss 32,910 ff 274–275.
[71] Considerations on the 1761 Supply, 4 Oct 1760, Add. Mss 33,040 ff 39–47.
[72] Newcastle to Hardwicke, 16 Aug 1760, Add. Mss 32,910 ff 120–130.

One means of easing the burden was the suggestion of the Treasury Lord, James Oswald, that departmental expenditures might be cut. The ending of hostilities in North America meant that some reductions there ought to be possible. At the beginning of September, West accordingly produced a series of papers for the War Office and Admiralty suggesting places where savings might be made.[73] The first to respond was Barrington on 9 September. As Newcastle feared, the War Office held out little hope of any reduction. Prince Ferdinand was now facing the brunt of France's effort and an increase in Germany was to be anticipated. Even in America there was little prospect of economies. Although fighting in Canada was about to end, most of the troops would be required for service elsewhere. The Admiralty was even less accommodating. All its units were required for service.[74] The general message from both services was that even to carry on the war was certain to lead to increased costs.

Newcastle was despondent, not least because responsibility for the nation's solvency seemed to be solely his. He told Mansfield that he had been alone now for many months with 'scarce the assistance of a clerk'. The only person he could talk to confidentially was Pitt and that was little consolation, given his lack of interest in finance. The other ministers were of no help, for everyone was only 'concerned for his own department'.[75] Years later North made a similar complaint: he told Charles James Fox in 1783 that only by having 'one man, or Cabinet, to govern the whole and direct every measure' could the burden of the Treasury be made bearable. 'Government by Department was not brought in by me . . . I found it so and had not the vigour . . . to put an end to it.'[76]

One minor threat to the administration was the poor condition of Ligonier's health. In 1759 he had on several occasions been confined to bed. During 1760 he appeared to have staged a recovery, but late in August he was struck down by the need to have a stone removed from his gall-bladder. For a few days his life was despaired of.[77] However, the business of the government had to proceed and it only seemed prudent to agree on a successor. The old fears about Cumberland were still strong, in part because his return might embarrass Prince Ferdinand, while Pitt was anxious to 'have some General to consult with' to 'share in any measure of expeditions'. On a suitable replacement there was less agreement, though the discussion was friendly when the respective merits of Generals Tyrawley, Granby and Sinclair were mentioned outside the closet. Pitt wanted Sinclair or Granby,

[73] Some Observations relating to the Supplies, 3 Sept 1760, Add. Mss 32,911 ff 46–48.
[74] Lord Barrington – Answer to the Queries, 9 Sept 1760, Add. Mss 32,911 ff 263–264.
[75] Newcastle to Mansfield, 16 Sept 1760, Add. Mss 32,911 ff 342–346.
[76] Quoted in Sir Thomas Erskine May, *The Constitutional History of England since the Accession of George III, 1760–1860* (London, 1861), 1, 55.
[77] Major Ramsden to Hotham, 5 Sept 1760, Hotham Papers, DDHO 4/11, East Riding Record Office. Napier to Hotham, 9 Sept 1760, Hotham Papers, DDHO 4/11.

but Newcastle was strongly opposed to the former. He was 'no great general', and, given his birth, 'would fill the Army with all Scotch'. When Pitt pointed out that distinguished officers like the Duke of Argyle and Lord Stair were of that nation, Newcastle replied that none of them had been 'at the head of the civil Army' with power 'to go into the King and recommend vacancies'.[78] The debate proved academic, however, as Ligonier recovered, ready to play his part.

The other ministerial upsets were less direct though no less distressing for those concerned. Earlier, Lady Anson had died, leaving Anson inconsolable. Fortunately, he managed to immerse himself in the business of the Admiralty so that naval affairs did not suffer.[79] The Pelhams too were not without bereavement, as Lady Lincoln, a niece of Newcastle, whose husband was heir to his estate, died unexpectedly on 27 July.[80]

III

One item of increasing concern in the summer of 1760 was the changing nature of the Anglo-Spanish relationship. Since the offer of Gibraltar, relations with that power had remained correct, though marred by the same commercial and maritime disputes that existed between Britain and Holland. A particularly contentious incident had occurred the previous year when a British frigate had seized a French vessel that was attempting to seek the protection of a Spanish warship, the *Guerrero*. The Spanish affected to see the incident as a gross insult to their flag: the British as an unfriendly act by a neutral, giving aid to the King's enemies.[81] The incident was alarming since it remained a fixed tenet of British policy not to offend Spain to avoid extending the war.

Nevertheless, historians have usually cast Pitt as a man who was contemptuous of Spain, seeing her as a power in decline. This was not the view he had taken in 1757 during the negotiations over Gibraltar, and it was not his position now. He fully recognized the need to prevent a union of the Bourbon powers if Britain was to secure her objectives in Europe and North America. Hence, in conformity with established policy, he took a conciliatory tone over the *Guerrero*, stressing to Lord Bristol, the British ambassador at Madrid, how distressed he was at the incident.[82] There was good reason for his concern. Anglo-Spanish relations were at a delicate stage in view of the imminent death of Ferdinand IV and his succession by Charles IX of Naples. While dealing with the *Guerrero*, Pitt was approached by the

---

[78] Newcastle to Hardwicke, 17 Sept 1760, Add. Mss 32,911 ff 361–366.
[79] Yorke, ii, 580.
[80] Memorandum of a Conversation with the King, 31 July 1760, Add. Mss 32,909 f 162.
[81] Bristol to Pitt, 6 Aug 1759, SP 94/160.
[82] Pitt to Bristol, 31 Aug 1759, SP 94/160.

Neapolitan minister in London, the Prince de San Severino, with the suggestion that his master should act as a mediator in the disputes between Britain and France. The offer placed the ministry in a dilemma. Though anxious to maintain good relations with the future King of Spain, none of the ministers felt inclined to trust so delicate a negotiation to a man who was related to the French royal family and had his own interests in America. By way of excuse, Pitt suggested to San Severino that the proposal was premature. France ought to make the first move but had not done so because a number of objectives still had to be decided, and she recognized that the field of battle was the place for determining them.[83]

Pitt, however, had continued to be conciliatory. In November 1759 he told Bristol to communicate confidentially to the Spanish the details of the pending Anglo-Prussian peace initiative. He did this as a sign of Britain's desire to reciprocate the Spanish wish for a settlement.[84] Pitt was hence all the more disconcerted when, early in December, the Marqués de Abreu, the temporarily acting Spanish and Neapolitan representative in London, presented him with a memorial that not only raised once more the question of mediation, but also included – in a far from friendly tone – another unexpected demand. The court of Madrid now claimed rights under the Treaty of Utrecht to the Newfoundland fishery, asserting ominously that it could not witness further British 'success in America with indifference'.[85] The subject was so important that Pitt naturally referred it to his fellow ministers. In his verbal reply to Abreu, he merely noted that the Treaty of Utrecht did not concern Spain with respect to the fishery, an opinion in which all the ministers agreed. However, in his more lengthy formal reply to the ambassador, Pitt still tried to be conciliatory, emphasizing how Britain had helped the King's family to secure the Bourbon title to the Kingdom of Naples. Peace, he asserted, was still uppermost in George II's thoughts. This letter was 'highly approved' by the ministers on 10 December, with only Granville saying anything of a derogatory nature.[86] Hardwicke thought Pitt's handling of the affair 'not only a fine performance, but a very judicious one' too.[87]

One reason for the apparently erratic course of Spanish diplomacy was the uncertainty on whose behalf Abreu was acting; whether for the court of Madrid or that of Naples. Pitt wisely sent a covering letter to Bristol explaining the British position, and asking him if he could find out how the recent memorial had been concocted.[88] He also recognized that the ministry knew too little about the new incumbent on the Spanish throne. He

---

[83] Pitt to Bristol, 14 Sept 1759, SP 94/160.
[84] Pitt to Bristol, 2 Nov 1759, SP 94/160.
[85] Pitt to Bristol, 14 Dec 1759, SP 94/160.
[86] State of Affairs, 10 Dec 1759, DPC.
[87] Hardwicke to Newcastle, 12 Dec 1759, Add. Mss 32, 900 ff 14–15.
[88] Pitt to Bristol, 14 Dec 1759, SP 94/160.

therefore wrote a long letter to the ambassador in Naples, Stanier Porten, requesting him to supply all the information he could about the new king, his former ministers and their views. More knowledge was essential to shed light on the direction Spain's new ruler was likely to take.[89]

During the next few months relations appeared to mend. In March 1760 Wall assured Bristol that Spain had no intention of changing the present system, despite the incidents on the high seas.[90] Undoubtedly, one reason for this more moderate tone was the hope that the Anglo-Prussian peace initiative might bear fruit, at least on the quarrels between the two maritime contestants. But, after the final rejection of the proposed congress at Augsburg, the Spanish attitude hardened again, as was demonstrated on the arrival of a new ambassador in London, Count Fuentes. With Pitt ill once more of the gout and Holdernesse away in Yorkshire, the initial interviewing had to be undertaken by Newcastle.[91] The portents were distinctly alarming. Fuentes began by assuring Newcastle of the continued desire of his master for a more perfect understanding: together, Britain and Spain could defy the powers of Europe. For this reason the new King had retained General Wall with instructions to continue the old system. But Fuentes affirmed that Spain could no longer tolerate the illegal cutting of logwood in Honduras. He also stated that Spain had irrefutable rights to the fishery in Newfoundland. To continue to deny justice on these must destroy the understanding that had been so beneficial to both nations. The only one to gain would be France.[92]

Newcastle found Pitt in a strangely disconcerting mood when he gave him his report of the negotiations on 3 July. For the first time, Pitt hinted that he was less than conciliatory towards Spain. The reason for this change of heart cannot be ascertained with accuracy. Probably the crushing of the French navy and other military success made him less sensitive to what the powers of Europe were thinking. But as yet the conversion was incomplete, and to Newcastle he simply confessed that he 'did not apprehend the consequences of a breach with Spain so much as others might do'. He still wished to avoid any provocation 'in order to secure an alliance with that Crown with regard to the affairs of Europe'. On the claim to the fishery, Pitt was confident it had been raised simply as an expedient to extract concessions on the logwood dispute. Rather curiously, he then suggested that the question would have to be determined by Newcastle and Hardwicke. His position would not enable him to withstand 'either breaking with Spain or the giving up of the rights of this country'. Pitt was almost certainly

[89] Porten's reply is printed in Taylor and Pringle (eds.), *Chatham Correspondence*, II, 31–40.
[90] Bristol to Pitt, 10 Mar 1760, SP 94/116.
[91] Robert Wood to Newcastle, 24 May 1760, Add. Mss 32,906 f 246.
[92] Account of my conference with the Spanish Ambassador, 3 July 1760, Add. Mss 32,908 ff 34–35.

anticipating the political and military difficulties that were likely to arise should the disputes with that country degenerate into war. Perhaps he was preparing to shuffle responsibility off on to others. Remarkably, it was the Spanish issue that caused his resignation twelve months later. But Newcastle for the moment affected to be undisturbed. He attributed the Secretary of State's 'ill humour to the Spanish Ambassador's having talked so fully to me upon a point in his department', since Pitt himself had been indisposed.[93]

In the meantime, the policy of conciliating Spain continued. Though the French navy had been crushed, no one wanted to extend the war. In August 1760, Pitt sent a directive to the Admiralty for circulating to all ships that they were to respect territorial waters, in particular those of Spain. Furthermore, all care was to be taken to treat the commerce of that power according to the Treaty of 1667.[94] The southern Secretary also arranged for the release of a Spanish vessel detained at Portsmouth, after representations by Abreu in Paris.[95] Unfortunately, nothing was done about the logwood dispute, and if the administration thought the Spanish problem would go away they were to be disappointed. In September, Fuentes renewed the Spanish claim to the Newfoundland fishery, and, in a more truculent tone than ever, pressed for an end to the British presence in Honduras. But perhaps most disturbing of all, the ambassador informed Pitt that his government had given the French the details of the affair. The two Bourbon powers were acting in concert.[96]

Since the Spanish demands contained nothing new, Pitt did not refer them to a formal meeting of the ministers. To Fuentes, he merely protested verbally about the communication of the disputed matters to a third party.[97] But, in a more formal reply through Bristol, Pitt reaffirmed the British view that Spain could have no pretensions to the fishery under the Treaty of Utrecht. Concerning Honduras, he could only regret the peremptory tone of the Spanish demand, which seemed to preclude all negotiation.[98] In his management of these difficult matters Pitt had so far received nothing but praise from his colleagues. Hardwicke noted approvingly: 'Nothing could be more wise or agreeable to the King's dignity than the *response verbale* which you gave to the Spanish ambassador.'[99]

It was at this time that the ministers heard that Canada had finally fallen. Amherst had from the start adopted a comprehensive plan. Murray was to advance up the St Lawrence from Quebec, while Colonel Haviland

[93] Newcastle to Hardwicke, 4 July 1760, Add. Mss 32,908 ff 80–82.
[94] Pitt to the Admiralty, 4 Aug 1760, SP 94/162.
[95] Admiralty to Commodore Hanway, 4 Aug 1760, Adm 2/85.
[96] Fuentes to Pitt, 9 Sept 1760, SP 94/162. Yorke, III, 250–251.
[97] Response Verbale, 16 Sept 1760, SP 94/164.
[98] Pitt to Bristol, 26 Sept 1760, SP 94/164.
[99] Hardwicke to Pitt, 29 Sept 1760, Yorke, III, 250.

completed Amherst's work of the previous year by taking the Isle aux Noix and entering the St Lawrence near Montreal. Finally, Amherst himself would cross Lake Ontario from Oswego and approach the French settlements from the west, thus sealing their escape.[100] The plan, of course, had nearly miscarried when Murray precipitously attacked the main enemy army, but after Lévis's retreat the French could only wait for the British to make their final assault. This was a matter of time. Amherst, with the main force of regulars and provincials, first had to get to Oswego and win control of Lake Ontario. Then he had to force the passage of the St Lawrence.[101] Hence it was not until September that he finally camped before Montreal, having established contact with Murray and Haviland on the other side. The position of the French was now hopeless and they had little choice but to capitulate: the result was the final cessation of arms on the northern part of the American continent.[102] Britain now had complete control of the French colony and her original objectives had been more than attained. The possibility of a good peace was greatly increased.

Historians have commonly acclaimed the conquest of Canada as one of Pitt's greatest achievements. Certainly, in terms of creating resources he and the other ministers had done well. The shipping had been provided, the ordnance supplied and the support facilities ensured. Nevertheless the conduct of the war was hardly farsighted. Even Pitt rarely looked beyond the immediate needs and this produced a cyclical effect that largely explains why the war was so long, despite Britain's material advantage. Plans for America were rarely considered before December, and by the time the details had been forwarded there, it was spring. The military authorities then had to build boats, hire wagons, raise transports, buy supplies and dispatch them to the front, by which time it was too late to achieve the ambitious programmes laid down in London. But the consequences of this late preparation did not end here. The failure to anticipate any prolongation of the war meant that at the close of each season the men, ships and supplies were invariably dispersed, so that when news of this reached London there was scarcely time to organize a campaign the following year. Thus, as Professor Pargellis noted, a war which should have taken two or three campaigns required six.[103] Of course, there were limits in the eighteenth century to anticipation and foresight. Nevertheless, the cyclical nature of that conflict illustrates just how little planning there was in a twentieth-century sense.

---

[100] Amherst to Pitt, 19 May 1760, Kimball, II, 288–289.
[101] Amherst to Pitt, 26 Aug 1760, Kimball, II, 324–329.
[102] Amherst to Pitt, 8 Sept 1760, Kimball, II, 329–332.
[103] S. M. Pargellis (ed.), *Military Affairs in North America, 1748–1765: Selected Documents from the Cumberland Papers in Windsor Castle* (New York, 1936), ix–xxi. S. M. Pargellis, *Lord Loudoun in North America* (New Haven, 1933), 337–365.

IV

At home the war was about to undergo a change, as there was for once disenchantment with Ferdinand. All the ministers, especially Pitt, had expected something from the substantial reinforcements earlier in the year. These hopes had not been realized. Despite the urgings of the government, Ferdinand had remained on the defensive. The only success was by his brother, the Hereditary Prince of Brunswick, with a small force on the lower Rhine.[104] This was more than offset by the loss of Cassell at the beginning of August, resulting in the destruction of one of the commissariat's magazines.[105] The picture brightened a little with news of the King of Prussia's victory over the Austrians at Liegnitz, but this only increased the dissatisfaction with Ferdinand, especially when he requested yet more troops.[106] By mid September Pitt was telling his fellow ministers that unless Ferdinand fought a decisive battle, he would oppose continuing the war in Germany. The people of England would only be convinced of its utility if they could see some return for the vast sums and numbers of troops employed.[107] Not all the ministers were so condemnatory. Hardwicke remembered a maxim of the Duke of Alva that it was the 'business of a general always to get the better of his enemy, but not always to fight'. Hardwicke had not forgotten that Ferdinand was containing almost the whole military force of France, protecting Hanover and Prussia from attack.[108] A decisive battle in the sense of driving the French back into their own country was unrealistic. Even Marlborough and Eugene, with the united forces of Austria, Holland and England had not been able to do this. Ferdinand was doing as much as he could.

However, for Pitt the question was political, not military. He had detected that people were becoming disillusioned with victories that only led to disappointment. The failure to achieve anything decisive was reviving all those arguments in favour of an exclusively maritime conflict, and the advocates for such a conflict, though silenced, had never been convinced by the performances of Frederick II and Prince Ferdinand. The continental struggle might be distracting France from her maritime interests, but it was bleeding Britain to death. These views were soon put forcefully by Israel Mauduit in his pamphlet *Considerations on the Present German War*, in which he returned to the old theme that the Germans were the best people for fighting a continental war.[109] Mauduit asserted that it was mockery to

---

[104] Granby to Newcastle, 1 Aug 1760, Add. Mss 32,909 ff 191–192.
[105] Pierson to Newcastle, 6 Aug 1760, Add. Mss 32,909 f 286.
[106] Granby to Newcastle, 11 Aug 1760, Add. Mss 32,908 f 396. Granby to Newcastle, 5 Sept 1760, Add. Mss 32,911 ff 66–67.
[107] Newcastle to Hardwicke, 13 Sept 1760, Add. Mss 32,911 ff 269–270.
[108] Hardwicke to Newcastle, 14 Sept 1760, Add. Mss 32,911 ff 285–287.
[109] Mauduit's pamphlet first appeared early in November 1760.

pretend that the King of Prussia was a defender of the protestant religion. One had only to see what that monarch had done to Saxony. The one thing that Frederick II did for Britain was to find her new burdens. How much better if George II had observed the Convention of Klosterseven, for, by concentrating the resources of the nation overseas, the government could have completed the seizure of the French empire and held it as security for the return of Hanover.

Pitt's sudden change of view on the war was thus hardly coincidental. Reports from Germany all spoke of a significant reinforcement by the French of their armies on the Rhine, perhaps by 15,000 men. Since the nation could not make a comparable response, Pitt suggested the answer might lie in a diversion along the French coast. Initially, he proposed a demonstration against Boulogne or some part of Flanders in which he had the support of Newcastle. The latter had long thought this could only be useful, contiguous as it was to the German operations, especially as the troops could be recalled quickly for an emergency at home. But, in his discussions with Newcastle, Pitt also mentioned Belleisle. As Newcastle observed, Pitt had often talked of the island and the advantages which might accrue from its capture. It could be traded for the return of Minorca. It might provide the navy with a sheltered base from which to operate against Brest and Rochefort.[110] As an island it posed none of the dangers inherent on the mainland of being caught or surprised by the enemy, as had happened at St Cast.

Initially the Belleisle proposal was poorly received. Newcastle, remembering the likely expense, argued it would take troops out of the country and tie them up on a barren island without creating any kind of diversion.[111] Anson was concerned for the fleet after another long patrol off the coasts of France. Ligonier thought the measure would denude Britain of troops.[112] The feeling was that Germany was still the decisive theatre and that an operation so far away could only have the most marginal effect. However, Newcastle was agreeable to a demonstration by four battalions without a landing, as he informed the King on 30 September.[113] But, on returning to court after a short stay in the country, he was surprised to learn that Pitt had already issued instructions to the transport pool for the accommodation of 10,000, not 4,000, men.[114] Even more disturbing, Barrington told him that 'the whole thing was looked upon as a measure agreed'.[115]

To clear up the confusion, a ministerial meeting was arranged for the following day, 3 October. Present were the two Secretaries, Anson, Ligonier, Newcastle and Barrington. The proceedings were a good example of how

[110] Newcastle to Hardwicke, 3 Oct 1760, Add. Mss 32,912 ff 323–327.
[111] Memorandum for the King, 3 Oct 1760, Add. Mss 32,912 f 321.
[112] Newcastle to Hardwicke, 3 Oct 1760, Add. Mss 32,912 ff 323–327.
[113] Memorandum for the King, 30 Sept 1760, Add. Mss 32,912 f 259.
[114] Pitt to the Admiralty, 2 Oct 1760, Adm 1/4124.
[115] Newcastle to Hardwicke, 3 Oct 1760, Add. Mss 32,912 ff 323–327.

Pitt could cajole his colleagues into doing something they were inclined to reject. He began by pointing out the need for a diversion. He then followed this by artfully saying that the King was in favour, which was not strictly true. After this, Pitt got down to the details and advantages of the operation during which he elicited the attention of the service ministers, Ligonier and Anson. Without asking them to commit themselves, Pitt obtained from Ligonier the view that the troops could be ready in three weeks, though the Commander-in-Chief would have to make further enquiry about a battering train. In this spirit of constructive argument, Anson reflected that good weather was possible until the middle of November and that the fleet could shelter from the Atlantic storms on the eastern side of Belleisle. Holdernesse said little, except to ridicule Newcastle, who consequently found himself alone arguing for a demonstration off Boulogne. The majority accordingly agreed to meet again when Ligonier had had time to make his report.[116]

Newcastle tried to prepare for the next meeting by having a dinner beforehand with Anson and Mansfield, during which Anson seemed once more against the operation because of the lateness of the season. At the meeting itself on 8 October were Devonshire, Mansfield, Holdernesse, Pitt, Ligonier, Anson and Newcastle, together with Keppel, the designated commander of the naval squadron who had spent much of the preceding year in the vicinity of the island. His presence proved important. Though Ligonier now favoured the scheme, Keppel cast doubt over its practicality. The French had recently strengthened their defences and he was not certain that there was sufficient depth of water to permit ships to come inshore. With opinion running against him, Pitt played for time by suggesting that the question of the water's depth should be resolved by Hawke who was then cruising in the area, guarding the remnants of the enemy fleet in the Vilaine. This compromise was eagerly seized,[117] and the letter to Hawke was accordingly written the next day by Anson.[118] In the meantime, preparations were to continue in case of a favourable reply. These preparations proved to be salt in Newcastle's wounds, for some of the troops had to pass his country residence, Claremont, as he complained to Yorke, filling the roads with convoys of wagons and men. To avoid disclosing their destination he facetiously added: 'Where they go, God knows'. He personally wished that they were going to Prince Ferdinand. Then with tongue in cheek he concluded: 'I write treason.'[119]

The ministers now had to wait for Hawke to report, although Hardwicke thought that 'if His Majesty finds a difference of opinion in his Council and his own judgement is against it', he should decide the matter himself.[120]

[116] Ibid. [117] Newcastle to Hardwicke, 11 Oct 1760, Add. Mss 32,913 ff 45-54.
[118] Anson to Hawke, 9 Oct 1760, Add. Mss 15,956 ff 54-57.
[119] Newcastle to Yorke, 10 Oct 1760, Add. Mss 32,913 ff 8-9.
[120] Hardwicke to Newcastle, 12 Oct 1760, Add. Mss 32,913, ff 67-68.

George II, however, was not about to get involved. The issue did not interest him unless it could be used to bargain support for Hanover's claim to territorial compensation. Pitt and Newcastle meanwhile continued their discussions. Newcastle renewed all his arguments that the expedition was too late for a diversion. The operation would simply increase the expenses of the nation and ruin the health of the best regiments left in Britain. Pitt tried to appease him, saying that if Ligonier or Hawke were against the project, and 'if the Council shall finally be against', then he would not persist.[121]

There can be little doubt that Pitt expected a favourable reply. Hardwicke too thought Hawke would be diplomatic rather than forthright in his assessment.[122] Both men were wrong. Hawke's verdict was a blunt no. In his letter to Anson, dated 17 October, he reported that he had sent Captain Hotham to reconnoitre the island. From the latter's investigation it appeared that no vessel could come closer to the main fortifications of Pallais than two miles, except at one point which was totally dominated by enemy batteries impregnably situated on the surrounding cliffs. Elsewhere, at those few places where nature's own defences were wanting, the French had done everything practicable to make a landing impossible. Any disembarkation therefore must take place in the most unpromising circumstances. Hawke personally doubted whether 'the possession of a place detached by water from the Continent' would 'draw troops from any part', which seemed most unlikely in view of the current preponderance of the royal navy, which made any French counter-attack impossible. If the ministers wanted an expedition in that part of the world, Hawke had a better suggestion, an attack on the enemy vessels still in the Vilaine. This would complete the destruction of the French fleet begun at the battle of Quiberon Bay, for intelligence reports suggested that the enemy had few troops in the area to protect them.[123]

The letter from Hawke arrived in England on 24 October. Anson went directly to St James's to show it to the King, and, before entering the closet, he gave it to Newcastle. Shortly afterwards Pitt arrived and received a verbal account. He immediately grew angry with Anson for not first showing him the letter. After Anson had left the closet, Pitt insisted on seeing it before he went inside. To George II's gruff assertion that he would not send any troops, Pitt replied: 'He did not understand Sir Edward Hawke's letter. That he had not answered the only Question, which he was directed to return an Answer, viz whether there was depth of water to support the ships to come and land the troops.' Outside the closet once more Pitt bitterly attacked Hawke, stating that 'Sir Edward did not know what use to make of Belleisle... that he was a very good sea officer, but no minister'. He

121 Newcastle to Hardwicke, 18 Oct 1760, Add. Mss 32,913 ff 183–189.
122 Hardwicke to Newcastle, 12 Oct 1760, Add. Mss 32,913 ff 67–71.
123 Hawke to Anson, 17 Oct 1760, Add. Mss 32,913 ff 163–166.

certainly had reason to be angry, for Hawke had overstepped his brief. But, as so often, Pitt went to extremes, threatening one minute to bring the whole affair into Parliament, saying the next that the matter was finished, and that he would have nothing more to do with it. Ligonier and Anson must take the King's orders for recalling the troops and dismissing the transports. Later, at Lady Yarmouth's apartment, Pitt resumed his attack on Hawke, remembering that he had commanded the fleet during the Rochefort débâcle. Newcastle noted that Pitt seemed more angry than he had ever known.[124] But his rage was to be quickly superseded, for, though none of the ministers realized, they had had their last interview with the King.

[124] Newcastle to Hardwicke, 25 Oct 1760, Add. Mss 32,913 ff 326–332.

7

A New King

George II died early on the morning of 25 October from a stroke, so that, inevitably, further discussion of the expedition had to wait while the old King was buried and arrangements made to induct his successor. Technically all commissions had to be renewed, Parliament dissolved and another one elected. But first, George III had to be proclaimed King. This was a task for the Privy Council. At a preliminary meeting that afternoon, George III and Bute read to Pitt, Holdernesse and Newcastle the text of a proclamation they wished to publish under the auspices of the Council. The document was short, merely grieving the loss of the old King and stressing the determination of the new monarch to do his best. The only controversial point was a passing reference to the 'present bloody and expensive war' which Pitt later insisted should be changed to 'expensive but just and necessary'.[1] The incident was perhaps trivial, though indicative of the hostility of the new King and his confidant to the war in Europe.

The intention of the new monarch to abide by the existing arrangements was conveyed to Pitt by Bute in an interview that evening. Bute said it was the King's wish that all the ministers should continue to serve him. Fresh commissions would not be issued until a new Parliament had been summoned in the spring. Bute then affirmed that he planned to remain a private citizen: that he was not sincere Pitt well knew. Nevertheless, Pitt took him at his word, making clear his own position in language reminiscent of his first taking office: 'He must act as an independent minister or not at all: that his politics were like his religion, which would admit of no accommodation.' Surveying the present situation, Pitt warned 'that if the system of the war was to undergo the least . . . shadow of a change he could no longer be of any service'. Pitt particularly mentioned that part under the direction of Prince Ferdinand and his brother, making it clear he would not pander to Leicester House's anti-German views. He then approved the retention of Newcastle at the Treasury, and concluded by saying: 'He too

---

[1] Sir Lewis Namier, *England in the Age of the American Revolution* (London, 1930), 120–121.

wished to be a private man, if he could once see the country out of the present plunge', meaning a satisfactory end to the war.

Bute said little except to disagree about the necessity of retaining Newcastle to secure the financial stability of the government.[2]

Newcastle's response, when invited to stay, was naturally different. He affected to think of retiring, remembering that he had been in the service of the House of Hanover for nearly forty-five years.[3] But in his heart he was as keen to stay as Bute was to see him go. Most of his friends and associates urged him to remain, and their pleas proved decisive when joined to those of the 'considerable mony'd men in the City'. The latter declared that 'if the Duke of Newcastle continued in employment they would raise the money for the service of the year but feared that if that were not the case, there might be greater difficulty in doing it'.[4] However, in a letter to the King Newcastle begged permission to retire whenever necessary for his own 'ease and quiet'.[5]

. The other members of the administration made little fuss. To men like Anson and Ligonier it was unthinkable to desert the King when he had requested them to stay. In membership, therefore, the government was for the moment unchanged. The only difference was the attendance of Bute at the ministerial discussions. One of the first acts of George III had been to declare him a member of the Cabinet Council. George III clearly intended Bute to be a force in the government. Nevertheless, Devonshire thought that if Pitt and Newcastle stuck together they would have little difficulty in getting their way against such inexperienced operators.[6]

However, it was inevitable that some changes must occur. Indeed, the desire of George III that Bute should be his leading adviser made it unavoidable that there should be new tensions in the ministry and that these would, in due course, affect the running of the war. The ambitions of Bute had been spotted by Devonshire, who noted in his diary it was 'plain that he intended to be the Minister'. At the same time it was also clear that Bute 'had no plan of administration' beyond that of confining 'all the ministers to their separate departments'. In pursuit of this Bute and George III determined to reconstitute the Cabinet Council.[7] When Pitt suggested within two days of the new King's accession that there ought to be a discussion at Anson's house about the expedition to Belleisle, Bute told him that 'the King would have no meetings at which he [Bute] was not present . . . and that for the future everything should be considered and debated in his presence and then His Majesty would determine as he

---

[2] Ibid., 121.
[3] Hugh Valence Jones to the Duchess of Newcastle, 28 Oct 1760, Add. Mss 32,913 ff 405–408.
[4] Newcastle to Thomas Pelham, 1 Nov 1760, Add. Mss 32,914 ff 1–3.
[5] Newcastle to George III, 31 Oct 1760, Add. Mss 32,913 f 483.
[6] Memoranda on the State of Affairs, 27 Oct 1760, DPC. This is written in the form of a diary and will be referred to hereafter as the Devonshire Diary.   [7] Ibid.

thought proper'.[8] George III and his mentor wanted to recapture for the
Crown the initiative in the transaction of business. By controlling the inner
group they hoped to restore a proper constitutional balance. For, as Bute
privately confessed some months later, the new 'King would not be led or
governed by his Ministers as the late King had been'.[9] A week later Bute
reaffirmed his master's intentions. The meeting on the expedition would be
held on 11 November, and for the future the persons summoned were to
include the Lord Keeper, the Lord President, the two Secretaries of State,
Newcastle, Hardwicke, Anson, Ligonier, Mansfield, Bedford, Devonshire
and Halifax, if American affairs were pending.[10]

The new scheme was naturally upsetting for the existing personnel.
Nevertheless, an informal meeting on the speech was held on 5 November,
between Newcastle, Pitt, Bute and Hardwicke. Everything was amicable
until Pitt raised the question of the militia. The drafting, however, was left
to Hardwicke and the document fully reflected the Whig views of its
author.[11] It began by lamenting the death of the old king, since 'he was
the great Supporter of that System, by which alone the liberties of Europe,
and the weight and influence of these Kingdoms can be preserved'. The
speech then went on to make the familiar acknowledgements to the King
of Prussia and Prince Ferdinand. It noted the continuing success of that
King's arms and hoped that peace would soon be secured. Unfortunately,
this did not seem imminent, for the 'dangerous designs' of the enemy made
the continuation of the war both 'just and necessary'. Indeed, only by
prosecuting the 'War with Vigour' could 'that desirable Object, a safe and
honourable Peace' be obtained.[12] Clearly, no change in the conduct of
affairs was publicly envisaged.

After finishing his draft Hardwicke gave it to Newcastle who in turn
handed it over to Bute for the King's perusal.[13] Some minor alterations were
made, including the insertion of the line 'born and educated in this Country,
I glory in the Name of Briton'. Such sentiments could not but cause unease
to Newcastle and the other Whigs, reminiscent as they were of the patriot
element among the Tories and those who wanted to dispense with the
present continental system. But since the King personally insisted on the
sentence, the ministers had little option but to agree to it at the formal
reading in the Cabinet Council.[14]

   [8] Ibid.
   [9] Memorandum, 10 Aug 1761, Add. Mss 32,927 ff 352–353. Newcastle called the statement
        'offensive'.
   [10] Newcastle to Hardwicke, 7 Nov 1760, Add. Mss 32,914 ff 171–178.
   [11] Devonshire Diary, 6 Nov 1760, DPC.
   [12] *JHC*, xxviii, 935–936.
   [13] Hardwicke to Newcastle, 12 Nov 1760, Add. Mss 32,914 ff 275–277. Newcastle to Bute,
        14 Nov 1760, Add. Mss 32,914 f 339.
   [14] Bute to Newcastle, 15 Nov 1760, Add. Mss 32,914 f 345. Newcastle to Hardwicke, 16 Nov
        1760, Yorke, iii, 311. See also Paper written in the King's Hand, Add. Mss 32,914 f 359.

In the meantime, the Belleisle expedition had been finally settled at a meeting on 11 November, even though the circumstances on which it had been planned no longer pertained. Earlier the Austrians and Russians had occupied Berlin. The Russians then retreated, allowing Frederick II to gain yet another victory over the Austrians, at Torgau. As a result, Silesia and Saxony were evacuated. In the west the offensive of Broglie and the other French commanders had ended with little to show for their efforts as the armies prepared to go into winter quarters.[15] A diversion was thus no longer needed. But, as with the Rochefort expedition in 1757, it was easier to change the rationale than to stop the venture. Though a diversion could no longer be justified, an attempt to seize something negotiable at the peace was. The only outstanding problem was the operation's feasibility. Pitt admitted this depended on two points that only Anson and Ligonier could settle. The first was whether the ships of war could get sufficiently close to protect the troops on their landing; the second whether an operation of this kind could be sustained after the troops were ashore.[16] Newcastle remained firm in his opposition. Bute, however, would not commit himself beforehand, saying that he would be guided by the discussion.[17]

Present on 11 November were Henley, Granville, Temple, Bedford, Newcastle, Holdernesse, Bute, Pitt, Ligonier, Anson, Mansfield, Hardwicke and Legge. Also in attendance were Keppel and Captain Hotham, who had been recalled specially for the purpose.[18] Pitt opened the discussion by questioning Hotham about the waters around Belleisle, using all his arts to get Anson and Ligonier in favour of the project. After a time the two service chiefs appeared convinced of its feasibility, without questioning the utility. Their readiness to support the scheme proved decisive. Bute declared: 'It would be a blot on the King's reign to open it by laying aside such an expedition.' Mansfield, much to Newcastle's annoyance, quickly followed and although Temple had come declaring he was undecided, there was never much doubt where his support would lie.[19] Nevertheless, Pitt's success was to prove incomplete. The winter had set in, detaining the flotilla at Portsmouth for three weeks. On 11 December Pitt accordingly told Keppel to disembark the force, 'both horses and men having suffered considerably by extreme Badness of the weather'. But the return to quarters was to be only temporary. The operation was to proceed as soon as the weather improved.[20]

---

[15] Sir Reginald Savory, *His Britannic Majesty's Army in Germany during the Seven Years' War* (Oxford, 1966), 244–278.   [16] Devonshire Diary, 1 Nov 1760, DPC.

[17] Newcastle to Hardwicke, 7 Nov 1760, Add. Mss 32,914 ff 171–178.

[18] Cabinet Minute, 13 Nov 1760, CP PRO 30/8/79 f 201.

[19] Devonshire Diary, 14 Nov 1760, DPC. Lord Royston to Charles Yorke, 13 Nov 1760, Yorke, III, 311. Royston was Hardwicke's eldest son.

[20] Pitt to Keppel, 11 Dec 1760, printed in Reverend T. Keppel, *The Life of Augustus, Viscount Keppel, Admiral of the White and First Lord of the Admiralty in 1782–1783* (London, 1842), I, 295. Holdernesse to Granby, 19 Dec 1760, SP 87/32.

The one item of note before Christmas was the discussion on 9 December of a letter from Frederick II about a renewal of the peace initiative. The letter was addressed to Pitt, a symptom of Holdernesse's eclipse, despite his attempts to better himself at Leicester House. Pitt accordingly opened the subject in the 'Council'. Admitting it was not properly in his department, he proceeded to give an account of his discussion with Knyphausen, the Prussian ambassador, the previous week. During this recital he took the opportunity of letting the ministers know who were in his favour. According to Devonshire, he 'rapped Lord Holdernesse'; talked about his close union with Newcastle; mentioned communicating the matter to Devonshire and Hardwicke; 'apologized that he had not had an opportunity of talking with the Lord President', all the while taking no notice of Bedford.[21] On the Prussian negotiation itself Pitt explained he had informed the Prussians that they must be more specific. They must say how they wanted the negotiations opened, whether by a general congress, or by separate talks between Britain and France. They should also state whether they were prepared to make some territorial concessions to detach the Russians from the alliance. Despite the bombastic prelude, Pitt's handling of the negotiation was firmly approved.[22]

Although Bute had so far been inconspicuous in the deliberations the other members of the administration were by no means content. Newcastle in particular was upset at the failure to consult him over appointments. These were being made 'piecemeal', with 'no previous concert or plan', a foolish proceeding in view of the approaching election.[23] The problem was that Newcastle had no comprehension of the subtle changes that were now taking place. He had entered public life when the survival of the dynasty and the political settlement of 1689 were in doubt and the preservation of these was the goal to which all his actions tended. To the Whigs of Newcastle's generation, the British constitution was the most perfect yet devised. It was enough that the King's government ran smoothly and the Jacobites were kept in check.

He was hence nonplussed when George III began appointing Tories to court; announced his intention of having elections free of government interference; and refused electoral support for one of the administration's own members. To Newcastle's generation a Hanoverian could not be neutral, not when the sitting member was Legge, the Chancellor of the Exchequer. Fifty years in politics made such ideas anathema to him, and his immediate reaction was to resign.[24] From the Hague, Yorke tried to put matters into perspective, commenting that he could not expect to feel immediately 'the same tranquility and satisfaction as you had been used

[21] Devonshire Diary, 9 Dec 1760, DPC.   [22] Yorke, III, 315.
[23] Newcastle to Yorke, 25 Nov 1760, Add. Mss 32,915 ff 52–53.
[24] Namier, *England in the Age of the American Revolution*, 134–156.

to after a service of so many years under an old and tried master'.[25] But Newcastle was not alone in his despondency. Pitt too was unhappy, telling Hardwicke that 'for his part he knew no more of what was intended' than anyone else. 'That this he knew, he and my Lord Holdernesse dangled at court with a bag in their hands, but they were not the ministers.'[26] He repeated his sentiments to Newcastle, acknowledging the latter's previous value in the closet. 'Formerly my Lord, if I had not an opportunity to see the King, if you told me that you would answer for the King's consent, that was enough; I was satisfied. Where is that satisfaction to be had now?'[27]

Ligonier was also disgruntled, for the problem of aristocratic influence with the King had surfaced once more. One of the new appointments at court was that of Lord Shelburne to be *aide de camp* to George III. As Ligonier tried to remonstrate, this meant superseding 'many lieutenant-colonels' of 'great merit'. However, Ligonier's protests were to no avail, for Shelburne was a protégé of Bute.[28]

It was to clear up the uncertainties that Newcastle sought an audience with the favourite. He listed seven points, including the election of a new Parliament, the allocation of employments and the arrangements for the Cabinet Council. It was essential to find out 'who are to be called to the secret meetings'. There were rumours that George III and Bute intended 'to exclude some, perhaps the Chancellor of the Exchequer, the lord Chief Justice, and the Admiral and General except upon Maritime and Military considerations'.[29] Unfortunately, Bute had no clear plan, despite his pronouncements about the Cabinet Council. He accordingly made various excuses to Newcastle for not meeting him.[30]

The normal business of government, however, still had to be implemented, including the presentation of the estimates to the last session of the old Parliament. Those for the army were for an establishment of 107,000 men, a decrease of 2,000 on the previous year, a further reflection of the continuing difficulty in finding men.[31] The naval estimates also showed a similar tapering. Anson expected to have 288 vessels in commission, manned by 80,675 seamen, compared to 301 vessels and 82,000 men in 1759.[32] A number of ships had now reached the end of their usefulness. In addition, fewer vessels were building, partly for financial reasons. Only twenty-three were under construction, half the number in 1757, though another seven

[25] Yorke to Newcastle, 18 Nov 1760, Add. Mss 32,914 ff 407–409.
[26] Hardwicke to Newcastle, 29 Oct 1760, Add. Mss 32,913 ff 426–430.
[27] Newcastle to Hardwicke, 3 Dec 1760, Yorke, III, 315.
[28] Devonshire Diary, 3 Dec 1760, DPC.
[29] Heads for my Conference with Lord Bute, 16 Dec 1760, Add. Mss 32,916 f 105. See also ff 56–60.
[30] Namier, *England in the Age of the American Revolution*, 156–161.
[31] *JHC*, XXVIII, 943–946, 983–985.
[32] Monthly List and Progress of the Navy, 1 Jan 1761, Adm 7/567.

were soon to be ordered.[33] Then there was the difficulty of finding men. In addition Anson assumed that the navy was sufficient for its current requirements, being unlikely to face any new major burden.

The conquest of Canada meant that this time North America was not on the agenda. But expeditions were very much in the air, and not just to Belleisle. As Pitt explained to Newcastle when summoning him to a meeting on New Year's Eve: 'The object. . . will be to find if possible a proper and timely operation' without which the 'coming year will move very heavily under the load of twelve millions and not the most promising aspect of affairs in Germany'.[34] This latter was a reference to the recent attempt of Ferdinand to seize the town of Göttingen before going into winter quarters. The siege had not accomplished its purpose and the result had been that Ferdinand had had to surrender Hesse to the borders of Hanover.[35] Hence, even Newcastle was beginning to feel that Pitt was right in advocating a different approach. As he told Yorke on 30 December 1760: 'If we can't make peace, we must try our fate with expeditions...and beat France into a Peace.'[36]

In the event two main operations were approved. The first was another assault on Martinique. The ministry had already sanctioned this once and there was little reason not to try again, especially as the army in North America could be used, thus eliminating any depletion of the units at home. The military believed that 5,000 men would be enough to secure Canada. Most of the remainder of Amherst's army, therefore, could profitably be deployed elsewhere.[37] However, no immediate action would be possible until the hurricane season was over. In the meantime, Amherst was to prepare accordingly and should also take some of the smaller French islands, notably Dominique and St Lucia, which could be done more speedily by a limited force.[38]

The other main project was an attack on the naval base and colony of Mauritius. The previous year Pitt had received a plea from Clive in India for assistance. The enemy had proved difficult to defeat because they could operate from their island base.[39] What Pitt now proposed was a partial diversion of the Belleisle expedition. He argued that the breaking of French power in the Indian Ocean would be as much of a blow as the seizure of

[33] Account of Ships Building, 28 Oct 1760, Adm 2/228. Admiralty to the Navy Board, 18 Mar 1761, Adm 2/229. *JHC*, xxviii, 959.
[34] Pitt to Newcastle, 29 Dec 1760, Add. Mss 32,916 f 369.
[35] Savory, *Britannic Majesty's Army*, 280–282.
[36] Newcastle to Yorke, 30 Dec 1760, Add. Mss 32,916 ff 385–386.
[37] Newcastle to Hardwicke, 30 Dec 1760, Add. Mss 32,916 ff 385–392.
[38] Pitt to Amherst, 17 Dec 1760, Kimball, ii, 370–372. Pitt to Amherst, 7 Jan 1761, Kimball, ii, 384–387.
[39] Clive to Pitt, 7 Jan 1759, printed in W. S. Taylor and J. H. Pringle (eds.), *The Correspondence of William Pitt, Earl of Chatham* (London, 1838), i, 387–392.

Belleisle. The main need would be for a naval squadron with two or three regiments plus transports to arrive after the monsoon season was over. In the ministry there was general support for the idea, though George III did raise some objections when Ligonier discussed the matter with him. He was especially concerned about the dispatch of the regiments, which might imperil the kingdom when the target was so far away.[40] Hence, much to Pitt's annoyance, the preliminary orders from Anson to Steevens, warning him of the intended operation, made no mention of any military reinforcement. The admiral was to expect a squadron of ten battleships and transports for 6,000 men. The Company would have to find the necessary troops from its own resources and those royal forces already there.[41]

II

Otherwise, two matters were to dominate the ministers regarding the war in the first part of 1761: one was the condition of Prince Ferdinand's army, the other the possibility of peace. Despite the dissatisfaction with Ferdinand, more troops would have to be sent, for all the evidence suggested that the French would make another effort in Germany to improve their position at the negotiating table. Indeed, their plan was to have two armies totalling about 150,000 men on the upper and lower Rhine to catch Ferdinand in the middle.[42]

It was hence imperative for the ministry to ensure that the British contingents at least were up to strength. At the beginning of January 1761 Ligonier told Napier, the Adjutant-General, to join him so that they might devise some expedient for recruiting the ranks.[43] Initially the situation seemed so difficult that Ligonier considered disbanding some of the most understrength regiments. The officers could then be put on half pay and the men distributed elsewhere.[44] In the event he decided this would be too severe. He accordingly proposed that 1,500 men should be provided from the Irish establishment, 1,200 raised in England by independent companies, and a further 600 men drafted from the Guards to recruit their battalions in Germany. Also 400 men would be found by some undetermined means, probably in the Highlands.[45] According to Barrington, the army in Germany wanted 2,300 men. The scheme devised by Ligonier and Napier would more than meet this and mild optimism seemed not inappropriate.

[40] Barrington to Newcastle, 3 Jan 1761, Add. Mss 32,917 f 75.

[41] Admiralty to Steevens, 16 Jan 1761, Adm 2/1331.

[42] Newcastle to Yorke, 13 Jan 1761, Add. Mss 32,917 ff 271–274. Savory, *Britannic Majesty's Army*, 310.

[43] Napier to Hotham, 30 Jan 1761, Hotham Papers, DDHO 4/12, East Riding Record Office.

[44] Last Returns from Germany, 1 Dec [1760], Donoughmore Papers, T 3459/A/8, Public Record Office of Northern Ireland.

[45] Newcastle to Granby, 10 Feb 1761, Add. Mss 32,918 ff 402–403.

Equally important for the conduct of the campaign in Germany was the condition of the supply services. Here things were not so good. Though Pierson had initially made a good impression, he had not proved a man of business. One indication of this was the mounting expense of the commissariat, for, contrary to every expectation, by the end of 1760 the monthly allowance of £150,000 was proving insufficient.[46] The department had admittedly been hurt by the loss of Cassell, which had necessitated the making of additional contracts. Unfortunately accusations were soon being made that they had been negotiated with men of unsavoury character.[47]

These charges were not the only testimony that things were amiss there. At the turn of 1761, London was full of officers complaining that the army was inadequately supplied. Assertions were appearing in the newspapers that several recent scarcities had impeded Ferdinand in the execution of his plans.[48] But when Newcastle interrogated two senior officers, Lord Pembroke and General Waldegrave, they flatly denied this.[49] Their views were confirmed by Granby and Pierson. Granby suggested that the only possible cause for complaint had been the want of forage, which had admittedly made the department unpopular. But many reasons could explain this: the inclement weather; the difficult navigation of the Weser; the poor state of the roads; and the inevitable want of carriage.[50] Pierson said much the same, though he admitted that at times the supply of forage had not been as efficient as in Flanders. Regrettably, the Hanoverians had not shown that alacrity which a 'friendly army ought to expect from a country it comes to defend'.[51] Even so, to suggest that the army had dwindled to nothing for want of bread and forage' was a lie.[52]

Here for the moment the matter stood, Newcastle accepting that the charges were exaggerated. However, there was still the danger of opposition in Parliament. Pitt, always the political weathervane, ominously informed Newcastle that he could 'be of no use...explaining or defending' the estimates then pending. The Treasury must manage itself.[53] Newcastle was hence greatly relieved when the German figures were agreed to without a division.[54]

Meanwhile, relations inside the ministry remained tense because of the

46 Newcastle to Yorke, 19 Dec 1760, Add. Mss 32,916 ff 193–194.
47 Newcastle to Pierson, 26 Dec 1760, Add. Mss 32,916 ff 316–319. Newcastle to Granby, 26 Dec 1760, Add. Mss 32,916 ff 314–315.
48 *London Chronicle*, 8/10 Jan 1761. Newcastle to Granby, 8 Jan 1761, Add. Mss 32,917 ff 185–189.
49 Newcastle to Yorke, 20 Jan 1761, Add. Mss 32,917 ff 419–422.
50 Granby to Newcastle, 19 Jan 1761, Add. Mss 32,917 ff 391–394.
51 Pierson to Newcastle, 7 Jan 1761, Add. Mss 32,917 ff 40–41.
52 Pierson to Newcastle, 25 Jan 1761, Add. Mss 32,918 ff 59–60.
53 Pitt to Newcastle, 2 Feb 1761, Add. Mss 32,918 ff 188–189.
54 Charles Yorke to Newcastle, 16 Feb 1761, Add. Mss 32,919 ff 38–39. Newcastle had heard rumours that William Beckford and Sir John Philips would attack the estimates and he had asked Yorke to defend them, 15 Feb 1761, Add. Mss 32,919 ff 1–2.

uncertain position of Bute. Though not a minister, he had what the others lacked, the confidence of the King. Accordingly, Count Viry, the Sardinian ambassador and confidant of almost everyone, suggested that Bute should replace Holdernesse as Secretary of State. If the King was determined to confide in Bute, it was better he did so openly by making him minister.[55] There was much sense to the proposal and Newcastle readily agreed. The present secretarial team was far from effective. As he commented to George III, Pitt had 'such long interruptions by the Gout, as often deprived the King of his services for weeks or even months'.[56] Indeed, that February Pitt had once more been confined to bed and had to confess how ill fitted he was for the office to which he was entrusted by the King.[57] As to Holdernesse, Newcastle asserted, though he 'carried on His Majesty's foreign Correspondence' diligently, he 'entered very little into Home affairs... particularly the business of Parliament'. Since Pitt was politically indispensable, it made sense to replace Holdernesse with Bute.[58]

To make the scheme more acceptable, it was proposed to restore to the southern office some of the powers that had been allocated to the Board of Trade in 1751.[59] Unfortunately, Newcastle failed to discuss the matter with Pitt. The promotion of Bute was presented as a *fait accompli* which the King had insisted upon.[60] Pitt affected to be unconcerned, but he did not forgive Newcastle for his treachery, especially after he had so recently supported his retention of the Treasury. Pitt's immediate reaction, as always when he felt threatened, was to reiterate his need for personal access to the King without having to go through the channel of any other minister.[61] The longer-term effect was to set the scene for the destruction of the Pitt–Newcastle coalition.

The other major changes in the administration were the replacement of Bedford with Halifax as Lord-Lieutenant of Ireland and the removal of Legge. George III was averse to the Chancellor of the Exchequer for his intrigues in the previous reign.[62] Legge's place at the Treasury was taken by Barrington, a move that pleased Newcastle, and the War Office was given to Charles Townshend. Finally, Sir Robert Henley was made Lord Chancellor, filling a post that had lain vacant since 1756. Bedford for the moment had no office, though his standing with the King was reflected by his increasing attendance at the ministerial deliberations.

One indication of a change of style if not of substance was the restoration

[55] Devonshire Diary, 12 Jan 1761, DPC. Ibid., 29 Jan 1761.
[56] Account of what happened with the King, 6 Mar 1761, Add. Mss 32,919 ff 481–483.
[57] Pitt to Newcastle, 8 Feb 1761, Add. Mss 32,918 f 358.
[58] Account of what happened with the King, 6 Mar 1761, Add. Mss 32,919 ff 481–483.
[59] Memorandum – The Board of Trade, 12 Mar 1761, Add. Mss 32,920 ff 156–157.
[60] Substance of what passed with Lord Bute, 10 Mar 1761, Add. Mss 32,920 ff 64–70.
[61] Newcastle to Devonshire, 13 Mar 1761, Add. Mss 32,920 ff 166–170.
[62] Sir Lewis Namier and J. Brooke, *The History of Parliament. The House of Commons, 1754–1790* (London, 1964), iii, 30–31.

of Cumberland to esteem. George III was anxious to begin his reign in an appropriately benign spirit by conciliating his uncle. Recognition of officers well thought of by Cumberland was one means of doing this. Accordingly, Studholme Hodgson was nominated to command the expedition which was about to sail from Portsmouth.[63]

The plan to divert the expedition to Mauritius had now been abandoned, for various reasons. One was the improved military situation in India. The arrival of Draper's and Coote's regiments in the Carnatic had permitted Coote to take the offensive, leading to his victory at Wandewash in January 1760, which foreshadowed an end to French power there. But equally important was Hardwicke's point that the scene of action was too far away. With the possibility of peace talks in the offing, hostilities might be concluded before the results of the expedition could be known.[64] Another objection was the problem of to whose advantage the operation might accrue. As Pitt had earlier commented to Clive's emissary, the Company would benefit much: the expense would largely fall on the government.[65] Belleisle had none of these disadvantages. The orders to Steevens were accordingly cancelled on 4 March and new ones issued to Keppel and Hodgson.[66]

It was during these weeks that Parliament was dissolved and writs issued for a new one. Earlier, Newcastle had been afraid that George III and Bute were going to ruin matters because of their notion that it should be 'a Parliament of the people's own choosing'.[67] In the event their ideas for reforming British politics were naïve and impractical. The management of the election was left to Newcastle, the King and Bute seeking Treasury assistance for three innocuous candidates.[68] At the beginning of April 1761 Newcastle was forecasting to Devonshire 'the certainty of a better Parliament than the last'.[69] By all the normal criteria the administration was likely to be as secure politically as ever in the pursuit of its war aims.

Unfortunately, any pleasure Newcastle might have felt in this forecast was overshadowed by further difficulties with the commissariat. Initially, affairs there had taken a favourable turn. Ferdinand had opened his campaign early, driving the French back towards the Rhine. But these successes were not maintained. By the end of March it was Ferdinand who was in retreat, making for the security of the river Dymel. His disappointment was considerable and this time he attributed it to the commissariat. In a letter

[63] Hodgson to Lord Albemarle, 28 Mar 1761, printed in Keppel, *Life of Keppel*, I, 301.
[64] Hardwicke to Newcastle, 3 Jan 1761, Add. Mss 32,914 ff 94–96.
[65] B. Williams, *The Life of William Pitt, Earl of Chatham* (London, 1913), II, 29–30.
[66] Admiralty to Steevens, 4 Mar 1761, Adm 2/1331. George III to Keppel, 25 Mar 1761, printed in Keppel, *Life of Keppel*, I, 302–303.
[67] Yorke to Mitchell, 8 Jan 1761, Add. Mss 6836 ff 145–146.
[68] Namier, *England in the Age of the American Revolution*, 154–155.
[69] Newcastle to Devonshire, 2 Apr 1761, Add. Mss 32,921 ff 272–273.

dated 30 March 1761, he charged that 'the want of subsistence for the army had obstructed his...plan of operations'.[70] Newcastle had confined the earlier complaints to his department; this time, there was no avoiding a wider discussion. Pitt was quick to take it up, if only because of his estrangement over Bute.[71] The matter was eventually dealt with at a ministerial meeting on 23 April. Pitt demanded an enquiry. Newcastle asserted one was already in progress. On the first intimation he had written to Pierson demanding an explanation. He had also expressed similar sentiments to Ferdinand, but there had not yet been time for a reply. Bedford then suggested that the Prince was trying to cover up his own mistakes. After further discussion, the ministers asked Pitt to write to Ferdinand to ascertain his views more fully; Pitt demurred, saying 'it was Treasury business', but finally agreed. The incident convinced Devonshire that Pitt's conduct was entirely personal. He did 'not want to have the point cleared up...only that it might hang over the Treasury' as a stick with which to beat Newcastle.[72]

In addition to a reorganization of the commissariat, Ferdinand requested more troops. However, with the Belleisle expedition just departed, the ministry necessarily had to refuse. Hodgson's force was expected to create a useful diversion.[73]

No word had yet been received from Germany, which was unfortunate, since the replies of Ferdinand and Pierson did much to exonerate the Treasury. Pierson denied that the commissariat was to blame for the late retreat. The main reason had been the enemy superiority and the weakness of the allied forces, cut off as they had been from their supplies. Nevertheless, on the receipt of Newcastle's letter, he had gone immediately to Ferdinand to clear up the matter. The Prince had assured him that it 'was no part of his meaning to attribute the retreat of the army in any shape to the neglect of the Commissariat'. Newcastle must have misunderstood him, although Ferdinand admitted: 'The Commissariat wanted some improvement and alteration for the more easy and effectual carrying on of the service.' It was for this reason he had inserted 'that strong paragraph'.[74]

Further enquiry by the Treasury established Ferdinand's complaints to be twofold. One was a lack of commissaries: two were not enough when the army was divided into four or five corps. The other was the method of

---

[70] Ferdinand to Holdernesse, 30 Mar 1761, SP 87/40.

[71] Lord Bute, 21 Apr 1761, Add. Mss 32,922 ff 108–110.

[72] Devonshire Diary, 23 Apr 1761, DPC.

[73] Hodgson finally got away at the end of March, Keppel to Cleveland, 29 Mar 1761, Adm 1/91.

[74] Pierson to Newcastle, 20 Apr 1761, Add. Mss 32,922 ff 74–75. However, to Frederick II, Ferdinand expressed himself more freely: 'I have a monster of a commissariat, independent in some respects of me, and composed of several heads...each with its own chief or protector in England, but together as ignorant and as incapable, as they are avid to line their own pockets', quoted in Savory, *Britannic Majesty's Army*, 303.

settling the army's smaller purchases. Fifteen days were too long, being a discouragement to the 'country people'. The commissaries must have ready money, as in the Prussian system, with their own cashiers.[75]

Newcastle readily agreed to the appointment of five more commissaries.[76] However, the request for separate cashiers required further consideration. It had always been Treasury practice to restrict the power of issuing money to avert misappropriation. Several people issuing money made the possibilities for graft seem endless and, before taking so momentous a decision, Newcastle wanted to know more about the Prussian system. As Hardwicke pointed out, an autocrat like Frederick II could always ensure honesty among his servants by summarily hanging a few. Such ruthlessness was not possible in Britain. The sums being spent on the service were already immense and the greatest care must be taken to protect the public.[77] The Board had recently been furnishing the commissariat with £340,000 a month.[78] These massive outlays were contributing to the financial difficulties of the Treasury and threatening the war aims of the ministry.

Newcastle therefore would only consider the idea of separate cashiers simultaneously with another enquiry into how the existing costs of the army might be reduced. But examination revealed that the factors that were so damaging in the previous year were still prevalent. Further economies were not to be expected.[79] Nevertheless, Newcastle was determined that Ferdinand's new plan did not lead to any massive increases. To prevent this he decided to appoint an entirely new group of officials to be known as 'commissaries of control'. They were to be under the nominal direction of Pierson, but would otherwise operate separately with full powers to enquire into all dealings within the department. Pierson was in no circumstances to use them for other purposes.[80]

III

By now talk of peace was once more in the air.

A nation's foreign policy is customarily thought of as being one and indivisible, as expressed by the responsible minister. This view overlooks the complexities and contradictions that usually exist between one state and another. But in addition relations are often affected by domestic tensions that in themselves have little to do with foreign affairs. The new King and

[75] Treasury Board Minute, 28 Apr 1761, T 29/34.
[76] Treasury Board Minute, 30 Apr 1761, T 29/34.
[77] Hardwicke to Newcastle, 16 May 1761, Add. Mss 32,923 ff 123–125.
[78] Draft of a letter from the Treasury to Lord Granby, 23 Apr 1761, Add. Mss 32,922 ff 145–147.
[79] Treasury Board Minute, 1 May 1761, T 29/34. Ibid., 6 May 1761.
[80] Treasury Board Minute, 14 May 1761, T 29/34. Treasury to Bute, 19 May 1761, Add. Mss 32,923 ff 167–169, 179–181.

his favourite, Bute, were eager for peace so that they could begin the regeneration of British political life. However, they were terrified of appearing too pacific in case this increased Pitt's popularity. They were also scared that Pitt might resign before the conflict had ended. If that happened and the situation deteriorated, the events of 1756 might be repeated. The ministry would collapse and the King would be compelled to summon Pitt back on his own terms.[81] As a result, George III and Bute felt compelled to adopt an aggressive stance.

Without these tensions, peace might have been secured between Britain and France, and no war with Spain ensued. Initially, there seemed no cause for dispute. Bute acknowledged his inexperience, announcing that he would 'leave Mr Pitt master of foreign affairs, except when the Duke of Devonshire, my Lord Hardwicke and I [Newcastle] shall think Mr Pitt goes too far'.[82] Until the beginning of April the differences between the ministers were not great. All agreed that a recent approach by the French for talks should be explored, especially as the Prussians had given their consent once more to a separate negotiation, subject only to the same proviso that any agreement was not detrimental to their interest.[83] Concerning America, there was still some division of opinion whether to keep Canada or return it in exchange for Guadeloupe or some equivalent. However, everyone accepted that the minimum in America must be an acknowledgement of Britain's full claims to the continent under the Treaty of Utrecht. This would mean a frontier contiguous to the St Lawrence, incorporating the whole of Nova Scotia and New Brunswick, and including such strategic points as Ticonderoga, Crown Point, Frontenac, Niagara and Fort Duquesne. In Europe, Minorca must be returned and Germany evacuated, though this must not be secured at the expense of Britain's overseas acquisitions. Fortunately, compensation for Hanover was not an issue after the death of George II. His successor affected to be indifferent to the Electoral patrimony.

With these opinions Pitt seemed in close agreement. He had consistently acknowledged that the nation must be prepared to give up some of its conquests. After Wolfe's success, he told Newcastle that Quebec, Montreal and Louisburg should 'not be given up for nothing' but were certainly 'proper matters of negotiation'.[84] A year later he thought the nation should either retain Canada with exclusive right to the Newfoundland fishery, or keep what was claimed under the Treaty of Utrecht, plus the fishery, Guadeloupe and Goree. None was seemingly *sine qua non*.[85] As late as March 1761 he had observed to Hardwicke that concerning Canada 'it

---

[81] Devonshire Diary, 5 Nov 1760, DPC.

[82] Count Viry, 13 Mar 1761, Add. Mss 32,920 ff 158–159.

[83] Sir Richard Lodge, *Great Britain and Prussia in the Eighteenth Century* (Oxford, 1923), 110–115. Substance of a letter from the King of Prussia, 19 Dec 1760, Add. Mss 32,917 ff 45–47.

[84] Newcastle to Hardwicke, 31 Oct 1759, Yorke, III, 241–242.

[85] Newcastle to Hardwicke, 3 Dec 1760, Yorke, III, 314.

might be wiser and necessary (tho he hoped it would not become so) for the King under certain circumstances to give it up by Treaty, either in whole or in part'.[86] Like all the ministers, he seemed to believe that a good peace was now possible.

Then came the promotion of Bute and his estrangement from Newcastle. Suddenly, as if from wilful design, Pitt began to harden his attitude. He told Devonshire: 'Either we were in a situation to receive the law or to give it', and he rather 'thought the latter was our case'.[87] In a discussion with Newcastle on 9 April he announced that the minimum terms for a settlement must include the whole of Canada, together with an exclusive right to the Newfoundland fishery. Peace in any case was no longer his primary aim. More important was the need to inflict a lasting blow on the enemy, by diplomacy if possible, by hostilities if not.[88] This was the first time he had used such language or indicated such extensive views.

Pitt knew that the peace terms were a matter for all the ministers to decide. Foreign policy was one item that had always been discussed collectively. But he warned that if he was overruled on what he considered essential points, he would retire.[89]

The first moves for peace came, this time, from France. The ministry of Louis XV, disappointed at the failure of its commanders in Germany, was at last ready to consider a separate negotiation, even though this might mean abandoning its allies. The French were encouraged to treat by the knowledge that the court of Spain was ready to support them. There was a strong belief at both Bourbon courts that Britain was financially exhausted and might be ready to moderate her demands. Accordingly, at the end of March 1761, the French King issued a declaration to all the powers suggesting talks on the basis of possessions then held. The declaration was followed by a letter from Choiseul to Pitt proposing an exchange of envoys.[90] The response of the majority in the ministry was favourable, given the military situation. Ferdinand was on the defensive in Germany and, although Pitt affected to be optimistic because of the recently departed expedition to Belleisle, the rest felt that there was no certainty that the Prince would be able to resist the two armies then operating against him on the upper and lower Rhine.[91]

The next question was that of the epochs or time limits on which the talks were to be conducted. This was important if the discussions were held on

[86] Hardwicke to Newcastle, 17 Mar 1761, Add. Mss 32,920 ff 270–271.
[87] Devonshire Diary, 22 Apr 1761, DPC.
[88] Memorandum, 10 Apr 1761, Add. Mss 32,921 ff 381–382.
[89] Devonshire Diary, 9 Apr 1761, DPC.
[90] Declaration of the French King, 26 Mar 1761, SP 78/251. Choiseul to Pitt, 26 Mar 1761, SP 78/251.
[91] Pitt to Choiseul, 8 Apr 1761, SP 78/251. Newcastle to Hardwicke, 17 Apr 1761, Yorke, III, 315–317.

the basis of *uti possidetis*, or possessions in hand. The fortunes of war might alter dramatically during the negotiation and it was customary to set different limits on the various theatres to allow for the halting of more distant operations. Choiseul's initial proposals of 1 May for Europe, 1 July for America and 1 September for the East Indies immediately produced discord when they were discussed on 27 April. Pitt, with an eye to Belleisle, thought the dates too soon. The other ministers, with Germany in mind, disagreed. Pitt then renewed his threat to retire. In the end it was agreed to defer the matter.[92] In his next letter to Choiseul, Pitt simply announced the names of the three plenipotentiaries for the congress at Augsburg, and the man who was coming to Paris. The three plenipotentiaries were Lord Egremont, Lord Stormont and Yorke. The envoy for Paris was to be Hans Stanley.[93]

The instructions for the latter were considered at another meeting on 13 May when the general feeling was that the main talking ought to be done in London by the French envoy, Monsieur Bussy, since his government had requested the talks and presumably had proposals to make. However, Stanley could talk to Choiseul on the basis of *uti possidetis*, though he was not to sign anything without express instruction from one of the Secretaries of State. But when Pitt tried to clarify whether *uti possidetis* included the King's German possessions and those of his allies, the other ministers demurred, insisting that this be left until Bussy had arrived.[94] Pitt sulkily acquiesced, telling those present: 'Take my Lords which way you please. I shall give no opinion, I shall follow directions, but direction I must have.'[95] Further discussion then settled that any agreement between Britain and France must not depend on an understanding being reached at Augsburg; and that in the absence of any settlement there, Britain must be able to aid the King of Prussia as an auxiliary.[96]

In the third week of May, the British envoy set off for Paris. Stanley was well qualified for the task. Fluent in several languages, he had long been interested in foreign affairs. He had lived in Paris for a number of years and knew many of the people to whom he would be talking. Though he was attached to Newcastle, Pitt remembered his name when discussions were held about a suitable envoy.[97] There was a temporary halt while he waited at Calais for Bussy to appear, and this delay gave rise to fears that the French were stalling on the negotiations; Pitt accordingly ordered Stanley not to hurry. When he arrived in Paris he was to protest to Choiseul.[98] The fears

[92] Devonshire Diary, 27 Apr 1761, DPC.
[93] Pitt to Choiseul, 28 Apr 1761, SP 78/251.
[94] Devonshire Diary, 13 May 1761, DPC.
[95] Newcastle to Hardwicke, 14 May 1761, Add. Mss 32,923 ff 63–71.
[96] George II to Stanley, Instructions, 18 May 1761, SP 78/251.
[97] Namier and Brooke, *History of Parliament*, III, 468–469.
[98] Pitt to Stanley, 31 May 1761, SP 78/251.

proved unfounded, however. Bussy arrived in London on 5 June, properly contrite for his delay, while in Paris Choiseul disowned the conduct of his envoy. The first item of business was to settle the epochs under which the negotiations were to be conducted. Choiseul renewed his suggestion of 1 May for Europe, 1 July for America and 1 September for the East Indies.[99] The British countered with 1 July for Europe, 1 September for America, and 1 November for the East Indies.[100] Choiseul quickly agreed.

It was at this moment that the fall of Belleisle was announced. The conquest had by no means been easy. As Hawke had warned, getting ashore was the difficulty and Hodgson had only succeeded after several attempts. However, once ashore the enemy had had to retire to their fortress at Pallais, which had fallen on 8 June after a six-week siege.[101]

The operation did not pass without some criticism of Ligonier. Hodgson claimed that his artillery had been reduced to twenty-four rounds a day because his ammunition was low. Ligonier had been pressed several times to send extra stores, 'instead of which his Lordship . . . is pleased to insinuate that I used too much powder'. Hodgson was annoyed in part because Ligonier attributed to him 'three thousand more men' than he had. He told Albemarle: 'Facts advanced by one of His Lordships age and service, will if not timely contradicted, make impressions; for mankind are too ready to give credit to what old people are saying.'[102] Here was one officer at least who had no confidence in the octogenarian minister.

Another criticism was the performance of the engineers. Hodgson commented to Albemarle: 'It is impossible to tell you what a set of wretches I have for engineers.'[103] Despite Marlborough's reforms, this branch of the Ordnance had defied improvement since the beginning.

With the epochs settled, the respective parties could begin the more serious business of discussing terms. In London the talks were conducted by Pitt and Bute. Appearances were not promising. Bussy seemed reluctant to speak his mind. He also threw in some unacceptable conditions, notably the return of Belleisle without compensation.[104] Part of the problem may have been Pitt's domineering conduct, haranguing Bussy as though he were in the Commons.[105]

Hence, contrary to expectations, the discussions in Paris were to prove more productive. Initially, the talks there were equally slow. In the first

---

[99] Stanley to Pitt, 8 June 1761, SP 78/251.

[100] Paper to be submitted by Mr Pitt, 16 June 1761, SP 78/251.

[101] J. S. Corbett, *England in the Seven Years' War: A Study in Combined Strategy* (London, 1907), II, 160–170.

[102] Hodgson to Albemarle, 8 June 1761, printed in Keppel, *Life of Keppel*, I, 321–325.

[103] Hodgson to Albemarle, 17 May 1761, printed in Keppel, *Life of Keppel*, I, 317–320.

[104] Pitt to Stanley, 19 June 1761, SP 78/251.

[105] Memorandum, 15 July 1761, Add. Mss 32,925 ff 83–84. Stanley to Pitt, 28 June 1761, SP 78/251.

three interviews Stanley did not get beyond a discussion of philosophical principles, the cruel fortunes of war and the problems of conducting hostilities simultaneously by sea and land. But on 17 June, Choiseul, having established some rapport, began unfolding his thoughts on a settlement. Canada would be ceded entirely, except for Cape Breton Isle. This would be retained, unfortified, so that France's fishermen had a place to dry their catches and enjoy their rights under the Treaty of Utrecht. Guadeloupe, Marie Galante and Goree should be exchanged for Minorca. The French King would then evacuate the territory of George III and his allies in Germany, except that of Prussia. No mention was made of Belleisle or the demilitarization of Dunkirk, another potentially contentious issue.[106]

Stanley noted in his covering letter of 18 June the high price the French were placing on the return of Minorca and their obvious determination to fight for the fishery. He thought, however, that the proposals were only an opening gambit.[107] The French memoir was duly circulated by Pitt to the other ministers and a meeting to discuss them arranged for Wednesday 24 June. The initial reaction was one of satisfaction. Although Pitt disparaged the paper, the main outlines of an acceptable settlement were taking shape, judged by the original objectives of the war. The only point the ministers could not accept was the return of Cape Breton Island. Otherwise, the ceding of Canada was most acceptable, preempting as it did further debate on the keeping of that territory rather than Guadeloupe. But the ministers agreed that if the French were going to insist on the Treaty of Utrecht with respect to the fishery, they must be consistent and accept its provisions regarding the demilitarization of Dunkirk. For the rest, they thought Belleisle should be exchanged for Minorca, while Guadeloupe and Marie Galante would be the price for an evacuation by the French of their German conquests, including the Rhineland territories of Prussia.[108]

Unfortunately, as Newcastle reported to Devonshire, there was one serious point of disagreement, namely the fishery. Pitt was more than ever determined to exclude the French from this trade. The Treaty of Utrecht, he demanded, should in no circumstances be renewed regarding that article. If the French insisted, then the negotiation ought to be broken off. He would, however, submit to the opinion of the Council. Granville, for once taking an active part, replied that if the administration were to adopt so unaccommodating an attitude the nation would never have peace. Newcastle supported him, asserting it was foolish to put the chance of a good peace at risk. Bedford then stressed that while they argued over the fishery the position in Germany might collapse. But Pitt was not without support.

[106] French Proposals, 17 June 1761, SP 78/251. Marie Galante had been captured by Barrington shortly after his seizure of Guadeloupe in 1759.
[107] Stanley to Pitt, 18 June 1761, SP 78/251.
[108] Bedford to Lord Gower, 27 June 1761, PRO 30/29/1/14.

Temple took his position, as did Bute and Halifax, though both the latter thought the administration should not insist on the fishery if the French proved obdurate. At the end it was not clear what had been decided and Pitt was left to try and make sense of the discussion in a draft reply for the next meeting, which was fixed for Friday 26 June.[109]

On the renewal of the debate, Pitt first read his draft. Newcastle noted for the absent Devonshire: 'Some observations were made, but we agreed to hear the whole' before making any alteration. On most points the ministers agreed, especially over the cession of Canada and Cape Breton. When Pitt came to the fishery he suggested this should be left until the negotiators dealt with Dunkirk, linked as both were to the Treaty of Utrecht. In the meantime 'he had drawn that part agreeable to what he understood to be the sense of the Majority. . . He owned it was not his opinion; that he thought we ought to insist upon it, as a *sine qua non.*'[110] By so doing they would inflict a crushing blow on the old foe, for without the fishery the French would 'be incapacitated. . . from being any longer a naval power'. He admitted the demand was certain to lead to a breakdown in the talks. However, he was confident that 'another campaign of 16 millions would be buying it very cheaply', for 'his plan of operations on the coast of France during the Summer, and the conquest of Martinique before the winter would oblige them to it'.[111] The other ministers were not convinced. Bedford spoke about the rights of other nations. If Britain claimed a monopoly of the fishery, the ministry could 'not fail to alarm all the maritime powers of Europe and unite them against us'. The others then restated their views. Bute reaffirmed his idea of trying to get the fishery without making it a *sine qua non.*[112] Bedford believed he did this for purely domestic reasons. He informed Lord Gower confidentially: 'This behaviour of the Earl of Bute can be ascribed to nothing but the fear of Mr Pitt running away with all the popularity in the City.' Bedford was so disgusted that he left the meeting early, with the other ministers still 'hammering at a dispatch upon the middle system of civilly desiring the French to lie down quietly' so as to 'let us cut their throats'.[13]

In the event, the reply to Choiseul's first offer was closer in tone to what Pitt desired than what the more pacific members of the administration wanted. 'This little leaf is so loose and void of precision', Pitt informed Stanley in his dispatch of 26 June, that it could only be considered an opening proposition, not Choiseul's real terms.[114]

Militarily, Pitt's idea was to use the forces in Belleisle for a coastal

---

[109] Newcastle to Devonshire, 28 June 1761, Add. Mss 32,924 ff 310–315.
[110] Ibid., ff 315–317.
[111] Bedford to Gower, 27 June 1761, PRO 30/29/1/14.
[112] Newcastle to Devonshire, 28 June 1761, Add. Mss 32,924 ff 315–321.
[113] Bedford to Gower, 28 June 1761, PRO 30/29/1/14.
[114] Pitt to Stanley, 26 June 1761, SP 78/251.

demonstration, thereby forcing the French 'to make still further detachments from their armies in Germany'.[115] Even before the fall of Belleisle he had written to Keppel about Port L'Orient and Port Louis, both important bases for the French East India Company and used on occasion by the French navy. But the idea was no sooner raised than it was forgotten, for it was clear that there would not be enough troops to garrison Belleisle and engage in further coastal operations. The other part of the plan, the expedition to Martinique, met with more approval. With the enemy attempting to exert fresh pressure in Germany, it was only prudent to consider further operations to offset their efforts.[116] Indeed, the capture of this, the richest sugar island in the world, must speed the ruin of French trade, which had just received another blow with news of the fall of Pondicherry to the forces of Steevens and Coote.[117] The only objection was that the troops might be needed in Germany, where the armies of Soubise and Broglie were expected to unite shortly in one massive force. However, since the majority of the men for Martinique would be found in America, the ministers had little difficulty in agreeing to the proposal, especially since they had already accepted it in principle six months before.[118]

The decision was no sooner taken than the reassuring news arrived of Ferdinand's victory of Vellinghausen, where he had taken advantage of the personal antagonism between the two French commanders to inflict a sharp defeat on the forces of Broglie.[119] Militarily, the war still seemed to be going Britain's way.

Diplomatically too the situation seemed one for optimism, for Choiseul was ready to negotiate. On Canada he promised that the territory would be ceded unequivocally. The French King would also evacuate Germany and the barrier fortresses of Ostend and Nieuport, which had been garrisoned with Austrian permission since 1757. But he insisted in his response of 13 July that Louis XV could not suffer the indignity of allowing Dunkirk to be inspected by a foreign power, which was unnecessary since nature had made the place unfit for use by privateers. On Louisburg, Choiseul would accept another unfortified island, with no officials other than a judge and a few policemen. But he would sign no humiliating peace, which Pitt's reply seemed to require. Unless satisfaction were offered on the fishery, he would be forced into the arms of Austria, and by implication those of Spain. Choiseul several times hinted that a satisfactory peace could not be expected unless Spain's disputes with England were also settled.[120]

---

[115] Newcastle to Devonshire, 18 June 1761, Add. Mss 32,924 ff 151–159.
[116] Pitt to Keppel, 29 May 1761, printed in Keppel, *Life of Keppel*, I, 314. Keppel to Pitt, 10 July 1761, CP PRO 30/8/79.   [117] *London Chronicle*, 18/21 July 1761.
[118] Pitt to Amherst, 17 July 1761, Kimball, II, 452–454.
[119] *London Chronicle*, 25/28 July 1761.
[120] Stanley to Pitt, 1 July 1761, SP 78/251. Ibid., 14 July 1761. French Memoire, 13 July 1761, SP 78/251.

A meeting to consider these points and Pitt's reply was held on 24 July. The discussions began amicably enough. All the ministers agreed that the attempt to incorporate the Spanish claims into the negotiation was inadmissible. They reaffirmed that if France was going to claim her right to the fishery, then she must be consistent and accept the provisions of the Treaty of Utrecht regarding Dunkirk. But while there was general accord on the details, privately there was once more dissatisfaction with the tone of Pitt's draft. Newcastle commented that the letter to Stanley and the accompanying paper of points contained 'some very offensive expressions' which were not likely to conciliate the French or convince them of Britain's sincerity.[121] Hardwicke agreed. Both documents were 'very haughty and dictatorial', reminiscent of 'Louis XIV in the height of his glory and presumption'.[22] What upset the ministers was Pitt's insistence on inserting a protest at France's supposed delay in replying to the earlier paper. The southern Secretary affected to believe that this had been a deliberate move to gain time while France prosecuted the war in Germany. The only conciliatory part in the letter to Stanley was the instruction not to press the point about Dunkirk, if it meant breaking off the negotiation. Otherwise, he insisted, the earlier dispatch of 26 June still represented the King's final offer.[123]

Nevertheless, no alterations were effected and the results were as Newcastle feared. On reading the revised British paper of points, Choiseul complained that Pitt could have said the same in less offensive language. He then presented Stanley, on 5 August, with a copy of France's ultimate terms. It contained two main points. France must retain her rights to the fishery as guaranteed by the Treaty of Utrecht, with an *abri* or refuge for her fishermen. Secondly, France would evacuate the territories of George III, Hesse and Brunswick, but not those of Prussia which were being held in trust for her allies. Settlement of this matter could only be determined at the proposed congress at Augsburg.[124] In his covering letter Stanley tried to calm obviously troubled waters. He explained that the previous delay had not been deliberate, but caused by Choiseul being so overburdened with business. All the foreign ministers were complaining of inattention to their affairs. Stanley himself had done his best. But he could not conceal his feeling that Pitt's dispatches had not helped. 'Though you are extremely skilled in the French language', he told Pitt, there had been some ambiguities which a British translation had not entirely clarified.[125]

The receipt of this letter and the French ultimatum caused renewed dismay and despondency among the more pacific members of the ministry,

121 Newcastle to Hardwicke, 1 Aug 1761, Add. Mss 32,926 ff 125–131.
122 Hardwicke to Newcastle, 2 Aug 1761, Add. Mss 32,926 ff 139–142.
123 Pitt to Stanley, 25 July 1761, SP 78/251.
124 Ultimatum of France, 5 Aug 1761, SP 78/252.
125 Stanley to Pitt, 6 Aug 1761, SP 78/252.

and the next meeting on 13 August was accordingly acrimonious. Hardwicke began the discussion by observing that the paper of 25 July 'did not quite agree with the sense of the last meeting'. Its tone had obviously upset Choiseul and put the negotiations at risk. Pitt warmly defended himself, saying that he had only followed the advice of those present. Devonshire then suggested that to avoid future dispute, proper minutes ought to be taken, as formerly.[126] The point was as quickly forgotten as it had been raised, being overtaken by the issue of whether to continue the negotiations with Bussy in London. Pitt had not seen the ambassador since 6 August, ostensibly because of the offensive inclusion of the Spanish memorial, but in reality, Hardwicke thought, because Bussy had been ordered to make a strong protest at the recent tone of the British counter-proposals. 'After much altercation and some thumps of the fist on the table, it was at last carried . . . that the conference should be had.' A written invitation was considered desirable and Pitt was asked to draft it. Another meeting was held two days later to vet this. Once more there were unpleasantries. Hardwicke thought the letter was 'much too long and irritating'.[127] Granville agreed: 'The letter was a fine piece of oratory, a classical and elegant performance, but all his experience had taught him that in Negotiation, plain language and style did best.' Pitt, not surprisingly, 'flew into a great passion'. He asserted that his letter to Bussy had been written in 'the plainest language . . . he would not suffer an Iota in it to be altered – it should not be cobbled by anyone'. In the end the matter was put to the vote. With some support from Halifax and Bute, Pitt succeeded in carrying his version by six votes to five, with one abstention.[128]

So much time was spent debating the letter to Bussy that another meeting had to be arranged to consider Pitt's reply to Stanley concerning the French ultimatum of 5 August. Wednesday 19 August was accordingly fixed for this. The occasion proved comparatively harmonious. No one wanted a repetition of the earlier events. The ministers, Pitt included, rapidly agreed that to keep the negotiations going they would acknowledge the right of the French to the fishery and offer them a suitable place for drying their catches. However, Britain, like France, must insist on her rights under the Treaty of Utrecht. The fortifications around Dunkirk would have to be dismantled. Concerning Germany, both sides should assist their allies with money only.[129] Another meeting, however, proved necessary to fix an *abri* so that Pitt's dispatch to Stanley only left London on 27 August.[130] By now events had gone too far for these concessions to have effect. There can be little doubt that had they been offered a month earlier instead of in Pitt's letter of 25

[126] Devonshire Diary, 13 Aug 1761, DPC.
[127] Hardwicke to Lord Royston, 15 Aug 1761, Yorke, III, 320.
[128] Devonshire Diary, 15 Aug 1761, DPC.
[129] Hardwicke to Royston, 22 Aug 1761, Yorke, III, 321–322.
[130] Pitt to Stanley, 27 Aug 1761, SP 78/252.

July, peace would have been secured. Instead, as Newcastle explained to Yorke: 'We had, or pretended to have, such a diffidence of Monsieur Choiseul's sincerity at first as gave him such doubts of our *sincerity* that he found himself obliged, in interest, to adopt another system.'[131] Choiseul, as Stanley had repeatedly warned, was under intense pressure from Austria and Spain not to sign a peace detrimental to their interests. When it became clear that Pitt and the other elements in the British administration were seeking to inflict a humiliating peace on France, Choiseul had little option but to seek an understanding with Spain.

The Family Compact, signed on 15 August, did not commit Spain to a war with Britain. The main point of the treaty was the professed readiness of the two signatories to settle their disputes together. Spain would only take up arms if the two Crowns could not obtain a reasonable settlement of their claims. Both courts hoped that their agreement would make the British more moderate. Equally, they recognized that this might not happen, hence the secret clauses committing Spain after eight months to full diplomatic and military support for France.[132]

News of the signing of the Family Compact reached London in a dispatch from Stanley early in September. Even now the British envoy asserted that there was hope of an agreement. Choiseul had informed him that if the outstanding point of the fishery could be settled, then France might yet disengage herself from Spain. Unfortunately, the fishery continued to bedevil the negotiations. Choiseul asserted that St Pierre, the *abri* offered off the south-west coast of Newfoundland, was unknown to him. If suitable he would accept it, together with the other British proposals respecting Germany and Dunkirk.[133] But the spirit had gone out of the talks. Stanley reported on 4 September that Choiseul seemed irresolute, raising small difficulties as though he wanted an excuse for rejecting the whole. The envoy could not avoid suspecting that the French were delaying matters so that Spain could put her house in order before beginning hostilities.[134]

It was to consider these issues that a ministerial meeting was arranged for 15 September. Present with the two Secretaries of State were Henley, Granville, Devonshire, Newcastle, Halifax, Holdernesse, Hardwicke, Temple, Mansfield, Ligonier and Anson. The discussion began with the question of whether Stanley ought to be recalled from Paris, thus giving official recognition to the ending of the talks. Most of the ministers agreed: Stanley's presence was doing no good; he ought to be recalled.[135] Only Newcastle differed on this point, arguing that so long as talks continued there was an apparent prospect of peace, which would assist the raising of

---

[131] Newcastle to Yorke, 18 Sept 1761, Add. Mss 32,928 ff 211–215.
[132] C. Parry (ed.), *The Consolidated Treaty Series* (New York, 1969), XLII, 85–100.
[133] Stanley to Pitt, 2 Sept 1761, SP 78/252.
[134] Ibid., 4 Sept 1761.
[135] Devonshire Diary, 15 Sept 1761, DPC.

the supplies.[136] The meeting then turned to the issue of Spain. Pitt, supported by Temple, thought there ought to be an immediate declaration of war. Spain was clearly preparing for hostilities and the King's ministers ought to anticipate her by striking a blow before she was ready. An intercepted dispatch between Fuentes and the Marquis de Grimaldi, the ambassador in Paris, made it clear why there had been no public announcement of the recently concluded agreement: the court of Madrid wanted to avoid hostilities until the treasure fleet from America had arrived and the country was in a condition for war.[137] But, whatever the Spanish intentions, Pitt was no longer impressed by their military capacity. Indeed, he now wanted to inflict on Spain the same mortal blow he was seeking to give France. The present crisis was a golden opportunity to crush both branches of the Bourbon dynasty.

The majority of the ministers could not agree. The nation had not gone to war for so extravagant an aim. Other objections were voiced, too. Anson thought the navy was not yet ready to engage another major naval power and produced a paper to show how the fleet's 105 ships of the line and 82,000 men were fully employed. A war with Spain would mean an enormous extension of responsibilities in the Mediterranean, East and West Indies, as well as the area between Finisterre and Cape Verde. Bedford supported him, pointing out that the nation would have difficulty finding the money. Newcastle could only confirm this point. Despite Temple's assertion that the merchants were willing to lend £14,000,000, Newcastle reported that so far he had been unable to secure more than £12,000,000. He had also been warned that if war broke out with Spain, the City would not even vouch for that.[138]

The pessimism of Newcastle was not without reason. In May, there had been a banking crisis during which a number of City houses stopped payment; and in July a leading financier had suggested that the next instalment of the loan be deferred, since many subscribers were having to borrow to meet their payments.[139] The situation was so threatening that Newcastle had for once consulted the whole ministry, though to little effect. Bute could only suggest that the expenses in America be cut. Pitt strongly opposed this, thinking of the Martinique expedition. Newcastle supported him, since a 'million is a trifle now'.[140] But this did not mean that the nation could continue the war much longer. The paymaster was in difficulties

---

[136] Newcastle had expressed his views earlier to Bedford, 13 Sept 1761, Add. Mss 32,928 ff 131–134.

[137] Grimaldi to Fuentes, 31 Aug 1761, Add. Mss 32,927 ff 299–300.

[138] Memoranda, 15 Sept 1761, Add. Mss 32,928 ff 185–187.

[139] Watkins to Newcastle, 28 May 1761, Add. Mss 32,923 ff 282–283. Memorandum, 15 July 1761, Add. Mss 32,925 ff 83–84. Barrington to Newcastle, 21 July 1761, Add. Mss 32,925 f 231.

[140] Account of what Happened in the Council, 20 Aug 1761, Add. Mss 32,927 f 131. Newcastle to Mansfield, 22 Aug 1761, Add. Mss 32,927 ff 173–175.

again, having only £600,000 to meet anticipated demands of £1,200,000.[141] And, after the deficiencies of the current year had been met, a total supply of £20,000,000 would be needed in 1762, of which £14,000,000 would have to be borrowed.[142]

Nevertheless, when the diplomatic discussions were renewed on 18 September, Pitt and Temple reiterated their demand for an immediate break with Spain. The other ministers reaffirmed their opposition. They felt that war with Spain would not necessarily follow a breakdown of the Anglo-French negotiations or the signing of the Family Compact. The ministers still did not know the actual nature of the Bourbon commitment. The Spanish government had declared there was nothing of a hostile nature to Britain. The evidence was that the two powers were by no means anxious to fulfil their recently concluded agreement. In these circumstances it was foolish to anticipate a declaration of war. The majority felt that the sensible course was to try and keep Spain detached from France, not add her as an enemy of Britain. With this in mind they thought the best method would be the seeking of a categorical assurance from Spain of her friendly intentions. The demand should be coupled with a conciliatory offer to evacuate Honduras pending a final settlement of that dispute. If the reply was still unsatisfactory, an additional seven ships of the line with 3,000 troops would then be dispatched to the Caribbean, and a substantial reinforcement sent to Admiral Saunders in the Mediterranean.[143]

With these decisions Pitt and Temple could not agree. They therefore announced their intention of drawing up a separate minute for the King, emphasizing the hostile actions of Spain and advising an immediate opening of hostilities.[144]

The delivery of a separate minute was unusual. Dissenters normally noted their opposition on the same minute as that presented by the majority. The King could then question them if he desired.[145] In any case, George III refused to accept the paper when Pitt tried to present it on 21 September, stating that he would take no resolution until Stanley had returned from Paris. George III believed that the envoy might have additional information on the Family Compact that could alter the whole aspect of the affair.[146] Later that same day there was another meeting about Spain. The discussion, however, retrod the now stale ground of the two previous meetings. The only difference was a slight change of tone by Pitt. Previously he had declared that 'he would execute any resolution' the ministers should come

---

[141] State of the Paymaster's credit, 10 Sept 1761, Add. Mss 33,040 ff 68–73.

[142] State of the Several Expenses, [undated], Add. Mss 33,040 ff 251–255.

[143] Memoranda and Minute of the Meeting, 18 Sept 1761, Add. Mss 32,928 ff 227–233. Lord Hardwicke's Notes, 18 Sept 1761, Yorke III, 275–276.

[144] Paper signed by Lord Temple and Mr Pitt, 18 Sept 1761, Add. Mss 32,928 ff 225–226.

[145] Hardwicke to Newcastle, 22 Sept 1761, Add. Mss 32,928 ff 320–321.

[146] Newcastle to Hardwicke, 21 Sept 1761, Yorke III, 325–326.

to. Now he was saying 'he would not do it; that the other Secretary or Lords used to the business might'.[147] He acquiesced in the decision to await the arrival of Stanley, but insisted on giving Bute his paper for the King.

A discussion among a number of the ministers after Pitt had left revealed a general recognition that he might resign and that they ought to be ready with the name of a successor. This time there was little fear of such eventuality.[148] But the question still needed careful consideration and Devonshire, Granville, Bute, Newcastle, Anson and Mansfield held another, more private, meeting two days later to determine their course of action. After some deliberation they decided against presenting the King with a counter-minute: 'The drawing of papers against one another would be a very bad custom.'[149] Instead, the ministers would give the King their opinions verbally, one by one, which they did the following day.[150] Hardwicke, who had just been striken by the death of his wife, much approved. A paper war between the ministers would be most undesirable: 'The delivering of such formal papers might lay a foundation for calling for minutes of the Cabinet Council by Parliament.' The King's prerogative would be much undermined.[151]

Stanley did not reach England before the end of the month, so that no final decision on the matter of Spain was possible until 2 October, much as Pitt might press it. The meeting, emphasizing its importance, was for once held at St James's, Granville, Temple, Devonshire, Newcastle, Bute, Hardwicke, Ligonier, Anson, Mansfield and Pitt being present.[152] Pitt began the proceedings by reiterating his arguments for an immediate commencement of hostilities. Britain was prepared, Spain was not. The court of Madrid had forfeited any right to diplomatic courtesy by its clandestine negotiations with France. The nation must strike before it was too late. Newcastle the first to reply, stressed the huge expense that such action must entail. Bute supported him; war with Spain was for the moment inadvisable. Hardwicke then spoke about the folly of anticipating a union of the Bourbon powers which might yet be avoided. Anson too emphasized the unreadiness of the fleet to engage another naval power. Newcastle knew that the King put great store by Anson's views. Two days earlier he had asserted that if Anson spoke out this 'cuts short at once any consideration of immediate operations'.[153] Mansfield then dwelt on the danger of

---

[147] Devonshire Diary, 21 Sept 1761, DPC.
[148] Newcastle to Hardwicke, 21 Sept 1761, Yorke, III, 326.
[149] Devonshire Diary, 23 Sept 1761, DPC. Newcastle to Hardwicke, 23 Sept 1761, Add. Mss 32,928 ff 325–330.
[150] Devonshire Diary, 24 Sept 1761, DPC.
[151] Hardwicke to Newcastle, 24 Sept 1761, Add. Mss 32,928 ff 334–335.
[152] Devonshire Diary, 2 Oct 1761, DPC. Newcastle and Hardwicke also made lengthy notes of the meeting which are published in Yorke, III, 277–280. All three closely agree.
[153] Memorandum, 30 Sept 1761, Add. Mss 32,929 ff 2–6.

increasing the jealousies of the maritime powers. Finally, Ligonier stressed the by no means derisory strength of the Spanish army, with 70,000 men plus 20,000 Neapolitans. Spain had cut a great figure in Queen Anne's war and no one ought to forget it. Only Temple supported the southern Secretary.[154]

Pitt, recognizing the almost unanimous opinion of his colleagues, began what was effectively a resignation speech. He first recalled the circumstances of his rise to power, stating that he had been called 'by his Sovereign, and he might say, in some degree by the voice of the People, to assist the State, when others had *abdicated* the service of it'. He had answered that call and, despite much obstruction, had carried on a most singularly successful war. While good fortune had played its part, 'there was hardly one expedition which he had proposed, tho' the most probable and at last attended with the best success, that had not been before treated as chimerical and ridiculous'. Now unsupported he would not continue, convinced as he was that the only possible course was the one outlined in his paper of 18 September. He had in his bag such material that 'it would be criminal in him, as Secretary of State, to let this affair sleep in his office'. The conspiracy of the two Bourbon powers 'was the greatest indignity that ever had been offered to the Crown of Great Britain'. Such conduct could not be condoned. As southern Secretary he was responsible for Spanish affairs. This being the case 'nobody could be surprised that he could go on no longer'. He could only repeat: 'He would be responsible for nothing but what he directed' and with which he agreed.[155]

The speech is a good example of Pitt's frequent disregard of facts and love of exaggeration. There were a number of points the ministers might have refuted. Newcastle, Hardwicke and Anson had not abdicated their responsibilities in 1756: they had been forced from office by Fox's resignation and Pitt's refusal to work with them.[156] The voice of the people played no part in his admission to office. It had been Pitt's ability to halt the business of the government in the Commons that had led to his appointment as Secretary of State. Most of the expeditions had received the full support of the ministers: only the coastal operations had been questioned. Finally, it was ludicrous for Pitt to claim all the credit for the war's successes. Every action of government had been a collective one, from the ministers in Whitehall to the men on the battlefield.

Pitt's speech of course was not intended as a reasoned analysis. It was an impassioned plea in a highly emotional situation. The other ministers, well accustomed to these histrionics, let the diatribe pass. Granville, replying on

---

[154] Notes at a Meeting of the Lords, 2 Oct 1761, Yorke, III, 277–278.
[155] Minutes of the Meeting, 2 Oct 1761, Yorke, III, 279–280.
[156] J. C. D. Clark, *The Dynamics of Change: The Crisis of the 1750s and English Party Systems* (Cambridge, 1982), 231–282.

behalf of the majority, addressed himself simply to one point, Pitt's position as minister. He reminded him: 'The King might take a Foreign measure with his Secretary of State only, but that if the King referred the matter to the Council, the opinion of the majority of the Council was the measure, the rest was only execution.' Pitt of course was not disputing this. He was merely saying that he could not execute a measure in his department unless he was in agreement with it. There followed an exchange of civilities, in which Pitt admitted he had indeed received 'great support, in particular instances, from other Lords of the old administration'. He then withdrew, accompanied only by Temple, leaving the remainder to decide what to do on the question of Spain. For the moment they did not send a letter to Bristol, pending the appointment of a new Secretary. However, they decided not to delay taking further action. Anson was to inform George III that 'the Lords. . . were of opinion a considerable reinforcement be sent' immediately to Admiral Saunders at Gibraltar.[157]

The departure of Pitt was accepted as being inevitable if not desirable. No attempt was made to dissuade him. There was general recognition that the government could not continue as it had during the last five months. The ministry wanted peace and everyone agreed with Bedford that there was no prospect of this while Pitt remained Secretary.[158] Over Spain, most of the ministers were not prepared to extend the conflict gratuitously. Admittedly, Bute and Newcastle were a little nervous of the consequences. Though Pitt had promised the King he would not go into opposition, both were conscious that if affairs took a turn for the worse, the administration might be placed in a difficult parliamentary position. As Dupplin observed: 'Pitt goes out with all the glory of success, which whether justly or unjustly. . . will be attributed to him.'[159] Newcastle recognized too the value of Pitt's contribution to the war. He commented to Hardwicke: 'With all his faults, we shall want Mr Pitt. There is no one so able to push an expedition as he.'[160] But widespread feeling existed that the Secretary was not indispensable. One writer in the *London Chronicle* commented: 'It is to be hoped that more than one man, or one score of men, are to be found among us, that have capacity and ability for managing the helm of state, otherwise our case were indeed miserable.'[161] In the City there was even relief. Some financiers believed that the departure of the warlike Secretary would make it easier for the Treasury to secure the money needed for the next supply.[162]

Nevertheless, it has been customary to assert that Pitt left office to the

[157] Minutes of the Meeting, 2 Oct 1761, Add. Mss 32,929 ff 18–24.
[158] Bedford to Newcastle, 14 Sept 1761, Add. Mss 32,928 ff 158–161.
[159] Kinnoull to Newcastle, 13 Oct 1761, Add. Mss 32,929 ff 229–231.
[160] Newcastle to Hardwicke, 15 Nov 1761, Add. Mss 32,931 ff 45–47.
[161] *London Chronicle*, 10/13 Oct 1761.
[162] Memorandum – Deputy Governor, 6 Oct 1761, Add. Mss 32,929 ff 83–87.

dismay of the whole nation. Those making such assertions have too often overlooked the partisan nature of what was said and have been too selective. Even the press on this occasion was far from unanimous. Papers like the *Monitor*, which invariably praised him, eulogized him now. Those like the *London Chronicle* remained more critical.

Pitt explained his reasons for departing to George III in a final interview on 5 October. He stressed that his resignation was not intended to embarrass the ministry but to assist, since his continued membership could only induce disagreement and perplexity at a critical time.[163] These sentiments were accepted by George III. But when the King suggested some acknowledgement for his services, Pitt burst into tears, confirming his highly emotional state. The need to offer some reward was strengthened because Pitt's own financial circumstances were far from secure. That night Bute accordingly settled that Pitt should receive a pension of £3,000 and his wife a title.[164]

The offer and acceptance were unimpeachable. Nevertheless, many commentators placed the worst construction on the transaction: Pitt had sold his office for monetary gain. Various pieces appeared on the theme of the 'Right Honourable Annuitant', and there were references to 'Lady Cheatham'.[165] To counter these, Pitt published a letter to Beckford in the City. In this he explained that he had resigned on a matter of principle and was only offered the pension after his departure had been accepted. Then he had only taken it at the insistence of the King.[166]

In the heat of these exchanges, there were surprisingly few appreciations of Pitt's ministerial achievement. This may have been because most writers did not accept that his departure was permanent. The only significant exception was the Common Council which in mid-October voted its thanks to Pitt while expressing apprehension at what must follow the loss of 'so able and upright a minister' at this critical juncture.[167] Not until the middle of November did other tributes begin to appear. The City of York thanked Pitt 'for the signal advantages this nation has derived from his upright, wise and vigorous administration'.[168] The merchants of Dublin followed. It had been Pitt's 'patriot and singularly wise and upright administration' which had rescued the nation from ' the shameful infection of that ministerial panic which had called foreign mercenaries in' during 1756. Thereafter Pitt had inspired 'the Councils and Arms of Britain with that ancient and true spirit, which when duly exerted, ever has and ever must render the British name terrible to her foes'. Finally, the merchants believed that Pitt would be

---

[163] Newcastle to Bedford, 6 Oct 1761, Add. Mss 32,929 ff 80–81.

[164] G. F. S. Elliot, *The Border Elliots and the Family of Minto* (Edinburgh, 1897), 367–368.

[165] *London Chronicle*, 15/17 Oct 1761. M. Peters, *Pitt and Popularity: The Patriot Minister and London Opinion during the Seven Years' War* (Oxford, 1980), 205–208.

[166] Pitt to Beckford, 15 Oct 1761, printed in W. S. Taylor and J. H. Pringle (eds.), *The Correspondence of William Pitt, Earl of Chatham* (London, 1838), II, 158–159.

[167] Reprinted in the *London Chronicle*, 22/24 Oct 1761.   [168] Ibid., 10/12 Nov 1761.

remembered for leading an administration in which 'instead of private interest, merit was the only recommendation'. The merchants could only express grief at his departure mingled with admiration for his virtue.[169]

However, the most complete testimony to Pitt was that of Edmund Burke in the *Annual Register*. Burke wrote: 'We may affirm with truth and impartiality that no man was ever better fitted than Mr Pitt to be the minister in a great and powerful nation... There was in all his designs, a magnitude and even vastness which was not easily comprehended by every mind, and which nothing but success could have made to appear reasonable'. Remarkably, 'he was called to the ministry by the voice of the people and what is more rare, he held it with that approbation... Under him Great Britain carried on the most important war in which she was ever engaged, alone and unassisted with greater splendour and with more success than she had ever enjoyed at the the head of the most powerful alliances.' But admiration for Pitt did not blind Burke to his faults, especially his 'want of judgement'. He commented: 'Happy it had been for him, for his sovereign, and his country, if a temper less austere, and a disposition more practicable, more compliant and conciliating, had been joined to his other great virtues.'[170] Equally Burke was aware that Pitt was not indispensable, for he later commented after his resignation: 'There was a necessity of showing that the spirit of the nation and wisdom of its councils, were not confined to a single man', and 'it was shown effectually'.[171]

This eulogy is interesting in that it eloquently summarizes many of the more flattering things published while Pitt was in office.[172] Most of Burke's conclusions cannot now be accepted. Pitt was not called to office by the voice of the people. He did not maintain his position because of it. The nation had not fought the war single-handed. Finally, as Burke had to admit, the vastness of Pitt's designs was only apparent *after* the event.

[169] Ibid., 8/10 Dec 1761.
[171] *Annual Register for 1762*, 5.

[170] *Annual Register for 1761*, 42–48.
[172] Peters, *Pitt and Popularity*.

8

War with Spain: Conclusion

I

The first thing required on the resignation of Pitt and Temple was a reconstruction of the ministry. Plans were quickly made to effect this. The names most frequently mentioned for the Secretaryship were those of Grenville and Lord Egremont. The choice ultimately fell on Egremont, Grenville finding it too embarrassing to succeed his brother-in-law.[1] The promotion of Egremont, however, meant that both Secretaries were in the Lords, while none of the major office-holders had a seat in the Commons. This lack of ministerial representation in the lower House had caused much difficulty at the beginning of the war. Nevertheless, the government determined to persist in the plan. Bute, Newcastle, Hardwicke and Devonshire met Grenville, Fox, Townshend and Barrington to urge on them the need to exert themselves on the government's behalf. To ensure that they were properly informed, Grenville would be called to the Cabinet Council and act as leader of the House.[2]

This was not to be the only change. Bute and George III were dissatisfied with the manner in which the Cabinet Council was working. They were not alone in their opinion. At the time of the discussions over Ferdinand's campaign that spring, Hardwicke had confessed he thought it a most improper subject. The operations were too far away and, in so large a body, there was always the possibility of idle talk, 'babbled by accident or through vanity', leading to the plans becoming public.[3] Bute could only agree. He told Hardwicke that he was thinking in terms of an inner group of four: himself, Egremont, Grenville and Newcastle. Hardwicke, somewhat surprised, cautioned against anything too drastic. Otherwise those persons who had been accustomed to attending might take offence. Bute assured him 'he meant upon material points, to call a meeting something larger after the

---

[1] Narrative of events, Oct 1760, printed in W. J. Smith (ed.), *The Grenville Papers, being the Correspondence of Richard Grenville, Earl Temple, K.G., and the right Honourable George Grenville, their Friends and Contemporaries* (London, 1852), I, 409–411.
[2] Memorandum, 3 Oct 1761, Add. Mss 32,929 ff 48–50.
[3] Hardwicke to Newcastle, 22 Apr 1761, Add. Mss 32,922 ff 136–137.

first proposition'.[4] There would in effect be an inner and outer group, though not of the kind that Burke suggested later. Constitutionally, the proposal was unobjectionable and might mean the more efficient dispatch of important business. Only Newcastle objected, fearing he would be in a permanent minority of three to one.[5]

Meanwhile, the expedition for Martinique, which Pitt had organized, had departed. The plan was for four regiments from Belleisle plus a squadron of ships under Rodney to meet up with 8,000 troops in America at Barbados. The whole would then proceed to its objective.[6] The command of the army had been left to Amherst who had chosen Monckton, one sign that Cumberland's influence was by no means complete, for he had only a poor opinion of his abilities.[7]

During the ministerial changes, Newcastle had again been wrestling with the problems of the commissariat, for, contrary to all his hopes, the reforms that spring had not proved efficacious. During the summer, various charges were made about dealings in false receipts. One contractor had already fled to Holland.[8] Even so, Pierson was reluctant to act. The men accused were friends of Prince Ferdinand and the superintendent was fearful that any investigation might lead to his resignation.[9] However, if Pierson thought he could prevent an enquiry he was mistaken. Apart from concern for economy, Newcastle feared that the scandal might become public. The war in Germany was sufficiently unpopular. Revelations of widespread fraud could prove fatal. In the middle of October it was reported that the Common Council was about to call for an enquiry. This action appeared linked with the resolution thanking Pitt for his services on leaving the ministry. Everything seemed to suggest that the former minister would begin the new Parliament with an attack on the commissariat and Newcastle's handling of it.[10] In that case, Newcastle would have no choice but to lay the matter before Parliament. Indeed, he had given the junior Lords instructions to support any such motion if one came before the Commons. In the meantime, Newcastle would do his best to clean up the department himself.[11]

The investigations at the end of October made it all too plain that widespread deception had taken place. Those involved included not only the Prussian contractors but members of the commissariat as well. There

[4] Hardwicke to Newcastle, 9 Oct 1761, Add. Mss 32,929 ff 144–146.
[5] Newcastle to Hardwicke, 8 Oct 1761, Add. Mss 32,929 ff 116–117.
[6] J. S. Corbett, *England in the Seven Years' War: A Study in Combined Strategy* (London, 1907), II, 208–211.
[7] Cumberland to Newcastle, 10 Feb 1762, Add. Mss 32,934 f 267.
[8] Hulton to Martin, 18 Aug 1761, Add. Mss 32,927 ff 88–92. Fuhr to Martin, 22 Aug 1761, Add. Mss 32,927 ff 163–166. Both Hulton and Fuhr were officials in the commissariat.
[9] Pierson to Newcastle, 21 Sept 1761, Add. Mss 32,928 ff 292–294.
[10] Newcastle to Hardwicke, 18 Oct 1761, Add. Mss 32,929 ff 356–357. Resolutions of the Common Council, 22 Oct 1761, Add. Mss 32,929 f 442.
[11] Newcastle to Yorke, 23 Oct 1761, Add. Mss 32,929 ff 460–468.

were seemingly three areas of laxity. The first was in the deputy paymaster's department where a number of irregularities had been tolerated. Then there was the matter of poor hay, which a number of magazine-keepers had connived at accepting. But most serious of all was the traffic in forged receipts.[12] These illegalities seemed so extensive to Newcastle and his Treasury colleagues that after several meetings they decided on the appointment of yet another set of commissaries to enquire into the allegations. The man in charge was to be Sir James Cockburne, at present senior commissary of accounts.[13] Meanwhile, Pierson was to be given the first vacant regiment and relieved of his position. Though still personally above suspicion, the Board recognized that nothing could be done while he was still in control. These ideas were duly reported to Bute and the other ministers on 8 November.[14]

By now the ministry had returned to the matter of Spain. The letter to Bristol in Madrid was finally sent on 28 October, demanding assurances of that power's peaceful intentions, but offering to negotiate the logwood affair.[15] While awaiting the results of this initiative the ministry prepared for war. Anson sent Saunders instructions to explore the possibility of attacking Cadiz.[16] Steps were taken simultaneously to recruit the army, for it was recognized that any breakdown in relations was likely to lead to an invasion of Portugal by Spain. Britain was allied to that country and bound to assist.[17] The ministry realized that this time the expansion of the army could not be done by independent companies. Since normal recruitment was as unpromising as ever, the only solution appeared to be the formation of new corps by the nobility.

Soon, Ligonier and Townshend were hard at work on the details. The hope was that the army's establishment could be increased by 10,000 men. Most of the new augmentation was sought in Scotland. Among the corps to be raised was a regiment of Highlanders under Colonel Graham, made up of two battalions of 600 men each, and six other units of a similar size under Majors Nairn, Hamilton, Monckton, Ogle, Crauford and Deacon. In addition, three other normal-sized battalions were being formed under Colonels Barré, Beauclerk and McDowell, and another Highland corps under Major McClean. All were to be completed in five months at the expense of their commanding officers.[18] As to the ranks in Germany, this was left to Ligonier. The returns from Hanover revealed that the army there,

[12] Treasury Board Minute, 10 Nov 1761, T 29/34.
[13] Martin to Pierson, 3 Nov 1761, Add. Mss 32,930 ff 293–295.
[14] Newcastle to Bute, 8 Nov 1761, Add. Mss 32,930 ff 355–356.
[15] Egremont to Bristol, 28 Oct 1761, SP 94/164.
[16] Anson to Saunders, Oct 1761, Anson Papers, G 615/HMC/ Box U, Stafford Record Office.
[17] A Defensive Treaty between Great Britain and Portugal, 1703, printed in G. Chalmers, *A Collection of Treaties between Great Britain and Other Powers* (London, 1790), II, 296–303. C. Parry (ed.), *The Consolidated Treaty Series* (New York, 1969), XXIV, 401–407.
[18] Townshend to Egremont, 3 Nov 1761, WO 4/66. The new corps are listed in the estimates for 1762, *JHC* XXIX, 29.

nominally 100,000 men, mustered only 78,000 fit for duty.[19] The British contingents wanted 1,600 men. Ligonier proposed to find these by a draft on the Irish establishment.[20]

The determination of the ministry to act vigorously was reflected in a letter from Ligonier to Amherst, in which he affirmed that 'every measure will be pressed on the same plan it had been digested before Mr Pitt's retreat'.[21] Newcastle rather sadly noted this was being done not from principle but simply out of 'fear of Mr Pitt's popularity'. This, he believed, would prove utterly futile for, try as they might, they would not emulate the recently departed Secretary in this respect.[22] The desire to gain popularity by appearing belligerent was reflected in the King's speech. Though Hardwicke drafted the first outline, both Bute and Grenville made extensive changes. The speech promised 'the most vigorous Efforts in every part' as the best means of producing an appropriate peace.[23]

Parliament assembled on 3 November. The first business was the election of a speaker and normal proceedings did not begin for another three days. The speech was well received. The one item of contention was the lack of any mention of the militia, especially for Scotland. Pitt kept to his word about not going into opposition. In a series of statements he reaffirmed that he had resigned on a matter of principle concerning the direction of his department, a privilege that all ministers ought to enjoy. He then denied having been sole minister: 'In the Treasury, in the Military, in the Navy he had never assumed or claimed any direction', always applying 'to the ministers of those several departments . . . through the channels of each office'. This would be clear if the papers respecting the Spanish negotiations were laid before Parliament. However, he respected the wishes of the ministry that such delicate matters ought not to be revealed. But he could affirm that he personally had done everything possible to avoid a war with that power. He then paid tribute to the graciousness of the King; acknowledged that his own part in the ministry had largely been one of adding vigour to plans already laid; and pronounced that he intended to remain a private citizen, having no further desire of office.[24]

Sadly, the slide into war with Spain continued, for the distrust on all sides went too deep. In any case, Choiseul was determined to make Spain honour the Family Compact.[25] The Spanish were not eager for this, knowing the

[19] State of the Army under Prince Ferdinand, 1 Nov 1761, Add. Mss 33,048 f 180.
[20] Memorandum for Lord Bute, 25 Nov 1761, Add. Mss 32,931 f 262. Proposals for the completing of the Army in Germany, Add. Mss 32,931 f 277.
[21] Ligonier to Amherst, 28 Oct 1761, quoted in R. Whitworth, *Field Marshal Lord Ligonier* (Oxford, 1958), 355.
[22] Newcastle to Hardwicke, 23 Oct 1761, Yorke, III, 335.   [23] *JHC*, XXIX, 8–12.
[24] H. Walpole, *Memoirs of the Reign of King George III* (London, 1894), I, 74–76, 82–84, 91–94. Lord Royston to Hardwicke, 13 Nov 1761, Yorke, III, 338.
[25] J. O. Lindsay (ed.), *The New Cambridge Modern History*, VII, *The Old regime, 1713–1763* (Cambridge, 1957), 481–482.

unreadiness of their forces. On the other hand, they realized that no recognition of their rights in Honduras seemed likely, despite Spain's friendly attitude for the last few years. Apparently fear and force alone would bring the British to reason and justice. Hence, only a dramatic initiative could have halted hostilities, and this was impossible. The shadow of Pitt on the ministry was equally strong in or out of office. The King and Bute were still scared that Pitt would exploit national feeling on the issue to create a political crisis. The result was the peremptory demand to see the terms of the Family Compact: such conduct could not but be offensive. Bristol was told to leave Madrid whenever he liked.[26]

Fortunately, the nation was not unprepared for the crisis facing it. Anson expected to have 297 ships in service, manned by 82,400 seamen, almost as many as in 1759.[27] The army too was in good condition. The recent augmentations meant that the figures presented to Parliament for 1762 were for a record establishment of 120,000 men. Together with the foreign troops, there were now 186,000 men in British pay.[28] Even so, the number was barely sufficient for the tasks awaiting it. Apart from the demands of the German theatre, an expeditionary force of 7,000 men was about to depart for Portugal under Lord Loudoun. Several thousands more were locked up on Belleisle, while a similar force was committed to the capture of Martinique. If additional operations were to be undertaken in the Caribbean against Spain, the army in North America would have to be reinforced. The manpower as well as the financial resources of the nation seemed truly stretched.[29]

The decision to send troops to Portugal was taken at a meeting on 26 December. This had originally been called at Anson's house to draft orders for the commencement of hostilities against Spain. The matter of Portugal, however, left Newcastle angry, since he had been given no prior warning of it. Such action was inexcusable, as troops meant money. The incident led Newcastle to reflect: 'Even Mr Pitt, til towards the last always had that attention to me . . . as constantly to send me his Draught with Copies for my own use' before the meetings. 'These ministers act in a very different way.'[30]

But first a formal declaration of war had to be issued by the King and Privy Council. On 31 December Egremont informed Newcastle that this had been fixed for Saturday 2 January, at 2.00 p.m. However, there was to be a 'Cabinet Council to meet the same day at eleven' to resolve any problems.[31] More important was the gathering four days later of Bute,

---

[26] Wall to Bristol, 10 Dec 1761, SP 94/164. Bristol to Egremont, 11 Dec 1761, SP 94/164.
[27] Monthly List and Progress of the Navy, 1 Jan 1762, Adm 7/567.
[28] *JHC*, XXIX, 27–29.
[29] Newcastle to Yorke, 8 Jan 1762, Add. Mss 32,933 ff 112–116.
[30] Newcastle to Hardwicke, 30 Dec 1761, Add. Mss 32,932 ff 408–409.
[31] Egremont to Newcastle, 31 Dec 1761, Add. Mss 32,932 f 426.

Egremont, Newcastle, Anson, Grenville, Ligonier and Devonshire to discuss the 'most effectual methods of distressing and attacking the Spaniards'.[32] The meeting began with a consideration of 'Lord Anson's project of attacking Havannah', Newcastle later reported to Hardwicke: 'After hearing the facility, which his Lordship and Lord Ligonier apprehended there was in doing it, we all unanimously advised the undertaking.' The plan was for Lord Albemarle, the land commander, to take 4,000 men from Britain, sail to the West Indies and pick up the rest of Monckton's army, once the latter had finished in Martinique. Also joining would be 4,000 men from North America. The whole force would then proceed to Havana escorted by a formidable squadron of fifteen battleships under Admiral Pocock. The capture of Havana, a place 'of the greatest importance', would be a severe blow to Spain. Egremont then introduced a scheme put forward by Colonel Draper for taking Manila with troops already in the East Indies. This too was approved.[33]

The other main item was the deployment of the navy. Saunders now had a force of thirty battleships in the Mediterranean, based on Gibraltar, to prevent a union of the French and Spanish fleets.[34] However, there was always the danger that the enemy might elude him and try to repeat their manoeuvre of 1744 by sailing up the Channel, this time in support of an invasion. Anson accordingly suggested that the western squadron, which was then watching Brest, Quiberon Bay and Basque Road, should be ready to fall back to Plymouth. The entire force would be commanded by Hawke.[35]

Unfortunately, the meeting on 6 January did not end harmoniously, for Bute raised 'the Great Question, *for Consideration only*, of withdrawing all our troops from Germany and giving up the German war'. The situation of the King of Prussia appeared desperate and Bute noted that Newcastle had several times mentioned his doubts about the nation's ability to 'carry on the whole war'. But, although Newcastle had echoed these sentiments at the time of the discussions over Spain, he had used them to argue against extending, not contracting out of the war. To Newcastle a unilateral withdrawal from Germany would be tantamount to giving France the victory, leading as it would to the occupation of Hanover and destruction of Prussia. The nation would be undone, no matter how many maritime conquests it made, for the French would then be able to give their entire attention to the war overseas. It was better to risk the nation's fate in another campaign: £16,000,000 was as insupportable as £20,000,000. The country

---

[32] Devonshire Diary, 6 Jan 1762, DPC.
[33] Newcastle to Hardwicke, 10 Jan 1762, Add. Mss 32,933 ff 179–182.
[34] Admiralty to Saunders, 21 Nov 1761, Adm 2/1331.
[35] State of the Respective Fleets this side of Finisterre, 25 Jan 1762, Add. Mss 33,048 ff 230–232.

could surely fight for another year. Newcastle was supported by Devonshire, Bute by Grenville. The others remained silent.[36]

The financial position was certainly ominous, for the 1762 supply had been negotiated with difficulty. Newcastle had had to tempt subscribers with additional capital by charging them only £80 for every £100 of stock. He had also had to give them a £1 annuity, payable for ninety-nine years to themselves or their descendants. This meant an effective interest rate of 5 per cent. Moreover, he had only been able to borrow £12,000,000 of the £14,000,000 required.[37] The gap would have to be bridged by the issue of Exchequer bills, most likely without the assistance of the Bank. As Barrington pointed out, many of the potential subscribers were merchants whose financial position must be affected by the extension of the war. With the stocks losing in some cases 3 per cent in one day, bankruptcies were likely and the completion of the loan by no means certain. Another problem stemming from the new conflict was the certainty of a further decline in the revenues of the Sinking Fund, which were heavily dependent on receipts from trade with Spain and the Mediterranean. With less revenue there was a real danger of the government trying to do too much, especially if it had to fight a land war in Portugal.[38]

For the moment Bute did not press the matter. Newcastle responded by consulting several people to see how the commissariat in Germany might be run more economically. If enough savings could be made it might still be possible to finance both wars without the need for any withdrawals or requests for additional funds. As Newcastle told Yorke, it was shameful that 90,000 men should cost £3,000,000 for provision alone, especially when the total spending on the war in Germany was between £6,000,000 and £7,000,000.[39]

In these circumstances, the news of the sudden death of the Tsarina Elizabeth and her succession by a monarch eager to ally with Frederick II was almost miraculous. As Bute suggested, consideration could be given to dispensing with the subsidy to Prussia, since the fortunes of the war in that part of the world ought to improve dramatically. Enquiries to the court of Berlin were therefore made to find out its views.[40]

Another item to cheer the administration was the hopeful prospect of renewed peace talks. Viry, the Sardinian minister, reported from his court

---

[36] Newcastle to Hardwicke, 10 Jan 1762, Add. Mss 32,933 ff 179–182. Newcastle to Yorke, 8 Jan 1762, Add Mss 32,933 ff 112–116.

[37] Minute – 1762 Loan, 3 Dec 1761, Add. Mss 32,931 f 383. An Act for Raising by Annuities...the Sum of Twelve Million Pounds, *Statutes at Large*, Ch. x, 2 Geo III. J. J. Grellier, *The History of the National Debt from the Revolution in 1688 to the Beginning of 1800* (London, 1810), 254.

[38] Barrington to Newcastle, 5 Jan 1762, Add. Mss 32,933 ff 50–54.

[39] Memorandum for Lord Barrington, 8 Jan 1762, Add. Mss 32,933 f 128. Newcastle to Yorke, 8 Jan 1762, Add. Mss 32,933 ff 112–116.

[40] Bute to Mitchell, 6 Feb 1762, SP 90/79.

that Choiseul was still anxious to talk. If the British ministers sent proposals similar to those previously agreed by France, then peace might be concluded within six weeks.[41] Accordingly, on 26 March Bute summoned Newcastle, Hardwicke, Grenville and Devonshire to his office to discuss the matter.[42]

It was at this point that news arrived of the fall of Martinique. The capture of this, like that of Belleisle, had not proved easy. The terrain favoured the defenders. However, Monckton had with him an overwhelming force; he also had complete naval superiority, Rodney having eighteen ships of the line and several frigates in support. The expedition had revealed the formidable ability of the British to operate almost anywhere in the world.[43]

Nevertheless, any hopes that Newcastle might have had of avoiding a financial storm were to be inadvertently dashed by Barrington. At the end of March, the Chancellor came to the conclusion that the £1,000,000 vote of credit was insufficient to cover both the war in Germany and Portugal. The Treasury must insist on an additional £1,000,000 to ensure that it had sufficient reserves.[44] Somewhat taken aback, Newcastle asked West to look at the figures, well aware that such demand would give a handle to those members of the administration anxious to end the war in Germany. West was inclined to think that the Treasury might get by without adopting any of the actions so feared by Newcastle.[45] To make sure, Newcastle then asked Martin to scan both sets of figures. Martin equivocated, but implied that the war could be continued as at present.[46]

This division within the department led Newcastle to consult the other ministers. He did this at a meeting on 10 April 1762, at which Henley, Hardwicke, Egremont, Mansfield, Grenville, Newcastle, Bute and Ligonier were present. Newcastle introduced the problem as circumspectly as possible, telling the ministers that he wanted to discuss 'the state of the Expense that would attend the war in Portugal, and to consider the method of laying it before Parliament'. But when he aired the question of a further £1,000,000 vote of credit, objections were raised, principally by Grenville, who emphasized that savings in America and Belleisle would more than cover the costs of the war with Spain: to vote £2,000,000 would simply encourage extravagance in Germany. Newcastle was not unsupported. Devonshire asserted that he would retire from the 'Council' if so dishonourable a measure were taken as a unilateral withdrawal from Germany, as some ministers seemed to be arguing.[47] Newcastle could also count on Hardwicke and Anson, if the latter recovered from illness. But there was

---

[41] Devonshire Diary, 1 Feb 1762, DPC. [42] Ibid., 26 Mar 1762.
[43] Corbett, *Seven Years' War*, II, 217–226.
[44] Lord Barrington's Paper on the Supply for 1762, 31 Mar 1762, Add. Mss 33,040 ff 317–319.
[45] Mr West's Paper, 7 Apr 1762, Add. Mss 33,040 ff 329–330.
[46] Mr Martin's Observations, Apr 1762, Add. Mss 33,040 ff 336–337.
[47] Devonshire Diary, 10 Apr 1762, DPC. Ibid., 19 Apr 1762.

no disguising the depth of opposition, not only to the vote of credit, but to the struggle on the continent. Bute, Grenville, Halifax and Bedford, currently the brightest stars in the political firmament, all reflected the feelings of the King that continental engagements were expensive and of doubtful value.

However, on the vote of credit Barrington remained adamant. In a further letter to Newcastle he insisted that £1,000,000 would not be enough for the war in Portugal, North America and Germany. Unless the vote of credit were doubled, a contraction would be inevitable. The most likely area for cutting must be Germany.[48] This idea was something to which Newcastle was resolutely opposed and the crisis in the ministry was now as much political as financial. Newcastle knew that the King and Bute were anxious to scale down if not contract out of the continental war. Barrington's insistence on a further vote of credit simply provided an excuse for them to further deprecate operations there. Some historians have argued that the two men did this to force Newcastle out of the Treasury. Newcastle himself was inclined to think so. In a letter to Devonshire he recalled the methods used in the time of Sunderland and Stanhope for getting rid of ministers. The usual tactic had been to challenge them on matters pertaining to their department, which Grenville was clearly doing. By refusing the Treasury an additional vote of credit and by insisting on aid for Portugal, Bute and Grenville were making it necessary for Newcastle and Barrington to economize elsewhere and that could only mean Germany.[49]

There was no plot. At the beginning of the reign George III and Bute had reluctantly accepted that they must keep Newcastle for a while. Now that the supply for 1762 had been negotiated, there was less need for this. If the possibility of contracting out of the German war should cause a breach, George III himself was ready to see the minister go, as he told Bute at the beginning of January.[50] That eventuality was now at hand and he was in no way alarmed, for his desire to reduce the commitment in Germany was sincere.

On the financial aspect of the dispute, Newcastle supported Barrington, knowing well the experience of sitting at the Treasury with too little money and too many demands. But he was not insensible of the need to reduce costs, or of the burdens the nation would have to face on the conclusion of peace. Newcastle has often been accused of having no principles, but this was not so. He was firmly in favour of peace. He was equally convinced that this could only be achieved by a general, not unilateral, ending of the war.

---

[48] Lord Barrington, 3 May 1762, Add. Mss 33,040 ff 339–340.
[49] Newcastle to Devonshire, 17 Apr 1762, Add. Mss 32,937 ff 188–192. Newcastle to Devonshire, 30 Apr 1762, Add. Mss 32,937 ff 452–453.
[50] Sir Lewis Namier, *England in the Age of the American Revolution* (second edition, London, 1961), 308–309.

It was nonsense to suppose that the nation could withdraw from one theatre without upsetting its prospects elsewhere. If the war could not be sustained, then a general peace ought to be sought as the only honourable and sensible thing to do. Although he had indulged in jeremiads of approaching ruin, Newcastle was enough of a realist to recognize that the country could go on a little longer, however desperate the crisis might appear.[51]

The offer to continue was not appreciated. Newcastle was increasingly out of step on this and other questions facing the administration. He was not insensitive to his isolation. He had been sufficiently snubbed on several occasions to raise the question of his resignation with Hardwicke and his other friends.[52] The dispute over the vote of credit now offered him a chance of departing on a matter of principle. As usual, he spoilt the dignity of his position, for he only resigned after he had been publicly humiliated in the conduct of his department. On 5 May, Martin ordered the Treasury clerks to calculate the savings, should the troops be recalled from Germany. Martin did this without authorization from Newcastle and in the presence of several lords.[53] Like Pitt, Newcastle had always insisted that he remain master of his own department. He had for some time been irritated at the increasing interference of Grenville. He had affirmed to Devonshire on 17 April that this meddling must either stop or he would retire.[54] Clearly he was about to be overruled and reduced in his own words to a 'cypher'. Two days after the incident with Martin, Newcastle informed the King that he would retire. He hoped that even now a compromise might be arranged and waived his personal views on the need for a second vote of credit. The concession was to no avail. George III was confident that he could manage without Newcastle, and much to the latter's dismay, no opportunity was permitted for reconsidering his resignation.[55]

The resignation of Newcastle marks the real end to the government formed in June 1757. Along with Newcastle went the faithful Hardwicke, while Anson, the other member of the Pelham group, had, since Christmas, been in poor health and had only a few weeks to live. Granville was almost senile. Only Ligonier of the inner group was still in office and his days were numbered.

Newcastle left the ministry an unhappy man. Not least among his grievances was that the administration was about to squander everything he and Pitt had worked for. As he explained to Yorke in a long letter dated 14 May 1762: 'My scheme was to make our push this campaign, whatever it might have cost. I would have carried it on everywhere, whatever might

[51] Newcastle to Yorke, 8 Jan 1762, Add. Mss 32,933 ff 112–116.
[52] See Namier, *England in the Age of the American Revolution*, 283–316.
[53] Ibid., 317.
[54] Newcastle to Devonshire, 17 Apr 1762, Add. Mss 32,936 ff 188–192.
[55] Namier, *England in the Age of the American Revolution*, 318–323.

have been the expense; and I would have seen at the end of this campaign
what general peace we could then have made.' Now surely was the time
to encourage the King of Prussia to bring the Austrians to terms, deprived
as the Hapsburgs were of Russian support. 'In the meantime, I would have
carried on our secret negotiations with France', which must surely have
succeeded when 'the Duke of Choiseul saw we were so strong in Germany'.
Sadly, 'all these advantages we have flung away'.[56]

These gloomy predictions proved unfounded. Although Bute and Grenville failed to renew the subsidy, the country did not forfeit the goodwill of
Prussia for that reason.[57] Nor did the nation suffer militarily. The last few
months had convinced even the Austrians that it was time to negotiate.
Elsewhere the war went on despite the financial stringencies. Ferdinand was
able to campaign successfully, containing the last efforts of the French to
seize Hanover as a bargaining counter at the peace. In the maritime war
the Family Compact proved of little consequence, for neither Bourbon
power had the will to make an effort. Spain entered the war unprepared.
Of her forty-eight ships of the line, only twenty were in a condition to sail.
The year passed with little activity either in the Mediterranean or Atlantic.
However, the measures taken by the administration in Europe, the
Caribbean and Far East bore fruit. The dispatch of Loudoun's force proved
more than sufficient to contain the Spanish invasion of Portugal, while
success smiled on both colonial ventures. Havana and Manila fell, to
provide a fitting end to the war if not to the peace negotiations then in
progress.

The terms finally negotiated were similar to those of the previous year,
though some compensation had to be made to Britain for her recent gains.
France retained her right to the fishery, receiving the islands of St Pierre
and Miquelon as drying stations, though without fortifications. All the rest
of Canada, including Cape Breton island, was ceded to Britain. In the West
Indies, Britain returned Martinique, Guadeloupe and Marie Galante, but
retained Granada and several of the small neutral islands which had been
an issue at the start of hostilities. She also returned Goree but kept Senegal,
thus strengthening her presence in Africa, while in India there were substantial gains for the East India Company. With regard to Europe, Belleisle
and Minorca were exchanged, Dunkirk was returned to its former state,
while the French evacuated all the territories of George III and his allies
in Germany.

Elsewhere, Britain returned Cuba and Manila to Spain while she
reciprocated by evacuating Portugal. In addition Spain surrendered all
claims to the Newfoundland fishery and ceded Florida, thus completing

[56] Newcastle to Yorke, 14 May 1762, Yorke, III, 355–358.
[57] F. Spencer, 'The Anglo-Prussian Breach of 1762: An Historical Revision', *History*, XLI,
     100–112.

British control of the North American east coast. She also acknowledged the British right to cut logwood in Honduras, though no fortifications were allowed.[58]

The terms of this treaty have often been criticized as a surrender of all that the previous government, especially Pitt, had sought. This, as has been shown, cannot be sustained. Much of the criticism was the product of writers anxious to cast the actions of George III and Bute in the most hostile light. Even Pitt until the end had comparatively modest aims, and these did not include the total humiliation of France or Spain, however respectable such ideas may have become in the nineteenth century. Indeed, judged by the original objects of the war the terms were spectacularly successful. Not only had the security of the British colonies been assured in North America, but the vast expanse of Canada and lands to the Mississippi had been added to the King's dominions. Even in the light of Britain's subsequent military and naval success the terms were still eminently satisfactory, with important gains in Africa, Asia and the West Indies. The nation's efforts had not gone unrewarded.

II

The arguments in this book are at variance with much of the literature on the war, especially that written since the turn of the nineteenth century. The latter has generally focused on the role of Pitt, enthusing about his unique foresight and control. Careful study of the ministers' political, personal and departmental correspondence cannot substantiate this view. Government was a team affair and traditional accounts have unfairly ignored Pitt's debt to others, placing laurels on a brow that could scarcely have borne them all.

Historians have been much given to talking about Pitt's 'system'. However, by system he meant that Britain's interests should not be sacrificed to those of Hanover and was thinking in political not military terms. Otherwise he was far from having a comprehensive system for waging the war, as his attitude to the German conflict and relations with Spain suggest. Almost always he did things piecemeal, usually in response to some political or traditional consideration. Thus, the coastal expeditions were designed to avoid the necessity of sending British troops to Germany; and the operations in the Caribbean were a continuation of the mercantilist belief that the way to strike at France was through her trade. Historians have commended Pitt's command of naval strategy, but the principal arm of the fleet, the western squadron, played little part in his thinking, except as an adjunct to the coastal operations. His plan to capture Martinique and recommence the

---

[58] The Definitive Treaty of Peace between Britain, France and Spain, 10 Feb 1763, Parry (ed.), *The Consolidated Treaty Series*, XLII, 320–349.

coastal expeditions in June 1761 were certainly part of a wider scheme to make France accept his peace terms. Unfortunately, the forces available were insufficient for the task. Only rarely did Pitt look ahead to increase the resources of the nation in the matter of ship building, manning the fleet, recruiting the army or producing munitions. The coat always had to be cut according to the cloth. This failure to anticipate the war's requirements more than anything else vitiates the idea that Pitt had an integrated strategy or that his schemes were much more than thoughts of the moment.

As an executive agent there are also grounds for being sceptical about the nature of Pitt's achievement. A reading of the dispatches in G. S. Kimball's *Correspondence of William Pitt, when Secretary of State, with the Colonial Governors and Military and Naval Commissioners in North America* make it impossible not to be impressed with the apparent care, foresight and sense of urgency therein. But it is easy to overlook the collective planning that went into their composition: that Pitt's letters were the tip of the iceberg, not the whole substance of government activity. Moreover, though Pitt was capable of demonstrating great energy, it would be wrong to assume that this was typical of his period in office. Most ministers monotonously used the phrase 'with all expedition'.[59] Many of Pitt's deadlines remained unfulfilled. Some of his target dates for operations in America were far too optimistic. Lastly, his capacity to make the machinery of government work was limited by continuing ill health which meant frequent absences from office.

The contribution of Pitt to the success of Britain, therefore, was less than has been supposed. Pitt's talents, though considerable, were not those of an administrator or even military planner. Horace Walpole was not far from the truth when he commented: 'Pitt kept aloof from all details, drew magnificent plans and left others to find the magnificent means.' But even his plans were often imprecise and in practice he too followed the policies and commitments of his predecessors. His contribution was in any case limited by the departmental structure of government and there is no truth to the assertion that he directed every branch of government. Such power would have been unconstitutional, a fact all too often overlooked.

In reality the abilities of Pitt were primarily parliamentary. His brilliant if bombastic oratory mesmerized the members and captivated a large portion of the nation. It did not matter that his language was rhetorical and of little substance. It was what the nation wanted to hear when coupled with so much success. By 1761 people believed that his participation in government was vital. Events of course proved otherwise. The operations against Spain went as well as any during the war; and Hardwicke rightly commented how the fall of Havana, of which Anson and Ligonier were the architects, 'proves...that an expedition of great consequence, extent and

59 H. Walpole, *Memoirs of the Reign of King George II* (London, 1846–47), III, 173.

difficulty, might be well concerted without the counsel and consent of that gentleman'.[60] No one had been indispensable.

It has been customary to repeat Temple's remark that Newcastle was merely in charge of patronage. Certainly, the management of the government's supporters had been an important task, though by no means his only one. Paradoxically, it was often here that he was least successful, for, as Waldegrave noted, Newcastle too readily made promises, forgetting that he was 'under the same engagement to at least ten competitors'.[61] It was this 'want of resolution in conducting the common patronage of the Treasury', Shelburne concluded, that 'gave him the reputation of being a poor man of business'.[62]

Respecting his financial and administrative responsibilities, historians have been too willing to accept Pitt's assertion that Britain's credit was unlimited: that Treasury determination only was required to finance his multifarious projects. They, like Pitt, have failed to see the problems Newcastle faced in the management of the revenue: the want of co-operation from the Bank; the fear of paper money; the rise in interest rates; and the lack of control over departmental spending. Newcastle admittedly did give way to excessive fears about the nation's solvency: this is characteristic of any finance minister. National bankruptcy was a terrible spectre. The difficulty was that it was impossible to predict. Nations are not like individuals. They can renege on their obligations and survive, something that the Younger Pitt forgot when he made his famous prediction about the hour and the day when the French Republic must cease fighting. Yet by 1761 the limits of British borrowing, if not of taxation, appear to have been approached. The twelve million pounds raised that year and in 1762 represented approximately 60 per cent of all government expenditure. This was a far higher figure than anything achieved before. Under Newcastle's direction the war had been fought and paid for. No essential services or operations failed for want of money, as those of France had on occasion.

His achievement with the commissariat was of a similar order. Though his handling of the department may not have been inspired, it was honest, showing a commendable desire for economy compatible with military efficiency. The problem was that the demands of the army and the desire for economy were often in conflict. Also, Newcastle did not have the most reliable personnel. Nevertheless, despite occasional difficulties, the army was supplied with relatively plentiful and wholesome provisions.[63] There were few crucial breakdowns and Ferdinand's plans were not often circumscribed,

---

[60] Hardwicke to Newcastle, 2 Oct 1762, Yorke, III, 417–418.
[61] James Earl Waldegrave, *Memoirs from 1754 to 1758* (London, 1821), 13.
[62] Lord E. Fitzmaurice, *The Life of William, Earl of Shelburne* (London, 1875), I, 84.
[63] These are the conclusions of H. Little, 'The British Army Commissaries in Germany during the Seven Years' War' (London, Ph.D thesis, 1981).

unlike the French who were much hampered thereby. The result was that Hanover was secured, Frederick II given material assistance, while Britain fought her maritime war. For this, Newcastle and his Treasury colleagues deserve much praise, though their success was another demonstration of the extent of British credit.

Administratively, no minister made a greater contribution than Anson. Because of his endeavours before the war, the fleet was in an excellent condition and his continued supervision ensured that it undertook most of its assignments with an assured superiority. The good state of the navy in 1755 was one of the points remembered at his death. So too was his judicious choice of officers.[64]

But administratively the Anson era was not one of innovation. Though new classes of ship were introduced, the men were recruited and the ships built in the same manner as they had for many decades. Of course, problems like manning could only be tackled by legislation and Parliament was reluctant to sanction anything that strengthened the executive. The navy departments themselves, steeped in tradition, were rarely able to escape from the weight of precedent to think positively about their methods. The excuse that a precedent might be set was on occasion valid, but it encouraged the habit of judging present demands by past requirements.

Nevertheless, the achievement of Anson and his Admiralty colleagues was superficially impressive. They had produced the largest number of men and ships in the history of the navy. In manning the fleet they had broken the previous record by some 20,000 men or 30 per cent. The reader might well ask how this was possible by such traditional methods. One reason is provided by George Chalmers in his book *An Estimate of the Comparative Strength of Britain during the Present and Preceding Reigns*. Between 1689 and 1760 the number of men of military age had risen from 1,800,000 to 2,400,000, while the income of the nation had more than doubled. Equally substantial was the growth of the merchant marine. In 1695 this was 280,000 tons, manned by approximately 16,000 mariners who in turn provided the nucleus for a navy of 45,000 men. By 1760 the merchant marine had risen to 609,000 tons, implying a pool of 36,000 experienced sailors.[65] Chalmers's figures are very crude, but they do put Anson's achievement into perspective. New records were set as the century progressed, and this was as true for manning as it was for other government activities. The figures for the Seven Years' War were surpassed by the administration of Lord Sandwich; and they in turn were overshadowed by those of the Revolutionary era. Each generation set targets which the growth in national resources allowed the next to exceed.

---

[64] *London Chronicle*, 1/3 July 1762.
[65] G. Chalmers, *An Estimate of the Comparative Strength of Britain during the Present and Preceding Reigns, and of the Losses of her Trade from every War since the Revolution* (London, 1782), 16–37, 178–179.

The recruitment of the army was of a similar nature, though less spectacular, for Britain ended the war with a regular force not much more than half that of France. However, if the foreign corps are taken into account the country had close to 200,000 men under arms. British money if not British manpower ensured that the nation remained a military power. Since almost all these men had been obtained through voluntary enlistment, the performance was still remarkable, however haphazard it had been. Equally amazing was the high reputation of the forces, given the random method of recruitment and the difficulties in training them. With the exception of the independent companies, the British infantry and cavalry were as admired as any in Europe.[66] After the early disasters, the war had witnessed a truly remarkable flowering of the British military effort.

Credit for this achievement lies with all the ministry, not just Ligonier and Barrington. But their accomplishment has to be seen in perspective. They had no master plan for expanding the nation's forces. All the increases were in response to rather than in anticipation of demand. When the ministers did augment the army, they did so along traditional lines and in piecemeal fashion.

Regarding the Ordnance, Ligonier was perhaps too old to master all the complexities of the department. Nevertheless, the Ordnance did most of the things required of it. The two services were armed and equipped with few delays or failures in supply. The artillery was expanded and trains provided in many parts of the world, incurring the praise even of Ferdinand. The one arm to meet with extensive disapproval was the engineers. Nevertheless, Ligonier himself had no doubts about his overall contribution. When his own removal was under discussion after the war he commented: 'I have the vanity to think that neither Louisburg, Quebec, or perhaps the Havana had been taken had the Ordnance been in other hands.'[67]

The eighteenth century has been called the age of reason. If the machinery of government is considered, it might equally be called the age of irrationality. In practice, reason penetrated no further than the doors of fashionable society; and a study of eighteenth-century institutions shows how shallow was the belief in unimpeded progress. Of course, compared to France, Britain had an efficient means for mobilizing her resources. The country had experienced an administrative revolution in the latter half of the seventeenth century when new dockyards had been developed, the Victualling Board established, the means of long-term credit effected, colonial administration improved and the revenue increased. Nevertheless, few wars can have been fought so successfully with so little change in the structure of government.

---

[66] P. Mackesy, *The Coward of Minden: The Affair of Lord George Sackville* (London, 1979), 25.
[67] Memorandum of an Interview with His Majesty, 14 April 1763, Donoughmore Papers, T 3459/A/73, Public Record Office of Northern Ireland.

Lord Shelburne observed of both Britain and France for a slightly later period that the principle in both Kingdoms was to get through the common business without ever looking beyond the present moment'.[68] This was to be expected, given the conditions under which people had to operate. There could be no pretence of some grand design when poor communications, uncertain weather and other phenomenon could nullify the best schemes. As Sir Joseph Yorke told Newcastle in the summer of 1757, the forces in America were superior to the enemy: 'The rest depends upon the conduct of the officers who command and upon the blessing of Providence, for the ministers can only furnish the means, not decide the success.'[69]

Such fatalism might seem unpardonable to later generations accustomed to the idea of progress, but it was entirely natural in an age when man placed his trust in God. Luck was as important as planning and the results of a campaign could be unforeseen, as the capture of Guadeloupe rather than Martinique in 1759 demonstrated. Ligonier reminded Mordaunt at the time of the Rochefort expedition: 'There is chance in the best concerted military enterprize. . .what share then must be left to fortune' when 'neither the country nor the numbers of troops you are to act against is known with any precision'.[70] What share indeed! The expeditions to Quebec in 1711 and 1759 were launched on similar hopes and prospects. Fortune smiled on Wolfe's enterprise though at the cost of his life; Walker saved his life but his armament was dashed to pieces in the St Lawrence. Tolstoy's argument in *War and Peace* that men are rarely in control of events would seem to have much truth.

Nevertheless, the question remains why Britain was so successful if it were not primarily for Pitt and his colleagues. Part of the answer must be sought elsewhere, in impersonal factors. One important reason was the strength of British credit which allowed the nation to mobilize its resources. Another was French involvement in Europe. France never found it easy to wage a war simultaneously by land and sea, as Choiseul commented to Stanley. After the invasion of Saxony she had to neglect her maritime and colonial effort to assist her European allies. Her navy and colonial possessions were consequently starved of attention; the only time this was not the case was in 1756. Then, by a judicious manoeuvre, the French were able not only to capture Minorca, but also to hold their own in America. The opening of the war in Europe changed this, with the result that Britain was able to amass overwhelming forces for the conquest of Canada, and later for the West Indies. Pitt thus had a point when he claimed that America had been

---

[68] Quoted in L. Scott, 'The Under-Secretaries of State, 1755–1775' (M.A. thesis, The University of Manchester, 1953), 346.

[69] Yorke to Newcastle, 15 July 1757, Add. Mss 32,872 ff 200–201.

[70] *The Report of the General Officers appointed. . .to Enquire into the Causes of the Failure of the Late Expedition to the Coasts of France* (London, 1758), 20. (See Mordaunt.)

conquered in Germany. But British success cannot simply be explained in terms of faulty strategy by the French. France was still a wealthy country, the most populous in Europe, and it must be asked not only why she could not fight a war on two fronts, but why her performance was so abysmal. Detailed analysis of these questions is beyond the scope of this book. It must suffice to say that the imbalance of French society and government, which only a revolution could change, prevented her from mobilizing her resources. These weaknesses did not entirely escape the notice of contemporaries. One commentator noted how the French had fielded a much larger army in the time of Louis XIV. But the reasons for the decline of French power were not understood. Contemporaries merely suggested that in future they should cut their coat according to their cloth.[71]

The other main reason for the British success was the neutrality of Spain. Historians have generally decried that power in the eighteenth century. But Spanish involvement meant an immense extension to the responsibilities of the royal navy. Thousands of miles of additional coast had to be patrolled to protect British trade in the Atlantic, East and West Indies and the Mediterranean. As Edmund Burke emphasized in the *Annual Register* for 1762: 'Britain never was in such a doubtful and dangerous situation, for at this time she was engaged, directly or indirectly . . . with the most considerable part of the maritime strength of Europe. . . The navy of Spain consisted of more than one hundred men of war; and though the French navy was greatly reduced, it became a consideration when added to the Spanish.'[72] Fortunately, the earlier cultivation of good relations with Madrid meant that this union of the Bourbon powers did not take place until near the end of the war. The result was that the British reaped a rich reward. While Spain preserved her neutrality, Britain was able to destroy her chief maritime rival without interference. When Spain at last intervened, the French navy had been destroyed as a fighting force, leaving Spain to meet the main impact of Britain's victorious fleet.

The importance of these factors becomes more apparent if comparison is made with some of the other wars in which Britain was engaged during the eighteenth century. It took Britain eight years to master the combined fleets of France and Spain during the War of Austrian Succession, though both those powers had extensive commitments on the continent. In the War of American Independence Britain's performance was even worse, though she had a navy which was larger than any before and faster, too, because of copper-bottoming. The reasons for the British defeat then were cogently put by Lord Sandwich in the House of Lords: 'England till this time, was never engaged in a war with the House of Bourbon thoroughly united, their naval forces unbroken, and having no other war or object to draw off their

[71] *London Chronicle*, 17/20 Feb 1759.   [72] *The Annual Register for 1762*, 5.

attention and resources.[73] The task of the Pitt–Newcastle coalition between 1757 and 1762 was a relatively easy one, compared to that of other eighteenth-century administrations. The weakness of France, the ability of Frederick II and the neutrality of Spain all provided the ministers with a unique opportunity for advancing Britain's maritime claims. To their credit, the opportunity was not lost.

[73] Quoted in P. Mackesy, *The War for America, 1775–1783* (London, 1964), 314.

Pitt and the Historians

A persistent feature of historical writing on the war has been the adulation of Pitt. Curiously, this was by no means universal or complete during his lifetime. His colleagues and contemporaries had reservations about his genius, and even the most sycophantic admirers claimed less than many later writers. The historiography of Pitt marks the growth of a legend.

A good example of the early moderation is the work of John Entick. As a contributor to the *Monitor*, he was naturally favourable to Pitt. Nevertheless, his *General History of the Late War* is not sycophantic; for Entick used considerable documentary evidence and in his introduction assured the reader that it was the 'part of an historian to relate the facts', not pass judgement.[1] In general he succeeds in what is a simple, though comprehensive, narrative. He limits his criticism of Newcastle to a suggestion that it was his ministry's excessive, if understandable, concern for the Channel which made the invasion of Minorca possible.[2] Nevertheless, that government was culpable in not pressing the war vigorously, a situation which only changed with the arrival of Pitt. Then, with the nation behind him, he was able to embark on new measures and victory followed. But this was not a one-man performance, for Entick discusses events in an impersonal fashion, since of Pitt and the other ministers he rarely has much to say.

Another literary account was that of Tobias Smollett. Smollett, like Entick, used documentary material. However, he brought to his work the attitude of a Tory writer, recognizing the frailties of human nature and the difficulties under which man had to operate. He is accordingly commendatory of the early naval preparations of the Newcastle administration though, like Entick, he denounces the subsequent obsession with the Channel which led to a neglect of the Mediterranean and the fall of Minorca.[3] Concerning America, he commends Loudoun's energy, but is critical of Pitt's policy of dispersal, which exposed Wolfe and Amherst to

---

[1] J. Entick, *The General History of the Late War, Containing its Rise, Progress and Events, in Europe, Asia, Africa, and America* (5 vols., London 1763–1764), IV, 43.
[2] Ibid., I, 202, 233–250; II, 1–5.
[3] T. G. Smollett, *The History of England from the Revolution to the Death of George II* (5 vols., London, 1790), III, 437–438; IV, 64–66. The first edition appeared in 1763.

defeat before they could support each other.[4] But his history is not hostile to Pitt, for Smollett dedicated it to the statesman. In general he is factual and accurate.

Even more restrained are the accounts of participants, notably those of John Knox, Thomas Mante and Robert Beatson. Knox's *Historical Journal of the Campaigns in North America*, published in 1769, is, as the title suggests, the personal story of a captain in the 46th Foot Regiment, though by the use of documentary material Knox frequently transposes his account from the level of a regimental mess to that of general headquarters. But Knox's attention is riveted on America and there is no awareness of the ministers in Whitehall, except for one passage about the official delusion that the war would be short.[5]

Mante, an officer in the engineer corps, also has little to say of the ministers back home. Unlike Knox's journal, his *History of the Late War in North America*, published in 1772, contains nothing of a personal nature and consists simply of a narrative of the campaigns. Mante, aware of the difficulties of campaigning in North America, suggests that the expedition under Braddock was well equipped and that his instructions were as farsighted as any during the war. Unfamiliarity with the conditions and ill luck were the causes of the disaster on the Monongahela.[6] Like Knox, Mante becomes engrossed in the details of the war. He merely observes that Pitt had the confidence of the nation; and that his admission to power brought new officers to the fore and more spirit to the conduct of affairs.[7] Regarding Pitt's direction of the war in North America he had nothing to say.

Another more comprehensive account by a participant was that of Robert Beatson. Beatson was pre-eminently a compiler, spending much of his life gathering information about the political institutions of Britain. His first love, however, had been the army, having served on the expedition to Rochefort, and later in the attack on Guadeloupe.[8] Perhaps because of his experience at Rochefort, he was critical of coastal operations, feeling that they too often fell short of their objective.[9] Like other military writers, he had little to say about the central direction of the war, giving the impression that what happened on the field was quite divorced from anything that was done in Whitehall.

General histories and military chronologies were not the only works at this time. Eight years after the death of Pitt appeared the first full biography

[4] Ibid., IV, 104–107; V, 34–37.
[5] J. Knox, *Historical Journal of Campaigns in North America, 1757–1760*, ed., A. G. Doughty (3 vols., Toronto, 1914–1916), I, 272.
[6] T. Mante, *History of the Late War in North America* (London, 1772), 21–28.
[7] Ibid., 110–111.
[8] *Dictionary of National Biography*.
[9] R. Beatson, *Naval and Military Memoirs of Great Britain from 1727–1783* (6 vols., London, 1804), II, 265.

by William Godwin, a dissenting minister and political reformer. Godwin naturally warmed to a person who, like himself, had seemingly been a rebel, though he was not uncritical of his hero. He admitted that Pitt had had too much ambition, which had led him into error, notably his desertion of the popular cause on the fall of Carteret in 1744. In addition one could only draw a veil over Pitt's pitiful government from 1766.[10] However, the period of office from 1757 was one of the most glorious in the nation's annals. Here ambition was legitimately employed: 'Whatever comprehensive genius, extended intelligence, deep political knowledge, and indefatigable industry could effect, was ours...Not a ship, not a man was suffered to remain unemployed. Europe, America, Africa, felt the influence of Mr Pitt's character in an instant.'[11] Godwin introduced a new element, for he asserted that Pitt effected this transformation because he took 'in some manner, the oversight of every department of government'.[12] Here for the first time was the suggestion that one man was administratively responsible for the war.

Though laudatory in tone, the work of Godwin was to be overshadowed by the appearance, in 1795, of John Almon's *Anecdotes of the Life of the Right Honourable William Pitt, Earl of Chatham*. Unlike Entick, Beatson or Godwin, Almon was no scholar or thinker, being a printer who began writing pamphlets. One of his earliest pieces was the *Review of Mr Pitt's Administration*, defending the resignation in 1761. The pamphlet commended him to Temple, who set him up as his printer. Almon played a leading role in the newspaper defence of Wilkes. Afterwards he began work on topics of a less polemical and more scholarly nature.[13] Even so, his work on Pitt was well described, for it contains mainly gossip picked up from Temple some time after the events being described. Not surprisingly, the style and tone of the work were reminiscent of the *Monitor*. Nevertheless, the book was sufficiently removed from events to escape serious challenge, with the result that it was extensively used by later biographers of Pitt.

However, narrative history remained the most important form of historical writing, although by the end of the eighteenth century it was the reign of George III, not George II, which attracted attention. The public were now engrossed in other, more recent, events, for which many held their King responsible. But if Whig and Tory could not agree about George III, they were surprisingly unanimous in their treatment of Pitt. Both were critical of his actions at the beginning of the reign, especially his handling of the peace negotiations in 1761. This hostility reflected the difficulties the nation was undergoing in its war with France. The dangers of isolation in Europe were all too apparent, as were the advantages of peace. Thus William Belsham, in his *Memoirs of the Reign of George III*, commented that the

---

[10] W. Godwin, *The History of the Life of William Pitt, Earl of Chatham* (London, 1783), 44. Ibid., 165.   [11] Ibid., 80.   [12] Ibid., 121.
[13] *Dictionary of National Biography*.

resignation of Pitt 'savoured more of pride and passion than of wisdom or patriotism'. Spain was clearly the injured party and the 'thinking part' of the nation were not keen to be dragged into another conflict. In addition, Belsham acknowledged 'Newcastle's honourable career'.[14] Similar sentiments were expressed by John Adolphus in his *History of England, 1760–1783*. The equitable end of war, Adolphus suggested, was not the annihilation of opponents, but the honourable termination of disputes. This Pitt had signally failed to do.[15]

At the turn of the nineteenth century, therefore, the image of the Elder Pitt was by no means untarnished. Authors like Entick, Smollett, Mante and Belsham, though of very different professions and outlook, portray many similarities in their writings, not only in what they say, but in what they omit. None of them ascribe to Pitt any long-term strategy for defeating France, nor, except for Almon, do they suggest that Pitt's colleagues were mere stooges who were cowed by every outburst of the statesman. There are no claims that Pitt had qualities other than a fierce patriotism, a natural impatience and an irrepressible confidence that France could be crushed. Furthermore, though several authors are critical of Newcastle's early handling of the war, there is none of that virulent abuse which has been such a feature of later historical writing. In 1760 a Mr James Marriott had suggested that Newcastle ought to write an account of his life in the style of Clarendon. Marriott commented: 'With regard to Posterity, the lives of Great Men are made the subjects of lying histories unless they themselves transmit an account of their own actions.'[16] So far Marriott's predictions had proved unfounded.

But significant changes in the interpretation of the war and Pitt's role were not long in coming. Several new influences were at work. The final defeat of France in 1815 ended what had, on the whole, been a period of uncertainty and doubt. Englishmen could once more persuade themselves that they were a match for the rest of Europe. The reading public were readier to admire the policy of a man who would apparently have given the final blow to France had he not been prevented by timorous colleagues. Equally important was the development of Whig history. The tide of opinion that was to submerge the reputation of George III simultaneously carried Pitt to new heights. He appeared to embody so much that was dear to the Whig and later liberal order of things: a great orator and parliamentary debater; a popular leader and defender of liberty; a man of principle above the sordid temptations of office; above all, someone

---

[14] W. Belsham, *Memoirs of the Reign of George III* (5 vols., London, 1795), I, 11–12. Ibid., 43–47.
[15] J. Adolphus, *The History of England from the Accession of King George III to the Conclusion of the Peace* (3 vols., 1802), I, 40.
[16] Marriott to Newcastle, 26 Jan 1760, Add. Mss 32,901 f 483. Marriott probably intended to write the biography himself, but never did. See his entry in the *Dictionary of National Biography*.

independent of the Crown, although in claiming him for their own the Whigs managed to overlook his opposition to party and treatment of the Rockinghamites. Such contradictions did not matter for, as Lord Mahon later observed, all parties in dealing with Pitt's administration were now 'eager to claim its principles as their own'.[17]

One other factor was to influence work on the subject. With the advent of Napoleon, a number of writers on the continent began a systematic analysis of war in a way that had not been done before. Battles were dissected, tactics discussed and campaigns inspected for their strategic content. The new breed of military writers were probably justified in so treating the campaigns of Napoleon. The Revolutionary Wars were the first in modern times to involve whole nations at every level, affording a purpose and direction that had been lacking in the earlier, more limited, conflicts of the eighteenth century. But inevitably the new concepts began to be used as analytical tools for other eras by writers anxious to show how up to date they were in their scholarship. This fashion for systematizing war and reducing it to first principles was initiated by Andre Jomini, whose *Traité des Grandes Opérations Militaires* started appearing in Paris from 1811.[18] He was followed by a number of others, not least Carl von Clausewitz, whose masterpiece *Vom Kriege* was published posthumously between 1832 and 1837. Both works were translated into English, bringing with them a new word, 'strategy'.[19]

These several influences could not but affect anyone writing on Pitt in the first half of the nineteenth century. They were certainly present in the work of the Reverend Francis Thackeray, whose two-volume study in 1832 was the first full biography to appear since that of Godwin. Here for the first time are gathered all the ingredients which later historians were to use. Pitt was now elevated to the position of a great strategist and master planner. A dynamic administrator and compulsive innovator, he was an absolute war minister who brooked no opposition from colleagues or subordinates.[20] Thackeray's biography was a landmark in another respect. He was the first of many historians who persistently and consistently denigrated the character of Newcastle. The Duke was portrayed as a person of limited ability, if of unlimited ambition, who relied on intrigue to obtain

[17] P. H. Mahon, Earl Stanhope, *History of England from the Peace of Utrecht to the Peace of Versailles, 1713–1783* (7 vols., London, 1836–1845), IV, 161.

[18] A. Jomini, *Traité des Grandes Opérations Militaires, Contenant L'Histoire Critique des Campagnes de Frédéric II, Comparées à celles de L'Empereur Napoléon avec un Recueil des Principes Généraux de L'Art de Guerre* (8 vols., Paris, 1811–1816).

[19] Jomini was partially translated by J. A. Gilbert in *An Exposition of the First Principles of Grand Military Combinations* (1 vol., London, 1825). Clausewitz had to wait until 1873 for a full translation of his three-volume *On War*, edited by J. J. Graham, although John Murray, the publisher, brought out a single volume, *The Campaign of 1812* (London, 1843).

[20] F. Thackeray, *A History of the Right Honourable William Pitt, Earl of Chatham* (2 vols., London, 1827).

office and had no resolution to accomplish anything once he had obtained his heart's desire.

Thackeray claimed to have researched diligently in the state paper office when writing his work. He certainly quoted extracts from Pitt's dispatches and other material in the Chatham papers. But he relied heavily on a selective use of Horace Walpole, Edmund Burke and Almon. Indeed Thackeray was one of the first to use Walpole's recently published *Memoirs of the Reign of King George the Second*.[21] Though these were reasonably balanced in their treatment of Pitt, the case was quite otherwise with Newcastle. Thackeray, and those who followed him, ignored Walpole's strong personal reasons for maligning Newcastle, who, he believed, had engineered the downfall of his father, and who had later denied him financial security by refusing to make a sinecure that would be payable for life. Historians were not assisted subsequently in arriving at a more balanced assessment on the presentation of the Newcastle papers to the British Museum. The correspondence simply provided readers disposed to be critical of Newcastle with fresh material of his supposed incompetence and timidity. To the cost of his reputation, Newcastle committed too many of his innermost thoughts to paper which writers already hostile to him did not hesitate to exploit, missing at the same time his good if muddled sense. As a result, Walpole's posthumous publication perpetrated a masterly fraud on the Whigs, the real victims of which were George III and Newcastle.

The deficiencies of Walpole's memoirs were not unknown. John Wilson Croker, in a long review article that same year (1822), detailed Walpole's defects as a historian and a source.[22] Nevertheless, neither Thackeray nor later writers made any attempt to meet the problems posed by his evidence. Admittedly, the new fashion of according Pitt total adulation brought forth some pungent remarks from Thomas Babington Macaulay. He suggested, in a review of Thackeray's work in the *Edinburgh Review*, that the biographers of the statesman were beginning to suffer from what he called 'the disease of admiration'. Apparently, they were determined to make Pitt a 'poet in *esse*, a general in *posse*', and a great many other things besides, including the perfect father, husband and friend. Whatever one might think of Pitt the statesman, there could be no denying, Macaulay asserted, his less attractive features. Firstly, he had an undeniable tendency to act a part. Then there was his total inconsistency. Finally, he was utterly unscrupulous, as evidenced by his despicable attempt to barter the impeachment of Sir Robert Walpole for a promise of office. However, Macaulay did not

---

[21] H. Walpole, *Memoirs of the Last Ten Years of the Reign of King George the Second*, ed. Lord Holland (2 vols., London, 1822). All citations in this book however are to the later three-volume edition (London, 1846–1847).

[22] J. W. Croker, 'Walpole's Memoirs of the Reign of George II', *The Quarterly Review*, xxvii, 178–215. See also his review of Walpole's *Memoirs of the Reign of King George III*, ed. D. Le Marchant (4 vols., London, 1845) in *The Quarterly Review*, lxxvii, 253–298.

question the now accepted interpretation of Pitt the war leader. He was the true guardian of the people: a great patriot who had inspired the nation to victory. About Newcastle, Macaulay also agreed. The Duke was the epitome of cunning, timidity and incompetence.[23]

Macaulay set the tone for much of the more important writing that was to follow: some criticism, generally commendation. Lord Mahon, in his seven-volume *History of England from the Peace of Utrecht to the Peace of Versailles*, suggested that the government of Pitt, while 'the greatest and most glorious perhaps, that England has ever known', was nevertheless 'not always, indeed, free from haste or error in its schemes'.[24] William Hartpole Lecky, in his *History of England in the Eighteenth Century*, like Macaulay asserted that Pitt 'never unbent. . . He was always acting a part, always self conscious, always aiming at a false and unreal dignity.' Yet with all his faults he was still a very great man, especially as a war minister where 'his greatness was beyond question, and almost beyond comparison'.[25]

Though the adulation of Pitt was considerably increased, the written output on him was not large, for popular interest was greater in his son. The Victorians valued economy, and in this field the Elder Pitt had been a conspicuous failure. Moreover, the loss of the American colonies had reduced esteem for empire. In an era of free trade, dependencies seemed to be a burden, not an asset. However, all this changed towards the end of the century. Shrinking resources and increasing competition made the European powers once more value colonies. The new attitudes were expressed in the division of Africa and the intervention in China. This chauvinism contributed to a renaissance in the study of Pitt. Much of the new work was to come from scholars working in the universities, though it was not until the turn of the century that the revival began. Then, in a few short years, several major works appeared, dealing with different aspects of the war and Pitt's handling of it. Frederick Harrison began the process with a brief life, published in 1905.[26] The following year Gertrude S. Kimball produced her two-volume *Correspondence of William Pitt, when Secretary of State, with the Colonial Governors and Military and Naval Commissioners in America*, and twelve months later Sir Julian Corbett published his classic study, *England in the Seven Years' War*. In addition, Albert von Ruville produced a three-volume biography, indicating that scholars overseas were also influenced by the prevalent mood of imperialism. During the same period important articles were written by William Hunt and Hubert Hall.[27]

[23] T. B. Macaulay, 'William Pitt, Earl of Chatham', *Edinburgh Review*, LVIII, 508–544.
[24] Mahon, *History of England*, IV, 161.
[25] W. E. H. Lecky, *A History of England in the Eighteenth Century* (8 vols., London, 1878–1890), II, 483–489.   [26] F. Harrison, *Chatham* (London, 1905).
[27] W. Hunt, 'Pitt's Retirement from Office, 1761', *English Historical Review*, XXI, 119–132. H. Hall, 'Chatham's Colonial Policy', *American Historical Review*, V, 659–675. This latter topic was later enlarged upon by K. Hotblack, *Chatham's Colonial Policy* (London, 1917).

Finally, there appeared in 1913 another work which has remained, with Corbett, the standard authority, Basil Williams's two-volume biography, *The Life of William Pitt, Earl of Chatham*.

Curiously, although it had been fashionable since Thackeray to talk of Pitt the strategist, no one had attempted a full-scale analysis of the war in the manner of Jomini or Clausewitz. It was this omission that Corbett now rectified, showing how Pitt achieved victory by a military and naval strategy that was co-ordinated to the last detail. He asserted: 'Pitt's system is a most brilliant lesson of the way in which the weak army of a strong naval power can be used, of how great continental armies may be made to feel the shock of fleets, and how mere superiority at sea can be made to thwart continental . . . strategy and upset their moral balance.'[28] Of the Rochefort scheme, Corbett concluded: 'Nothing could be more modern or scientific.'[29] In writing his work, Corbett was subject to a number of influences beyond those of other writers. From 1902 he had been appointed lecturer at the newly established Royal Naval College, Greenwich, where in the words of G. A. R. Callendar, 'it was strategy rather than tactics his audience required'.[30] Corbett was primarily writing a text which would be useful for demonstrating the principles of naval warfare. Furthermore, he was writing at a time when steam power and the cable telegraph had made the co-ordination of distant operations possible. Nevertheless, his writings are still of great interest and value. He was one of the first scholars to use the Newcastle papers extensively. By the standards of his day, the work was well researched and fully convincing.

Another work to receive acclaim was that of Basil Williams. Like Corbett, Williams used the Newcastle papers, though his searches in the British Museum served mainly to reinforce the now traditional picture of Newcastle the interfering busybody. Williams agreed with Thackeray in portraying Pitt as the masterful and overriding minister who supervised every action of government. Williams asserted: 'When Pitt left office the Pope of Rome said that he esteemed it the highest honour to be born an Englishman. In Africa we had taken away all the French possessed; in Europe our troops had beaten the flower of their armies, while our expeditions had insulted their coasts from Dunkirk to Bordeaux and had even occupied a parcel of France; and on the high seas our fleets were supreme. In America we had won a continent. In India we were masters of Bengal, and in other parts had no European rivals left – victories which ensured that in these two vast portions of the world the Protestant Anglo-Saxon – not the French Roman Catholic – civilization should hereafter prevail. And in spite of the long war

[28] J. S. Corbett, *England in the Seven Years' War: A Study in Combined Strategy* (2 vols, London, 1907), I, 8–9.   [29] Ibid., 190.
[30] *Dictionary of National Biography*.

the commerce on which England's greatness then chiefly rested had never been so flourishing. To Pitt all this was due.'[31]

By now the 'disease of admiration' was the accepted test of orthodoxy. Thus, when von Ruville made some less than flattering remarks about the statesman, he was severely criticized by Frederick Harrison in his capacity as a Vice-President of the Royal Historical Society. Ruville suggested that Pitt was more indebted for his success to his predecessors than was commonly acknowledged, especially in the equipment of the navy. Worse, he raised the old point about Pitt's consistency and political sincerity.[32] Macaulay had written the same. Now, such sentiments amounted to the denigration of a British hero. In an address to the Fellows of the Society, Harrison suggested: 'Von Ruville, whilst recognizing the genius of Chatham and the marvellous achievements of his brief era of power. . . has so persistently sought to belittle his motives and his sincerity – and that by vague hypothesis and cynical innuendo in the absence of a shred of proof – that the Quarterly Reviewer correctly alludes to him as *advocatus diaboli*.' Harrison continued: 'It is impossible for Englishmen to accept a portrait which at times is little more than a caricature. The Prussian archivist, though a past master in documentary research, seems unable to understand the nature of our English hero. I had almost said he is unable to understand the genius of English politics, or indeed the true evolution of England.'[33]

Following the appearance of Williams's biography in 1913, the interpretation of Pitt and the conduct of the Seven Years' War has remained almost unaltered to the present time. One reason for this has been the decline of interest in the subject. Equally important, there seemed nothing left to say. The only work of biographical note to appear in the inter-war period was that by Brian Tunstall, published in 1938. Tunstall did considerable research in the Chatham, Newcastle and Hardwicke papers, but did not pretend to supersede the writings of Corbett and Williams.[34]

The other major publications during this period were those by S. M. Pargellis, whose *Lord Loudoun in North America* appeared in 1933, followed three years later by his *Military Affairs in North America*. Tunstall makes no mention of either and not surprisingly, for Pargellis is severely critical of Pitt. He argues that the conquest of North America took far too long. The main reasons for this were Pitt's readiness to change generals on every setback

[31] B. Williams, *The Life of William Pitt, Earl of Chatham* (2 vols., London, 1913), II, 124.
[32] A. von Ruville, *William Pitt, Earl of Chatham* (3 vols., London, 1907), II, 77–79.
[33] F. Harrison, 'Address to the Fellows of the Royal Historical Society', *Transactions of the Royal Historical Society*, 3rd Series, III (1909), 34–49.
[34] W. C. B. Tunstall, *William Pitt, Earl of Chatham* (London, 1938), 5.

and his tendency to interfere in matters that could only be determined by men on the spot.[35]

These criticisms by Pargellis have scarcely been noted. Certainly, the experiences of the Second World War did nothing to change the views of Pitt as the master planner and strategist. If anything they helped to confirm them, showing that a war could be planned from nothing and brought to a victorious conclusion. Although the empire was finished in Asia, hopes remained of reviving British fortunes elsewhere. Pitt could still be seen as the architect of an entity on which the sun would never set. Accounts of Wolfe scaling the Heights of Abraham, of Clive winning the battle of Plassey and of Pitt reviving the nation, had comforting parallels for a country that had just emerged from its greatest ordeal.

Only recently has the traditional interpretation come under scrutiny. Stanley Ayling, in the best modern biography, presents Pitt with all his contradictions.[36] Ayling, however, did not pretend to provide a new biography based on fresh material and his work is less novel than it might have been, especially on Pitt the war minister. Essentially he does no more than produce a portrait similar to the one by Macaulay.

Every work is necessarily the product of its environment. *The Bells of Victory* has been affected by several influences. The first is the trend towards an egalitarian society. The people who are admired today are the Lucky Jims and Rabbit Angstroms, the anti-heroes of society. Great men in the traditional sense are disparaged. Secondly, the present age is one that is beginning to question the ability of governments to control events. Tolstoy's view of history has never seemed more persuasive. If twentieth-century governments find human affairs difficult to direct, how much more impossible it must have been for eighteenth-century administrations. In addition, this book has been produced at a time when opinion has favoured European unity and international co-operation. The word 'imperialism' has become a pejorative term, making it difficult to write sympathetically about a man who seemingly wanted to seize for his country a monopoly of overseas territory and prostrate foreign rivals for good.[37] Lastly, there has been a tendency to see war in less heroic terms. Much greater emphasis is now placed on its misery and destructiveness. This too has made it more difficult to be sympathetic to a statesman who gloried in its conduct.

No doubt later generations will be influenced by different ideas and bring other values to bear on the past. They are, however, unlikely to return to

---

[35] S. M. Pargellis, *Military Affairs in North America, 1748–1765: Selected Documents from the Cumberland Papers in Windsor Castle* (New York, 1936), xvii–xxi. S. M. Pargellis, *Lord Loudoun in North America* (New Haven, 1933), 337–365.

[36] S. Ayling, *The Elder Pitt, Earl of Chatham* (London, 1976).

[37] Conversely, it is now easier to write sympathetically about Newcastle for favouring a negotiated settlement of the Anglo-French disputes.

the former eulogy of Pitt. A close analysis of the nineteenth- and early-twentieth-century works suggest how brittle were the foundations of Pitt's reputation as a war minister. Corbett had to admit about the plans for 1758: 'Of the process of thought by which Pitt and Anson settled the design not a trace remains. All we can know is the main considerations that must have been in their minds.'[38] Corbett would have done well to reflect that no such grand designs are to be found in Entick or Beatson, who did not credit Pitt with anything more than a full measure of self-confidence and a determination to succeed. He might then have postulated that such thinking was beyond the intellectual capacity of eighteenth-century ministers. However, in the intellectual climate of the early twentieth century, such reservations were unthinkable. At the time when Corbett was writing, Frederick Harrison asserted how recent publications 'reveal to us the real Chatham in a light in which he was not known down to the present century. We now know better than his contemporaries, that success was won by admirably planned combinations, worked out with consummate mastery of ways and means, of places and men.'[39] The writings of Entick, Smollett and Beatson could be dismissed as dilettante.

In reality, the achievement of Pitt has all too often rested on a number of unsubstantiated incidents that supposedly demonstrate his restless energy and control. It has been popular to tell how Pitt compelled the Admiralty to sign documents which the members of the Board were not even permitted to read.[40] Historians have also fondly related a statement, attributed to Sir James Porter, the ambassador to Turkey, that he would have known instantly of Pitt's dismissal or withdrawal from public office by the change of tone in the office dispatches.[41] Not all biographers of Pitt or historians of the war have necessarily used these stories every time, but they have been repeated often enough to be considered as more than window-dressing to the reality of Pitt the war minister. The references for these incidents are varied and it does not seem to have been noticed that their ultimate source is Almon. For reasons already described, Almon cannot be relied upon. The manuscript evidence in no way substantiates the anecdotes about Pitt's treatment of the Admiralty. Yet the story of how Pitt compelled the Admiralty to sign blank orders is to be found in Tunstall, Williams and Lecky, who took it from Thackeray, who in turn repeated it from Almon.[42]

---

[38] Corbett, *Seven Years' War*, I, 311.

[39] Harrison, 'Address', *Royal Historical Society Transactions*, 43–44.

[40] J. Almon, *Anecdotes of the Life of the Right Honourable William Pitt, Earl of Chatham, and of the Principal Events of his Time* (3 vols., London, 1793), I, 307. Thackeray, *Pitt*, I, 293. Lecky, *History of England*, II, 466. Williams, *Life of Pitt*, I, 327. Tunstall, *Pitt*, 191–192.

[41] Almon, *Anecdotes of Pitt*, I, 334–335. Thackeray, *Pitt*, I, 318–319. Williams, *Life of Pitt*, I, 329.

[42] See above, note 40. Williams and Tunstall certainly discount the story, but imply that it is symbolic of the dominance that Pitt exercised over his colleagues and their departments.

The same uncritical repetition is also true of a number of anecdotes which have their origin in the memoirs of Walpole. Perhaps the most famous is the statement he attributed to Pitt on the formation of his coalition with Devonshire: 'My Lord, I am sure I can save this country, and no one else can.'[43] Walpole related this anecdote as an example of Pitt's arrogance, but historians have repeated it as though it were fact. The statement should in any case have been challenged. More reliable evidence from Pitt's own correspondence shows that he was anything but self-confident at this time. The *Chatham Correspondence*, published in 1836, contains a letter from Pitt to Keene, the British ambassador in Madrid, dated 22 August 1757. This commented how 'the indefinite benefits of the Treaty of Utrecht', which had been the 'indelible reproach of the last generation, are become the necessary but almost unattainable wish of the present'.[14] These were hardly the words of a man brimming with self-assurance. Indeed, Pitt was so lacking in confidence that he was prepared to cede Gibraltar to entice Spain into the war. It is contradictions like these that discredit the traditional interpretation.

In general, nineteenth- and twentieth-century historians have been too ready to accept uncritically the evidence favourable to Pitt. For example, they have usually cited as a sign of his popularity the awarding of gold boxes to him and Legge in the spring of 1757 with the freedom of various towns and cities. But, as Paul Langford, in an article in the *English Historical Review*, points out, the total number of boxes presented was only twelve. Hundreds of other towns and corporations might have so honoured him, and at least one box was given not by the city corporation but by the guild of merchants. Moreover, most of the awards were hardly spontaneous. They were managed by patrons of boroughs who happened to be politically sympathetic.[45]

Another example of the selective use of evidence has been the quoting of Isaac Barré's statement that no man went into Pitt's office without coming out the braver.[46] Writers using it have rarely noted that this was made on the death of Pitt, and contradicts other sentiments uttered earlier. In 1761, just after he had entered Parliament, Barré delivered a bitter denunciation, describing Pitt as 'a profligate minister, who had thrust himself into power on the shoulders of the mob'.[47] Barré had personal reasons for speaking thus, believing Pitt was responsible for his not being promoted to the rank of colonel.[48] It is a moot point which comment best represents Barré's true

---

[43] Walpole, *Memoirs of George II*, III, 84.
[44] Pitt to Keene, 22 Aug 1757, W. S. Taylor and J. H. Pringle (eds.), *The Correspondence of William Pitt, Earl of Chatham* (4 vols., London, 1838–1840), I, 247–256.
[45] P. Langford, 'William Pitt and Public Opinion', *English Historical Review*, LXXXVIII, 54–79.
[46] Lecky, *History of England*, II, 489. Williams, *Life of Pitt*, I, 332. Tunstall, *Pitt*, 166.
[47] Walpole, *Memoirs of George III*, I, 86.
[48] See Taylor and Pringle, *Chatham Correspondence* II, 41–43.

feelings: the one uttered in the aftermath of disappointed ambition; the other when it is customary to speak no evil of the dead. Both should be treated with caution.

It is probably a truism that the further a writer is from his subject, the more research he needs to do to understand its premises. Nineteenth-century authors tended to rely on a few accessible sources, some of which can only be described as facile. Of course, much of the more crucial material was not always available. However, the establishment of the Public Record Office in 1838 meant that more might have been done. Particularly culpable was the neglect of departmental correspondence. With so little known about the inner workings of government, there was no substitute for an inspection of the archives. However, except for the State Papers, little or nothing was attempted. It was for this reason that Basil Williams was misled about the Secretarial powers. By restricting his research to the State Papers and Chatham's personal correspondence, he acquired a distorted picture of the administrative workings and failed to realize that the Secretary's office was a channel of communication, rather than the source of all activity. In general, there has been too little attention to the constitutional parameters in which all the ministers had to work.

Lastly, historians since the turn of the nineteenth century have been influenced in their assessment of Pitt by an excessively biographical approach to the subject. They have preoccupied themselves with the deeds of individuals rather than the impersonal factors of geography, demography and administration. Attention has been focused on the actions of a few prominent men like Chatham, Hardwicke and Newcastle, and changes of fortune have too readily been ascribed to a change of personnel. Historians have hence overlooked the fortunate timing of Pitt's admission to office, when France was being distracted from the maritime war by affairs in Europe and the preparations of the Newcastle ministry were beginning to take effect. It was easy for these writers to attribute subsequent setbacks at Rochefort, St Cast and Ticonderoga to other more culpable agents, leaving to Pitt the credit for all the success. The problem posed by this temptation to simplify events has been succinctly put by Eric McDermott when he said: 'Good reasons offer a tremendous obstacle to the discovery of the real reasons.'[49]

I have tried to avoid such pitfalls by first looking systematically at the departmental correspondence, next at the participants' personal letters and then at the contributions of bystanders like Walpole. I have tried always to use contemporary material, written at the time, not after the event. Human beings have poor memories. After an occurrence they reflect and reinterpret. What is written at the time is more likely to state accurately

---

[49] E. McDermott, 'The Elder Pitt and His Admirals and Generals', *Military Affairs*, xx, 65–77.

the intentions and achievement of the participant. Walpole, on whom so many historians have relied, is suspect on two counts. Except for the debates in Parliament, he was not involved in the events he was describing, being a mere observer dependent on hearsay. Secondly, he did not write his memoirs at the time. Indeed, they were published many years after with the specific intention of deceiving the reader on many points. I have not been able to dispense entirely with such work, since more reliable evidence has not always been available. But anything from a secondary authority has been used sparingly and with caution. I have tried for the rest to use the best primary material and it is my hope that the present work will provide a more convincing account of the war's management and the reasons for the British success. Pontius Pilate jested to Christ about the nature of truth. The historian must take the matter more seriously, though he can never achieve the truth completely.

BIBLIOGRAPHY

I: MANUSCRIPTS

Admiralty Library
Da. 95, Progress of the Navy.
American Antiquarian Society
Bradstreet Papers and Account Books.
Bedford Record Office
Robinson Papers.
Hardwicke–Lady Anson Correspondence.
British Library
Add. Mss 15,955–15,957, Anson Correspondence.
Add. Mss 31,959, Hardwicke Papers Relating to the Loss of Minorca.
Add. Mss 32,852–32,939, Newcastle Papers, General Correspondence.
Add. Mss 32,995–32,998, Newcastle Papers, Cabinet Memoranda.
Add. Mss 33,029–33,030, Newcastle Papers, North America and the West Indies.
Add. Mss 33,038–33,040, Newcastle Papers, Finance and Treasury.
Add. Mss 33,046–33,048, Newcastle Papers, Army and Navy.
Add. Mss 34,728–34,736, West Papers.
Add. Mss 35,359–35,909, Hardwicke Papers.
Add. Mss 41,346–41,356, Martin Papers.
Add. Mss 51,375–51,380, Holland House (Fox) Papers.
Egerton 3425–3490, Leeds Papers, Holdernesse Correspondence.
King's Mss 44, Survey of the Dockyards, 1688–1774.
King's Mss 70, Warrant Establishing the Government of the Ordnance.
Chatsworth
Papers of the Fourth Duke of Devonshire.
Clements Library
Amherst Papers.
Furness Letter Book.
Gage Papers.
Germain Papers.
Howe Papers.
Ligonier Letter Book.
Shelburne Papers.
East Riding Record Office
Hotham Papers.

Houghton Library
  Ms Eng 106 F, Gage–Bradstreet Correspondence.
  Ms Cam 64, Loudoun Correspondence.
Huntington Library
  Abercromby Papers.
  Grenville Papers.
  Loudoun Papers.
Library of Congress
  Monckton Papers.
National Library of Scotland
  Mss 305, Letter Book of General Bland.
  Mss 7,090, Military Returns.
National Maritime Museum
  Adm A/2444–2476, Admiralty to the Navy Board.
  Adm B/149–168, Navy Board to the Admiralty.
  Adm C/536–557, Admiralty to the Victualling Board.
  Adm N/237–240, Transport Orders.
  Admiralty Dimension Book, 1660–1760.
  Duff Papers.
  Hawke Papers.
  Roddam Letter Book.
  Rochefort Letter Case.
New York Public Library
  Frederick Papers.
Public Record Office
  Adm 1, Admiralty In-Letters.
  Adm 2, Admiralty Out-Letters.
  Adm 3, Admiralty Minutes.
  Adm 7, Admiralty–Privy Council Correspondence, Progress of the Navy etc.
  Adm 8, List Books of Ships' Officers, Names and Stations, etc.
  Adm 106, Navy Board Papers.
  Adm 110, Victualling Board Papers.
  C. 66, Letters Patent.
  CO 5, Colonial Office, Correspondence of the Secretaries of State with the
    Governors and Commanders in America.
  PC 1, Privy Council In-Letters.
  PC 2, Privy Council Registers (Out-Letters).
  SP 41, Secretaries of State, In-Letters from the War Office and Ordnance.
  SP 42, In Letters from the Admiralty and Naval Commanders.
  SP 44, Military and Naval Entry Books (Out-Letters).
  SP 54, Scottish Correspondence.
  SP 63, Ireland, In-Letters.
  SP 67, Ireland, Out-Letter Books.
  SP 78, French Correspondence.
  SP 84, Dutch Correspondence.
  SP 87, Correspondence with the Commanders in Germany.

SP 90, Prussian Correspondence.
SP 91, Russian Correspondence.
SP 94, Spanish Correspondence.
SP 97, Turkish Correspondence.
SP 104, Diplomatic Entry Books.
T 1, Calendar of In-Letters to the Treasury.
T 27, Treasury Out-Letters
T 29, Treasury Board Minutes.
T 64, Treasury, Miscellaneous, the Commissariat etc.
WO 1, War Office In-Letters.
WO 4, War Office Out-Letters.
WO 5, Marching Orders.
WO 7, Clothing Board, Commissary of Musters, etc.
WO 8, War Office Correspondence with Ireland.
WO 25, Commission Books, Embarkation Returns etc.
WO 26, Warrants and Precedents.
WO 27, Inspection Returns.
WO 30, Papers relating to the Defence of Britain and Ireland.
WO 34, Amherst Papers.
WO 47, Ordnance Board Minutes.
PRO 30/8, Chatham Papers.
PRO 30/29, Granville Papers.
Public Record Office of Northern Ireland
  DOD 678, Diary and Letters of an officer on the staff of Brigadier Murray.
  T 2812, Conway Correspondence.
  T 2915, Bedford Correspondence (photostat transcripts).
  T 3459, Donoughmore (Ligonier) Papers.
Royal Archives, Windsor
  Cumberland Papers.
Scottish Record Office
  Dalhousie Papers.
Staffordshire Record Office
  Anson Papers.

II: PRINTED PRIMARY MATERIALS

Admiralty, *The Laws, Ordinances, and Institutions of the Admiralty*, 2 vols., London, 1746.
Almanacs etc., *The Court and City Register for 1754–1763*.
Bisset, A., ed., *The Memoirs and Papers of Sir Andrew Mitchell, K.B., Envoy Extraordinary and Minister Plenipotentiary from the Court of Great Britain to the Court of Prussia, 1756–1771*, 2 vols., London, 1850.
Board of Trade, *Journal of the Commissioners for Trade and Plantations, 1704–1782*, 14 vols., London, 1920–1938.
Bradshaw, J., ed., *The Letters of Philip Dormer Stanhope, Earl of Chesterfield*, 3 vols., London, 1893.
Bromley, J. S., ed., *The Manning of the Royal Navy: Selected Public Pamphlets, 1693–1873*, Navy Record Society Publications, cxix, London, 1974.

Brown, P. D. and Schweizer, K. W., eds., *The Devonshire Diary: William Cavendish, Fourth Duke of Devonshire, Memoranda on State of Affairs, 1759–1762*, Camden Society Publications, Fourth Series, xxvii, London, 1982.

Bullocke, J. G., ed., *The Tomlinson Papers*, Navy Records Society Publications, lxxiv, London, 1935.

Chalmers, G., ed., *A Collection of Treaties between Great Britain and Other Powers*, 2 vols., London, 1790.

Chamberlayne, J., *Magnae Britanniae Notitia: or the Present State of Great Britain*, London, 1726.

Chance, J. F., ed., *British Diplomatic Instructions, 1689–1789*, vol. iii, *Denmark*, Camden Society Publications, Third Series, vol. xxxiv, London, 1926.

Cushner, N. P., *Documents Illustrating the British Conquest of Manila, 1762–1763*, Camden Society Publications, Fourth Series, viii, London, 1971.

Doughty, A., and Parmalee, G. W., eds., *The Siege of Quebec and the Battle of the Plains of Abraham*, 6 vols., Quebec, 1901.

Erskine, D., ed., *Augustus Hervey's Journal*, London, 1953.

Graham, G. S., ed., *The Walker Expedition to Quebec*, Navy Records Society Publications, xciv, London, 1953.

Gwyn, J., ed., *The Royal Navy and North America: The Warren Papers 1736–1752*, Navy Records Society Publications, cxviii, London, 1973.

Historical Manuscripts Commission, *Appendix to the Twelfth Report*, Part 5, *Rutland Manuscripts*, 2 vols., London 1889.

Appendix to the Twelfth Report, Part 10, *Charlemont Manuscripts*, 2 vols., London, 1891.

Report on the Manuscripts of Mrs Stopford-Sackville, 2 vols., London, 1904–1910.

Report on Manuscripts Various, vol. vi, *Eyre Matcham Manuscripts*, London, 1909.

House of Commons, *Journal of the House of Commons*, vols. xxvii–xxix.

James, A. P., ed., *The Writings of General John Forbes*, Wisconsin, 1938.

Kimball, G. S., *The Correspondence of William Pitt, when Secretary of State, with the Colonial Governors and Military and Naval Commissioners in North America*, 2 vols., London, 1906.

Lloyd, C., ed., *The Naval Miscellany*, iv, Navy Records Society Publications, xcii, London, 1952.

The Health of Seamen: Selections from the Works of Dr James Lind, Sir Gilbert Blane and Dr Thomas Trotter, Navy Records Society Publications, cvii, London, 1965.

Mordaunt, Sir J., *The Report of the General Officers appointed by His Majesty's Warrant . . . to Enquire into the Causes of the Failure of the Late Expedition to the Coasts of France*, London, 1758.

The Proceedings of a General Court Martial held in the Council Chamber at Whitehall . . . upon the trial of Lieutenant General Sir John Mordaunt, London, 1758.

Newman, A., ed., *Leicester House Politics, 1750–1760, from the Papers of John Second Earl of Egmont*, Camden Society Miscellany Fourth Series, vii, London, 1969.

New York Historical Society Publications, l–lvi, *The Letters and Papers of Cadwallader Colden*, 7 vols., New York, 1917–1923.

iv–vii, *The Lee Papers*, 4 vols., New York, 1871–1874.

xiv, *The Montresor Journals*, New York, 1881.

Northcliffe, *The Northcliffe Collection: Papers presented to the Government of Canada by Sir Leicester Harmsworth*, Toronto, 1926.

Operations of the Allied Army under the Command of his Serene Highness, Prince Ferdinand, Duke of Brunswick . . . by an Officer who Served in the British Forces, London, 1764.

Pargellis, S. M., ed., *Military Affairs in North America, 1748–1765: Selected Documents from the Cumberland Papers in Windsor Castle*, New York, 1936.

Parry, C., ed., *The Consolidated Treaty Series*, 225 vols., New York 1969–.

Phillimore, R., ed., *Correspondence of George, Lord Lyttelton, 1734–1773*, 2 vols., London, 1845.

Privy Council, *Acts of the Privy Council, Colonial Series*, 6 vols., London, 1908–1912.

Richmond, Sir Herbert, *Papers Relating to the Loss of Minorca in 1756*, Navy Records Society Publications, XLII, London, 1913.

Russell, Lord J., ed., *Correspondence of John, Fourth Duke of Bedford*, 3 vols., London, 1842–1846.

Sedgwick, R. *Letters from George III to Lord Bute, 1756–1766*, London, 1939.

Smith, D. B., ed., *The Barrington Papers*, Navy Records Society Publications, LXXVII, London, 1937.

Smith, W. J., ed., *The Grenville Papers, Being the Correspondence of Richard Grenville, Earl Temple, K.G., and the Right Honourable George Grenville, Their Friends and Contemporaries*, 4 vols., London, 1852.

Statutes, *The Statutes at Large*, 9 vols., London, 1769–1770.

Syrett, D., ed., *The Siege and Capture of Havana, 1762*, Navy Records Society Publications, CXIV, London, 1970.

Taylor, W. S. and Pringle, J. H., eds., *The Correspondence of William Pitt, Earl of Chatham*, 4 vols., London, 1838–1840.

Toynbee, P., ed., *The Letters of Horace Walpole, Fourth Earl of Oxford*, 19 vols., Oxford, 1903–1925.

Waldegrave, James Earl, *Memoirs from 1754 to 1758*, London, 1821.

Webster, J. C., ed., *The Journal of Jeffery Amherst*, Toronto, 1931.

Yorke, P. C., *The Life and Correspondence of Philip Yorke, Earl of Hardwicke*, 3 vols., Cambridge, 1913.

III: CONTEMPORARY NEWSPAPERS AND JOURNALS

The Annual Register
The Contest
The Gentleman's Magazine
The New York Mercury
The London Chronicle
The London Gazette
The Monitor
The Test
The Westminster Journal

IV: PAMPHLETS

Anonymous, *A Letter from the Honourable L---t G---l B--gh to the Right Honourable W---m P--t Esquire*, London, 1758.

A Letter to the Right Honourable Lord A----, London, 1757.

Candid Reflections on the report of the General Officers, London, 1758.

A Journal of the Campaign on the Coast of France, London, 1758.

Conway, H. S., *The Military Arguments in the Letter to a Right Honourable Author Fully Considered*, London, 1758.
Dalrymple, C., *A Military Essay, Containing Reflections on the Raising, Arming, Clothing and Discipline of the British Infantry and Calvary: with Proposals for the Improvement of the Same*, London, 1761.
Mallet, D., *Observations on the Twelfth Article of War*, London, 1757.
Mauduit, I., *Considerations on the Present German War*, London, 1760.
Shebbeare, J., *Fifth Letter to the People of England on the Subversion of the Constitution and the Necessity of it being Restored*, London, 1757.
Thompson, W., *The Royal Navy-Men's Advocate: The Corrupt Practices of Victualling the Royal Navy*, London, 1757.

V : PRINTED SECONDARY SOURCES

Adolphus, J., *The History of England from the Accession of King George III to the Conclusion of the Peace*, 3 vols., London, 1802.
Albion, R. G., *Forests and Sea Power: The Timber Problem of the Royal Navy, 1652–1862*, Cambridge, Mass., 1926.
Almon, J., *Anecdotes of the Life of the Right Honourable William Pitt, Earl of Chatham, and of the Principal Events of his Time*, 3 vols., London, 1793.
Anson, W., *The Life of Admiral Lord Anson, the Father of the British Navy 1697–1762*, London, 1912.
Ayling, S., *The Elder Pitt, Earl of Chatham*, London, 1976.
Baker, N., *Government and Contractors: The British Treasury and War Supplies, 1775–1783*, London, 1971.
Ballantyne, A., *Lord Carteret*, London, 1887.
Banbury, P., *Shipbuilders of the Thames and Medway*, Newton Abbot, 1971.
Barnett, C. D., *Britain and her Army, 1509–1970*, London, 1970.
Barrington, S., *The Political Life of William Wildman, Viscount Barrington*, London, 1814.
Barrow, Sir J., *Life of George, Lord Anson*, London, 1839.
Basye, A. H., *The Lords Commissioners of Trade and Plantations, Commonly Known as the Board of Trade, 1748–1782*, New Haven, 1925.
Baugh, D. A., *British Naval Administration in the Age of Walpole*, Princeton, 1965.
Baxter, S. B., *The Development of the Treasury, 1660–1702*, London, 1957.
England's Rise to Greatness, 1660–1763, Berkeley, 1983.
Beatson, R., *Naval and Military Memoirs of Great Britain from 1727–1783*, 6 vols., London, 1804.
Beers, H. P., 'The Papers of the British Commanders-in-Chief in North America, 1754–1783', *Military Affairs*, XIII (1949), 79–94.
Belsham, W., *Memoirs of the Reign of George III*, 5 vols., London, 1795.
Beveridge, W. H., *Prices and Wages in England from the Twelfth to the Nineteenth Century*, London, 1939.
Binney, J. E. D., *British Public Finance and Administration, 1774–1792*, Oxford, 1958.
Blackstone, W., *Commentaries on the Laws of England*, 4 vols., Oxford, 1765–1769.
Bonfils, M. Le Comte de, *Histoire de la Marine Française*, 3 vols., Paris, 1845.
Boyce, D. G., 'Public Opinion and Historians', *History*, LXIII (1978), 214–228.

Brown, P. D., *William Pitt, Earl of Chatham: The Great Commoner*, London, 1978.

Browning, R., *The Duke of Newcastle*, New Haven, 1975.

'The Duke of Newcastle and the Financing of the Seven Years' War', *Journal of Economic History*, XXXI (1971), 344–377.

'The Duke of Newcastle and the Financial Management of the Seven Years' War in Germany', *Journal of the Society for Army Historical Research*, XLIX (1971), 20–35.

Bruce, A., *The Purchase System in the British Army, 1660–1871*, London, 1980.

Burrows, M., *Life of Edward, Lord Hawke*, London, 1883.

Carter, A., *The Dutch Republic during the Seven Years' War*, London, 1971.

Carver, P. L., 'The Letters of James Wolfe to the Duke of Richmond', *University of Toronto Quarterly*, VIII (1938), 1–23.

Chalmers, G., *An Estimate of the Comparative Strength of Britain in the Present and Preceding Reigns, and of the Losses of her Trade from every War since the Revolution*, London, 1782.

Chandaman, C. D., *The English Public Revenue, 1660–1688*, Oxford, 1975.

Charnock, J., *A History of Marine Architecture*, 3 vols., London, 1802.

Charteris, Sir Evan, *William Augustus, Duke of Cumberland and the Seven Years' War*, London, 1925.

Christie, I. R., *Myth and Reality in Late Eighteenth Century British Politics: and Other Papers*, London, 1970.

Clapham, Sir John, *The Bank of England: A History*, 2 vols., Cambridge, 1944.

Clark, J. C. D., *The Dynamics of Change: The Crisis of the 1750s and English Party Systems*, Cambridge, 1982.

Clode, C. M., *The Military Forces of the Crown: Their Administration and Government*, 2 vols., London, 1869.

Cobbett, W. (ed.), *The Parliamentary History of England*, vol. XII, *1752–1763*, London, 1811.

Colley, L., *In Defiance of Oligarchy: The Tory Party, 1714–60*, Cambridge, 1982.

Corbett, J. S., *England in the Seven Years' War: A Study in Combined Strategy*, 2 vols., London, 1907.

Croker, J. W., 'Walpole's Memoirs of the Reign of George II', *The Quarterly Review*, XXVII (1822), 178–215.

'Walpole's Memoirs of the Reign of George III, *The Quarterly Review*, LXXVII (1845), 253–298.

Crowhurst, P., *The Defence of British Trade, 1689–1815*, Folkestone, 1977.

Curtis, E. E., *The Organization of the British Army in the American Revolution*, New Haven, 1926.

Dalton, C., *George I's Army, 1714–1727*, 2 vols., London, 1910–1912.

Dickson, P. G. M., *The Financial Revolution in England: A Study in Development of Public Credit, 1688–1756*, London, 1967.

Dorn, W. L., *The Competition for Empire, 1740–1763*, New York, 1940.

Duncan, F., *History of the Royal Regiment of Artillery*, 2 vols., London, 1879.

Ehrman, J., *The Navy in the War of William III: Its State and Direction, 1689–1697*, Cambridge, 1953.

Eldon, C. W., *England's Subsidy Policy towards the Continent during the Seven Years' War, 1756–1763*, Philadelphia, 1938.

Elliot, G. F. S., *The Border Elliots and the Family of Minto*, Edinburgh, 1897.

Entick, J., *The General History of the Late War, Containing its Rise, Progress and Events, in Europe, Asia, Africa and America*, 5 vols., London, 1763–1764.

Ernst, J. A., *Money and Politics in America, 1755–1775*, Chapel Hill, 1973.

Evans, F. G., *The Principal Secretary of State, 1558–1680*, Manchester, 1923.

Fitzmaurice, Lord E., *The Life of William, Earl of Shelburne*, 3 vols., London, 1875–1876; two-volume revised edition, London, 1912.

Forbes, A., *A History of the Army Ordnance Services*, 3 vols., London, 1929.

Forrest, Sir George, *The Life of Lord Clive*, 2 vols., London, 1918.

Fortescue, Sir John, *A History of the British Army*, 13 vols., London, 1899–1930.

Fregault, G., *Canada: The War of the Conquest*, Toronto, 1969.

Gipson, L. H., *The British Empire before the American Revolution*, 15 vols., New York, 1936–1970.

Glover, R., *Memoirs of a Celebrated Literary and Political Character*, London, 1814.

Godwin, W., *The History of the Life of William Pitt, Earl of Chatham*, London, 1783.

Gradish, S., *The Manning of the British Navy during the Seven Years' War*, London, 1980.

Graham, G. S., *Empire of the North Atlantic: The Maritime Struggle for America*, Toronto, 1950.

'The Naval Defence of British North America, 1739–1763', *Transactions of the Royal Historical Society*, Fourth Series, xxx (1948), 95–110.

Grellier, J.J., *The History of the National Debt from the Revolution in 1688 to the Beginning of 1800*, London, 1810.

Haffenden, P., 'Colonial Appointments and Patronage under the Duke of Newcastle, 1724–1739', *English Historical Review*, LVIII (1963), 417–435.

Hall, H., 'Chatham's Colonial Policy', *American Historical Review*, v (1900), 659–675.

Hansard, T. C. (ed.), *The Parliamentary History of England*, vol. xv, 1753–65, London, 1813.

Harrison, F., *Chatham*, London, 1905.

'Address to the Fellows of the Royal Historical Society', *Transactions of the Royal Historical Society*, Third Series, III (1909), 34–49.

Hayter, T., *The Army and the Crowd in Mid-Georgian England*, London, 1978.

Hogg, O. F. G., *The Royal Arsenal: Its Background, Origin and Subsequent History*, 2 vols., London, 1963.

Horn, D. B., *Great Britain and Europe in the Eighteenth Century*, Oxford, 1967.

Hotblack, K., *Chatham's Colonial Policy*, London, 1917.

Houlding, J. A., *Fit for Service: The Training of the British Army, 1715–1795*, Oxford, 1981.

Hunt, W., 'Pitt's Retirement from Office, 1761', *English Historical Review*, XXI (1906), 119–132.

Hutchinson, J. R., *The Press Gang Afloat and Ashore*, London, 1913.

Ilchester, Earl of, *Henry Fox, First Lord Holland*, 2 vols., London, 1920.

Jackson, Sir George, *Naval Commissioners, 1660–1760*, Lewes, 1889.

James, C., *A New and Enlarged Military Dictionary or Alphabetical Exposition of Technical Terms*, 2 vols., London, 1810.

Jomini, A., *Traité des Grandes Opérations Militaires, Contenant L'Histoire Critique des Campagnes de Frédéric II, Comparées à celles de L'Empereur Napoléon avec un Recueil des Principes Généraux de L'Art de Guerre*, 8 vols., Paris, 1811–1816.

Kelch, R. A., *Newcastle: A Duke without Money: Thomas Pelham-Holles, 1693–1768*, London, 1974.

Keppel, Lord T., *The Life of Augustus, Viscount Keppel, Admiral of the White and First Lord of the Admiralty in 1782–1783*, 2 vols., London, 1842.

Kingsford, W., *The History of Canada*, 10 vols., Toronto, 1887–1898.

Knox, J., *Historical Journal of the Campaigns in North America, 1757–1760*, ed., A. G. Doughty, 3 vols., Toronto, 1914.

Lacour-Gayet, G., *La Marine Militaire de La France sous le Règne de Louis XV*, Paris, 1902.

Langford, P., 'William Pitt and Public Opinion', *English Historical Review*, LXXXVIII (1973), 54–79.

Lecky, W. E. H., *A History of England in the Eighteenth Century*, 8 vols., London, 1878–1890.

Lindsay, J. O. ed., *The New Cambridge Modern History*, VII, *The Old Regime 1713–1763*, Cambridge, 1957.

Lloyd, C. and Coulter, J. L. S., *Medicine and the Navy, 1200–1900*, 4 vols., London, 1957–1963.

Lloyd, E. M., 'The Raising of the Highland Regiments in 1757', *English Historical Review*, XVII (1902), 466–469.

Lodge, Sir Richard, *Great Britain and Prussia in the Eighteenth Century*, Oxford, 1923.

Long, J. C., *Lord Jeffery Amherst, A Soldier of the King*, New York, 1933.

Macaulay, T. B., 'William Pitt, Earl of Chatham', *Edinburgh Review*, LVIII (1834), 508–544.

McCardell, L., *Ill-Starred General: Braddock of the Coldstream Guards*, Pittsburgh, 1958.

McCormac, E. I., *Colonial Opposition to Imperial Authority during the French and Indian War*, Berkeley, 1914.

McCracken, E., *The Irish Woods since Tudor Times*, Newton Abbot, 1971.

McDermott, E., 'The Elder Pitt and his Admirals and Generals', *Military Affairs*, XX (1956), 65–77.

McLachlan, J. O., *Trade and Peace with Old Spain, 1667–1750*, Cambridge, 1940.

Mackay, R., *Admiral Hawke*, Oxford, 1965.

Mackesy, P., *The War for America, 1755–1783*, London, 1964.

The Coward of Minden: The Affair of Lord George Sackville, London, 1979.

McLennen, J. S., *Louisburg, from its Foundation to its Fall, 1713–1758*, London, 1918.

Mahan, A. T., *The Influence of Sea Power upon History, 1660–1783*, Boston, 1890.

Mahon, P. H., Earl Stanhope, *The History of England from the Peace of Utrecht to the Peace of Versailles, 1713–1783*, 7 vols., London, 1836–54.

Manners, W. E., *Some Account of the Military, Political and Social Life of the Right Honourable John Manners, Marquis of Granby*, London, 1899.

Mante, T., *The History of the Late War in North America*, London, 1772.

Marcus, G., *A Naval History of England*, London, 1961.

Quiberon Bay: the Campaign in the Home Waters, 1759, London, 1960.

'Hawke's Blockade of Brest', *Journal of the Royal United Services Institute*, CIV (1959), 475–488.

Marshall, D. W., 'The British Engineers in America, 1775–1783', *Journal of the Society for Army Historical Research*, LI (1971), 155–163.

May, Sir Thomas, *The Constitutional History of England since the Accession of George III, 1760–1860*, 2 vols., London, 1861.
Middleton, R., 'A Reinforcement for America, Summer 1757', *Bulletin of the Institute of Historical Research*, XLI (1968), 58–72.
'Pitt, Anson and the Admiralty, 1757–1761', *History*, LV (1970), 189–198.
Molyneux, T. M., *Conjunct Expeditions or Expeditions that have been carried on jointly by the Fleet and Army, with a Commentary on a Littoral War*, 2 vols., London, 1759.
Murray, Sir Oswyn, 'The Admiralty', *Mariner's Mirror*, XXIII (1937), 13–35, 129–147, 316–331; XXIV (1938), 101–104, 204–225, 329–352.
Namier, Sir Lewis, *The Structure of Politics at the Accession of George III*, London, 1929, 2nd edition, 1957.
England in the Age of the American Revolution, London, 1930, 2nd edition, 1961.
The Crossroads of Power: Essays on Eighteenth Century England, London, 1962.
Namier, Sir Lewis and Brooke, J., *The History of Parliament: The House of Commons, 1754–1790*, 3 vols., London, 1964.
Charles Townshend, London, 1964.
Oppenheim, M., *A History of the Administration of the Royal Navy, 1509–1660*, London, 1896.
Pares, R., *War and Trade in the West Indies, 1739–1763*, Oxford, 1936.
'American versus Continental Warfare, 1739–1763', *English Historical Review*, LI (1936), 429–465.
Pares, R., and Taylor, A. J. P., eds., *Essays presented to Sir Lewis Namier*, London, 1956.
Pargellis, S. M., *Lord Loudoun in North America*, New Haven, 1933.
'Braddock's Defeat', *American Historical Review*, XLI (1936), 253–269.
Parkman, F. *Montcalm and Wolfe*, 2 vols., London, 1884.
Pease, T. C., *Anglo-French Boundary Disputes in the West, 1749–1763*, Springfield, 1936.
Peckham, H., *The Colonial Wars, 1689–1762*, Chicago, 1964.
Peters, M., *Pitt and Popularity: The Patriot Minister and London Opinion during the Seven Years' War*, Oxford, 1980.
Plumb, J. H., *Chatham*, London, 1953.
'The Organization of the Cabinet in the Reign of Queen Anne', *Transactions of the Royal Historical Society*, 5th Series, VII (1957), 137–157.
Pool, B., *Navy Board Contracts, 1660–1832: Contract Administration under the Navy Board*, London, 1966.
Porter, W., *A History of the Corps of Royal Engineers*, 2 vols., London, 1889.
Rashed, Z. E., *The Peace of Paris, 1763*, London, 1951.
Reilly, T., *The Rest to Fortune: The Life of Major-General James Wolfe*, London, 1960.
Richmond, Sir Herbert, *The Navy in the War of 1739–1748*, 3 vols., Cambridge, 1920.
Statesmen and Seapower, Oxford, 1946.
Riker, T. W., *Henry Fox, First Lord Holland*, 2 vols., Oxford, 1911.
Ritchie, M. K. and C. A., 'The Troubles of a Commissary during the Seven Years' War', *Journal of the Society for Army Historical Research*, XXXVI (1956), 157–164.
Robertson, C. G., *Chatham and the British Empire*, London, 1946.
Rogers, A., *Empire and Liberty: American Resistance to British Authority, 1755–1763*, Berkeley, 1974.
Rogers, H. C. B., *The British Army of the Eighteenth Century*, London, 1977.
Rosebery, Lord, *Chatham: His Early Life and Connections*, London, 1910.

Roseveare, H. G., *The Treasury: The Evolution of a British Institution*, London, 1969.

Ruville, A. von, *William Pitt, Earl of Chatham*, 3 vols., London, 1907.

Savory, Sir Reginald, *His Britannic Majesty's Army in Germany during the Seven Years' War*, Oxford, 1966.

Schutz, J. *William Shirley, King's Governor of Massachusetts*, New York, 1961.

Scouller, R. E., *The Armies of Queen Anne*, Oxford, 1966.

Sedgwick, H. R., 'The Inner Cabinet from 1739 to 1741', *English Historical Review*, XXXIV (1919), 290–302.

Sherrard, O. A. *Lord Chatham*, 3 vols., London, 1952–1959.

Shy, J., *Toward Lexington: The Role of the British Army in the Coming of the American Revolution*, Princeton, 1965.

Smelser, M. T., *The Campaign for the Sugar Islands, 1759: A Study of Amphibious Warfare*, New York, 1955.

Smollett, T. G., *The History of England from the Revolution to the death of George II*, 5 vols., London, 1790.

Spector, R. D., *English Literary Periodicals and the Climate of Opinion during the Seven Years' War*, The Hague, 1966.

Spenser, F., 'The Anglo-Prussian Breach of 1762: An Historical Revision', *History*, XLI (1956), 100–112.

Stacey, C. P., *Quebec, 1759*, Toronto, 1959.

Stanley, G. F. G., *New France, The Last Phase, 1744–1760*, London, 1968.

Sutherland, L. S., 'The City of London and the Pitt–Devonshire Administration, 1756–1757', *Proceedings of the British Academy*, XLVI (1960), 148–193.

(ed.), *The Correspondence of Edmund Burke* (Cambridge, 1960), II.

Sykes, N., 'The Duke of Newcastle as an Ecclesiastical Minister', *English Historical Review*, LVII (1942), 59–89.

Thackeray, F., *A History of the Right Honourable William Pitt, Earl of Chatham*, 2 vols., London, 1827.

Thomas, P. M. G., *The House of Commons in the Eighteenth Century*, Oxford, 1971.

Thomson, M. A., *The Secretaries of State, 1681–1782*, Oxford, 1932.

Torrens, W. M., *A History of Cabinets*, 2 vols., London, 1894.

Townshend, C. V. F., *The Military Life of Field Marshal George First Marquis Townshend, 1724–1807*, London, 1901.

Tunstall, W. C. B., *William Pitt, Earl of Chatham*, London, 1938.

Admiral Byng and the Loss of Minorca, London, 1928.

Turner, E. R., *The Privy Council of England in the Seventeenth and Eighteenth Centuries, 1603–1784*, 2 vols., Baltimore, 1928.

The Cabinet Council of England in the Seventeenth and Eighteenth Centuries, 1622–1784, 2 vols., Baltimore, 1930.

Valentine, A., *The British Establishment, 1760–1784: An Eighteenth Century Biographical Dictionary*, 2 vols., Norman, 1970.

Waddington, R., *La Guerre de Sept Ans*, 4 vols., Paris, 1899–1904.

Walpole, H., *Memoirs of the Reign of King George II*, 3 vols., London, 1846–1847.

Memoirs of the Reign of King George III, 4 vols., London, 1894.

Waugh, W. T., *James Wolfe, Man and Soldier*, Montreal, 1928.

Western, J. R., *The English Militia in the Eighteenth Century: The Story of a Political Issue, 1660–1802*, London, 1965.

244 The Bells of Victory

Wheeler, O., *The War Office Past and Present*, London, 1914.

Whitton, F. E., *Wolfe and North America*, London, 1914.

Whitworth, R., *Field Marshal Lord Ligonier: A Story of the British Army, 1702–1770*, Oxford, 1958.

Wickwhire, F., 'The Admiralty Secretaries and the British Civil Service', *Huntington Library Quarterly*, xxviii (1965), 240–256.

Williams, B., *The Life of William Pitt, Earl of Chatham*, 2 vols., London, 1913.

Carteret and Newcastle, Cambridge, 1943.

The Whig Supremacy, 1714–1760, Oxford, 1962.

Williams, E. N., *The Eighteenth Century Constitution, 1688–1815*, Cambridge, 1960.

Willson, B., *The Life and Letters of James Wolfe*, London, 1909.

'Fresh Light on the Quebec Campaign: From the Missing Journal of General Wolfe', *Nineteenth Century and After*, lxvii (1905), 448–457.

Wylly, H. C., *A Life of Lieutenant General Sir Eyre Coote, K.B.*, Oxford, 1922.

VI THESES

Bassett, J. H. 'The Purchase System in the British Army, 1660–1871', Ph.D., Boston University, 1969.

Fraser, E. J. S., 'The Pitt–Newcastle Coalition and the Conduct of the Seven Years' War, 1757–1760', D. Phil., Oxford University 1976.

Hackman, W., 'English Military Expeditions to the Coast of France 1757–1761', Ph.D., Michigan University, 1968.

Little, H., 'The British Army Commissaries in Germany during the Seven Years' War', Ph.D., London University, 1981.

Middleton, R., 'The Administration of Newcastle and Pitt: The Departments of State and the Conduct of the War, 1754–1760, with particular reference to the campaigns in North America', Ph.D., Exeter University, 1969.

Scott, L., 'The Under-Secretaries of State, 1755–1775', M.A., Manchester University, 1950.

INDEX

Made in the USA
Middletown, DE
25 June 2016